WildFly Configuration, Deployment, and Administration

Second Edition

Build a functional and efficient WildFly server with this step-by-step, practical guide

Christopher Ritchie

[PACKT] open source*
PUBLISHING community experience distilled

BIRMINGHAM - MUMBAI

WildFly Configuration, Deployment, and Administration
Second Edition

Copyright © 2014 Packt Publishing

All rights reserved. No part of this book may be reproduced, stored in a retrieval system, or transmitted in any form or by any means, without the prior written permission of the publisher, except in the case of brief quotations embedded in critical articles or reviews.

Every effort has been made in the preparation of this book to ensure the accuracy of the information presented. However, the information contained in this book is sold without warranty, either express or implied. Neither the author, nor Packt Publishing, and its dealers and distributors will be held liable for any damages caused or alleged to be caused directly or indirectly by this book.

Packt Publishing has endeavored to provide trademark information about all of the companies and products mentioned in this book by the appropriate use of capitals. However, Packt Publishing cannot guarantee the accuracy of this information.

First published: December 2011

Second edition: November 2014

Production reference: 1221114

Published by Packt Publishing Ltd.
Livery Place
35 Livery Street
Birmingham B3 2PB, UK.

ISBN 978-1-78328-623-2

www.packtpub.com

Credits

Author
Christopher Ritchie

Reviewers
Alexis Hassler
Michael S. Jo
Jan Kalina

Commissioning Editor
Usha Iyer

Acquisition Editor
Meeta Rajani

Content Development Editor
Vaibhav Pawar

Technical Editor
Pramod Kumavat

Copy Editors
Sarang Chari
Adithi Shetty

Project Coordinator
Kranti Berde

Proofreaders
Ameesha Green
Lauren E. Harkins
Kevin McGowan

Indexers
Hemangini Bari
Mariammal Chettiyar
Rekha Nair

Graphics
Disha Haria
Abhinash Sahu

Production Coordinator
Komal Ramchandani

Cover Work
Komal Ramchandani

About the Author

Christopher Ritchie is a Sun Certified Programmer with over 10 years of software experience. Having worked in both the UK and South Africa markets, he has worked on a variety of software applications, ranging from online gaming to telecoms and Internet banking. He has a keen interest in the WildFly application server and is an advocate of Java EE technologies.

He currently works as a technical lead at the company he cofounded, Sports Science Medicine Software, in South Africa. The company's core product is a research-based application that allows the profiling of soccer players through injury and exposure assessment.

Christopher was a technical reviewer for *WildFly Performance Tuning, Packt Publishing*. You can find him at `www.chris-ritchie.com`.

> I would like to thank my wife, Samantha, for her unwavering support and patience, and my parents for their continued encouragement and support. I would also like to give special thanks to both my dad and Patrick Dzvoti for their help and advice throughout my professional career.

About the Reviewers

Alexis Hassler lives in Beaujolais, France but, unlike his neighbors, he isn't a winemaker. He's a freelance software developer and trainer (http://www.sewatech.fr). Apart from his main activities, he cofounded the Java User Group of Lyon (http://www.lyonjug.org) and assists the organization of the Mix-IT conference (http://mix-it.fr).

Michael S. Jo is a technical architect with 14 years of enterprise Java web application development experience. Michael is an enthusiast of new technology and a lifelong learner. Currently, he works at Fujitsu Canada as an application architect. He likes to learn and share his experience through his blog at http://mjtoolbox.wordpress.com.

> A big thank you to my love, Aramireu, Ayin, and Kristina. Also, a thank you to Packt Publishing and its staff for giving me this opportunity to be a part of this project.

Jan Kalina is student of informatics in the Faculty of Information Technology, Brno University of Technology. He got familiarized with WildFly on the occasion of writing his bachelor thesis, the result of which was a subsystem of WildFly that allows the deployment of Java security policies on a WildFly domain. On the basis of this, while reviewing this book, he was recruited as a developer of WildFly Elytron at Red Hat.

www.PacktPub.com

Support files, eBooks, discount offers, and more

For support files and downloads related to your book, please visit www.PacktPub.com.

Did you know that Packt offers eBook versions of every book published, with PDF and ePub files available? You can upgrade to the eBook version at www.PacktPub.com and as a print book customer, you are entitled to a discount on the eBook copy. Get in touch with us at service@packtpub.com for more details.

At www.PacktPub.com, you can also read a collection of free technical articles, sign up for a range of free newsletters and receive exclusive discounts and offers on Packt books and eBooks.

PACKTLiB

https://www2.packtpub.com/books/subscription/packtlib

Do you need instant solutions to your IT questions? PacktLib is Packt's online digital book library. Here, you can search, access, and read Packt's entire library of books.

Why subscribe?

- Fully searchable across every book published by Packt
- Copy and paste, print, and bookmark content
- On demand and accessible via a web browser

Free access for Packt account holders

If you have an account with Packt at www.PacktPub.com, you can use this to access PacktLib today and view 9 entirely free books. Simply use your login credentials for immediate access.

Table of Contents

Preface	**1**
Chapter 1: Installing WildFly	**7**
What's new in WildFly 8?	**7**
Getting started with the application server	**9**
Installing the Java environment	9
Installing Java on Linux	10
Installing Java on Windows	11
Installing WildFly 8	12
Starting WildFly	13
Connecting to the server with the command-line interface	15
Stopping WildFly	16
Locating the shutdown script	17
Stopping WildFly on a remote machine	17
Restarting WildFly	17
Installing the Eclipse environment	18
Installing JBoss tools	19
Exploring the application server filesystem	**21**
The bin folder	22
The docs folder	22
The domain folder	22
The standalone folder	23
The welcome-content folder	24
The modules folder	24
Understanding WildFly's kernel	26
Loading application server modules	27
Summary	**29**

Table of Contents

Chapter 2: Configuring the Core WildFly Subsystems — 31
Configuring our application server — 31
- Extensions — 33
- Paths — 33
- Management interfaces — 34
- Profiles and subsystems — 35
- Interfaces — 35
- The socket-binding groups — 37
- System properties — 38
- Deployments — 38
- Configuring core subsystems — 38
- Configuring the thread pool subsystem — 39
  - Configuring the thread factory — 40
  - The bounded-queue thread pool — 40
  - The blocking bounded-queue thread pool — 42
  - The unbounded-queue thread pool — 44
  - The queueless thread pool — 45
  - The blocking queueless thread pool — 45
  - The scheduled thread pool — 46

Configuring application server logging — 47
- Choosing your logging implementation — 48
  - Configuring the logging subsystem — 49
- The console-handler — 49
- The periodic-rotating-file-handler — 50
- The size-rotating-file-handler — 51
- The async-handler — 51
- The syslog-handler — 52
- Custom handlers — 52
  - Configuring loggers — 55
  - Per-deployment logging — 56
  - Bypassing container logging — 57

Summary — 57

Chapter 3: Configuring Enterprise Services — 59
Connecting to a database — 59
- Installing the JDBC driver — 60
- Adding a local datasource — 62
  - Configuring the connection pool — 64
  - Configuring the statement cache — 65
  - Adding an xa-datasource — 65
- Installing the driver as a deployment unit — 66
  - Choosing the right driver deployment strategy — 68
- Configuring a datasource programmatically — 69

Configuring the Enterprise JavaBeans container	**70**
Configuring the EJB components	71
Configuring the stateless session beans	72
Configuring the stateful session beans	74
Configuring the message-driven beans	76
Configuring the timer service	77
Configuring the messaging system	78
Configuring the transport	80
Configuring connection factories	84
Configuring JMS destinations	85
Customizing destinations with an address	86
HornetQ persistence configuration	87
Configuring the transactions service	89
Configuring concurrency	**91**
Configuring the context service	92
Configuring the managed thread factory	92
Configuring the managed executor service	93
Configuring the managed schedule executor service	94
Summary	**94**
Chapter 4: The Undertow Web Server	**97**
An overview of Undertow	**97**
The Undertow architecture	98
Configuring Undertow	99
Configuring the server	99
Configuring the listener	100
Configuring the host	102
Serving static content	103
Configuring the servlet container	104
Configuring JSP	105
Configuring the session cookie	105
Saving the session state	106
Configuring the buffer cache	106
Creating and deploying a web application	**107**
Creating a new Maven web project	**107**
Adding JSF components	111
Adding the EJB layer	114
Choosing the web context of the application	116
Deploying the web application	117
Deploying a web application to the root context	118
Adding a remote EJB client	119
Configuring the client using a properties file	122
Configuring the client programmatically	123

Table of Contents

Configuring data persistence	124
Using a default datasource for the JPA subsystem	126
Configuring entities	126
Configuring persistence in other application archives	129
Switching to a different provider	130
Using Jipijapa	130
Summary	**131**
Chapter 5: Configuring a WildFly Domain	**133**
Introducing the WildFly domain	**133**
Understanding the default domain configuration	**134**
Starting up and stopping a domain	**136**
Configuring the domain	**137**
Overriding the default configuration files	137
Configuring the domain.xml file	138
Configuring the host.xml file	139
Configuring the management interfaces	140
Configuring the network interfaces	141
Configuring the domain controller	142
Configuring the JVM	142
Adding JVM options to a server definition	143
Order of precedence between elements	144
Configuring server nodes	145
Applying domain configuration	146
Creating our very own domain configuration	**147**
Changing the domain configuration at runtime	153
Summary	**156**
Chapter 6: Application Structure and Deployment	**159**
Deploying resources on the application server	**159**
The JAR file	160
The WAR file	160
The EAR file	161
Deploying applications on a standalone WildFly server	**161**
Automatic application deployment	162
Deploying applications to a custom folder	163
Changing the behavior of the deployment scanner	163
Deployment rollback	164
Deploying an application using the CLI	164
Deploying an application using the web admin console	165
Deploying an application using the WildFly Eclipse plugin	168
Manual application deployment	170

[iv]

Table of Contents

Deploying applications on a WildFly domain	**172**
Deploying to a domain using the CLI	173
Deploying to all server groups	173
Deploying to a single server group	174
Deploying to a domain using the Admin console	175
Explaining WildFly classloading	**178**
Getting to know module names	179
Finding the isolation level	180
Implicit dependencies	180
Explicit dependencies	182
Setting up global modules	184
Advanced deployment strategies	185
Setting up a single module dependency	185
Excluding the server's automatic dependencies	186
Isolating sub-deployments	187
Using the Class-Path declaration to solve dependencies	190
Summary	**191**
Chapter 7: Using the Management Interfaces	**193**
The command-line interface (CLI)	**194**
Reloading the server configuration	195
Employing the CLI	195
Navigating through the resources and executing operations	196
Executing commands with the CLI	204
Executing CLI scripts in batch	210
Advanced batch commands	211
Executing scripts in a file	212
Redirecting non-interactive output	213
Taking snapshots of the configuration	213
What the application server saves for you	215
Taking your own snapshots	215
History of CLI	216
The web admin console	**217**
Accessing the admin console	218
Configuring server profiles	220
Configuring datasources	220
Configuring JMS destinations	224
Configuring socket-binding groups	226
The CLI or web console?	**227**
Summary	**228**

[v]

Chapter 8: Clustering — 229

- Setting up a WildFly cluster — 230
  - Setting up a cluster of standalone servers — 230
    - A cluster of nodes running on different machines — 231
    - A cluster of nodes running on the same machine — 233
  - Setting up a cluster of domain servers — 236
    - Troubleshooting the cluster — 239
- Configuring the WildFly cluster — 241
  - Configuring the JGroups subsystem — 242
    - Customizing the protocol stack — 244
- Configuring the Infinispan subsystem — 245
  - Configuring session cache containers — 247
  - Choosing between replication and distribution — 250
  - Configuring the hibernate cache — 252
    - Using replication for the hibernate cache — 254
  - Advanced Infinispan configuration — 254
    - Configuring the Infinispan transport — 255
    - Configuring the Infinispan threads — 255
- Clustering the messaging subsystem — 257
  - Configuring messaging credentials — 259
- Configuring clustering in your applications — 260
- Clustering session beans — 261
- Clustering entities — 263
- Caching entities — 264
  - Using JPA annotations — 265
  - Using Hibernate annotations — 265
- Caching queries — 266
- Clustering web applications — 267
- Summary — 267

Chapter 9: Load-balancing Web Applications — 269

- Benefits of using the Apache web server with WildFly — 270
  - Using the mod_jk library — 270
    - Installing Apache — 271
    - Installing mod_jk — 271
  - Configuring mod_proxy — 274
- Load-balancing with mod_cluster — 276
- Installing mod_cluster libraries — 278
  - The mod_cluster configuration — 281
  - Testing mod_cluster — 284
- Managing mod_cluster via the CLI — 284

Table of Contents

Managing your web contexts with the CLI	286
Adding native management capabilities	287
Managing web contexts using the configuration file	288
Troubleshooting mod_cluster	288
Load-balancing between nodes	290
Using load metrics	293
An example for setting dynamic metrics on a cluster	295
Summary	296
Chapter 10: Securing WildFly	**299**
Approaching Java security API	300
The WildFly security subsystem	302
Using the UsersRoles login module	305
Using the Database login module	306
Encrypting passwords	307
Using an LDAP login module	309
Connecting LDAP to WildFly	310
Securing web applications	313
Securing EJBs	316
Securing web services	317
Securing the management interfaces	318
Role-based access control	321
Configuring groups	322
Securing the transport layer	323
Enabling the Secure Socket Layer	325
Certificate management tools	326
Securing HTTP communication with a self-signed certificate	327
Securing the HTTP communication with a certificate signed by a CA	329
Summary	331
Chapter 11: WildFly, OpenShift, and Cloud Computing	**333**
Introduction to cloud computing	333
Cloud computing versus grid computing	334
Advantages of cloud computing	335
Cloud computing options	336
Types of cloud services	337
Getting started with OpenShift Online	339
Installing OpenShift client tools	340
Accessing your OpenShift account from a different computer	342

[vii]

Creating our first OpenShift application	**342**
Installing your first cartridge	343
Understanding the workflow	346
Building the application	346
Viewing the OpenShift server logfiles	**351**
Tailing the logfile	351
Viewing logs via SSH	352
Managing applications in OpenShift	**352**
Configuring your applications	**354**
Adding a database cartridge	355
Using OpenShift Tools and Eclipse	357
Scaling your application	359
Summary	**360**
Appendix: CLI References	**363**
Startup options	**363**
General commands	**363**
The domain-mode commands	**364**
Commands related to application deployment	**365**
JMS	**366**
Datasources	**366**
Datasources (using operations on resources)	366
Mod_cluster	**367**
Batch	**368**
Snapshots	**368**
Index	**369**

Preface

WildFly is the new name for the community version of JBoss AS. WildFly is still the most popular Java Enterprise server out there. It is easy to use, has a clean management interface, a powerful command-line tool, a modular architecture, is light, and is lightning quick. If you need product support, it is very easy to move from WildFly to JBoss EAP Server and, importantly, the license and support costs won't break the bank.

This book gently introduces you to WildFly by looking at how to download and install the server. We then move on to look at configuring enterprise services and the various subsystems, and securing your server and applications. The topics become more advanced as the book progresses, so in the later part of the book, we look at high availability, which is achieved through clustering and load balancing.

Whether you are a Java developer who wishes to improve their knowledge of WildFly, or you are a server administrator who wants to gain a better understanding of the inner workings of WildFly, there is something in this book for everyone.

What this book covers

Chapter 1, *Installing WildFly*, introduces you to the WildFly server. You are taken through the installation of Java and WildFly and learn to start, stop, and restart the server. You will also discover the purpose of the various folders within the WildFly install directory and gain a basic understanding of the WildFly kernel. Lastly, you will learn to install the WildFly server adaptor in Eclipse.

Chapter 2, *Configuring the Core WildFly Subsystems*, provides a detailed description of the anatomy of the standalone configuration file. You will be introduced to the concepts of modules and subsystems, and then you will learn in detail how to configure two of the core subsystems, the logging subsystem, and the thread-pool subsystem.

Preface

Chapter 3, Configuring Enterprise Services, teaches you to configure enterprise services and components, such as transactions, connection pools, Enterprise JavaBeans, and JMS. You will also learn to install JDBC drivers and configure database connections.

Chapter 4, The Undertow Web Server, explains the architecture of Undertow and teaches you how to configure the servlet container. You will also learn how to serve static content and configure JSPs. In this chapter, we create a simple web application using JSF, EJB, and JPA and teach you to deploy the application using the Eclipse WildFly Server adaptor.

Chapter 5, Configuring a WildFly Domain, teaches you how to manage a WildFly domain. It covers the domain and host controller configuration and outlines the differences between a server domain and multiple standalone server instances.

Chapter 6, Application Structure and Deployment, explains the structure of web and enterprise archives and how they are packaged. You will also learn in detail about the various ways to deploy your application to the WildFly server. We also explain how class loading works in WildFly.

Chapter 7, Using the Management Interfaces, introduces more advanced command-line interface commands, such as those for adding datasources and configuring JMS. We also provide a high-level overview of the web admin console.

Chapter 8, Clustering, provides detailed examples on clustering standalone and domain servers. You will also learn about JGroups and how to cluster the enterprise components, such as Messaging and Hibernate.

Chapter 9, Load-balancing Web Applications, explains the benefits of using the Apache web server with WildFly. You will also learn how to load-balance your web applications with mod_jk, mod_proxy, and mod_cluster.

Chapter 10, Securing WildFly, teaches you how to configure the security subsystem. We cover various login modules, such as database login and LDAP. We also look at securing enterprise components, such as Enterprise JavaBeans and web services. We then look at securing the management interfaces.

Chapter 11, WildFly, OpenShift, and Cloud Computing, discusses the advancement of cloud computing and the benefits it offers to your company. We see how OpenShift can be used to ease software development and aid rapid deployment of your applications to cloud servers.

Appendix, CLI References, provides a quick reference to some of the more commonly used commands in the CLI.

What you need for this book

Prior knowledge of Java is expected. Some knowledge of Enterprise Java would be beneficial, although not essential. To run WildFly, you will need the following software:

- JDK 8
- WildFly 8
- MySQL (if you configure a MySQL datasource)

If you wish to run the Java code examples in this book, you will also need:

- Maven 3
- An IDE (Eclipse is used in the book)
- MySQL

Who this book is for

This book is aimed at Java developers, system administrators, and anyone who wants to learn more about how to configure the WildFly 8 server. It will suit people who are new to WildFly server, as no prior experience is assumed. The book progresses to advanced concepts, which means it will also suit the more experienced system administrators and developers.

Conventions

In this book, you will find a number of styles of text that distinguish between different kinds of information. Here are some examples of these styles, and an explanation of their meaning.

Code words in text, database table names, folder names, filenames, file extensions, pathnames, dummy URLs, user input, and Twitter handles are shown as follows: "The content of this file will include the custom Web context, as specified by the context-root element."

A block of code is set as follows:

```
<servers>
    <server name="server-one" group="other-server-group">
        <socket-bindings socket-binding-group="ha-sockets"/>
    </server>
</servers>
```

When we wish to draw your attention to a particular part of a code block, the relevant lines or items are set in bold:

```
public class RemoteEJBClient {
    static {
        Security.addProvider(new JBossSaslProvider());
    }
    public static void main(String[] args) throws Exception {
        super();
    }
}
```

Any command-line input or output is written as follows:

[standalone@localhost:9990 /] data-source remove --name=MySQLPool

New terms and **important words** are shown in bold. Words that you see on the screen, in menus or dialog boxes for example, appear in the text like this: "Agree to the terms and click on **OK**."

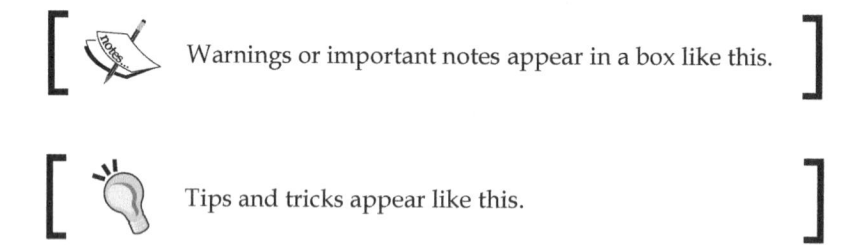

> Warnings or important notes appear in a box like this.

> Tips and tricks appear like this.

Reader feedback

Feedback from our readers is always welcome. Let us know what you think about this book—what you liked or may have disliked. Reader feedback is important for us to develop titles that you really get the most out of.

To send us general feedback, simply send an e-mail to feedback@packtpub.com, and mention the book title via the subject of your message.

If there is a topic that you have expertise in and you are interested in either writing or contributing to a book, see our author guide on www.packtpub.com/authors.

Customer support

Now that you are the proud owner of a Packt book, we have a number of things to help you to get the most from your purchase.

Downloading the example code

You can download the example code files for all Packt books you have purchased from your account at http://www.packtpub.com. If you purchased this book elsewhere, you can visit http://www.packtpub.com/support and register to have the files e-mailed directly to you.

Errata

Although we have taken every care to ensure the accuracy of our content, mistakes do happen. If you find a mistake in one of our books—maybe a mistake in the text or the code—we would be grateful if you would report this to us. By doing so, you can save other readers from frustration and help us improve subsequent versions of this book. If you find any errata, please report them by visiting http://www.packtpub.com/submit-errata, selecting your book, clicking on the **errata submission form** link, and entering the details of your errata. Once your errata are verified, your submission will be accepted and the errata will be uploaded on our website, or added to any list of existing errata, under the Errata section of that title. Any existing errata can be viewed by selecting your title from http://www.packtpub.com/support.

Piracy

Piracy of copyright material on the Internet is an ongoing problem across all media. At Packt, we take the protection of our copyright and licenses very seriously. If you come across any illegal copies of our works, in any form, on the Internet, please provide us with the location address or website name immediately so that we can pursue a remedy.

Please contact us at copyright@packtpub.com with a link to the suspected pirated material.

We appreciate your help in protecting our authors, and our ability to bring you valuable content.

Questions

You can contact us at questions@packtpub.com if you are having a problem with any aspect of the book, and we will do our best to address it.

Installing WildFly

The Java language has undergone many changes since its first release and will continue to adapt to meet the needs of the developer. Oracle, which acquired Sun in 2010, stated that its high-level Java strategy is to enhance and extend the reach of Java to new and emerging software development objectives; simplify, optimize, and integrate the Java platform into new deployment architectures; and invest in the Java developer community allowing for increased participation.

This has certainly been true in the Enterprise edition of Java, the main focus of which has been improved developer productivity, providing support for HTML5, and meeting enterprise demands. Out of all the Enterprise Java releases, Java EE 7 has been the most transparent and open to community participation. By allowing public feedback, the demands of the community can be realized and used to help shape Java EE 7 for the better, ultimately adding to the growth and success of Enterprise Java.

In addition, a large number of open source projects are used within the application server, such as Hibernate and Undertow. Integrating all these libraries does not come without a price because each library has evolved with complexity and requires more and more additional libraries to work.

As most IT experts agree, the challenge for today's application servers is to combine a rich set of features requested by customers along with a lightweight and flexible container configuration.

What's new in WildFly 8?

WildFly 8 is the direct continuation to the JBoss AS project. The renaming of the community version of JBoss AS was done to reduce confusion between the open source JBoss server, the JBoss community, and the **JBoss Enterprise Application Platform (JBoss EAP)**. WildFly 8 is free and open source, with support coming from the JBoss community, whereas JBoss EAP is a licensed product that comes with support from RedHat.

Installing WildFly

The most notable updates in WildFly 8 from earlier versions are as follows:

- **Java EE7 certification**: WildFly is a fully compliant Java EE enterprise server, which means that it provides reference implementations for all **Java Specification Requests (JSRs)** that make up Java EE 7. JSRs are basically change requests for the Java language. For more information on how JSRs work, refer to https://www.jcp.org/en/jsr/overview.
- **Arrival of Undertow**: JBoss Web has been completely removed and replaced with Undertow. Undertow is a cutting-edge web server that supports non-blocking and blocking handlers, web sockets, and asynchronous servlets. It has been designed for scalability and maximum throughput. It is easy to use, easy to configure, and is highly customizable.
- **Port Reduction**: The number of open ports has been greatly reduced in WildFly. Only two ports are open: 8080 and 9990. This has been achieved by multiplexing protocols over HTTP using the HTTP upgrade feature of Undertow.
- **Security Manager**: You can now configure per-deployment security permissions.
- **Logging**: Several enhancements have been made to WildFly logging. You can now view logfiles via the management interface, define custom formatters, and configure logging per-deployment.
- **Clustering**: Clustering in WildFly is heavily refactored and includes many new features, including web sessions, single sign-on, and mod_cluster support for Undertow. There is also a new public clustering API and new @Stateful EJB caching implementation.
- **Command-line interface (CLI)**: You now have the ability to define an alias when connecting to a server, and the CLI GUI has additional functionality allowing you to explore any node in the tree.

In this chapter, we will cover the following topics:

- Installing the Java environment
- Installing WildFly 8
- Installing JBoss tools
- Exploring the application server filesystem
- Understanding the WildFly kernel

Getting started with the application server

As far as hardware requirements are concerned, you should be aware that the server distribution, at the time of writing, requires about 150 MB of hard disk space and allocates a minimum of 64 MB and a maximum of 512 MB for a standalone server.

In order to get started, we are going to perform the following steps:

1. Download and install the Java Development Kit.
2. Download and install WildFly 8.
3. Download and install the Eclipse development environment. While we will use Eclipse in this book, you are free to use your IDE of choice.

At the end of this chapter, you will have all the required software installed and will be ready to start working with the application server.

Installing the Java environment

WildFly is written in Java; therefore it needs a **Java Virtual Machine (JVM)** in which to run, along with the standard edition Java libraries. So, before we can get started setting up or learning about WildFly, we first need to install the **Java Development Kit (JDK)**.

To use WildFly, you will need at least Java SE 7 or above. Although there is no plan to use Java 8 language changes within the WildFly 8.x source code, WildFly is compiled against Java 8. It is recommended that you use the latest version of Java SE 8 to run WildFly.

So, let's move to the Oracle download page, `http://www.oracle.com/technetwork/java/javase/downloads/index.html`, which now hosts all JDK downloads, as shown in the following screenshot:

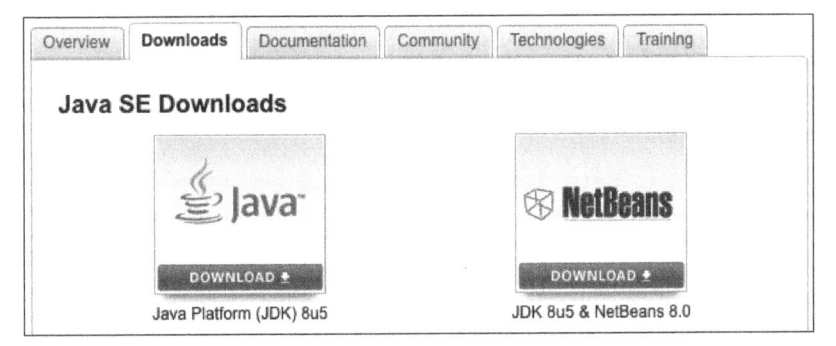

Installing WildFly

This will take you to the download page for the latest JDK. At the time of writing, this was Java 8 update 5. You will need to accept the license agreement before downloading the JDK. Choose to download the latest version of Java for your operating system. Have a look at the following screenshot:

Java SE Development Kit 8u5
You must accept the Oracle Binary Code License Agreement for Java SE to download this software.

Thank you for accepting the Oracle Binary Code License Agreement for Java SE; you may now download this software.

Product / File Description	File Size	Download
Linux x86	133.58 MB	jdk-8u5-linux-i586.rpm
Linux x86	152.5 MB	jdk-8u5-linux-i586.tar.gz
Linux x64	133.87 MB	jdk-8u5-linux-x64.rpm
Linux x64	151.64 MB	jdk-8u5-linux-x64.tar.gz
Mac OS X x64	207.79 MB	jdk-8u5-macosx-x64.dmg
Solaris SPARC 64-bit (SVR4 package)	135.68 MB	jdk-8u5-solaris-sparcv9.tar.Z
Solaris SPARC 64-bit	95.54 MB	jdk-8u5-solaris-sparcv9.tar.gz
Solaris x64 (SVR4 package)	135.9 MB	jdk-8u5-solaris-x64.tar.Z
Solaris x64	93.19 MB	jdk-8u5-solaris-x64.tar.gz
Windows x86	151.71 MB	jdk-8u5-windows-i586.exe
Windows x64	155.18 MB	jdk-8u5-windows-x64.exe

The download will take a few minutes depending how fast your network is.

Installing Java on Linux

Installing Java on Linux is very straightforward. Once the download is complete, extract the `tar.gz` file to your chosen install location. This command extracts the archive to your current directory:

```
tar -xzvf jdk-8u5-linux-x64.tar.gz
```

Next, you need to add the path as an environment variable. This can be achieved by adding the following lines to your user profile script (the `.profile` file found in your home directory):

```
export JAVA_HOME=/installDir/jdk1.8.0_05
export PATH=$JAVA_HOME/bin:$PATH
```

Installing Java on Windows

Windows users can simply run the executable (.exe) file to start the installation. The name of the installer varies depending on the operating system and your system architecture (32-bit or 64-bit); however, the steps will be the same—just the name will change. At the time of writing, the installer for the latest version of Java for 64-bit Windows is called `jdk-8u5-windows-x64.exe`.

When using Windows, you should stay away from installation paths that include empty spaces, such as `C:\Program Files`, as this leads to some issues when referencing the core libraries. An installation path such as `C:\Software\Java` or simply `C:\Java` is a better alternative.

When the installation is complete, you will need to update a couple of settings on the computer so that it will know where to find Java. The most important setting is `JAVA_HOME`, which is directly referenced by the WildFly startup script.

If you are running Windows XP/2000, follow these steps:

1. Right-click on **My Computer**, and select **Properties** from the context menu.
2. On the **Advanced** tab, click on the **Environment Variables** button.
3. Then, in the **System variables** box, click on **New**.
4. Name the new variable `JAVA_HOME`, and give a value of the path to your JDK installation; I recommend something like `C:\Java\jdk1.8.0_05`.

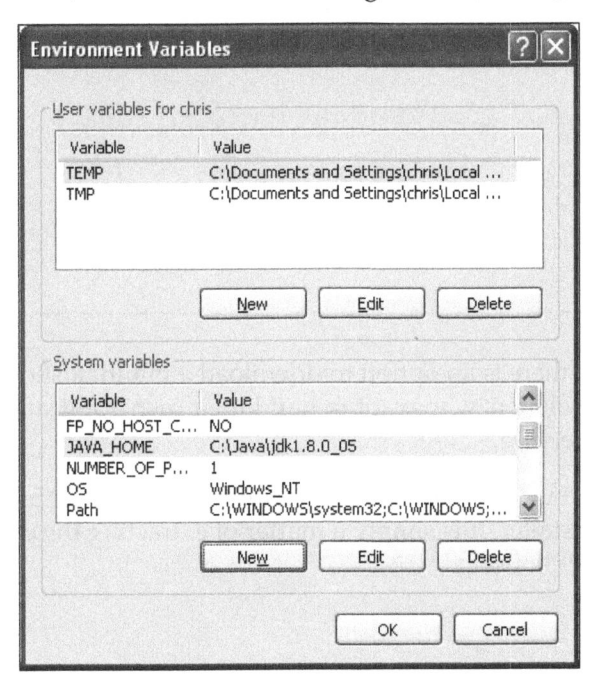

Installing WildFly

> **Windows 7 tip**
> Because of increased security in Windows 7, standard users must have **User Account Control** (**UAC**) turned on to change the environment variables, and the change must be completed via user accounts. In the **User Accounts** window, under **Tasks**, select **Change my environment variables**. Use the **New**, **Edit**, or **Delete** button to amend environment variables

5. Now it's time to modify the system's `PATH` variable. Double-click on the `PATH` system variable. In the box that pops up, navigate to the end of the **Variable Value** line, add a semicolon to the end, and then add the path to your JDK. This will be something like `%JAVA_HOME%\bin`.

Installing WildFly 8

The WildFly application server can be downloaded for free from the WildFly site, `http://www.wildfly.org/downloads/`. Have a look at the following screenshot:

Downloads

Version	Date	Description	License	Size	Format
8.1.0.Final	2014-05-30	Java EE7 Full & Web Distribution	LGPL	124 MB	ZIP
				111 MB	TGZ
		Update Existing 8.0.0.Final Install	LGPL	110 MB	ZIP
		Minimalistic Core Distribution	LGPL	15 MB	ZIP
		Application Server Source Code	LGPL	30 MB	ZIP
				17 MB	TGZ

You will notice that there is an option to download a minimalistic core distribution. This is aimed at developers who want to build their own application runtime using the WildFly 8 architecture.

Choose to download the full Java EE7 distribution. Like JBoss AS 7, WildFly does not come with an installer. It is simply a matter of extracting the compressed archive to a location of your choosing.

[12]

Linux users can extract the file using the `tar` or `unzip` command (depending on the type of compressed file you downloaded):

```
tar -xzvf wildfly-8.1.0.Final.tar.gz
unzip wildfly-8.1.0.Final.zip
```

For those of you using Windows, you can use WinZip or WinRAR, taking care to choose a folder that does not contain empty spaces.

> **Security warning**
> Unix/Linux users should be aware that WildFly does not require root privileges, as none of the default ports used by WildFly are below the privileged port range of 1024. To reduce the risk of users gaining root privileges through WildFly, install and run WildFly as a non-root user.

Starting WildFly

After installing WildFly, it is wise to perform a simple startup test to validate that there are no problems with your Java configuration. To test your installation, move to the `bin` directory of your WildFly install and issue the following command:

- For Linux/Unix users:
    ```
    $ ./standalone.sh
    ```

- For Windows users:
    ```
    > standalone.bat
    ```

The following screenshot shows a sample WildFly 8 startup console:

Installing WildFly

The preceding command starts up a WildFly standalone instance that's equivalent to starting the application server with the run.sh script used by releases prior to JBoss AS 7. The run.sh file remains in the WildFly bin directory but is merely a placeholder and will not start the application server.

Notice how fast the application server starts. This is due to the modular architecture of WildFly. Essential services are started concurrently on boot-up, and non-critical services are started only when needed, resulting in an exceptionally fast startup. Local caching means that the server will start even quicker second time round!

If you need to customize the startup properties of your application server, then you need to open and modify the standalone.conf file (or standalone.conf.bat for Windows users). This file contains the memory requirements of WildFly. The following is the Linux core section of it:

```
if [ "x$JAVA_OPTS" = "x" ]; then
    JAVA_OPTS="-Xms64m -Xmx512m -XX:MaxPermSize=256m -Djava.net.preferIPv4Stack=true"
    JAVA_OPTS="$JAVA_OPTS -Djboss.modules.system.pkgs=$JBOSS_MODULES_SYSTEM_PKGS -Djava.awt.headless=true"
fi
```

> **Java SE 8 users**
> PermGen has been replaced with Metaspace in Java 8. If you are using Java 8, then remove the -XX:MaxPermSize=256m property from the standalone.conf file, and replace it with -XX:MaxMetaspaceSize=256m. This will prevent VM warnings being printed to your WildFly logs on startup.

By default, the application server starts with a minimum heap space memory requirement of 64 MB and a maximum requirement of 512 MB. This will be just enough to get started; however, if you need to run a core Java EE application on it, you will likely require a minimum of 1 GB of heap space. More realistically, you will need 2 GB or more depending on your application type. Generally speaking, 32-bit machines cannot execute a process whose space exceeds 4 GB; however, on 64-bit machines, there's essentially no limit to process the size.

You can verify that the server is reachable from the network by simply pointing your browser to the application server's welcome page, which is reachable by default at the well-known address: http://localhost:8080. Have a look at the following screenshot:

Welcome to WildFly 8

Your WildFly 8 is running.

Documentation | Quickstarts | Administration Console

WildFly Project | User Forum | Report an issue

JBoss | JBoss Community

To replace this page simply deploy your own war with / as its context path.
To disable it, remove "welcome-content" handler for location / in undertow subsystem

Connecting to the server with the command-line interface

If you have been using releases of the application server prior to JBoss AS 7, you might have heard about the `twiddle` command-line utility that queries the MBeans installed on the application server. This utility was replaced in JBoss AS 7 and is still used in WildFly. Its replacement is a more sophisticated interface named the **command-line interface (CLI)**, which can be found in the `JBOSS_HOME/bin` folder.

> **References to JBOSS_HOME**
>
> Although the community version of JBoss AS has been renamed to WildFly, you will see that the properties in the startup scripts continue to use the property, `JBOSS_HOME`, to reference the install directory of WildFly. For this reason, we will continue to use `JBOSS_HOME` when referring to the root install of WildFly.

Installing WildFly

Just launch the `jboss-cli.sh` script (or `jboss-cli.bat` for Windows users), and you will be able to manage the application server via a shell interface, as shown in the following screenshot. Bear in mind that the server needs to be running in order to connect via the CLI.

```
chris-macbook:bin chris$ ./jboss-cli.sh
You are disconnected at the moment. Type 'connect' to connect to the server or 'help' for the list of supported commands.
[disconnected /] connect
[standalone@localhost:9990 /]
```

Once you are in the shell session, if you are unsure of what commands can be issued, you can simply press the *Tab* button to display all possible commands. If your command is partly typed, and there is only one possible matching command, your command will be autocompleted. Those of you who use Linux will be used to this type of command-line assistance.

In the preceding screenshot, we have just connected to the server using the `connect` command, which, by default, uses the loopback server address and plugs into port number 9990.

> The CLI is discussed in depth in *Chapter 7, Using the Management Interfaces*, which is all about the server-management interfaces. We will have an initial taste of its basic functionalities in the following sections, to get you accustomed to this powerful tool.

Stopping WildFly

Probably the easiest way to stop WildFly is to send an interrupt signal using *Ctrl* + *C*. This should be done in the same console window in which you issued the startup command, that is, where the server is running.

However, if your WildFly process was launched in the background or is running on another machine (see in the following sections), then you can use the CLI interface to issue an immediate `shutdown` command as follows:

```
[disconnected /] connect
[standalone@localhost:9990 /] shutdown
[disconnected /]
```

Locating the shutdown script

There is actually one more option to shut down the application server, which is pretty useful if you need to shut down the server from within a script. This option consists of passing the `--connect` option to the admin shell, thereby switching off the interactive mode as follows:

```
jboss-cli.sh --connect command=:shutdown       # Unix / Linux
jboss-cli.bat --connect command=:shutdown      # Windows
```

Stopping WildFly on a remote machine

Shutting down an application server running on a remote machine is just a matter of connecting and providing the server's remote address to the CLI:

```
[disconnected /] connect 192.168.1.10

[192.168.1.10:9990 /] shutdown
```

> Remotely accessing WildFly via the CLI requires authentication. Check out *Chapter 10, Securing WildFly*, for more information about it. It also requires that the management interface on the remote WildFly install is opened to allow remote connections. This is covered in detail in *Chapter 7, Using the Management Interfaces*.

Restarting WildFly

The CLI contains a lot of useful commands. One of the most helpful options is the ability to reload all or part of the server configuration using the `reload` command.

When issued on the **root node path** of the server, WildFly reloads all the services configuration, as shown in the following command:

```
[disconnected /] connect
```

```
[standalone@localhost:9990 /] reload
```

Installing the Eclipse environment

Although the main focus of this book is the administration of the WildFly application server, we are also concerned with application packaging and deployment. For this reason, we will sometimes add examples that require a development environment to be installed on your machine.

The development environment used in this book is Eclipse. Eclipse is known by developers worldwide and contains a huge set of plugins, building on its core functionality. If you are comfortable with another IDE, then feel free to use it, but this book will demonstrate Eclipse only. At the time of writing this, only Eclipse and NetBeans have plugins for WildFly.

So let's move to the Eclipse download page, located at http://www.eclipse.org/downloads.

From this page, download the latest Enterprise edition. The compressed package contains all the Java EE plugins already installed and requires about 248 MB of disk space. Have a look at the following screenshot:

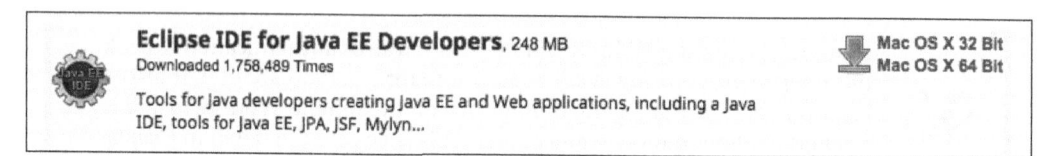

Eclipse IDE for Java EE Developers, 248 MB
Downloaded 1,758,489 Times

Tools for Java developers creating Java EE and Web applications, including a Java IDE, tools for Java EE, JPA, JSF, Mylyn...

Mac OS X 32 Bit
Mac OS X 64 Bit

> If you are using Java 8, you should make sure you download Eclipse Luna (4.4) or the patched Version of 4.3.

Once you have downloaded Eclipse, unzip it to a folder of your choice. The extracted folder will be called `eclipse`. To start Eclipse, navigate to the `eclipse` folder and run:

```
$ ./eclipse
```

Windows users can simply double-click on the executable file contained in the `eclipse` folder (the one with the big, blue, round eclipse icon).

Installing JBoss tools

The next step is to install the WildFly 8 adapter, which is a part of the suite of plugins named JBoss tools. Installing new plugins in Eclipse is pretty simple; just perform the following steps:

1. From the menu, navigate to **Help** | **Eclipse Marketplace**.
2. Then, search for the plugin you want to install (in this case, type `jboss tools`).
3. Finally, click on **Install** as shown in the following screenshot:

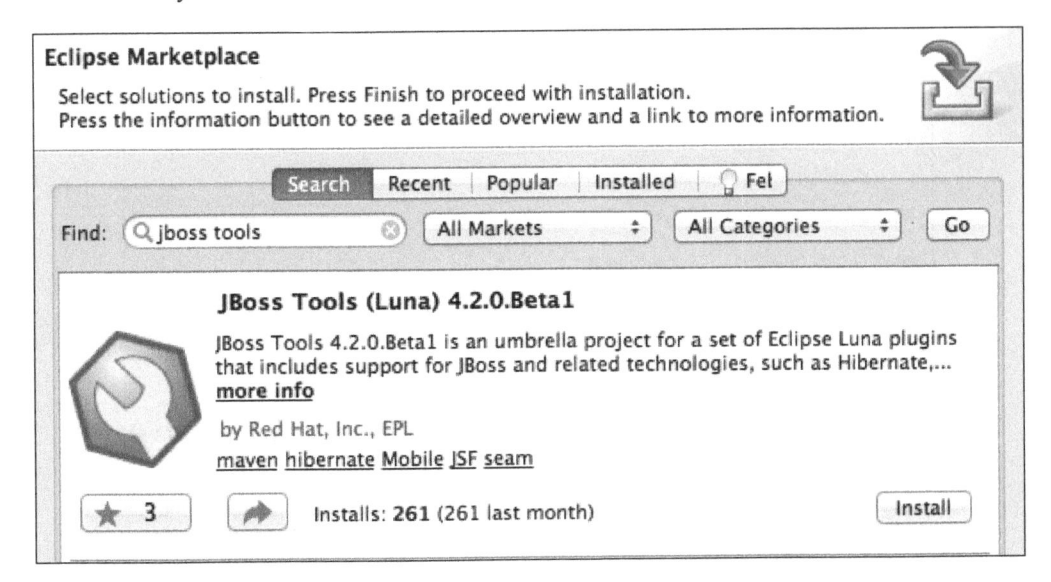

Make sure you select the version of JBoss tools that matches your version of Eclipse, for example, Luna or Kepler. In this case, we are using Eclipse Luna, so I have selected the Luna version of JBoss tools. If you want to install just the WildFly adapter, select **JBossAS Tools**. Agree to the terms and click on **OK**. Restart Eclipse when prompted to do so.

You can now set up the WildFly server in Eclipse by performing the following steps:

1. Navigate to **New** | **Server**.
2. Expand the **JBoss Community** node.

Installing WildFly

3. Select the option, **WildFly 8**, as shown in the following screenshot:

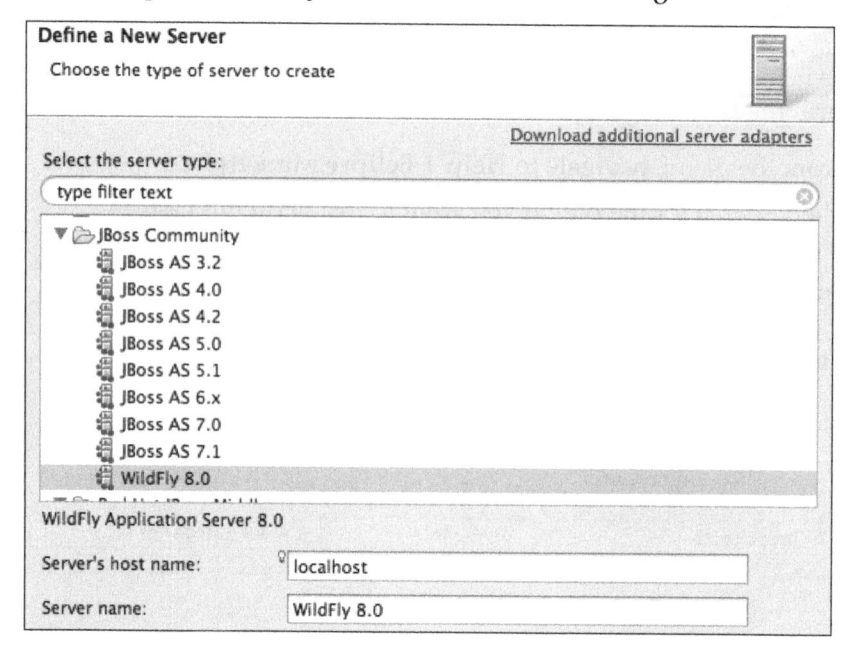

4. Make sure you select your installed Java 8 JRE.
5. Point the home directory to that of your WildFly root directory, as shown in the following screenshot:

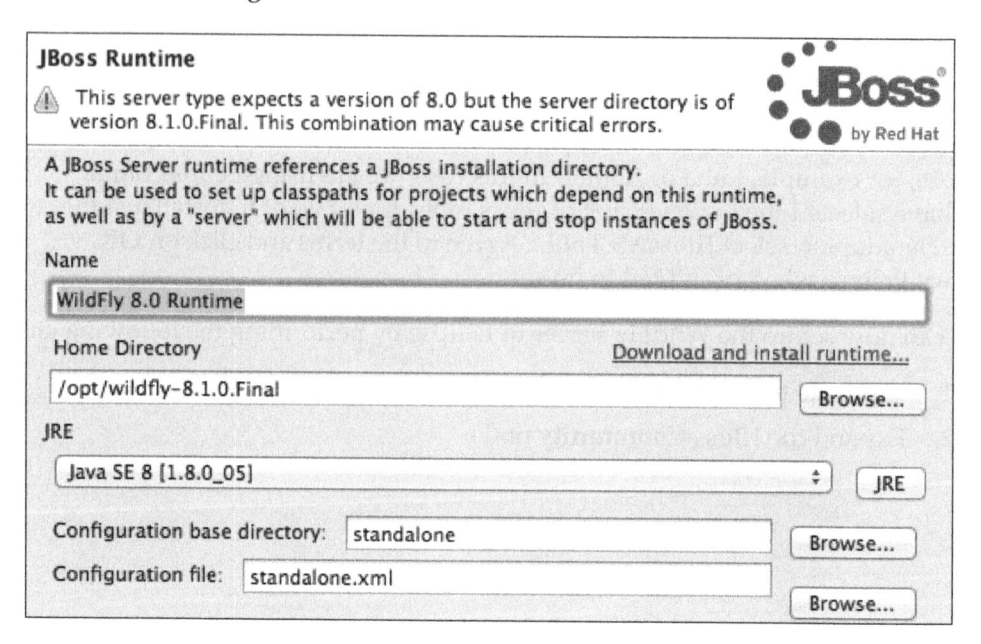

Exploring the application server filesystem

Now that we are done with the installation of all the necessary tools, we will concentrate on the application server structure. The first thing you'll notice when you browse through the application server folders is that its filesystem is basically divided into two core parts: the dichotomy reflects the distinction between **standalone** servers and **domain** servers.

The concept of a domain server is not new in the market of application servers, however, it was only introduced in JBoss with AS 7 as a way to *manage and coordinate* a set of instances of the application server. An application server node which is not configured as part of a domain is qualified as a standalone server. A standalone server resembles, in practice, a single instance of the application server you used to see in releases of the application server prior to JBoss AS 7.

We will discuss the concept of domains in detail in *Chapter 5, Configuring a WildFly Domain*. For the time being, we will explore the different filesystem structures for both kinds of servers.

From a bird's-eye perspective, we can see that the main filesystem is split in two: one section that is pertinent to domain servers and another that is relative to standalone servers. The following diagram depicts the tree of the application server:

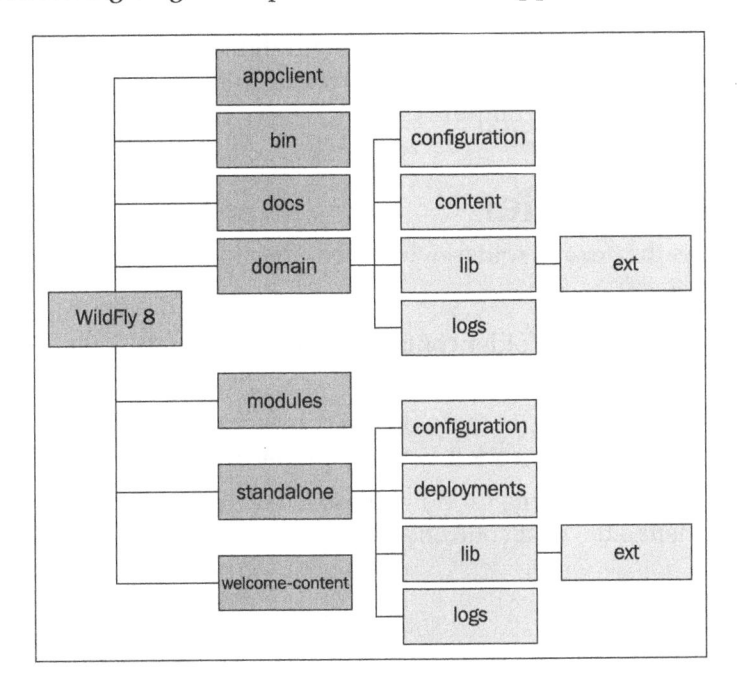

Installing WildFly

In the next section, we will dig deeper into the folder structure of the WildFly application server, dissecting its content and looking at what it is used for.

The bin folder

The bin folder is where you will find all your startup scripts, such as standalone.sh and domain.sh. In addition to the startup scripts, you can find standalone.conf, which can be used to customize WildFly's bootstrap process.

As you saw earlier, the bin folder also includes the jboss-cli.sh script (jboss-cli.bin for Windows users), which starts the interactive CLI. You will also find various other useful scripts, such as add-user.sh and vault.sh. This folder also contains the web services utility scripts (wsconsume.sh and wsprovide.sh) used to generate the web services definition language and the corresponding Java interfaces.

There are several subfolders within the bin directory. The service folder and the init.d folder contain programs that allow you to install WildFly as service on Windows and Linux, respectively.

The docs folder

The docs folder contains two subfolders, examples and schema. The schema folder contains all the .xsd schema definition files used by the configuration as schema.

The examples folder contains numerous configuration examples, from a minimalistic standalone example to an ec2 HA example (HA meaning high availability, and ec2 referring to Amazon Elastic Compute Cloud).

The domain folder

The next folder is the domain folder, which contains the domain structure split across a set of folders:

- The configuration folder contains all the configuration files:
    - The main configuration file is domain.xml, which contains all services that are used by the nodes of the domain. It also configures the socket-binding interfaces for all services.
    - Another key file for domains is host.xml, which is used to define the **host** controller (**HC**).

[22]

- The last file contained in the configuration folder is `logging.properties`, which is used to define the logging format of the bootstrap process for both the **process** controller (**PC**) and host controller.

- The `content` folder is used as a repository to store deployed modules.
- The `lib` folder hosts the subfolder `ext`, which is there to support Java SE/EE style extensions. Some of the application server deployers are able to scan this folder for additional libraries that are picked up by the local class loader. Nevertheless, this approach is not recommended and is maintained only for compliance with the language specifications. The `modules` folder should be used to install your libraries within WildFly.
- The `log` folder, as you might imagine, contains the logging output of the domain. The file, by default, is truncated every time the server is rebooted.
- The `servers` folder holds a set of subfolders for each server defined in the configuration file. The most useful directory contained beneath each server is the `log` folder, which is the location where single instances emit their log.
- The `data` folder is used by the application server to store its runtime data, such as transaction logging.
- Finally, the `tmp` folder is used to store temporary files written by the server.

The standalone folder

If you are running the application server in standalone mode, this is the part of the filesystem you will be interested in. Its structure is quite similar to the `domain` folder with the notable exception of a `deployment` folder. Let's proceed with order. Just below the `standalone` folder, you will find the following set of subdirectories:

- configuration
- data
- deployments
- lib
- log
- tmp

The content and use of these subdirectories is explained as follows:

- The `configuration` folder contains the application server configuration files. As a matter of fact, the application server ships with a set of different configuration files, each one using a different set of extensions. Launching the standalone startup script without passing in any parameters will, by default, use the `standalone.xml` configuration file.

  Besides `standalone.xml`, this folder contains the `logging.properties` file that configures the logging of the bootstrap process. The other files you will find here are `mgmt-users.properties` and `mgmt-group.properties`, which can be used to secure the management interfaces. Security is discussed in detail in *Chapter 10, Securing WildFly*.

- The `data` folder is used by the application server to store its runtime data, such as transaction logging.

- The `deployments` folder is the location in which users can place their deployment content (for example, WAR, EAR, JAR, and SAR files) to have it automatically deployed in the server runtime. Users, particularly those running production systems, are encouraged to use WildFly's management APIs to upload and deploy deployment content instead of relying on the deployment scanner subsystem that periodically scans this directory. See *Chapter 6, Application Structure and Deployment*, for more details.

- The `lib` folder hosts the subfolder `ext`, which is used to define extensions of the application server. The same considerations for the domain's `lib` path apply here.

- The `log` folder contains the logs emitted by the standalone instance of the application server. The default logfile, named `server.log`, is, by default, truncated every time the server is rebooted. This can be configured within the `standalone.xml` file.

- The `tmp` folder is used to save temporary files written by WildFly.

The welcome-content folder

The `welcome-content` folder contains the default page, which is loaded when you browse to the root of your application server (`http://localhost:8080`). In terms of web server configuration, this is the **Web root context**.

The modules folder

Beneath the `modules` folder, you will find the application server's set of libraries, which are a part of the server distribution.

Historically, JBoss AS releases used to manage their set of libraries in different ways. Let's recap to bring about some order. Earlier, Release 4.x was used to define the core server libraries into the `JBOSS_HOME/server` libraries. Thereafter, each server definition had its specific library in the `server/<servername>/lib` folder.

This approach was pretty simple, however, it led to a useless proliferation of libraries that were replicated in the `default/all` server distribution.

Releases 5.x and 6.x had the concept of the `common/lib` folder, which was the main repository for all modules that were common to all server definitions. Each server distribution still contained a `server/<servername>/lib` path for the libraries that were specific to that server definition. Unchanged from the earlier release was the repository for core server modules comprised by `JBOSS_HOME/server`.

JBoss AS 7 followed a more modular approach improving over all the earlier approaches. This modular approach remains unchanged in WildFly. The server bootstrap library, `jboss-modules.jar`, can be found in the root of the application server. This single archive is all you need to bootstrap WildFly's application server kernel.

The main system modules are located in the `system/layers/base` folder under the `modules` folder. This has changed slightly in WildFly as, in JBoss AS 7, all modules were defined directly in the `modules` folder.

The following table outlines the diverse approaches used across different server releases:

AS release	Bootstrap libraries	Server libraries
4.x	`JBOSS_HOME/server`	`JBOSS_HOME/server/<server>/lib`
5.x and 6.x	`JBOSS_HOME/server`	`JBOSS_HOME/common/lib` and `JBOSS_HOME/server/<server>/lib`
7.x and 8.x	`JBOSS_HOME/jboss-modules.jar`	`JBOSS_HOME/modules`

Listing all the modules will take up too much space, however, the module repository layout is often the same as the module name. For example, the `org.jboss.as.ejb3` module can be found in the `org/jboss/as/ejb3` subfolder of the `modules` folder. This approach to organizing the modules certainly makes sense, and if you are used to a maven repository layout structure, you will have no problem getting your head around it.

In the last section of this chapter, we will see how modules are actually loaded by the application server.

Understanding WildFly's kernel

WildFly's kernel was redesigned in JBoss AS 7. Understanding the details of the modular kernel will help you understand concepts introduced later in the book. The kernel is based on two main projects, as follows:

- **JBoss Modules**: This project handles class loading of resources in the container. You can think about JBoss modules as a thin bootstrap wrapper for executing an application in a modular environment.
- **Modular Service Container** (**MSC**): This project provides a way to install, uninstall, and manage services used by a container. MSC further enables resource injection into services and dependency management between services.

The following diagram depicts the basic architecture of WildFly's server kernel:

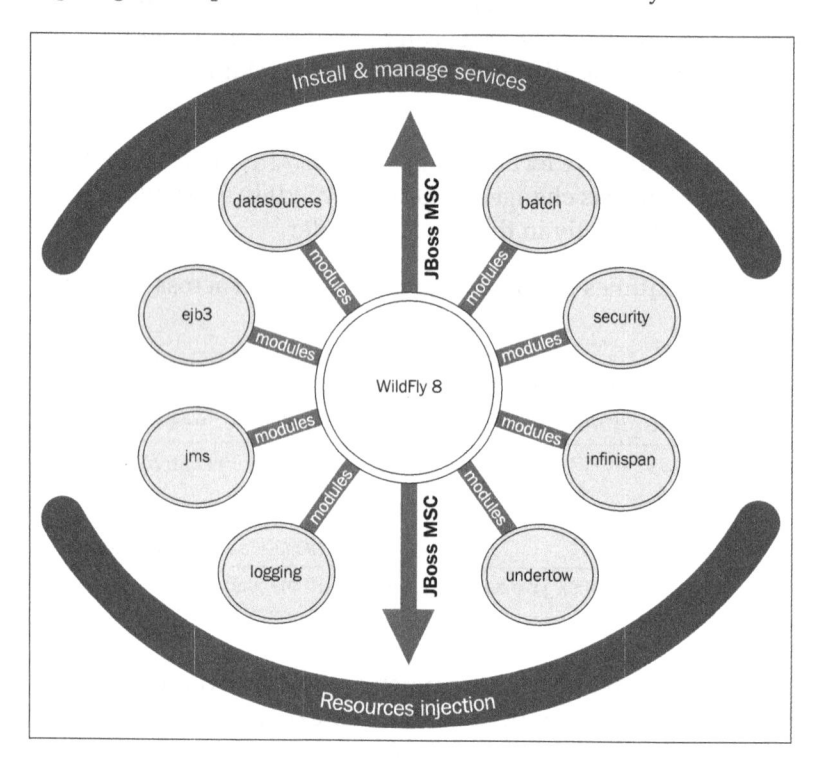

With this information, we can now progress to the loading of server modules.

Loading application server modules

Learning more about JBoss modules is essential if you want to understand the server configuration discussed in the next few chapters. At its heart, a module is really just a wrapper for a JAR file but treated by the application container as a module. The reason for this is class loading and dependency management, as each module can be treated as a pluggable unit, as depicted by the next diagram. WildFly has two different types of modules; the only difference between them is the way they are packaged:

- Static modules
- Dynamic modules

Have a look at the following screenshot:

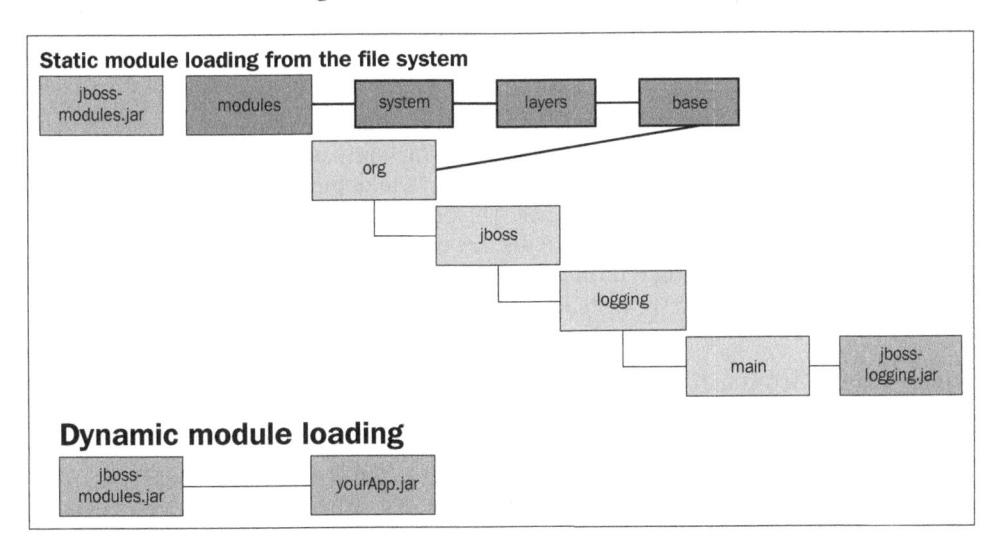

Static module loading from the file system

jboss-modules.jar → modules → system → layers → base
                                          ↓
                                         org
                                          ↓
                                        jboss
                                          ↓
                                       logging
                                          ↓
                                        main → jboss-logging.jar

Dynamic module loading

jboss-modules.jar → yourApp.jar

Using a static module is the simplest way to load a module, and it's used as the default module when starting up the application server. Static modules are defined within the `JBOSS_HOME/modules/system/layers/base` directory. Each module has a configuration file called `module.xml`. The following example shows the contents of the `javax.batch.api module.xml` file:

```
<module xmlns="urn:jboss:module:1.3" name="javax.batch.api">
    <resources>
        <resource-root path="jboss-batch-api_1.0_spec-1.0.0.Final.jar"/>
    </resources>
    <dependencies>
```

```xml
        <module name="javax.api"/>
        <module name="javax.enterprise.api"/>
    </dependencies>
</module>
```

As you can see, a module definition contains two main elements, the **resources** defined in the module (and their path) and the module's **dependencies**. In this example, the main resource is `jboss-batch-api_1.0_spec-1.0.0.Final.jar`, contained in the same folder as the `module.xml` file. It has dependencies on two other modules, `javax.api` and `javax.enterprise.api`.

A module which is defined with a `main-class` element is said to be **executable**. In other words, the module name can be listed on the command line, and the standard static `main(String[])` method in the named module's `main-class` will be loaded and executed.

> Creating custom static modules is useful should you have many applications deployed to your server, which rely on the same third-party libraries. This means that you do not have to deploy multiple applications with the same bundled libraries. The other benefit to creating custom static modules is that you can declare explicit dependencies on other static modules. Installing modules is covered in *Chapter 3, Configuring Enterprise Services*, in which we install a JDBC driver as a module.

The other way to approach the module repository is by using dynamic modules. This can be achieved in two ways, as follows:

- Firstly, we can add the module information, such as its dependencies, within the MANIFEST file within your JAR, for example, in the Main class `mypackage/MyClass`:

    ```
    Dependencies: org.jboss.logging
    ```

- The second way to do this is by adding the dependency to the `jboss-deployment-structure.xml` file, as shown in the following code:

    ```xml
    <jboss-deployment-structure>
      <deployment>
        <dependencies>
          <module name="org.jboss.logging" />
        </dependencies>
      </deployment>
    </jboss-deployment-structure>
    ```

We will cover this in more detail in *Chapter 6, Application Structure and Deployment*, in which we explain class loading.

Summary

In this chapter, we outlined the latest features that come shipped with WildFly.

We have seen that WildFly is composed of modular architecture, and that the kernel of WildFly is made up of two separate projects: JBoss Modules and MSC.

This modular architecture results in an exceptionally light kernel that is able to load modules as required, resulting in a quicker startup time.

The physical structure of the application server reflects the dichotomy between standalone servers and domain servers, the former being a single node instance and the latter a set of managed resources controlled by a domain controller and a host controller.

In the next chapter, we will dig deeper into the details of how to configure the application server, focusing our attention on the standalone server configuration file (`standalone.xml`), which contains the configuration for both the core application server and the stack of enterprise services running on top of it.

2
Configuring the Core WildFly Subsystems

The first chapter gave us the basis to get started with WildFly 8. It is time for us to dive right into the configuration of WildFly and see how to manage a standalone instance of the application server. You will see that the entire server is configured within a single file.

The configuration file is made up of a list of subsystems, including the application server core services and standard Java EE services. It is not possible to discuss all the subsystems within a single chapter, so they have been divided over a couple of chapters. By the end of this chapter, you should understand and be able to configure:

- The server configuration file `standalone.xml`
- The application server's thread pool
- The application server's logging subsystem

Configuring our application server

The default configuration files are named `standalone.xml`, for standalone servers, and `domain.xml` for an application server domain. An application server domain can be seen as a specialized server configuration, which also includes the domain and host controller setup. We will discuss the application server domain in *Chapter 5, Configuring a WildFly Domain*. However, as far as the core services configuration is concerned, what we cover here will be suitable for the domain configuration as well. The configuration files (`standalone.xml` and `domain.xml`) are non-static files, which means that runtime changes are persisted to them, for example, adding a new component, such as a JMS destination, or deploying an application.

Configuring the Core WildFly Subsystems

You can define as many configuration files as you need. The WildFly 8.1.0 release provides a few variants of `standalone.xml` (web profile), such as `standalone-full.xml` (full profile), and the `standalone-ha.xml` (web profile with high availability). You can also find some example configuration files in `JBOSS_HOME/docs/examples/configs`. If you want to start the server with a different configuration file, you can start the server with the following parameters:

```
./standalone.sh --server-config standalone-full-ha.xml
```

> The `standalone.xml` file is located in the `JBOSS_HOME/standalone/configuration` folder. This configuration file is in XML format and is validated by a set of `.xsd` files found in the `JBOSS_HOME/docs/schema` folder.

If you want to check the single `.xsd` files, you can find them in the `JBOSS_HOME/docs/schema` folder of your server distribution. You can get to know all the available server parameters with a simple inspection of these files or by importing them into your Eclipse environment. Once they are located in your project, right-click on your file, and navigate to **Generate | XML File**.

The application server configuration follows a tree-like structure that contains, at the root element, the server definition, as shown in the following diagram:

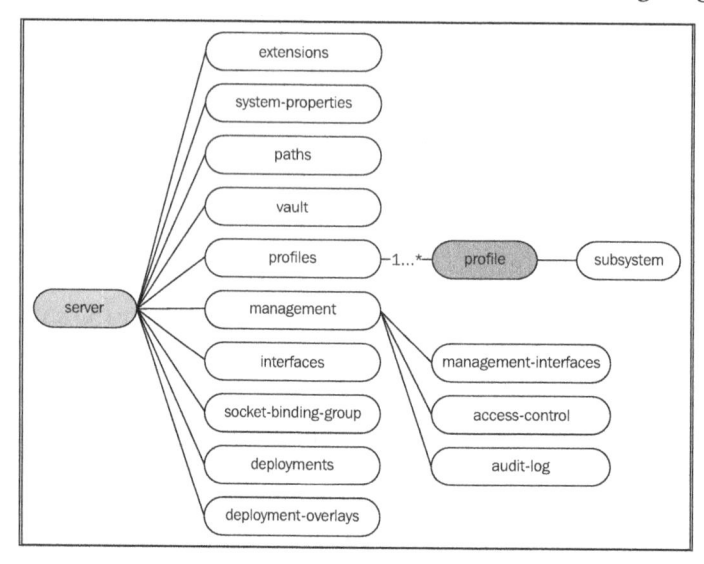

In the following sections, we will show in detail the important parts of the server configuration. This will be helpful to understand the role of each single component in the application server, although you are advised not to manually change the configuration file.

Manually changing the configuration file can lead to unchecked data modifications. This can corrupt the format of the file, preventing WildFly from starting up. If you do need to update the file manually, you should consider making a backup copy first.

> The best practice for changing the server configuration is to use the **command-line interface** (**CLI**) or the web admin console, which are described in *Chapter 7, Using the Management Interfaces*.

Extensions

The application server contains a list of modules that are used to extend the core of the application server. The core of WildFly is very light, and these extensions provide much of the functionality you expect from an application server. Just like regular static modules, they are stored in the JBOSS_HOME/modules folder. Each extension defined in the standalone.xml or domain.xml file is picked up by the WildFly class loader when you start the server, before any applications are deployed. The following code shows an extract from the server configuration:

```xml
<extensions>
    <extension module="org.jboss.as.clustering.infinispan"/>
    <extension module="org.jboss.as.connector"/>
    <extension module="org.jboss.as.deployment-scanner"/>
    <extension module="org.jboss.as.ee"/>
    <extension module="org.jboss.as.ejb3"/>
    ...
</extensions>
```

Paths

Logical names for a filesystem path can be defined using the paths element. These paths can then be referenced by their logical name, rather than having to type the full path each time within the configuration file. By default, the path entry is excluded from the configuration. If you want to include it, you will have to manually add the full configuration. The following example defines a path relative to the WildFly server log with the logical name of log.dir. For a standalone server, this directory translates into JBOSS_HOME/standalone/log/mylogdir:

```xml
<paths>
    <path name="log.dir" path="mylogdir" relative-to="jboss.server.log.dir"/>
</paths>
```

To reference this path in other sections of the configuration file, simply use the logical name as the path. The following example shows the path being used to store the logging, rotating file handler:

```
<periodic-rotating-file-handler name="FILE" autoflush="true">
  <file relative-to="log.dir" path="myserver.log"/>
</periodic-rotating-file-handler>
```

> Please note that the property relative-to is not mandatory. If you don't include it in your path configuration, the path is assumed to be an absolute path.

WildFly provides a set of system paths that are available for you to use without the need to configure them manually. The pre-configured paths are outlined in the following table. The first five paths cannot be overridden, but the rest can be overridden using the path element as shown in the preceding code snippet.

Path	Meaning
jboss.home	The root directory of the WildFly distribution
user.home	The user's home directory
user.dir	The user's current working directory
java.home	The Java installation directory
jboss.server.base.dir	The root directory for an individual server instance
jboss.server.data.dir	The directory the server will use for persistent data file storage
jboss.server.log.dir	The directory the server will use for logfile storage
jboss.server.tmp.dir	The directory the server will use for temporary file storage
jboss.domain.servers.dir	The directory under which a host controller will create the working area for individual server instances

Management interfaces

The management interfaces are configured within the management element. This configuration is used by the CLI, the administration console, and by JMX. Both the native CLI interface and the web console run on admin port number 9990. The following example is taken from the default server configuration and highlights the ports used for the management interfaces:

```
<socket-binding-group name="standard-sockets" default-interface="public">
    <socket-binding name="management-http" interface="management" port="9990"/>
```

```
    <socket-binding name="management-https" interface="management"
       port="9993"/>
</socket-binding-group>
```

In the following code snippet, we show the preceding `socket-binding` configuration being referenced by the `management-interfaces` section of the `standalone.xml` file:

```
<management-interfaces>
    <http-interface security-realm="ManagementRealm" http-upgrade-
       enabled="true">
        <socket-binding http="management-http"/>
    </http-interface>
</management-interfaces>
```

Management interfaces are discussed in detail in *Chapter 7, Using the Management Interfaces*, which provides detailed coverage of the application server management tools.

Profiles and subsystems

A profile can be seen as a collection of subsystems, and each subsystem in turn contains a subset of functionalities added to the application server by means of extensions (see the *Extensions* section). For example, the web subsystem contains the definition of a set of connectors used by the container, the messaging subsystem defines the JMS configuration and modules used by the AS's messaging provider, and so on.

One important difference between a standalone file and a domain configuration file is the number of profiles contained in it. When using a standalone configuration, there's a single profile that contains the set of subsystem configurations. Domain configuration can, on the other hand, provide multiple profiles.

Interfaces

Interfaces define a logical name for where network interfaces/IP address or host names can be bound.

By default, the standalone application server defines two available network interfaces, the `management` interface and the `public` interface:

```
<interfaces>
    <interface name="management">
        <inet-address value="${jboss.bind.address.
            management:127.0.0.1}"/>
    </interface>
```

```xml
<interface name="public">
    <inet-address value="${jboss.bind.address:127.0.0.1}"/>
</interface>
</interfaces>
```

The `public` network interface is intended to be used for the application server core services:

```xml
<socket-binding-group name="standard-sockets" default-interface="public">
    ...
</socket-binding-group>
```

The `management` network interface is referenced by the AS management interfaces, as shown in the *Management interfaces* section.

By default, both network interfaces resolve to the loop back address `127.0.0.1`. This means that the application server public services and the management services are accessible only from the local machine. By changing the `inet-address` value, you can bind the network interface to another IP address. The following example shows the server listening on IP `192.168.1.1`:

```xml
<interface name="public">
    <inet-address value="192.168.1.1"/>
</interface>
```

If, on the other hand, you want to bind the network interface to all available sets of IP addresses, you can use the `<any-address />` element, as follows:

```xml
<interface name="public">
    <any-address />
</interface>
```

Another useful variation of network interface is the **Network Interface Card (nic)** element, which gathers the address information from the network card name:

```xml
<interface name="public">
    <nic name="eth0" />
</interface>
```

> **Binding management interfaces via CLI**
>
> You can also bind your public interface using the `-b` switch, followed by a valid host/IP address. This will cause the server to listen on the host/IP address provided. For example, to bind all public interfaces to all IPv4 addresses, you will use `$JBOSS_HOME/bin/standalone.sh -b=0.0.0.0`.

The socket-binding groups

A socket-binding group defines a logical name for a socket. Each socket-binding name can be referenced in other parts of the configuration file. In this section, you are able to configure the network port that will be listening for incoming connections. Every socket-binding group references a network interface through the default-interface attribute. Have a look at the following code snippet:

```
<socket-binding-group name="standard-sockets" default-
interface="public">
        <socket-binding name="management-http" interface="management"
port="9990"/>
        <socket-binding name="management-https" interface="management"
port="9993"/>
        <socket-binding name="ajp" port="8009"/>
        <socket-binding name="http" port="8080"/>
        <socket-binding name="https" port="8443"/>
<socket-binding name="jacorb" interface="unsecure" port="3528"/>
        <socket-binding name="jacorb-ssl" interface="unsecure"
port="3529"/>
        <socket-binding name="txn-recovery-environment" port="4712"/>
        <socket-binding name="txn-status-manager" port="4713"/>
</socket-binding-group>
```

In order to change the port where a service is bound, you can change the port attribute of its service, but a better approach is to use one of the management interfaces. This will provide an immediate outcome of the affected change. In the following example, we are going to change the default port for the http connector using the CLI:

```
[standalone@localhost:9990 /] /socket-binding-group=
  standard-sockets/socket-binding=http:write-attribute(name="port",
  value="8090")
{
  "outcome" => "success",
  "response-headers" => {
    "operation-requires-reload" => true,
    "process-state" => "reload-required"
  }
}
```

You may have noticed in the response shown above that a reload is required. This can be achieved by executing the following command:

```
[standalone@localhost:9990 /] :reload
```

System properties

This section contains a set of system-wide properties, which can be added to the application server as part of the booting process. By default, the `system-properties` entry is excluded from the configuration. If you want to use this feature, you will need to add the full configuration. The following configuration snippet sets the property named example to `true`:

```
<system-properties>
    <property name="myboolean" value="true"/>
</system-properties>
```

The property can be later retrieved on the application server using the following code:

```
String s = System.getProperty("myboolean");
```

Deployments

The last section of the configuration file contains all the deployed applications that have been registered on the application server. Each time a new application is deployed or undeployed, this section is updated to reflect the new application stack.

Configuring core subsystems

Now that you have grasped the basic concepts of the WildFly configuration file, we will look in more detail at single services.

In the following diagram, you can find a rough representation of core WildFly 8 subsystems (for the sake of simplicity, we are including just the subsystems that are covered throughout this book):

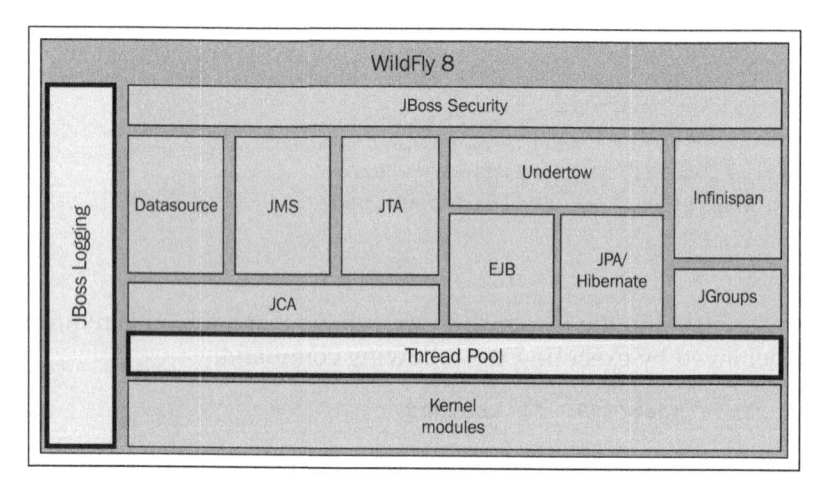

As a first taste of configuring the application server, we will explore the areas that are highlighted in bold in the preceding diagram. These include the following core application server subsystems:

- The thread pool subsystem
- The JBoss logging subsystem

Let's move straight to the first subsystem, the thread pool.

Configuring the thread pool subsystem

Thread pools address two different problems. Firstly, they usually deliver improved performance when executing large numbers of asynchronous tasks due to reduced per-task invocation overhead. Secondly, they provide a means of bounding and managing resources, including threads, consumed when executing a collection of tasks.

In releases of JBoss server prior to JBoss AS 7, the thread pool configuration was centralized in a single file or deployment descriptor. In WildFly, any subsystem that uses thread pools manages its own thread configuration.

By appropriately configuring the thread pool section, you can tune the specific areas that use that kind of pool to deliver new tasks. The application server thread pool configuration can include the following elements:

- Thread factory configuration
- Bounded-queue thread configuration
- Blocking bounded-queue thread configuration
- Unbounded-queue thread configuration
- Queueless thread pool configuration
- Blocking queueless thread pool configuration
- Scheduled thread configuration

> It is important to note that the thread subsystem will probably be marked for deprecation in WildFly 9, but in WildFly 8 this configuration is completely valid.

Let's look at each single element in detail.

Configuring the thread factory

A **thread factory** (implementing `java.util.concurrent.ThreadFactory`) is an object that creates new threads on demand. Using thread factories removes the hardwiring of calls to a new thread, enabling applications to use special thread subclasses, priorities, and so on.

The thread factory is not included in the server configuration by default, as it relies on default values that you will rarely need to modify. Nevertheless, we will provide a simple configuration example for the experienced user who may require complete control of the thread configuration.

The following is an example of a custom thread factory configuration:

```
<thread-factory name="MyThreadFactory"
  thread-name-pattern="My Thread %t"
  group-name="dummy" />
```

The following are the possible attributes that you can use when defining a thread factory:

- The `name` attribute is the name of the created thread factory
- The optional `priority` attribute may be used to specify the thread priority of created threads
- The optional `group-name` attribute specifies the name of the thread group to create for this thread factory
- The `thread-name-pattern` is the template used to create names for threads. The following patterns can be used:

Pattern	Output
%%	Emits a percentage sign
%g	Emits the per-factory thread sequence number
%f	Emits the global thread sequence number
%i	Emits the thread ID
%G	Emits the thread group name

The bounded-queue thread pool

A bounded-queue thread pool is the most common kind of pool used by the application server. It helps prevent resource exhaustion by defining a constraint on the thread pool's size. It is also the most complex to use. Its inherent complexity derives from the fact that it maintains both a fixed-length queue and two pool sizes: a **core size** and a **maximum size**.

If, each time a new task is submitted, the number of running threads is less than the core size, a new thread is created. Otherwise, if there is room in the queue, the task is queued.

If none of these options are viable, the executor needs to evaluate if it can still create a new thread. If the number of running threads is less than the maximum size, a new thread is created. Otherwise, the task is assigned to the designated `hand-off` executor, if one is specified. In the absence of a designated `hand-off` executor, the task will be discarded.

The following diagram summarizes the whole process, showing how all the pieces fit together:

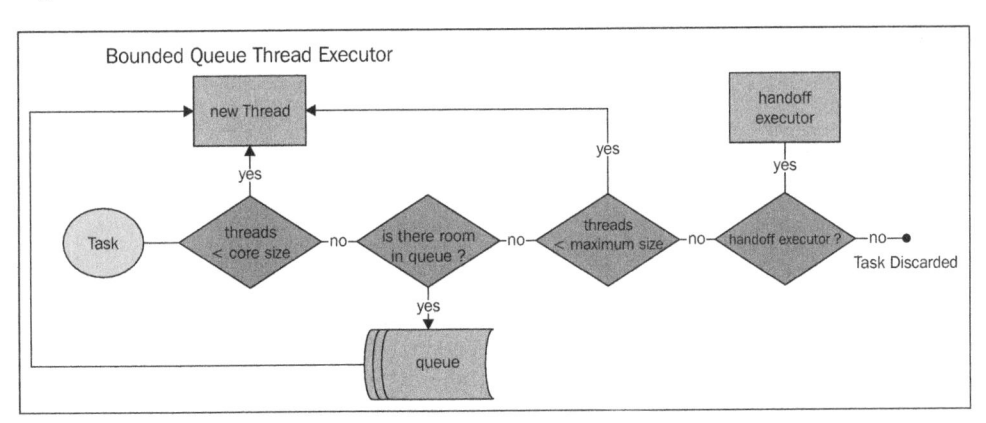

The following is a sample configuration of a bounded-queue thread pool taken from the configuration file:

```
<bounded-queue-thread-pool name="jca-short-running">
   <core-threads count="10"/>
   <queue-length count="10"/>
   <max-threads count="10"/>
   <keepalive-time time="10" unit="seconds"/>
</bounded-queue-thread-pool>
```

> **Downloading the example code**
>
> You can download the example code files for all Packt books you have purchased from your account at http://www.packtpub.com. If you purchased this book elsewhere, you can visit http://www.packtpub.com/support and register to have the files e-mailed directly to you.

The following table gives a short description of each attribute/element:

Attribute/element	Description
name	Specifies the bean name of the created executor
allow-core-timeout	Specifies whether core threads time out or not; if false, only threads above the core size will time out
core-threads	Specifies the core thread pool size, which is smaller than the maximum pool size
max-threads	Specifies the maximum thread pool size
queue-length	Specifies the executor queue length
keepalive-time	Specifies the amount of time that threads beyond the core pool size should be kept running when idle
thread-factory	Specifies the bean name of a specific thread factory to use to create worker threads
handoff-executor	Specifies an executor to delegate tasks to in the event that a task cannot be accepted

> **Performance focus**
>
> **Queue size** and **pool size** values are a performance tradeoff, and the right balance needs to be found between the two. When using a small pool with a large queue, you minimize CPU usage, OS resources, and context-switching overhead. It can, however, produce an artificially low throughput. If tasks are strongly I/O bound (and thus frequently blocked), a system may be able to schedule time for more threads than you otherwise allow. The use of small queues generally requires larger pool sizes, which keep the CPUs busier but may encounter unacceptable scheduling overhead, which also decreases throughput.

The blocking bounded-queue thread pool

The blocking bounded-queue thread pool has a very similar configuration to the bounded-queue thread pool; it has a slightly different workflow. The difference being, rather than attempting to hand off to the designated hand-off executor, the caller blocks until room becomes available in the queue.

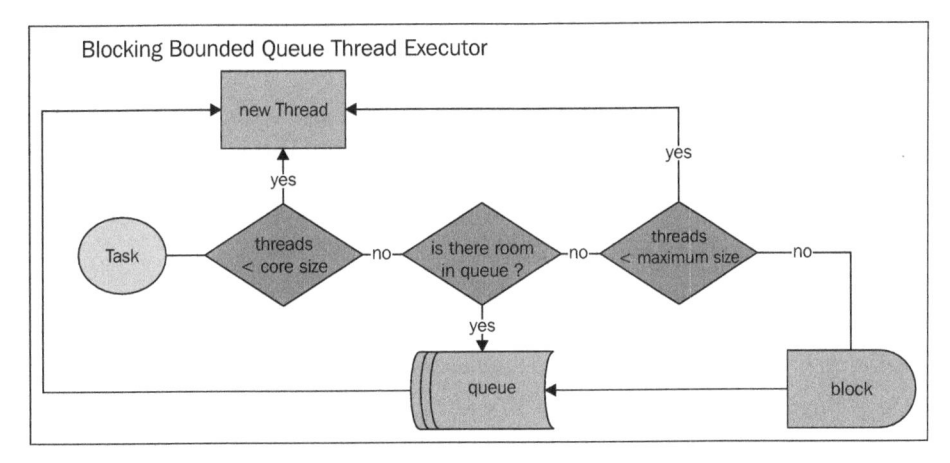

The flowchart for this thread pool is shown as follows:

The following is an example configuration for a blocking bounded-queue thread pool:

```
<blocking-bounded-queue-thread-pool name="jca-short-running">
    <core-threads count="10"/>
    <queue-length count="10"/>
    <max-threads count="10"/>
    <keepalive-time time="10" unit="seconds"/>
</bounded-queue-thread-pool>
```

Please see the following table for the bounded-queue thread pool for a description of each attribute/element. The attributes/elements available for the blocking bounded-queue thread pool are shown in the following table:

Attribute/element	Description
name	Specifies the bean name of the created executor
allow-core-timeout	Specifies whether core threads may time out or not; if `false`, only threads above the core size will time out
core-threads	Specifies the core thread pool size, which is smaller than the maximum pool size
max-threads	Specifies the maximum thread pool size
queue-length	Specifies the executor queue length
keepalive-time	Specifies the amount of time that threads beyond the core pool size should be kept running when idle
thread-factory	Specifies the bean name of a specific thread factory to use to create worker threads

The unbounded-queue thread pool

The unbounded-queue thread pool executor follows a simpler but more risky approach than the bounded thread pool; that is, it always accepts new tasks.

In practice, the unbounded thread pool has a core size and a queue with no upper limit. When a task is submitted, if the number of running threads is less than the core size, a new thread is created. Otherwise, the task is placed in a queue. If too many tasks are allowed to be submitted to this type of executor, an out-of-memory condition may occur. Have a look at the following flowchart:

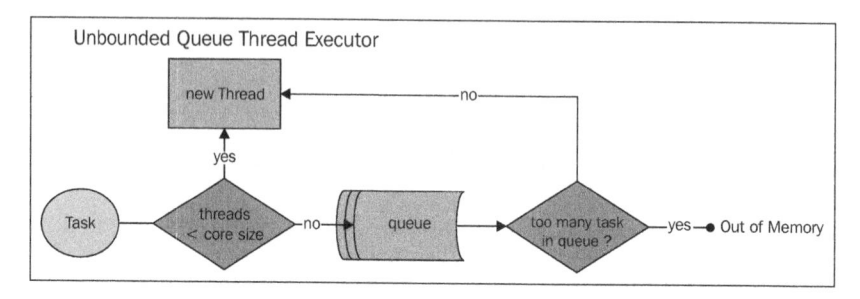

Due to its inherent risk, unbounded thread pools are not included by default in the server configuration. We will provide a sample here, with only one recommendation: don't try this at home, kids!

```
<unbounded-queue-thread-pool name="unbounded-threads">
    <max-threads count="10" />
    <keepalive-time time="10" unit="seconds"/>
</unbounded-queue-thread-pool>
```

If you want to know more about the meaning of each thread pool element/attribute, you can refer to the bounded thread pool table.

The attributes/elements available for the unbounded-queue thread pool are shown in the following table:

Attribute/element	Description
name	Specifies the bean name of the created executor
max-threads	Specifies the maximum thread pool size
keepalive-time	Specifies the amount of time that threads beyond the core pool size should be kept running when idle
thread-factory	Specifies the bean name of a specific thread factory to use to create worker threads

The queueless thread pool

As its name implies, the queueless thread pool is a thread pool executor with no queue. Basically, this executor short-circuits the logic of the bounded thread executor, as it does not attempt to store the task in a queue.

So, when a task is submitted, if the number of running threads is less than the maximum size, a new thread is created. Otherwise, the task is assigned to the designated `hand-off` executor if one is specified. Without any designated `hand-off`, the task will be discarded. Have a look at the following flowchart:

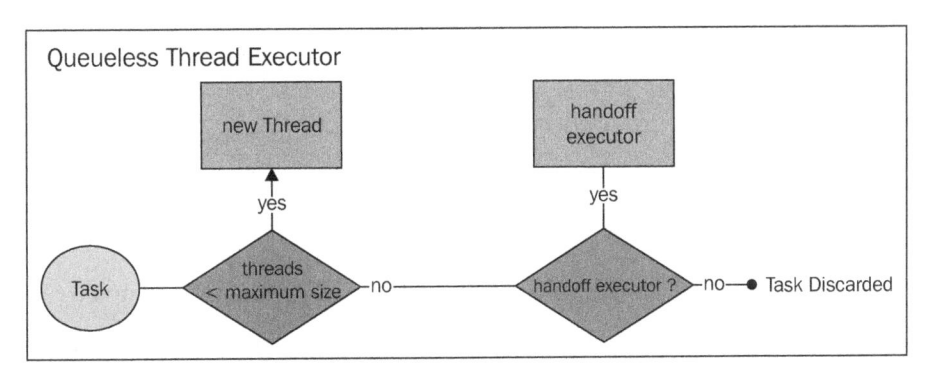

Queueless executors are also not included by default in the configuration file. However, we will provide a sample configuration here:

```
<queueless-thread-pool
  name="queueless-thread-pool" blocking="true">
  <max-threads count="10"/>
  <keepalive-time time="10" unit="seconds"/>
</queueless-thread-pool>
```

The blocking queueless thread pool

The blocking queueless thread pool has a similar configuration to the queueless thread pool. Similar to the blocking queue thread pool, the difference is that rather than attempting to hand off to the designated hand-off executor, the caller blocks until room becomes available in the queue.

Have a look at the following diagram:

Blocking Queueless Thread Executor — Task → (threads < maximum size?) — yes → new Thread; no → block.

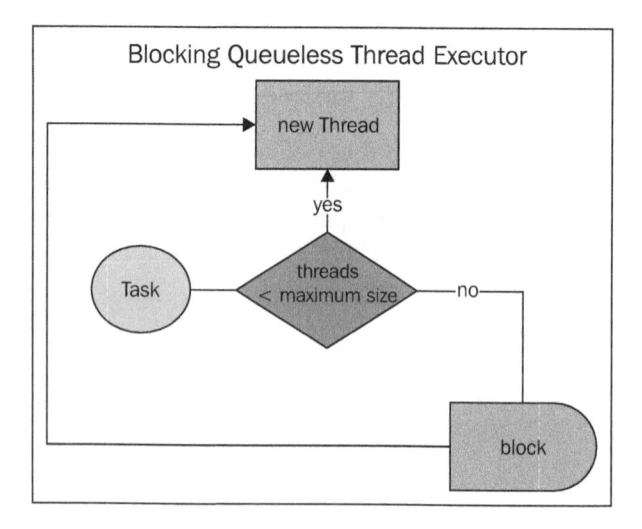

Although not included in the default configuration file, here is an example:

```xml
<blocking-queueless-thread-pool name="queueless-thread-pool">
    <max-threads count="10" />
    <keepalive-time time="10" unit="seconds"/>
</blocking-queueless-thread-pool>
```

The attributes/elements available for the unbounded-queue thread pool are `name`, `max-threads`, `keepalive-time`, and `thread-factory`.

The scheduled thread pool

The server-scheduled thread pool is used for activities on the server side that require running periodically or with delays. It maps internally to a `java.util.concurrent.ScheduledThreadPoolExecutor` instance. Have a look at the following diagram:

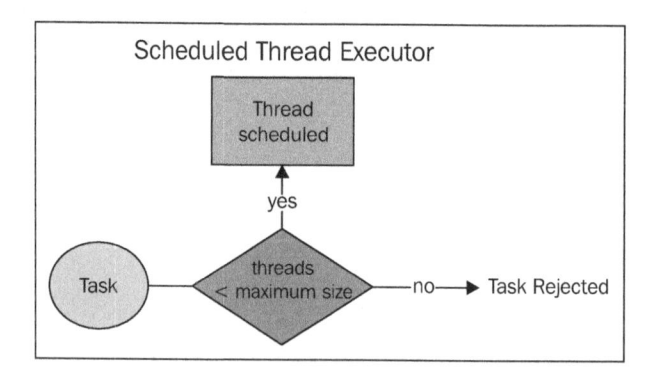

Scheduled Thread Executor — Task → (threads < maximum size?) — yes → Thread scheduled; no → Task Rejected.

This type of executor is configured with the `scheduled-thread-pool` executor element, as follows:

```
<scheduled-thread-pool name="remoting">
   <max-threads count="10"/>
   <keepalive-time time="10" unit="seconds"/>
</scheduled-thread-pool>
```

The scheduled thread pool is used by the `remoting` framework and by the HornetQ subsystem, which uses both a bounded JCA thread executor and a scheduled pool for delayed delivery.

Configuring application server logging

Every application needs to trace logging statements. At the moment, there are several implementations of logging libraries for Java applications, the most popular ones are:

- **Log4j**: It is a flexible open source logging library from Apache. Log4j is widely used in the open source community, and it was the default logging implementation on earlier releases of JBoss AS.
- **Java SE logging libraries (JUL)**: It provides the logging classes and interfaces as part of the Java SE platform's standard libraries.

Log4j and JUL have very similar APIs. They differ conceptually only in small details, but do more or less the same thing, with the exception of log4j, which has more features. You may or may not need these features.

The JBoss logging framework is based on JUL, which is built around three main concepts: **loggers**, **handlers**, and **formatters**. These concepts allow developers to log messages according to their type and priority and to control where messages end up and how they look when they get there.

The following diagram shows the logging cycle using the JUL framework. The application makes logging calls on the logger objects. These logger objects allocate the `LogRecord` objects, which are passed to the handler objects for publication. Both logger and handler may use the formatter to arrange the layout of logs and filter to decide whether they are interested in a particular log record.

Have a look at the following diagram:

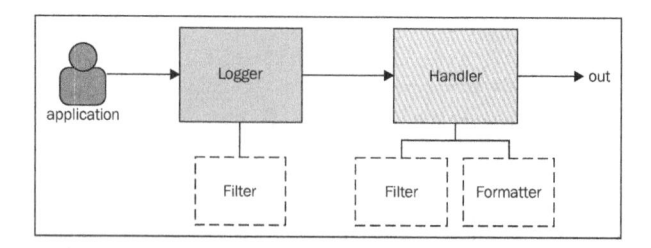

Choosing your logging implementation

The WildFly/JBoss application server, through its releases, has used different frameworks to handle application server logs. In JBoss AS 5 and earlier, log4j was the default logging API used by the application server.

Since JBoss AS 6, the logging provider switched to JBoss's own implementation, which is based on the JDK 1.4 logging system. However, it provides several fixes and workarounds for many shortcomings in the default JDK implementation.

For example, the default implementation of `java.util.logging` provided in the JDK does not have per-web application logging, as the configuration is per-VM.

As a result, WildFly replaces the default JUL log manager implementation with its own implementation, which addresses these issues. The following diagram illustrates the modules that make up the WildFly 8 logging subsystem:

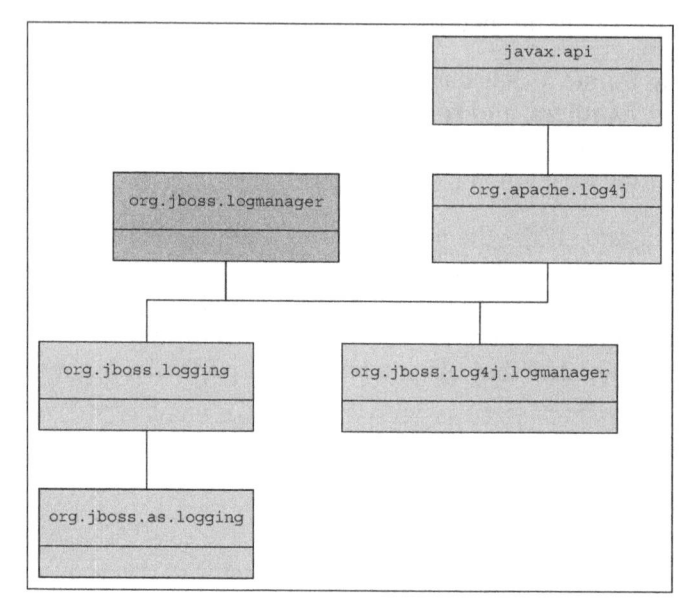

At the top of the hierarchy, there's the `org.jboss.logmanager` module, which is the top-level library that manages logs for the JBoss logging subsystem. Under jboss logmanager, you can find concrete implementations, such as the `org.jboss.logging` and `org.jboss.log4j.logmanager` modules. By default, the application server uses the former module (`org.jboss.logging`), which is implemented in turn by `org.jboss.as.logging` to manage your logs inside the application server. However, if you want to switch to the log4j implementation, the `org.jboss.log4j.logmanager` module is what you need (in the last section of this chapter, we will include an example of how to use log4j in your application).

> WildFly is not limited to JBoss logging or log4j. You can use any logging library, including slf4j or commons logging.

Configuring the logging subsystem

The logging subsystem contains a set of log handlers out of the box. A handler object takes log messages from a logger and exports them. For example, it might write them to a console or a file, send them to a network logging service, or forward them to an OS log. By default, the following handlers are defined:

- `console-handler`
- `periodic-rotating-file-handler`
- `size-rotating-file-handler`
- `async-handler`
- `syslog-handler`
- `custom-handler`

The console-handler

The `console-handler` defines a handler that simply writes log messages to the console, as follows:

```
<console-handler name="CONSOLE" autoflush="true">
  <level name="INFO"/>
  <formatter>
    <pattern-formatter pattern="%d{HH:mm:ss,SSS} %-5p [%c] (%t)
      %s%E%n"/>
  </formatter>
</console-handler>
```

The optional `autoflush` attribute determines if buffered logs are flushed automatically. The default value for this option is `true`.

The `level` element defines the lowest log level associated with the handler, which means that anything with this log level and a higher value will be logged. The full range of log levels, from lowest to highest, are: `OFF`, `FINEST`, `FINER`, `FINE`, `CONFIG`, `INFO`, `WARNING`, `SEVERE`, and `ALL`.

The `formatter` element provides support to format `LogRecords`. The log formatting inherits the same pattern strings as that of the layout pattern of `log4j`, which was in turn inspired by dear old C's `printf` function. Check the log4j documentation at http://logging.apache.org/log4j/1.2/apidocs/org/apache/log4j/PatternLayout.html.

Here, we will just mention that `%d{HH:mm:ss,SSS}` outputs the date of the logging event using the conversion included in brackets.

- The string `%-5p` outputs the priority of the logging event
- The string `[%c]` is used to output the category of the logging event
- The string `(%t)` outputs the thread that generated the logging event
- The string `%s` outputs the log message
- Finally, the `%n` string outputs the platform-dependent line separator character or characters

The periodic-rotating-file-handler

The `periodic-rotating-file-handler` defines a handler that writes to a file and rotates the log after a time period derived from the given suffix string, which should be in a format understood by `java.text.SimpleDateFormat`.

Here's the definition of it:

```
<periodic-rotating-file-handler name="FILE" autoflush="true">
  <level name="INFO"/>
  <formatter>
    <pattern-formatter pattern="%d{HH:mm:ss,SSS} %-5p [%c] (%t)
      %s%E%n"/>
  </formatter>
  <file relative-to="jboss.server.log.dir" path="server.log"/>
  <suffix value=".yyyy-MM-dd"/>
  <append value="true"/>
</periodic-rotating-file-handler>
```

This handler introduces the file element containing the path, which is the actual filename and its `relative-to` position. In our case, the relative position corresponds to the `jboss.server.log.dir` application server parameter.

> With the default suffix configuration, logs are rolled at 12 PM. By changing the value of `SimpleDateFormat`, you can also change the period when logs are rotated, for example, the suffix yyyy-MM-dd-HH will rotate the logs every hour.

The size-rotating-file-handler

The `size-rotating-file-handler` defines a handler that writes to a file, rotating the log after the size of the file grows beyond a certain point. It also keeps a fixed number of backups.

There's no size handler defined in the standard configuration. However, we can find out its basic configuration from the JBOSS_HOME/docs/schema/jboss-as-logging_2_0.xsd file. Have a look at the following code:

```xml
<size-rotating-file-handler name="FILESIZE" autoflush="true" >
  <rotate-size value="500k" />
  <level name="INFO"/>
  <formatter>
    <pattern-formatter pattern="%d{HH:mm:ss,SSS} %-5p [%c] (%t)
      %s%E%n"/>
  </formatter>
  <file relative-to="jboss.server.log.dir" path="server.log"/>
</size-rotating-file-handler>
```

The async-handler

The `async-handler` is a composite handler that attaches to other handlers to produce asynchronous logging events. Behind the scenes, this handler uses a bounded queue to store events. Every time a log is emitted, the asynchronous handler appends the log into the queue and returns immediately. Here's an example of asynchronous logging for the FILE appender:

```xml
<async-handler name="ASYNC">
  <level name="INFO" />
  <queue-length>1024</queue-length>
  <overflow-action>block</overflow-action>
  <sub-handlers>
    <handler-ref name="FILE" />
  </sub-handlers>
</async-handler>
```

In this handler, we also specify the size of the queue, where events are sent, and the action to take when the `async` queue overflows. You can opt between `block`, causing the calling thread to be blocked, and `discard`, causing the message to be discarded.

> **When should I use the asynchronous handler?**
>
> The asynchronous handler produces a substantial performance benefit to applications that are heavily I/O bound. Conversely, CPU-bound applications may not benefit from asynchronous logging, as it will put additional stress on the CPU.

The syslog-handler

A `syslog-handler` can be used to write logs to a remote logging server. This allows multiple applications to send their log messages to the same server, where they can all be parsed together. Both RFC3164 and RFC5424 formats are supported. Here is an example of a `syslog-handler`:

```xml
<syslog-handler name="SYSLOG" enabled="true">
    <level name="INFO" />
    <port value="514" />
    <server-address value="192.168.0.56" />
    <formatter>
        <syslog-format syslog-type="RFC5424" />
    </formatter>
</syslog-handler>
```

Custom handlers

So far, we have seen just a few basic log handlers, which are usually included in your server configuration. If you need a more advanced approach to managing your logs, you can define a custom logging handler. In order to add a custom handler, you need to define a class that extends the `java.util.logging.Handler` interface and then override its abstract methods. For example, the following class, named `JdbcLogger`, is used to write the logs to a database (full code is available at http://community.jboss.org/wiki/CustomLogHandlersOn701).

> Note that, although this article was written for JBoss AS 7, it remains valid for WildFly 8.

Have a look at the following code snippet:

```
public class JdbcLogger extends Handler{
  @Override
  public void publish(LogRecord record){
    try{
      insertRecord(record);
    }
    catch (SQLException e)  {
      e.printStackTrace();
    }
  }
  @Override
  public void flush() {      . . . .     }
  @Override
  public void close() {      . . . .     }
}
```

Once compiled, this class needs to be packaged in an archive (for example, `logger.jar`) and installed as a module in the application server. We will name the module `com.JDBCLogger`, which requires the following structure under the `modules` folder:

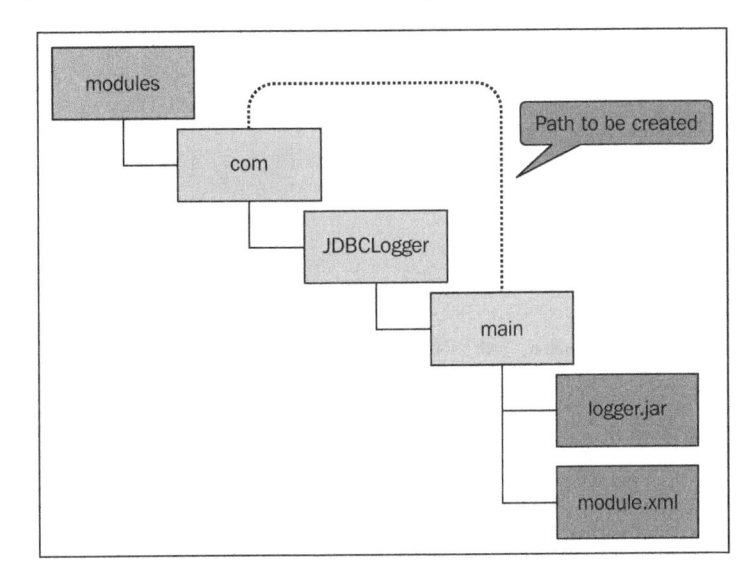

Configuring the Core WildFly Subsystems

The label **Path to be created** shows the directory structure under which we will place the `logger.jar` archive and its configuration file (`module.xml`), which follows here:

```xml
<module xmlns="urn:jboss:module:1.3" name="com.JDBCLogger">
    <resources>
        <resource-root path="logger.jar"/>
    </resources>
    <dependencies>
        <module name="javax.api"/>
        <module name="org.jboss.logging"/>
        <module name="com.mysql"/>
    </dependencies>
</module>
```

Note that this module has a dependency on another module, `com.mysql`. In the next chapter, we will show how to connect to a database after installing the appropriate module.

We are almost done. Now, insert the handler in the logging subsystem, which contains within its properties the database connection strings and the statement that will be used to insert logs into the database:

```xml
<custom-handler name="DB" class="com.sample.JdbcLogger" module="com.JDBCLogger">
    <level name="INFO"/>
    <formatter>
        <pattern-formatter pattern="%d{HH:mm:ss,SSS} %-5p [%c] (%t)
           %s%E%n"/>
    </formatter>
    <properties>
        <property name="driverClassName" value="com.mysql.jdbc.
            Driver"/>
        <property name="jdbcUrl" value="jdbc:mysql://localhost:3306/
            mydb"/>
        <property name="username" value="root"/>
        <property name="password" value="admin"/>
        <property name="insertStatement" value="INSERT INTO into
            log_table VALUES (?, $TIMESTAMP, $LEVEL, $MDC[ip],
            $MDC[user], $MESSAGE, hardcoded)"/>
    </properties>
</custom-handler>
<root-logger>
    <level name="INFO"/>
    <handlers>
        <handler name="CONSOLE"/>
        <handler name="FILE"/>
```

```
        <handler name="DB"/>
    </handlers>
</root-logger>
```

The new `handler`, named `DB`, is enlisted in the `root-logger` to collect all logging statements that have a priority of `INFO` or higher. Before testing the logger, don't forget to create the required tables on your MySQL database, as follows:

```
CREATE TABLE log_table(
    id INT(11) NOT NULL AUTO_INCREMENT,
    `timestamp` VARCHAR(255) DEFAULT NULL,
    level VARCHAR(255) DEFAULT NULL,
    mdc_ip VARCHAR(255) DEFAULT NULL,
    mdc_user VARCHAR(255) DEFAULT NULL,
    message VARCHAR(1500) DEFAULT NULL,
    hardcoded VARCHAR(255) DEFAULT NULL,
    PRIMARY KEY (id)
)
ENGINE = INNODBAUTO_INCREMENT = 1
```

If you have carefully followed all the required steps, you will notice that `log_table` contains the logging events that have been triggered since server startup. Have a look at the following screenshot:

id	timestamp	level	mdc_ip	mdc_user	message
40	2011-09-16	INFO	(null)	(null)	11:35:33,425 INFO [org.jboss.as.connector.subsystems.datasources] (Controller Boot Thread) Deploying JDBC-compliant driver cl...
41	2011-09-16	INFO	(null)	(null)	11:35:33,831 INFO [org.jboss.as.clustering.infinispan.subsystem] (Controller Boot Thread) Activating Infinispan subsystem.
42	2011-09-16	INFO	(null)	(null)	11:35:34,004 INFO [org.jboss.as.naming] (Controller Boot Thread) Activating Naming Subsystem
43	2011-09-16	INFO	(null)	(null)	11:35:34,044 INFO [org.jboss.as.naming] (MSC service thread 1-5) Starting Naming Service
44	2011-09-16	INFO	(null)	(null)	11:35:34,047 INFO [org.jboss.as.osgi] (Controller Boot Thread) Activating OSGi Subsystem
45	2011-09-16	INFO	(null)	(null)	11:35:34,109 INFO [org.jboss.as.security] (Controller Boot Thread) Activating Security Subsystem
46	2011-09-16	INFO	(null)	(null)	11:35:34,116 INFO [org.jboss.remoting] (MSC service thread 1-3) JBoss Remoting version 3.2.0.Beta2
47	2011-09-16	INFO	(null)	(null)	11:35:34,163 INFO [org.xnio] (MSC service thread 1-3) XNIO Version 3.0.0.Beta3
48	2011-09-16	INFO	(null)	(null)	11:35:34,211 INFO [org.xnio.nio] (MSC service thread 1-3) XNIO NIO Implementation Version 3.0.0.Beta3

Configuring loggers

A logger object is used to log messages for a specific system or application components. Loggers are normally named using a hierarchical dot-separated namespace. Logger names can be arbitrary strings, but they should normally be based on the package name or class name of the logged component. For example, the logger instructs the logging system to emit logging statements for the package `com.sample` if they have the log level `WARN` or higher:

```
<logger category="com.sample">
  <level name="WARN"/>
</logger>
```

At the top of the hierarchy, there's the `root-logger`. There are two important things to note about `root-logger`:

- It always exists
- It cannot be retrieved by name

In the default server configuration, the root-logger defines two handlers that are connected to `CONSOLE` and to the `FILE` handler:

```xml
<root-logger>
    <level name="INFO"/>
    <handlers>
        <handler name="CONSOLE"/>
        <handler name="FILE"/>
    </handlers>
</root-logger>
```

Per-deployment logging

WildFly has the ability to configure per-deployment logging. This is enabled by default. This means that if you add a logging configuration file to your deployment, its configuration will be used to log for that deployment. The valid logging configuration files are as follows:

- `logging.properties`
- `jboss-logging.properties`
- `log4j.properties`
- `log4j.xml`
- `jboss-log4j.xml`

If you package your application into an EAR, your logging configuration file should go into the `META-INF` directory. If you are packaging your application into a JAR or WAR, then it can be placed into either the `META-INF` directory or the `WEB-INF` directory.

Should you want to disable per-deployment logging, you will need to set the `use-deployment-logging-config` value to `false`. Have a look at the following code snippet:

```xml
<subsystem xmlns="urn:jboss:domain:logging:2.0">
    <use-deployment-logging-config value="false"/>
    <console-handler name="CONSOLE">
        <level name="INFO"/>
        <formatter>
```

```
            <named-formatter name="COLOR-PATTERN"/>
        </formatter>
    </console-handler>
    ...
</subsystem>
```

> The system property `org.jboss.as.logging.per-deployment` has been deprecated in WildFly 8. You should use `use-deployment-logging-config` instead.

Bypassing container logging

You may, for some reason, wish to bypass container logging altogether. To do this, add the `add-logging-api-dependencies` property to your logging configuration and set its value to `false`. This will disable the adding of the implicit server logging dependencies, as shown in the following code:

```
<subsystem xmlns="urn:jboss:domain:logging:2.0">
    <add-logging-api-dependenciesuse-deployment-logging-config value="false"/>
    <console-handler name="CONSOLE">
        <level name="INFO"/>
        <formatter>
            <named-formatter name="COLOR-PATTERN"/>
        </formatter>
    </console-handler>
    ...
</subsystem>
```

To bypass logging on per-application basis only, you will need to use the `jboss-deployment-structure.xml` file to exclude the logging subsystem. We will cover the `jboss-deployment-structure.xml` file in detail in *Chapter 6, Application Structure and Deployment*.

Summary

In this chapter, we've gone through the basics of the application server configuration, which is now composed of a single monolithic file that contains the configuration for all the installed services.

Although this main configuration file will be your main point of reference to get a full understanding of the WildFly infrastructure, we must stress the importance of modifying it via one of the management interfaces.

We have examined each of the sections within the thread pool configuration in detail. We have also seen that the thread pool relies on the Java Standard Edition Thread Executor API to define a set of pools, and that these pools are used by the application servers' core services.

Next, we discussed the JBoss logging framework, which is built on top of the Java Util Logging framework and addresses some known shortcomings of JUL. We described how to configure per-application logging in your applications.

In the next chapter, we will take a look at some core enterprise service configurations, such as the datasource and messaging subsystems. These services are the backbone of many enterprise applications.

3
Configuring Enterprise Services

This chapter covers the configuration of the Java Enterprise services that ship with the application server. Many of the services are configured within their own subsystem. These subsystems can be added or removed depending on whether or not the service is required in your application. We will look at the most common ones in the following order:

- Connecting to a database
- Configuring the Enterprise JavaBeans container
- Configuring the messaging service
- Configuring the transaction service
- Configuring concurrency

Connecting to a database

To allow your application to connect to a database, you will need to configure your server by adding a datasource. Upon server startup, each datasource is prepopulated with a pool of database connections. Applications acquire a database connection from the pool by doing a `JNDI` lookup and then calling `getConnection()`. Take a look at the following code:

```
Connection result = null;
try {
    Context initialContext = new InitialContext();
    DataSource datasource =
    (DataSource)initialContext.lookup("java:/MySqlDS");
    result = datasource.getConnection();
} catch (Exception ex) {
    log("Cannot get connection: " + ex);}
```

After the connection has been used, you should always call `connection.close()` as soon as possible. This frees the connection and allows it to be returned to the connection pool—ready for other applications or processes to use.

Releases prior to JBoss AS 7 required a datasource configuration file (`ds.xml`) to be deployed with the application. Ever since the release of JBoss AS 7, this approach has no longer been mandatory due to the modular nature of the application server.

Out of the box, the application server ships with the H2 open source database engine (http://www.h2database.com), which, because of its small footprint and browser-based console, is ideal for testing purposes.

However, a real-world application requires an industry-standard database, such as the Oracle database or MySQL. In the following section, we will show you how to configure a datasource for the MySQL database.

Any database configuration requires a two step procedure, which is as follows:

- Installing the JDBC driver
- Adding the datasource to your configuration

Let's look at each section in detail.

Installing the JDBC driver

In WildFly's modular server architecture, you have a couple of ways to install your JDBC driver. You can install it either as a module or as a deployment unit.

The first and recommended approach is to install the driver as a module. In the *Installing the driver as a deployment unit* section, we will look at a faster approach to installing the driver. However, it does have various limitations, which we will cover shortly.

> Please see the source code for this chapter for the complete module example.

The first step to install a new module is to create the directory structure under the modules folder. The actual path for the module is `JBOSS_HOME/modules/<module>/main`.

The `main` folder is where all the key module components are installed, namely, the driver and the `module.xml` file. So, next, we need to add the following units:

- JBOSS_HOME/modules/com/mysql/main/mysql-connector-java-5.1.30-bin.jar
- JBOSS_HOME/modules/com/mysql/main/module.xml

The MySQL JDBC driver used in this example, also known as Connector/J, can be downloaded for free from the MySQL site (http://dev.mysql.com/downloads/connector/j/). At the time of writing, the latest version is 5.1.30.

The last thing to do is to create the `module.xml` file. This file contains the actual module definition. It is important to make sure that the module name (`com.mysql`) corresponds to the `module` attribute defined in the your datasource.

You must also state the path to the JDBC driver resource and finally add the module dependencies, as shown in the following code:

```
<module xmlns="urn:jboss:module:1.3" name="com.mysql">
    <resources>
        <resource-root path="mysql-connector-java-5.1.30-bin.jar"/>
    </resources>
    <dependencies>
        <module name="javax.api"/>
        <module name="javax.transaction.api"/>
    </dependencies>
</module>
```

Here is a diagram showing the final directory structure of this new module:

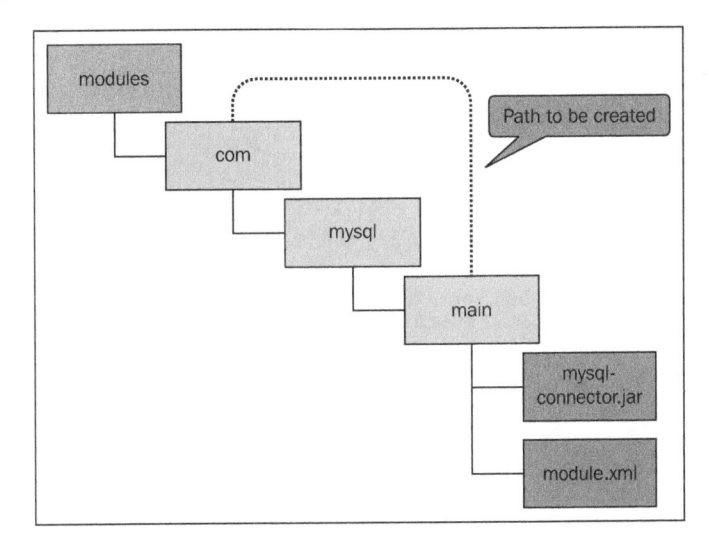

> You will notice that there is a directory structure already within the `modules` folder. All the system libraries are housed inside the `system/layers/base` directory. Your custom modules should be placed directly inside the `modules` folder and not with the system modules.

Adding a local datasource

Once the JDBC driver is installed, you need to configure the datasource within the application server's configuration file. In WildFly, you can configure two kinds of datasources, **local datasources** and **xa-datasources**, which are distinguishable by the element name in the configuration file.

> A local datasource does not support two-phase commits using a `java.sql.Driver`. On the other hand, an xa-datasource supports two-phase commits using a `javax.sql.XADataSource`.

Adding a datasource definition can be completed by adding the datasource definition within the server configuration file or by using the management interfaces. The management interfaces are the recommended way, as they will accurately update the configuration for you, which means that you do not need to worry about getting the correct syntax.

In this chapter, we are going to add the datasource by modifying the server configuration file directly. Although this is not the recommended approach, it will allow you to get used to the syntax and layout of the file. In *Chapter 7, Using the Management Interfaces*, we will show you how to add a datasource using the management tools.

Here is a sample MySQL datasource configuration that you can copy into your datasources subsystem section within the `standalone.xml` configuration file:

```xml
<datasources>
  <datasource jndi-name="java:/MySqlDS" pool-name="MySqlDS_Pool"
    enabled="true" jta="true" use-java-context="true" use-ccm="true">
    <connection-url>
      jdbc:mysql://localhost:3306/MyDB
    </connection-url>
    <driver>mysql</driver>
    <pool />
    <security>
```

```xml
      <user-name>jboss</user-name>
      <password>jboss</password>
    </security>
    <statement/>
    <timeout>
      <idle-timeout-minutes>0</idle-timeout-minutes>
      <query-timeout>600</query-timeout>
    </timeout>
  </datasource>
  <drivers>
    <driver name="mysql" module="com.mysql"/>
  </drivers>
</datasources>
```

As you can see, the configuration file uses the same XML schema definition from the earlier `-*.ds.xml` file, so it will not be difficult to migrate to WildFly from previous releases.

> In WildFly, it's mandatory that the datasource is bound into the `java:/` or `java:jboss/` JNDI namespace.

Let's take a look at the various elements of this file:

- `connection-url`: This element is used to define the connection path to the database.
- `driver`: This element is used to define the JDBC driver class.
- `pool`: This element is used to define the JDBC connection pool properties. In this case, we are going to leave the default values.
- `security`: This element is used to configure the connection credentials.
- `statement`: This element is added just as a placeholder for statement-caching options.
- `timeout`: This element is optional and contains a set of other elements, such as `query-timeout`, which is a static configuration of the maximum seconds before a query times out. Also the included `idle-timeout-minutes` element indicates the maximum time a connection may be idle before being closed; setting it to 0 disables it, and the default is 15 minutes.

Configuring the connection pool

One key aspect of the datasource configuration is the `pool` element. You can use connection pooling without modifying any of the existing WildFly configurations, as, without modification, WildFly will choose to use default settings. If you want to customize the pooling configuration, for example, change the pool size or change the types of connections that are pooled, you will need to learn how to modify the configuration file.

Here's an example of pool configuration, which can be added to your datasource configuration:

```
<pool>
    <min-pool-size>5</min-pool-size>
    <max-pool-size>10</max-pool-size>
    <prefill>true</prefill>
    <use-strict-min>true</use-strict-min>
    <flush-strategy>FailingConnectionOnly</flush-strategy>
</pool>
```

The attributes included in the `pool` configuration are actually borrowed from earlier releases, so we include them here for your reference:

Attribute	Meaning
`initial-pool-size`	This means the initial number of connections a pool should hold (default is 0 (zero)).
`min-pool-size`	This is the minimum number of connections in the pool (default is 0 (zero)).
`max-pool-size`	This is the maximum number of connections in the pool (default is 20).
`prefill`	This attempts to prefill the connection pool to the minimum number of connections.
`use-strict-min`	This determines whether idle connections below `min-pool-size` should be closed.
`allow-multiple-users`	This determines whether multiple users can access the datasource through the `getConnection` method. This has been changed slightly in WildFly. In WildFly, the line `<allow-multiple-users>true</allow-multiple-users>` is required. In JBoss AS 7, the empty element `<allow-multiple-users/>` was used.
`capacity`	This specifies the capacity policies for the pool – either `incrementer` or `decrementer`.

Attribute	Meaning
`connection-listener`	Here, you can specify `org.jboss.jca.adapters.jdbc.spi.listener.ConnectionListener` that allows you to listen for connection callbacks, such as activation and passivation.
`flush-strategy`	This specifies how the pool should be flushed in the event of an error (default is `FailingConnectionsOnly`).

Configuring the statement cache

For each connection within a connection pool, the WildFly server is able to create a statement cache. When a prepared statement or callable statement is used, WildFly will cache the statement so that it can be reused. In order to activate the statement cache, you have to specify a value greater than 0 within the `prepared-statement-cache-size` element. Take a look at the following code:

```
<statement>
    <track-statements>true</track-statements>
    <prepared-statement-cache-size>10</prepared-statement-cache-size>
    <share-prepared-statements/>
</statement>
```

Notice that we have also set `track-statements` to `true`. This will enable automatic closing of `statements` and `ResultSets`. This is important if you want to use prepared statement caching and/or don't want to prevent cursor leaks.

The last element, `share-prepared-statements`, can only be used when the prepared statement cache is enabled. This property determines whether two requests in the same transaction should return the same statement (default is `false`).

Adding an xa-datasource

Adding an `xa-datasource` requires some modification to the datasource configuration. The `xa-datasource` is configured within its own element, that is, within the datasource. You will also need to specify the `xa-datasource` class within the `driver` element.

In the following code, we will add a configuration for our MySQL JDBC driver, which will be used to set up an `xa-datasource`:

```
<datasources>
    <xa-datasource jndi-name="java:/XAMySqlDS" pool-name="MySqlDS_Pool"
        enabled="true" use-java-context="true" use-ccm="true">
        <xa-datasource-property name="URL">
```

```xml
      jdbc:mysql://localhost:3306/MyDB
    </xa-datasource-property>
    <xa-datasource-property name="User">jboss
    </xa-datasource-property>
    <xa-datasource-property name="Password">jboss
    </xa-datasource-property>
    <driver>mysql-xa</driver>
  </xa-datasource>
  <drivers>
    <driver name="mysql-xa" module="com.mysql">
      <xa-datasource-class>
        com.mysql.jdbc.jdbc2.optional.MysqlXADataSource
      </xa-datasource-class>
    </driver>
  </drivers>
</datasources>
```

> **Datasource versus xa-datasource**
>
> You should use an xa-datasource in cases where a single transaction spans multiple datasources, for example, if a method consumes a **Java Message Service (JMS)** and updates a **Java Persistence API (JPA)** entity.

Installing the driver as a deployment unit

In the WildFly application server, every library is a module. Thus, simply deploying the JDBC driver to the application server will trigger its installation.

> If the JDBC driver consists of more than a single JAR file, you will not be able to install the driver as a deployment unit. In this case, you will have to install the driver as a core module.

So, to install the database driver as a deployment unit, simply copy the `mysql-connector-java-5.1.30-bin.jar` driver into the `JBOSS_HOME/standalone/deployments` folder of your installation, as shown in the following image:

Chapter 3

[Diagram: JBOSS_HOME → standalone → deployments → mysql-connector.jar]

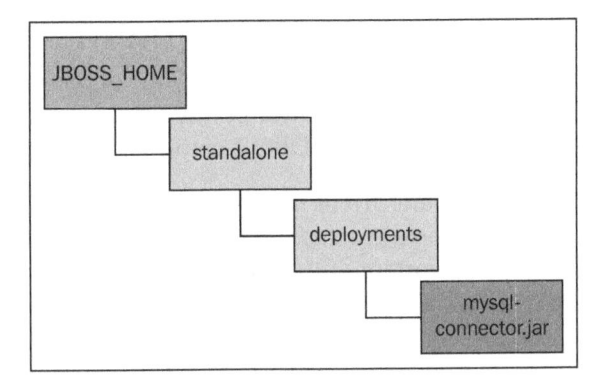

Once you have deployed your JDBC driver, you still need to add the datasource to your server configuration file. The simplest way to do this is to paste the following datasource definition into the configuration file, as follows:

```
<datasource jndi-name="java:/MySqlDS" pool-name="MySqlDS_Pool"
  enabled="true" jta="true" use-java-context="true" use-ccm="true">
  <connection-url>
    jdbc:mysql://localhost:3306/MyDB
  </connection-url>
  <driver>mysql-connector-java-5.1.130-bin.jar</driver>
  <pool />
  <security>
    <user-name>jboss</user-name>
    <password>jboss</password>
  </security>
</datasource>
```

Alternatively, you can use the **command-line interface** (**CLI**) or the web administration console to achieve the same result, as shown later in *Chapter 7, Using the Management Interfaces*.

> **What about domain deployment?**
>
> In this chapter, we are discussing the configuration of standalone servers. The services can also be configured in the domain servers. Domain servers, however, don't have a specified folder scanned for deployment. Rather, the management interfaces are used to inject resources into the domain. *Chapter 5, Configuring a WildFly Domain*, will detail all the steps to deploy a module when using a domain server.

Choosing the right driver deployment strategy

At this point, you might wonder about a best practice for deploying the JDBC driver. Installing the driver as a deployment unit is a handy shortcut; however, it can limit its usage. Firstly, it requires a JDBC 4-compliant driver.

Deploying a non-JDBC-4-compliant driver is possible, but it requires a simple patching procedure. To do this, create a `META-INF/services` structure containing the `java.sql.Driver` file. The content of the file will be the driver name. For example, let's suppose you have to patch a MySQL driver—the content will be `com.mysql.jdbc.Driver`.

Once you have created your structure, you can package your JDBC driver with any zipping utility or the `.jar` command, `jar -uf <your -jdbc-driver.jar> META-INF/services/java.sql.Driver`.

> The most current JDBC drivers are compliant with JDBC 4 although, curiously, not all are recognized as such by the application server. The following table describes some of the most used drivers and their JDBC compliance:

Database	Driver	JDBC 4 compliant	Contains java.sql.Driver
MySQL	`mysql-connector-java-5.1.30-bin.jar`	Yes, though not recognized as compliant by WildFly	Yes
PostgreSQL	`postgresql-9.3-1101.jdbc4.jar`	Yes, though not recognized as compliant by WildFly	Yes
Oracle	`ojdbc6.jar/ojdbc5.jar`	Yes	Yes
Oracle	`ojdbc4.jar`	No	No

As you can see, the most notable exception to the list of drivers is the older Oracle `ojdbc4.jar`, which is not compliant with JDBC 4 and does not contain the driver information in `META-INF/services/java.sql.Driver`.

The second issue with driver deployment is related to the specific case of xa-datasources. Installing the driver as deployment means that the application server by itself cannot deduce the information about the `xa-datasource` class used in the driver. Since this information is not contained inside `META-INF/services`, you are forced to specify information about the `xa-datasource` class for each xa-datasource you are going to create.

When you install a driver as a module, the `xa-datasource` class information can be shared for all the installed datasources.

```
<driver name="mysql-xa" module="com.mysql">
  <xa-datasource-class>
    com.mysql.jdbc.jdbc2.optional.MysqlXADataSource
  </xa-datasource-class>
</driver>
```

So, if you are not too limited by these issues, installing the driver as a deployment is a handy shortcut that can be used in your development environment. For a production environment, it is recommended that you install the driver as a static module.

Configuring a datasource programmatically

After installing your driver, you may want to limit the amount of application configuration in the server file. This can be done by configuring your datasource programmatically This option requires zero modification to your configuration file, which means greater application portability. The support to configure a datasource programmatically is one of the cool features of Java EE that can be achieved by using the `@DataSourceDefinition` annotation, as follows:

```
@DataSourceDefinition(name = "java:/OracleDS",
  className = " oracle.jdbc.OracleDriver",
  portNumber = 1521,
  serverName = "192.168.1.1",
  databaseName = "OracleSID",
  user = "scott",
  password = "tiger",
  properties = {"createDatabase=create"})
@Singleton
public class DataSourceEJB {
  @Resource(lookup = "java:/OracleDS")
  private DataSource ds;
}
```

In this example, we defined a datasource for an Oracle database. It's important to note that, when configuring a datasource programmatically, you will actually bypass JCA, which proxies requests between the client and the connection pool.

The obvious advantage of this approach is that you can move your application from one application server to another without the need for reconfiguring its datasources. On the other hand, by modifying the datasource within the configuration file, you will be able to utilize the full benefits of the application server, many of which are required for enterprise applications.

Configuring the Enterprise JavaBeans container

The **Enterprise JavaBeans (EJB)** container is a fundamental part of the Java Enterprise architecture. The EJB container provides the environment used to host and manage the EJB components deployed in the container. The container is responsible for providing a standard set of services, including caching, concurrency, persistence, security, transaction management, and locking services.

The container also provides distributed access and lookup functions for hosted components, and it intercepts all method invocations on hosted components to enforce declarative security and transaction contexts. Take a look at the following figure:

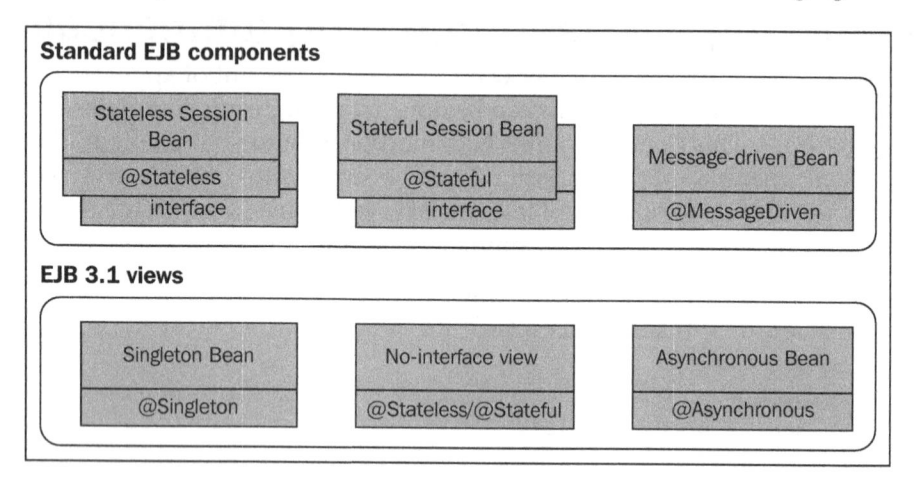

Standard EJB components

Stateless Session Bean	Stateful Session Bean	Message-driven Bean
@Stateless interface	@Stateful interface	@MessageDriven

EJB 3.1 views

Singleton Bean	No-interface view	Asynchronous Bean
@Singleton	@Stateless/@Stateful	@Asynchronous

As depicted in this image, you will be able to deploy the full set of EJB components within WildFly:

- **Stateless session bean (SLSB)**: SLSBs are objects whose instances have no conversational state. This means that all bean instances are equivalent when they are not servicing a client.
- **Stateful session bean (SFSB)**: SFSBs support conversational services with tightly coupled clients. A stateful session bean accomplishes a task for a particular client. It maintains the state for the duration of a client session. After session completion, the state is not retained.
- **Message-driven bean (MDB)**: MDBs are a kind of enterprise beans that are able to asynchronously process messages sent by any JMS producer.

- **Singleton EJB**: This is essentially similar to a stateless session bean; however, it uses a single instance to serve the client requests. Thus, you are guaranteed to use the same instance across invocations. Singletons can use a set of events with a richer life cycle and a stricter locking policy to control concurrent access to the instance. In the next chapter, which is about web applications, we will illustrate a Java EE 7 application that makes use of a Singleton EJB to hold some cached data.
- **No-interface EJB**: This is just another view of the standard session bean, except that local clients do not require a separate interface, that is, all public methods of the bean class are automatically exposed to the caller. Interfaces should only be used in EJB 3.x if you have multiple implementations.
- **Asynchronous EJB**: These are able to process client requests asynchronously just like MDBs, except that they expose a typed interface and follow a more complex approach to processing client requests, which are composed of:
    - The `fire-and-forget` asynchronous void methods, which are invoked by the client
    - The `retrieve-result-later` asynchronous methods having a `Future<?>` return type

> EJB components that don't keep conversational states (SLSB and MDB) can be optionally configured to emit timed notifications. See the *Configuring the timer service* section for more information about it.

Configuring the EJB components

Now that we have briefly outlined the basic types of EJB, we will look at the specific details of the application server configuration. This comprises the following components:

- The SLSB configuration
- The SFSB configuration
- The MDB configuration
- The Timer service configuration

Let's see them all in detail.

Configuring the stateless session beans

EJBs are configured within the `ejb3.2.0` subsystem. By default, no stateless session bean instances exist in WildFly at startup time. As individual beans are invoked, the EJB container initializes new SLSB instances.

These instances are then kept in a pool that will be used to service future EJB method calls. The EJB remains active for the duration of the client's method call. After the method call is complete, the EJB instance is returned to the pool. Because the EJB container unbinds stateless session beans from clients after each method call, the actual bean class instance that a client uses can be different from invocation to invocation. Have a look at the following diagram:

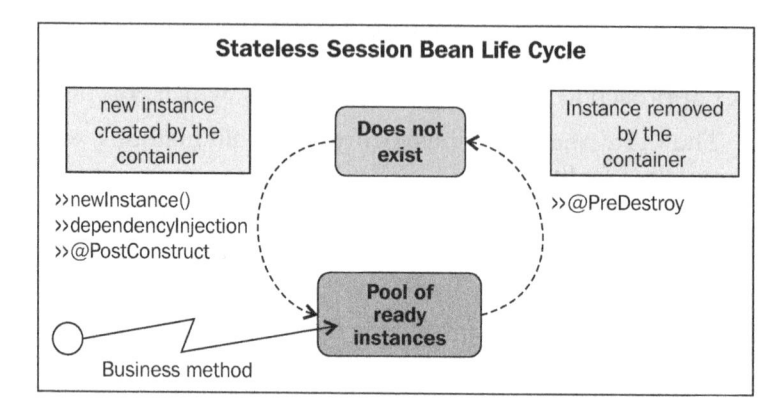

Stateless Session Bean Life Cycle

- new instance created by the container
  - »newInstance()
  - »dependencyInjection
  - »@PostConstruct
- Does not exist
- Instance removed by the container
  - »@PreDestroy
- Pool of ready instances
- Business method

If all instances of an EJB class are active and the pool's maximum pool size has been reached, new clients requesting the EJB class will be blocked until an active EJB completes a method call. Depending on how you have configured your stateless pool, an acquisition timeout can be triggered if you are not able to acquire an instance from the pool within a maximum time.

You can either configure your session pool through your main configuration file or programmatically. Let's look at both approaches, starting with the main configuration file.

In order to configure your pool, you can operate on two parameters: the maximum size of the pool (`max-pool-size`) and the instance acquisition timeout (`instance-acquisition-timeout`). Let's see an example:

```
<subsystem xmlns="urn:jboss:domain:ejb3:2.0">
  <session-bean>
    <stateless>
      <bean-instance-pool-ref pool-name="slsb-strict-max-pool"/>
    </stateless>
```

```
    ...
  </session-bean>
    ...
  <pools>
   <bean-instance-pools>
    <strict-max-pool name="slsb-strict-max-pool" max-pool-size=
      "25" instance-acquisition-timeout="5" instance-acquisition-
      timeout-unit="MINUTES"/>
   </bean-instance-pools>
  </pools>
    ...
</subsystem>
```

In this example, we have configured the SLSB pool with a *strict* upper limit of 25 elements. The strict maximum pool is the only available pool instance implementation; it allows a fixed number of concurrent requests to run at one time. If there are more requests running than the pool's strict maximum size, those requests will get blocked until an instance becomes available. Within the pool configuration, we have also set an `instance-acquisition-timeout` value of 5 minutes, which will come into play if your requests are larger than the pool size.

You can configure as many pools as you like. The pool used by the EJB container is indicated by the attribute `pool-name` on the `bean-instance-pool-ref` element. For example, here we have added one more pool configuration, `largepool`, and set it as the EJB container's pool implementation. Have a look at the following code:

```
<subsystem xmlns="urn:jboss:domain:ejb3:1.2">
  <session-bean>
    <stateless>
      <bean-instance-pool-ref pool-name="large-pool"/>
    </stateless>
  </session-bean>
  <pools>
    <bean-instance-pools>
      <strict-max-pool name="large-pool" max-pool-size="100"
        instance-acquisition-timeout="5"
        instance-acquisition-timeout-unit="MINUTES"/>
      <strict-max-pool name="slsb-strict-max-pool"
        max-pool-size="25" instance-acquisition-timeout="5"
        instance-acquisition-timeout-unit="MINUTES"/>
    </bean-instance-pools>
  </pools>
</subsystem>
```

Using CLI to configure the stateless pool size

We have detailed the steps necessary to configure the SLSB pool size through the main configuration file. However, the suggested best practice is to use CLI to alter the server model.

Here's how you can add a new pool named `large-pool` to your EJB 3 subsystem:

```
/subsystem=ejb3/strict-max-bean-instance-pool=large-pool:
   add(max-pool-size=100)
```

Now, you can set this pool as the default to be used by the EJB container, as follows:

```
/subsystem=ejb3:write-attribute(name=default-slsb-instance-pool,
   value=large-pool)
```

Finally, you can, at any time, change the pool size property by operating on the `max-pool-size` attribute, as follows:

```
/subsystem=ejb3/strict-max-bean-instance-pool=large-pool:write-
   attribute(name="max-pool-size",value=50)
```

Configuring the stateful session beans

SFSBs are bound to a particular client. The application server uses a cache to store active EJB instances in memory so that they can be quickly retrieved for future client requests. The cache contains EJBs that are currently in use by a client and instances that were recently in use. Take a look at the following diagram:

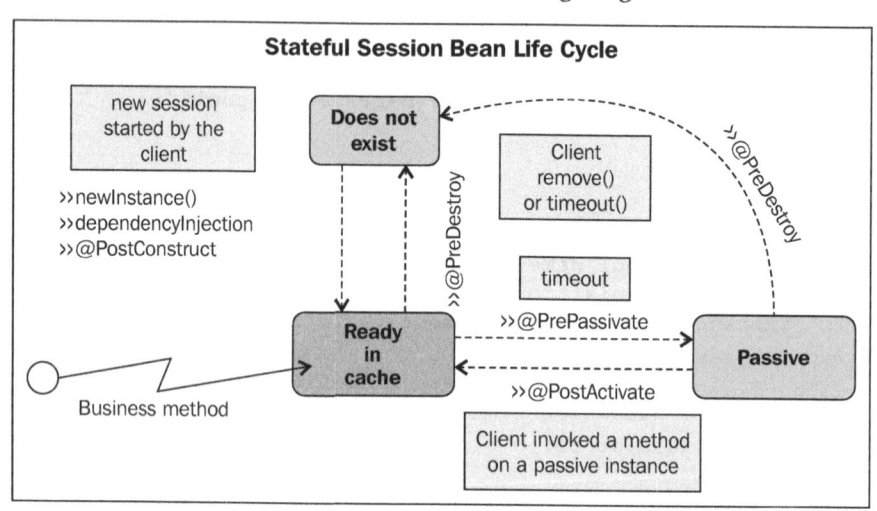

Having EJBs in memory is a costly operation, so you should move them out of memory as soon as possible by either passivating them or removing them.

Passivation is a process by which the EJB container ensures that idle SFSB instances are freed from the cache by having their state saved to disk.

Removing a bean from the cache, on the other hand, is a process that can be triggered programmatically for the EJB container. To remove the EJB programmatically, add the `@javax.ejb.Remove` annotation to your method. When this method is invoked, the EJB will be removed. Take a look at the following code:

```
@Remove
public void remove() {}
```

The following example shows a section of the `ejb3:2.0` subsystem, which shows the configuration of a SFSB along with its cache and passivation store configuration. Have a look at the following code:

```
<subsystem xmlns="urn:jboss:domain:ejb3:2.0">
  <session-bean>
    <stateful default-access-timeout="5000" cache-ref="distributable"
      passivation-disabled-cache-ref="simple"/>
  </session-bean>
  ...
  <caches>
    <cache name="simple"/>
    <cache name="distributable" passivation-store-ref="infinispan"
      aliases="passivating clustered"/>
  </caches>
  <passivation-stores>
    <passivation-store name="infinispan" cache-container="ejb" max-
      size="10000"/>
  </passivation-stores>
  ...
</subsystem>
```

As you can see, the stateful bean element references a cache definition (named `distributable`), which in turn is connected to a passivation store (named `infinispan`). Notice the optional `max-size` attribute that limits the amount of SFSBs that can be contained in the cache. You can also see that the clustered cache uses infinispan's `passivation-store` (see *Chapter 8, Clustering*, for more information about the infinispan cache).

> In WildFly, the `file-passivation-store` and `cluster-passivation-store` elements have been deprecated in favor of `passivation-store`. Both deprecated elements will be removed completely in future releases.

Configuring the message-driven beans

Message-driven beans (**MDBs**) are stateless, server-side, transaction-aware components that are used to process asynchronous JMS messages.

One of the most important aspects of MDBs is that they can consume and process messages concurrently.

This capability provides a significant advantage over traditional JMS clients, which must be custom-built to manage resources, transactions, and security in a multithreaded environment.

Just as the session beans have well-defined life cycles, so does an MDB. The MDB instance's life cycle is pretty much the same as the stateless bean. An MDB has two states: **Does not Exist** and **Method ready Pool**. Take a look at the following figure:

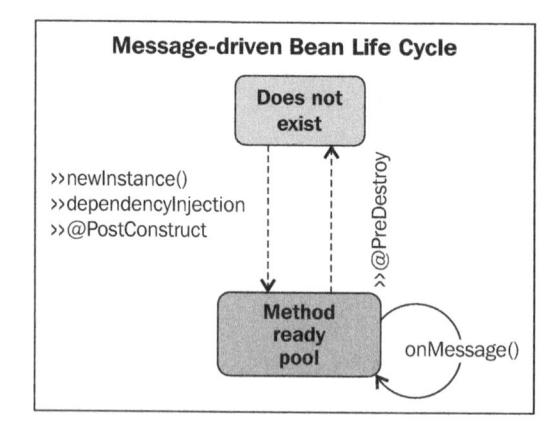

When a message is received, the EJB container checks whether any MDB instance is available in the pool. If a bean is available, WildFly uses that instance. After an MDB instance's onMessage() method returns, the request is complete, and the instance is placed back in the pool. This results in the best response time, as the request is served without waiting for a new instance to be created.

If no bean instances are available, the container checks whether there is room for more MDBs in the pool by comparing the MDB's MaxSize attribute with the pool size.

If MaxSize still has not been reached, a new MDB is initialized. The creation sequence, as pointed out in the preceding diagram, is the same as that of the stateless bean. Failure to create a new instance, on the other hand, will imply that the request will be blocked until an active MDB completes. If the request cannot acquire an instance from the pool within the time defined in instance-acquisition-timeout, an exception is thrown.

Chapter 3

The configuration of the MDB pool is exactly the same as for the SLSB, so we will just include it here without further explanation:

```xml
<subsystem xmlns="urn:jboss:domain:ejb3:2.0">
  <mdb>
    <resource-adapter-ref resource-adapter-name="hornetq-ra"/>
    <bean-instance-pool-ref pool-name="mdb-strict-max-pool"/>
  </mdb>
  <pools>
    <bean-instance-pools>
      <strict-max-pool name="mdb-strict-max-pool" max-pool-size="20"
        instance-acquisition-timeout="5"
        instance-acquisition-timeout-unit="MINUTES"/>
    </bean-instance-pools>
  </pools>
</subsystem>
```

> To learn more about the various types of enterprise beans, you can refer to the Java EE 7 tutorial at http://docs.oracle.com/javaee/7/tutorial/doc/ejb-intro002.htm.

Configuring the timer service

The EJB 3 timer service provides a way to allow methods to be invoked at specific times or time intervals. This is useful should your application business process need periodic notifications.

The EJB timer service can be used in any type of EJB 3, except for stateful session beans. Using the timer services is as simple as annotating a method with @javax.ejb.Timeout. This method will then be triggered by the container when the time interval expires.

The following example shows you how to implement a very simple timer, which will be started by invoking the scheduleTimer(long milliseconds) method. Take a look at the following code:

```java
import java.time.LocalDate;
import java.time.temporal.ChronoUnit;
import javax.annotation.Resource;
import javax.ejb.*;

@LocalBean
@Stateless
public class TimerSampleBean {

    @Resource
```

[77]

```
    private SessionContext ctx;

    public void scheduleTimer(long milliseconds) {
        LocalDate date = LocalDate.now().plus(milliseconds,
          ChronoUnit.MILLIS);
        ctx.getTimerService().createTimer(date.toEpochDay(), "Hello
          World");
    }

    @Timeout
    public void timeoutHandler(Timer timer) {
        System.out.println("* Received Timer event: " + timer.
          getInfo());
        timer.cancel();
    }
}
```

As far as configuration is concerned, you can store planned executions within the filesystem or in a database. To save them in the filesystem, you need to reference the `default-data-store` attribute from the `file-data-store` attribute (both called `file-store` in this example). The number of threads reserved for the timer service can be configured with the `thread-pool-name` attribute, which needs to reference a `thread-pool` element. Have a look at the following code:

```
<subsystem xmlns="urn:jboss:domain:ejb3:2.0">
    <timer-service default-data-store="file-store" thread-pool-
      name="default">
        <data-stores>
            <file-data-store name="file-store" path="timer-service-
              data" relative-to="jboss.server.data.dir"/>
        </data-stores>
    </timer-service>
    <thread-pools>
        <thread-pool name="default">
            <max-threads count="10"/>
            <keepalive-time time="100" unit="milliseconds"/>
        </thread-pool>
    </thread-pools>
</subsystem>
```

Configuring the messaging system

Message-oriented middleware has always been an integral part of the application server. Messaging systems allow you to loosely couple heterogeneous systems together while typically providing reliability, transactions, and many other features.

Messaging is not part of the Java EE web profile, so you will not find a configuration for the messaging subsystem in the `standalone.xml` file. However, the messaging subsystem is included in the configuration file named `standalone-full.xml`.

> Messaging systems normally support two main styles of asynchronous messaging: **Queues** (point-to-point messaging) and **Topics** (publish/subscribe messaging).

In the point-to-point model, a sender posts messages to a particular queue, and a receiver reads messages from the queue. Here, the sender knows the destination of the message and posts the message directly to the receiver's queue.

The publish/subscribe model supports the publishing of messages to a particular message topic. Subscribers may register interest in receiving messages on a particular message topic. In this model, neither the publisher nor the subscriber know about each other.

The following table shows the characteristics of the two different models:

Point-to-point messaging	Publish/Subscribe
Only one consumer gets the message.	Multiple consumers (or none) will receive the message.
The producer does not need to run at the time the consumer consumes the message, nor does the consumer need to run at the time the message is sent.	The publisher has to create a message topic for clients to subscribe. The subscriber has to remain continuously active to receive messages unless he has established a durable subscription. In that case, messages published while the subscriber is not connected will be redistributed whenever he reconnects.
Every message successfully processed is acknowledged by the consumer.	

JBoss AS has used different JMS implementations across its releases. Since the release of Version 6.0, the default JMS provider is HornetQ (http://www.jboss.org/hornetq), which provides a multi-protocol, embeddable, high-performance, clustered, asynchronous messaging system.

At its core, HornetQ is designed simply as a set of **Plain Old Java Objects** (**POJOs**). It has only one JAR dependency, the Netty library, which leverages the Java **Non-blocking Input/Output** (**NIO**) API to build high-performance network applications.

> Because of its easily adaptable architecture, HornetQ can be embedded in your own project or instantiated in any dependency injection framework, such as Spring or Google Guice.

In this book, we will cover the scenario where HornetQ is embedded into a WildFly subsystem as a module. The following diagram shows how the HornetQ server fits in the overall picture:

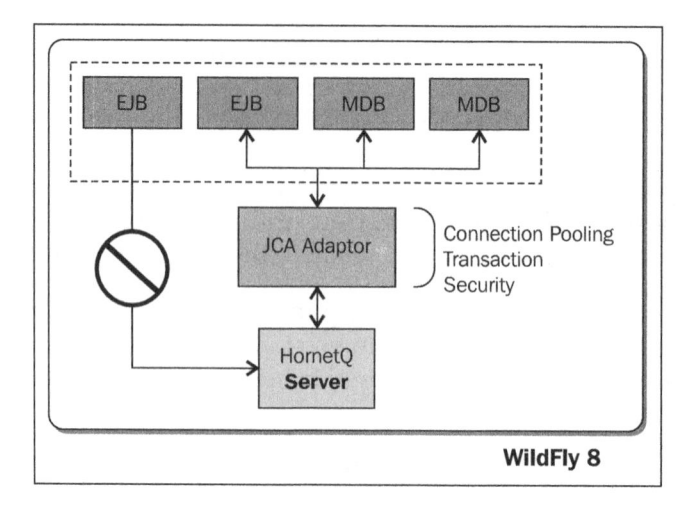

As you can see, a key part of the HornetQ integration is the **JCA Adaptor** that handles the communication between the application server and the HornetQ server.

> **Why can't you simply connect your resources to the HornetQ server?**
>
> This is theoretically possible; however, it violates Java EE specifications and will result in the loss of functionalities provided by the application server's JCA layer, such as connection pooling and automatic transaction enlistment. These functionalities are desirable when using messaging, say, from inside an EJB. For a description of JCA thread-pooling configuration, refer to the *The bounded-queue thread pool* section in *Chapter 2, Configuring the Core WildFly Subsystems*.

Configuring the transport

Configuring the transport of a JMS message is a key part of the messaging system tuning. Out of the box, HornetQ uses Netty as its high-performance, low-level network library. Netty is a NIO client-server framework, which enables quick and easy development of network applications, such as **protocol servers** and **clients**. It greatly simplifies and streamlines network programming, such as those of the TCP and UDP socket servers.

One of the most important concepts in HornetQ transport is the definition of acceptors and connectors.

An **acceptor** defines which type of connection is accepted by the HornetQ server. On the other hand, a **connector** defines how to connect to a HornetQ server. The connector is used by a HornetQ client.

HornetQ defines three types of acceptors and connectors:

- **inVM**: This type can be used when both the HornetQ client and the server run in the same virtual machine (inVM stands for intra virtual machine)
- **Netty**: This type defines a way for remote connections to be made over TCP (uses the Netty project to handle the I/O)
- **http**: This type is the default configuration in WildFly and defines a way for remote connections to be made to HornetQ over HTTP (it uses Undertow to upgrade from the HTTP protocol to the HornetQ protocol)

To communicate, a HornetQ client must use a connector compatible with the server's acceptor. A compatible client-server communication requires that it is carried out using the same type of acceptor/connector shown by the following diagram:

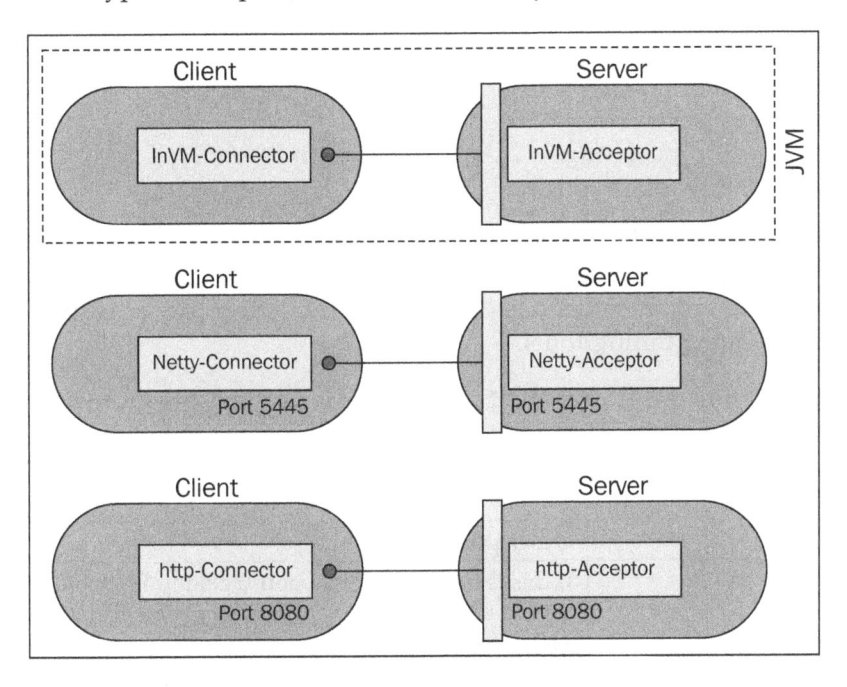

We can see that it's not possible to connect an InVM client connector to a Netty server acceptor. On the other hand, it's possible to connect a HTTP client connector to a HTTP server acceptor provided they are configured to run on the same host and port.

WildFly 8 comes with a preconfigured acceptor/connector pair that is part of the WildFly messaging subsystem, as shown in the following code:

```
<connectors>
    <http-connector name="http-connector" socket-binding="http">
        <param key="http-upgrade-endpoint" value="http-acceptor"/>
    </http-connector>
    <http-connector name="http-connector-throughput" socket-binding="http">
        <param key="http-upgrade-endpoint" value="http-acceptor-throughput"/>
        <param key="batch-delay" value="50"/>
    </http-connector>
    <in-vm-connector name="in-vm" server-id="0"/>
</connectors>
<acceptors>
    <http-acceptor name="http-acceptor" http-listener="default"/>
    <http-acceptor name="http-acceptor-throughput" http-listener="default">
        <param key="batch-delay" value="50"/>
        <param key="direct-deliver" value="false"/>
    </http-acceptor>
    <in-vm-acceptor name="in-vm" server-id="0"/>
</acceptors>
```

As you can see, besides the `in-vm` acceptor/connector pair, each section defines two kinds of acceptors/connectors, one of which relies on the default configuration, `http-connector`, and the other one (`http-acceptor-throughput`) is specialized for higher messaging throughputs.

You can further tune HTTP transport when you have a more complete knowledge of the parameters that can be added to the acceptor/connector section. Here's a comprehensive list of all parameters and their meanings:

Parameter	Description
use-nio	If this is `true`, then Java non-blocking I/O will be used. If set to `false`, then the old blocking Java I/O will be used. The default value is `true`.
host	This specifies the host name or IP address to connect to (when configuring a connector) or to listen on (when configuring an acceptor). The default value for this property is `localhost`. Multiple hosts or IP addresses can be specified by separating them with commas.

Parameter	Description
port	This specifies the port to connect to (when configuring a connector) or to listen on (when configuring an acceptor). The default value for this property is 5445.
tcp-no-delay	If this is true, then Nagle's algorithm will be disabled. The default value for this property is true.
tcp-send-buffer-size	This parameter determines the size of the TCP send buffer in bytes. The default value for this property is 32768 bytes.
tcp-receive-buffer-size	This parameter determines the size of the TCP receive buffer in bytes. The default value for this property is 32768 bytes.
batch-delay	This parameter lets you configure HornetQ so that messages are batched up to be written for a maximum of batch-delay milliseconds before sending them for transport. This can increase overall throughput for very small messages. The default value for this property is 0 ms.
direct-deliver	This parameter lets you configure whether message delivery is done using the same thread as the one that carried the message. Setting this to true (default) reduces the thread context switch's latency at the expense of message throughput. If your goal is a higher throughput, set this parameter to false.
nio-remoting-threads	When using NIO, HornetQ will, by default, use a number of threads equal to three times the number of core processors required to process incoming packets. If you want to override this value, you can set the number of threads by specifying this parameter. The default value for this parameter is -1, which means use the value derived from Runtime.getRuntime().availableProcessors() * 3.
http-client-idle-time	This determines how long a client can be idle before sending an empty HTTP request to keep the connection alive.
http-client-idle-scan-period	This determines how often we can scan for idle clients, in milliseconds
http-response-time	This determines how long the server can wait before sending an empty HTTP response to keep the connection alive.
http-server-scan-period	This determines how often we can scan for clients needing responses, in milliseconds.
http-requires-session-id	If true, the client will wait after the first call to receive a session ID.

One frequent source of confusion among HornetQ users is why connectors are included in the server configuration if the server is in charge of accepting connections and delivering messages. There are two main reasons for this:

- Sometimes the server acts as a client itself when it connects to another server, for example, when one server is bridged to another or when a server takes part in a cluster. In these cases, the server needs to know how to connect to other servers. That's defined by connectors.
- If you're using JMS and the server-side JMS services to instantiate JMS ConnectionFactory instances and bind them in JNDI then, when creating the HornetQConnectionFactory, it needs to know what server that connection factory will create connections to.

Configuring connection factories

A JMS ConnectionFactory object is used by the client to make connections to the server. The definition of connection-factory instances is included in the default server configuration. Take a look at the following code:

```
<connection-factory name="InVmConnectionFactory">
    <connectors>
        <connector-ref connector-name="in-vm"/>
    </connectors>
    <entries>
        <entry name="java:/ConnectionFactory"/>
    </entries>
</connection-factory>
<connection-factory name="RemoteConnectionFactory">
    <connectors>
        <connector-ref connector-name="http-connector"/>
    </connectors>
    <entries>
        <entry name="java:jboss/exported/jms/
RemoteConnectionFactory"/>
    </entries>
</connection-factory>
```

You can find two connection factory definitions, which are as follows:

- InVmConnectionFactory: This connection factory is bound under java:/ConnectionFactory and is used when the server and the client are running in the same JVM (and hence in the same WildFly server)

- `RemoteConnectionFactory`: This connection factory, as the name implies, can be used when JMS connections are provided by a remote server. By default, this uses `http-connector` and is bound by the JNDI name, `java:jboss/exported/jms/RemoteConnectionFactory`.

Configuring JMS destinations

Along with the definition of connection factories in the JMS subsystem, you can find the JMS destinations (queues and topics), which are part of the server distribution. Have a look at the following code:

```
<jms-destinations>
    <jms-queue name="ExpiryQueue">
        <entry name="java:/jms/queue/ExpiryQueue"/>
    </jms-queue>
    <jms-queue name="DLQ">
        <entry name="java:/jms/queue/DLQ"/>
    </jms-queue>
</jms-destinations>
```

The `name` attribute of a queue defines the name of the queue. At the JMS level, the actual name of the queue follows a naming convention, so it will be `jms.queue.ExpiryQueue`.

The `entry` element configures the name that will be used to bind the queue to JNDI. This is a mandatory element, and the queue can contain many of these to bind the same queue to different names.

So, for example, here's how you would configure a `MessageDrivenBean` component to consume messages from the `ExpiryQueue`:

```
@MessageDriven(name = "MessageMDBSample", activationConfig = {
  @ActivationConfigProperty(propertyName = "destinationType",
    propertyValue = "javax.jms.Queue"),
  @ActivationConfigProperty(propertyName = "destination",
    propertyValue = "java:/jms/queue/ExpiryQueue"),
  @ActivationConfigProperty(propertyName = "acknowledgeMode",
    propertyValue = "Auto-acknowledge") })

public class SampleMDBean implements MessageListener {
  @Resource
  private MessageDrivenContext context;
}
```

> **Why is it useful to know the actual destination name?**
>
> Apparently, it seems not important at all to know the server's destination name (in the example, `jms.queue.ExpiryQueue`). Rather, we would be concerned about the JNDI entry where the destination is bound. However, the actual destination name plays an important role if you want to define some properties across a set of destinations. See the next section, *Customizing destinations with an address*, for more information.

Queues and topic definitions can optionally include some non-mandatory elements, such as `selector` and `durable`:

```
<jms-queue name="selectorQueue">
    <entry name="/queue/selectorQueue"/>
    <selector>name='john'</selector>
    <durable>true</durable>
</jms-queue>
```

The `selector` element defines what JMS message selector the predefined queue will have. Only messages that match the selector will be added to the queue. This is an optional element with a default value of `null` when omitted.

The `durable` element specifies whether or not the queue will be persisted. This again is optional and defaults to `true` if omitted.

Customizing destinations with an address

If you want to provide some custom settings for JMS destinations, you can use the `address-setting` block, which can be applied both to a single destination and to a set of destinations. The default configuration applies a set of minimal attributes to all destinations. Have a look at the following code:

```
<address-settings>
  <!--default for catch all-->
  <address-setting match="#">
    <dead-letter-address>jms.queue.DLQ</dead-letter-address>
    <expiry-address>jms.queue.ExpiryQueue</expiry-address>
    <redelivery-delay>0</redelivery-delay>
    <max-size-bytes>10485760</max-size-bytes>
    <message-counter-history-day-limit>10</message-counter-history-day-limit>
    <address-full-policy>BLOCK</address-full-policy>
  </address-setting>
</address-settings>
```

Here is a brief description of the address settings.

The address setting's `match` attribute defines a filter for the destinations. When using the wildcard, `#`, the properties will be valid across all destinations. For example:

```
<address-setting match="jms.queue.#">
```

Here, the settings would apply to all queues defined in the `destination` section:

```
<address-setting match="jms.queue.ExpiryQueue ">
```

The settings would apply to the queue named `jms.queue.ExpiryQueue`.

A short description of the destination's properties is as follows:

Property	Description
`dead-letter-address`	This specifies the destination for messages that could not be delivered.
`expiry-address`	This defines where to send a message that has expired.
`expiry-delay`	This defines the expiration time that will be used for messages using the default expiration time.
`redelivery-delay`	This defines how long to wait before attempting redelivery of a cancelled message.
`max-size-bytes`	This specifies the maximum size of the message in bytes before entering the `page` mode.
`page-size-bytes`	This specifies the size of each page file used on the paging system.
`max-delivery-attempts`	This defines how many times a cancelled message can be redelivered before it is sent to the `dead-letter-address`.
`message-counter-history-day-limit`	This specifies how many days the message counter history will be kept.
`address-full-policy`	This is used when a destination maximum size is reached. When set to `PAGE`, further messages will be paged to the disk. If the value is `DROP`, further messages will be silently dropped. When `BLOCK` is used, client message producers will be blocked when they try to send further messages.

HornetQ persistence configuration

The last HornetQ topic we need to cover is message persistence. HornetQ has its own optimized persistence engine, which can be further configured when you know all about its various components.

> The secret of HornetQ's high data persistence consists in appending data to the journal files instead of using the costly random-access operations, which require a higher degree of disk-head movement.
>
> Journal files are precreated and filled with padding characters at runtime. By precreating files, as one is filled, the journal can immediately resume with the next one without pausing to create it.

The following are the default journal values for the messaging subsystem. Although these values are not explicitly set in the `standalone-full.xml` file, their absence causes these default values to be used.

```
<journal-file-size>102400</journal-file-size>
<journal-min-files>2</journal-min-files>
<journal-type>NIO</journal-type>
<persistence-enabled>true</persistence-enabled>
```

The default `journal-file-size` (expressed in bytes) is `100 KB`. The minimum number of files the journal will maintain is indicated by the property `journal-min-files`, which states that at least two files will be maintained.

The property `journal-type` indicates the type of input/output libraries used for data persistence. The valid values are `NIO` or `ASYNCIO`.

Choosing `NIO` sets the Java NIO journal. Choosing `AIO` sets the Linux asynchronous I/O journal. If you choose `AIO` but are not running Linux or you do not have `libaio` installed, then HornetQ will detect this and automatically fall back to using `NIO`.

The `persistence-enabled` property, when set to `false`, will disable message persistence. That means no binding data, message data, large message data, duplicate ID caches, or paging data will be persisted. Disabling data persistence will give to your applications a remarkable performance boost; however, the other side of it is that your data messaging will inevitably lose reliability.

For the sake of completeness, we include some additional properties that can be included if you want to customize the messages/paging and journal storage directories. Have a look at the following code:

```
<bindings-directory relative-to="jboss.server.data.dir"
  path="hornetq/bindings" />
```

```xml
<large-messages-directory relative-to="jboss.server.data.dir"
    path="hornetq/largemessages" />

<paging-directory relative-to="jboss.server.data.dir"
    path="hornetq/paging" />

<journal-directory relative-to="jboss.server.data.dir"
    path="hornetq/journal" />
```

For best performance, we recommend that the journal be located on its own physical volume in order to minimize disk-head movement. If the journal is on a volume that is shared with other processes, which might be writing other files (for example, bindings journal, database, or transaction coordinator), then the disk-head might move rapidly between these files as it writes them, thus drastically reducing performance.

Configuring the transactions service

A transaction can be defined as a group of operations that must be performed as a unit and can involve persisting data objects, sending a message, and so on.

When the operations in a transaction are performed across databases or other resources that reside on separate computers or processes, this is known as a distributed transaction. Such enterprise-wide transactions require special coordination between the resources involved and can be extremely difficult to program reliably. This is where **Java Transaction API (JTA)** comes in, providing the interface that resources can implement and to which they can bind in order to participate in a distributed transaction.

The EJB container is a transaction manager that supports JTA and so can participate in distributed transactions involving other EJB containers as well as third-party JTA resources, such as many database management systems.

Within WildFly 8, transactions are configured in their own subsystem. The transactions subsystem consists mainly of four elements:

- Core environment
- Recovery environment
- Coordinator environment
- Object store

The core environment includes the `TransactionManager` interface, which allows the application server to control the transaction boundaries on behalf of the resource being managed. Have a look at the following diagram:

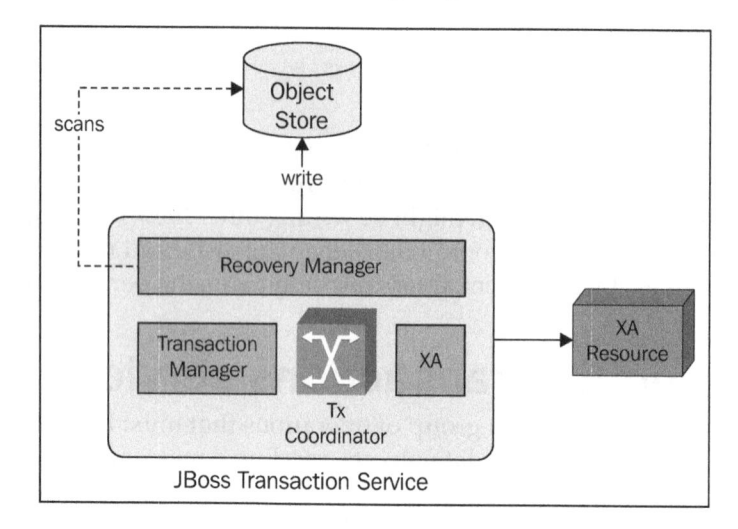

A transaction coordinator, in turn, manages communication with transactional objects and resources that participate in transactions.

The recovery subsystem of JBossTS ensures that the results of a transaction are applied consistently to all resources affected by the transaction even if any of the application processes or the machine hosting them crashes or loses network connectivity.

Within the transaction service, JBoss transaction service uses an object store to persistently record the outcomes of transactions for failure recovery. As a matter of fact, the recovery manager scans the object store and other locations of information looking for transactions and resources that require or might require recovery.

The core and recovery environments can be customized by changing their socket-binding properties, which are referenced in the `socket-binding-group` configuration section.

You might find it more useful to define custom properties in the coordinator environment section, which might include the default timeout and logging statistics. Here's a sample custom transaction configuration:

```
<subsystem xmlns="urn:jboss:domain:transactions:2.0">
  <core-environment>
    <process-id>
      <uuid/>
    </process-id>
```

```
            </core-environment>
            <recovery-environment socket-binding="txn-recovery-environment"
              status-socket-binding="txn-status-manager"/>
            <coordinator-environment default-timeout="300"
            statistics-enabled="true" />
        </subsystem>
```

The value of `default-timeout` specifies the default transaction timeout to be used for new transactions, which is specified as an integer in seconds.

> **How does the transaction timeout impact your applications?**
>
> The transaction timeout defines the timeout for all JTA transactions enlisted and thus severely affects your application behavior. A typical JTA transaction might be started by your EJBs or by a JMS session. So, if the duration of these transactions exceeds the specified timeout setting, the transaction service will roll back the transactions automatically.

The value of `statistics-enabled` determines whether or not the transaction service should gather statistical information. The default is to not gather this information.

> In WildFly, the `enable-statistics` property has been deprecated in favor of `statistics-enabled`. If you are migrating from JBoss AS 7, the deprecated property will still work but may be removed in future releases.

Configuring concurrency

Concurrency utilities is new to WildFly 8. As part of Java EE 7, are aim is to ease the task of multithreading within enterprise applications. Prior to Java EE 7, there was no safe way to create a new thread programmatically in your application.

With the new concurrency utilities, your new threads are now guaranteed to have access to other enterprise services, such as transactions, and security.

The main concurrency components are:

- `ContextService`
- `ManagedThreadFactory`
- `ManagedExecutorService`
- `ManagedScheduledExecutorService`

Configuring the context service

The context service is used to create contextual proxies from existent objects and is configured within the `ee` module of WildFly. The following is the default configuration in WildFly:

```xml
<subsystem xmlns="urn:jboss:domain:ee:2.0">
    ....
    <concurrent>
        <context-services>
            <context-service name="default" jndi-name="java:jboss/ee/
                concurrency/context/default"
                use-transaction-setup-provider="true"/>
        </context-services>
        ....
    </concurrent>
</subsystem>
```

The `name` attribute is the name of your context service, and the `use-transaction-setup-provider` attribute states whether or not the contextual proxies should suspend and resume active transactions.

Configuring the managed thread factory

The `ManagedThreadFactory` component is used to create threads that are managed by the container. The default configuration is as follows:

```xml
<concurrent>
    ...
    <managed-thread-factories>
        <managed-thread-factory name="default" jndi-name="java:jboss/
            ee/concurrency/factory/default" context-service="default"/>
    </managed-thread-factories>
    ...
</concurrent>
```

To use the default thread factory in your Java code, simply use the `@Resource` annotation without providing a value for the `lookup` attribute, as follows:

```java
@Stateless
public class ReportBean {
    @Resource
    private Managed ;
    public void runReports() {
        MyTask myTask = new MyTask();
```

```
        Future<Report> future = executorService.submit(myTask);
    }
}
```

Configuring the managed executor service

This class is used to execute tasks in a second thread within your enterprise application. You should always use this in preference over the executor service found within Java SE libraries. Here is an example of the configuration in WildFly:

```
<concurrent>
    ...
    <managed-executor-services>
        <managed-executor-service name="default"
            jndi-name="java:jboss/ee/concurrency/executor/default"
            context-service="default" hung-task-threshold="60000"
            core-threads="5" max-threads="25" keepalive-time="5000"/>
    </managed-executor-services>
    ...
</concurrent>
```

The following is the full list of attributes you can use to configure your `managed-executor-service` in WildFly:

`context-service`	This defines which context service to use.
`core-threads`	This defines the number of threads within the executors thread pool, including idle threads.
`hung-task-threshold`	This specifies how long, in milliseconds, the threads can be allowed to run before they are considered unresponsive.
`jndi-name`	This specifies the JNDI name for this resource.
`keepalive-time`	This specifies how long threads can remain idle when the number of threads is greater than the core thread size.
`long-running-tasks`	This checks whether the thread is a short-running or long-running thread.
`max-threads`	This specifies the maximum number of threads to allow in the executor's pool.
`name`	This specifies the name of the resource.
`queue-length`	This specifies the number of tasks that can be stored in the input queue. Zero means unlimited.
`reject-policy`	This defines how you can handle a failed task. An `ABORT` value will cause an exception to be thrown; `RETRY_ABORT`, which will cause a retry, and then an abort if the retry fails.
`thread-factory`	This specifies the name of the thread factory. If it's not supplied, the default thread factory is used.

Configuring the managed schedule executor service

This is the same as the `ManagedExecutorService`, except that it has additional functionality allowing you to schedule a thread to start at specific times. Here is an example of the configuration:

```
<concurrent>
    ...
    <managed-scheduled-executor-services>
        <managed-scheduled-executor-service name="default"
            jndi-name="java:jboss/ee/concurrency/scheduler/default"
            context-service="default" hung-task-threshold="60000"
            core-threads="2" keepalive-time="3000"/>
        </managed-scheduled-executor-services>
    ...
</concurrent>
```

The following is the list of attributes that can be used to configure your `managed-scheduled-executor-service`. Please see the preceding table in the `managed-executor-service` section for details of each property.

- `context-service`
- `core-threads`
- `hung-task-threshold`
- `jndi-name`
- `keepalive-time`
- `long-running-tasks`
- `name`
- `reject-policy`
- `thread-factory`

Summary

In this chapter, we continued the analysis of the application server configuration by looking at Java's enterprise services.

We first learned how to configure datasources, which can be used to add database connectivity to your applications. Installing a datasource in WildFly 8 requires two simple steps: installing the JDBC driver and adding the datasource into the server configuration.

We then looked at the enterprise JavaBeans subsystem, which allows you to configure and tune your EJB container. We looked at the basic EJB component configurations (SLSB, SFSB, and MDB) and then looked at the EJB timer service configuration that can be used to provide time-based services to your applications.

Next, we described the configuration of the message-oriented middleware, which allows you to loosely couple heterogeneous systems together while typically providing reliability, transactions, and various other features.

Then we moved on to the transaction subsystem configuration, which can be used to collect transaction logs and define the timeout for all JTA transactions enlisted.

Finally, we completed our journey by taking a look at how to configure concurrency within WildFly using the `ee` subsystem.

In the next chapter, we will discuss the web container configuration, providing a complete example, that uses a variety of enterprise technologies, and focusing on the structure and the packaging of the application.

4
The Undertow Web Server

In this chapter, we are going to look at how to configure Undertow, the web server shipped with WildFly 8. This will complete our overview of the standalone server configuration.

We will then look at the structure of a typical enterprise application by creating, packaging, and deploying a sample Java EE 7 project. It will include JavaServer Faces components, Enterprise JavaBeans, and CDI, and will also use the **Java Persistence API (JPA)**. This will give you a feel of working with a complete Java EE 7 application.

By the end of this chapter, you will have learned about:

- The architecture of Undertow
- The Undertow host configuration
- Serving static content
- The servlet container configuration
- The JSP configuration
- Configuration of session cookies
- How to create a simple web application

An overview of Undertow

Those of you who have worked with previous versions of WildFly will know that historically, JBoss has always included Tomcat, or a fork of Tomcat (named JBoss Web), as the application server's web container.

The decision to replace JBoss Web came about as a new web container was required, one that supports new Java EE 7 requirements, such as web sockets and an HTTP upgrade. It was also decided that the new web server should be lightweight and flexible, and have better performance. The resulting server is super responsive, can scale to over a million connections, and has exceptional throughput.

The Undertow architecture

Undertow is written in Java and based on the **Non-blocking Input/Output** API (often referred to as **New Input/Output** or just **NIO**). With a composition-based architecture and built using a fluent builder API, Undertow can be easily configured, giving you as much or as little functionality as you need. By chaining handlers together, you can build anything from a simple HTTP handler to a full Java EE 3.1 container.

There are three core parts that make up the Undertow server:

- **XNIO worker instances**: These instances form a thin abstraction layer over Java NIO, providing a channel API, management of IO and worker threads, and SSL support.
- **Listeners**: These handle incoming connections and the underlying protocol.
- **Handlers**: These are chained together to provide the main functionality for Undertow. They define how incoming requests are handled.

The following diagram shows how these components fit together to create the web server, and demonstrates how the handlers are chained together:

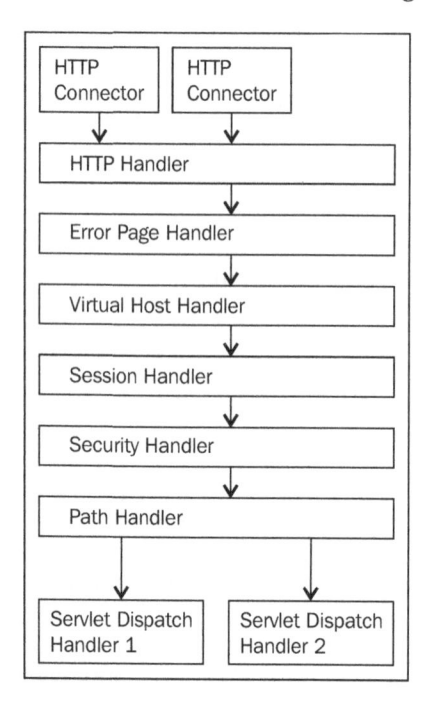

Configuring Undertow

In this section, we are going to look at how to configure the different components of Undertow. Undertow is configured within the Undertow subsystem found in the `standalone.xml` file. Here's an extract from the Undertow subsystem:

```xml
<subsystem xmlns="urn:jboss:domain:undertow:1.1">
    <buffer-cache name="default"/>
    <server name="default-server">
        <http-listener name="default" socket-binding="http"/>
        <host name="default-host" alias="localhost">
            <location name="/" handler="welcome-content"/>
            <filter-ref name="server-header"/>
            <filter-ref name="x-powered-by-header"/>
        </host>
    </server>
    <servlet-container name="default">
        <jsp-config/>
    </servlet-container>
    <handlers>
        <file name="welcome-content" path="${jboss.home.dir}/welcome-content"/>
    </handlers>
    ...
</subsystem>
```

The majority of the Undertow web server is configured within the `server` and `servlet-container` elements, both of which we are going to look at next.

Configuring the server

Within the `server` element, you can configure hosts and listeners. The attributes to configure your main server instance are as follows:

Name	Meaning
`default-host`	This is the virtual host to be used if a request has a no host header
`servlet-container`	This is the servlet container to be used, as configured in the `servlet-container` element

Configuring the listener

As we stated earlier, Undertow is made up of listeners and handlers. The listeners are configured within the `server` element, as highlighted in the following code. The default configuration in the `standalone.xml` file has just a single connector defined, which is the HTTP connector:

```xml
<server name="default-server">
    <http-listener name="default" socket-binding="http"/>
    <host name="default-host" alias="localhost">
        <location name="/" handler="welcome-content"/>
        <filter-ref name="server-header"/>
        <filter-ref name="x-powered-by-header"/>
    </host>
</server>
```

Notice that the `socket-binding` attribute points to a configuration defined in the `socket-binding-group` section:

```xml
<socket-binding-group name="standard-sockets" default-interface="public">
    <socket-binding name="http" port="8080"/>
</socket-binding-group>
```

> WildFly also supports AJP and HTTPS connection protocols; we will cover these in detail in *Chapter 9, Load-balancing Web Applications* and *Chapter 10, Securing WildFly*, respectively.

There are a lot of options when it comes to the configuration of the listener. The attributes for the HTTP listener element are outlined as follows:

Property	Description	Default value
allow-encoded-slash	When set to true, this property allows the server to decode percent-encoded slash characters (%2F). Only enable this option if you have a legacy application that requires it, as it can have security implications due to different servers interpreting the slash differently.	false
always-set-keep-alive	This property determines whether the `Connection: keep-alive` header should be added to all responses, even if not required by spec.	true

Property	Description	Default value
buffer-pipelined-data	This property determines whether responses to HTTP pipelined requests should be buffered and sent out in a single write. This can improve performance if the HTTP pipelining is in use and responses are small.	true
buffer-pool	This property references a buffer pool as defined in the I/O subsystem, which is used internally to read and write requests. In general, these should be at least 8 KB, unless you are in a memory-constrained environment.	default
certificate-forwarding	If this property is enabled, then the listener will take the certificate from the SSL_CLIENT_CERT attribute. This property should only be enabled if the client is behind a proxy and the proxy is configured to always set these headers.	
decode-url	This property determines whether the URL should be decoded. If this property is set to false, the percent-encoded characters in the URL will be left as is.	true
enabled	This property states whether this listener is enabled	true
max-cookies	This property defines the maximum number of cookies allowed. If a client sends more cookies than this value, the connection will be closed. This exists to prevent DOS attacks based on hash collision.	200
max-header-size	This property defines the maximum allowed HTTP header block size in bytes. Any request header with a value greater than this will be closed.	5120
max-headers	This property defines the maximum number of headers allowed. It exists to prevent DOS attacks based on hash collision.	200
max-parameters	This property defines the maximum number of query or path parameters allowed. If more parameters are sent, the connection will be closed. It exists to prevent DOS attacks based on hash collision.	1000
max-post-size	This property defines the maximum size allowed for incoming post requests.	0 (unlimited)
name	This property defines the name given to the listener.	
proxy-address-forwarding	This property enables x-forwarded-host and similar headers and sets a remote IP address and hostname.	

Property	Description	Default value
redirect-socket	This property, when enabled, automatically redirects a request to the specified socket binding port if the listener supports non-SSL requests and a request is received for which a matching security constraint requires SSL transport.	
socket-binding	This property determines the address and port the listener listens on.	
url-charset	This property defines the charset to decode the URL to.	UTF-8
worker	This property references an XNIO worker as defined in the IO subsystem. The worker that is in use controls the IO and blocking thread pool.	default

Configuring the host

The host configuration within the `server` element corresponds to a virtual host and is nested directly under the `server` element, as shown in the following code. Virtual hosts allow you to group web applications according to the DNS names by which a machine running WildFly is known.

```
<server name="default-server">
    ...
    <host name="default-host" alias="localhost">
        <location name="/" handler="welcome-content"/>
        <filter-ref name="server-header"/>
        <filter-ref name="x-powered-by-header"/>
    </host>
</server>
```

The elements nested within the host are explained here:

- `location`: This element defines the URL path to the content, such as `welcome-content`.
- `access-log`: This element allows you to configure the location and format of the access log.
- `filter-ref`: This element defines the filters that are applied to the current host.
- `single-sign-on`: This element allows you to configure the cookies to use for authentication.

The access log can be fully configured by changing the default attributes, as shown in the following code:

```
<access-log directory="${jboss.server.log.dir}" pattern="common"
prefix="access_log" rotate="true" suffix=".log" worker="default"/>
```

The `filter-ref` element states the filters applied by referencing the name of the filters defined in the `filters` element, as shown in the following highlighted code:

```
<server name="default-server">
    <host name="default-host" alias="localhost">
        <location name="/" handler="welcome-content"/>
        <filter-ref name="server-header"/>
        <filter-ref name="x-powered-by-header"/>
    </host>
</server>
<filters>
    <response-header name="server-header" header-name="Server"
        header-value="Wildfly 8"/>
    <response-header name="x-powered-by-header" header-name="X-
        Powered-By" header-value="Undertow 1"/>
</filters>
```

Serving static content

You may not want to deploy all your static content with your application. These may be images, PDF documents, or other types of files. You can configure Undertow to look for these files on the local filesystem. This example shows you how to do this by adding a file handler and location to the Undertow subsystem:

```
<server name="default-server">
    <http-listener name="default" socket-binding="http"/>
    <host name="default-host" alias="localhost">
        <location name="/" handler="welcome-content"/>
        <location name="/img" handler="images"/>
    </host>
</server>
<handlers>
    <file name="welcome-content" path="${jboss.home.dir}/welcome-
        content" directory-listing="true"/>
    <file name="images" path="/var/images" directory-listing="true"/>
</handlers>
```

With this additional configuration, any request for resources to www.yourdomain.com/contextroot/img will be redirected to the filesystem on your hard disk.

Configuring the servlet container

An instance of a servlet container is defined within a single `servlet-container` element. You can have more than one `servlet-container` element if you wish to have multiple servlet containers; however, for most setups, a single instance will suffice. The default configuration in `standalone.xml` is shown as follows:

```
<servlet-container name="default">
    <jsp-config/>
</servlet-container>
```

An explanation of the attributes available for the `servlet-container` are detailed in the following table:

Property	Description	Default value
`allow-non-standard-wrappers`	This property relaxes the servlet specification, which requires applications to only wrap the request/response with wrapper classes that extend the `ServletRequestWrapper` and `ServletResponseWrapper` classes.	`false`
`default-buffer-cache`	This is the buffer cache used to cache static resources in the default servlet.	
`default-encoding`	This is the default encoding for the requests and responses.	
`eager-filter-initialization`	By setting this property to `true`, the init method of filters defined in your `web.xml` file are called upon the first request, and not on server startup.	`false`
`ignore-flush`	This ignores flushes on the servlet output stream.	`false`
`stack-trace-on-error`	The available options for this property are `all`, `none`, or `local-only`. The `all` value will display all traces (should not be used in a production environment), while `none` means stack traces are not shown, and `local-only` means only requests from local addresses are shown and there are no headers to indicate that the request has been proxied. This feature uses the Undertow error page rather than the default error page specified in `web.xml`.	`local-only`
`use-listener-encoding`	This uses the default encoding used by the listener that received the request.	`false`

Several child elements can be added to the `servlet-container` element, which will allow you to configure your JSPs, session cookies, and persistent sessions.

Configuring JSP

The JSP element is provided in the default configuration. As no additional attributes are added, the default configuration is applied, as shown in the following code:

```
<jsp-config
check-interval="0"
development="false"
disabled="false"
display-source-fragment="true"
dump-smap="false"
error-on-use-bean-invalid-class-attribute="false"
generate-strings-as-char-arrays="false"
java-encoding="UTF8"
keep-generated="true"
mapped-file="true"
modification-test-interval="4"
recompile-on-fail="false"
smap="true"
source-vm="1.6"
tag-pooling="true"
target-vm="1.6"
trim-spaces="false"
x-powered-by="true"/>
```

Configuring the session cookie

You will probably be interested in configuring the Undertow session cookie. By default, there is no configuration text included in the `standalone.xml` file, so you will need to add it as a child element of the `servlet-container` configuration:

```
<servlet-container name="default">
    <jsp-config/>
    <session-cookie name="default" domain="yourdomain.com" http-
        only="true" max-age="60" secure="true"/>
</servlet-container>
```

The possible attributes for the `session-cookie` element are shown in the following table. If you do not set these values explicitly, no value will be set, as there are no defaults:

Property	Description	Default value
`name`	This property defines the name of a cookie	
`domain`	This property defines the cookie domain	
`comment`	This property defines the cookie comment	
`http-only`	This property determines whether the cookie is HTTP-only	`true`
`secure`	This property determines whether the cookie is marked as secure	`true`
`max-age`	This property defines the maximum age of a cookie (in minutes)	0 (infinite)

Saving the session state

Saving sessions allows session data to be stored when the server is restarted or the application is redeployed. To enable this, you need to add the `persistent-sessions` element to the configuration file, as shown in the following code. This property should be used in your development environment rather than in production.

```
<servlet-container name="default">
    <jsp-config/>
    <persistent-sessions path="/session"
      relative-to="${jboss.server.tmp.dir}"/>
</servlet-container>
```

> If you do not specify the `path` variable, then the session will only be persistent across redeploys and not across server restarts.

Configuring the buffer cache

The buffer cache is used to cache content, for example, static files. A buffer cache consists of one or more regions, and each region is split into smaller buffers. Here's an example configuration of the `buffer-cache` element:

```
<subsystem xmlns="urn:jboss:domain:undertow:1.1">
    <buffer-cache name="default" buffer-size="1024"
      buffers-per-region="2048" max-regions="10" />
    ...
</subsystem>
```

> The total cache size can be calculated by multiplying the buffer size by the buffers per region and the maximum number of regions. In our example, it would be:
>
> *1024 bytes * 2048 * 10 = 20971520 bytes*

Creating and deploying a web application

As you can see, the application server provides a relatively straightforward way to configure the web container. In order to build and deploy a web application, it would be good for you to learn how to organize an application along with its specific configuration files.

WildFly 8 is a Java EE 7 compliant application server and thus, can be used to deploy a wide range of web applications. One way of building a web application is to use the **JavaServer Faces (JSF)** technology, which is an evolution of the JSP technology. It is also part of Enterprise Java, meaning that WildFly supports it out of the box. WildFly 8 supports the JSF release 2.2 using the Mojarra implementation.

> The purpose of this example is to show you how to create, configure, and deploy a Java EE 7 application on WildFly 8. If you want to learn more about the various Java EE 7 technologies, you should check out the many Java EE 7 examples created by Arun Gupta, which have been configured specifically for WildFly. The GitHub URL is https://github.com/javaee-samples/javaee7-samples.

Next, we are going to create a simple application. The purpose of this is to demonstrate how to configure each of the various enterprise components found within a typical enterprise application.

Creating a new Maven web project

There are several ways in which you can create a web application project using Eclipse. Since Maven is the de facto build tool, it makes sense to use the Maven project structure in this example.

Let's start by creating the project file structure. Go to **File** | **New** | **Maven Project**, select **skip archetype selection**, create a simple project, and proceed to the next page. Then, complete the artifact details as shown in the following screenshot, ensuring that you select **war** as the packaging:

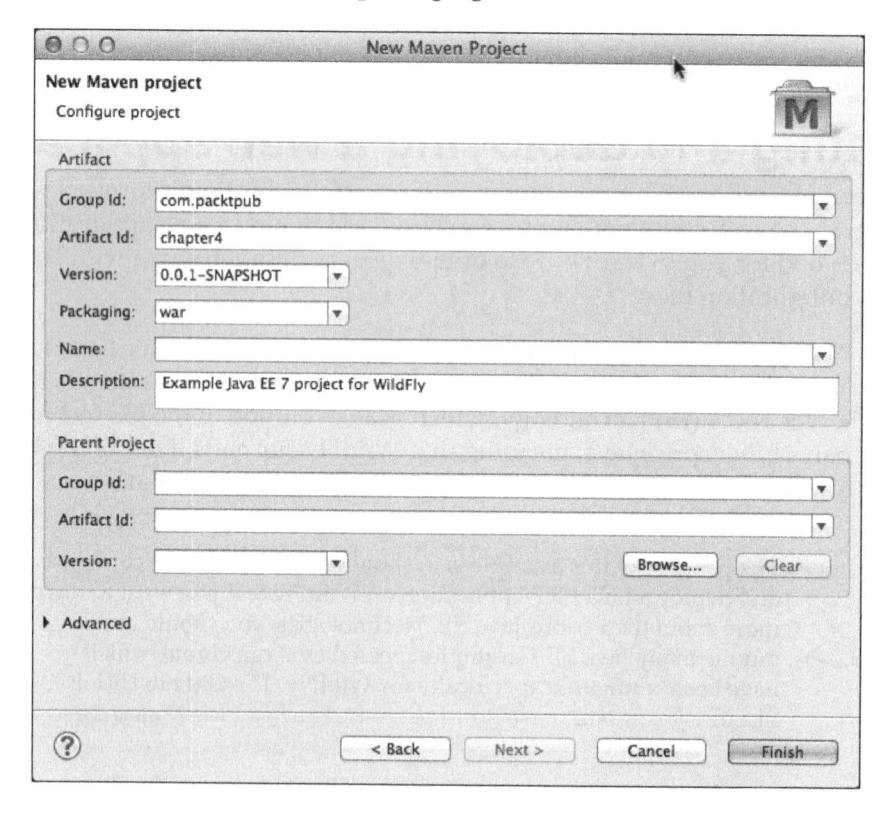

After clicking on **Finish**, Eclipse will generate a default folder structure for your application:

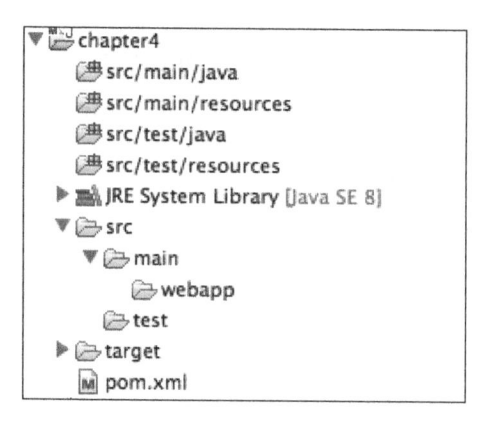

Chapter 4

We are going to use JSF to create the view. Configuring the JSF 2.2 web application requires very little effort. You can achieve this with the following steps:

1. Create a file called web.xml and place it in the WEB-INF folder of your application.
2. Add the FacesServlet to your web.xml file and specify what kind of URL patterns will be directed to it.
3. Create a faces-config.xml file and place it in the WEB-INF folder.

> The FacesServlet is a servlet that manages the request processing life cycle for web applications that are utilizing JavaServer Faces to construct the user interface.

Here's the complete web.xml file. You can see that we specified the URL patterns that the FacesServlet will process:

```xml
<?xml version="1.0" encoding="UTF-8"?>
<web-app xmlns:xsi="http://www.w3.org/2001/XMLSchema-instance"
  xmlns="http://xmlns.jcp.org/xml/ns/javaee/"
  xmlns:web="http://xmlns.jcp.org/xml/ns/javaee/web-app_3_1.xsd"
  xsi:schemaLocation="http://xmlns.jcp.org/xml/ns/javaee
  http://xmlns.jcp.org/xml/ns/javaee/web-app_3_1.xsd"
  id="WebApp_ID" version="3.1">
  <display-name>Java EE 7 - WildFly 8</display-name>
  <welcome-file-list>
    <welcome-file>index.xhtml</welcome-file>
  </welcome-file-list>
  <context-param>
    <param-name>
      com.sun.faces.enableRestoreView11Compatibility
    </param-name>
    <param-value>true</param-value>
  </context-param>
  <servlet>
    <servlet-name>Faces Servlet</servlet-name>
    <servlet-class>javax.faces.webapp.FacesServlet</servlet-class>
    <load-on-startup>1</load-on-startup>
  </servlet>
  <servlet-mapping>
    <servlet-name>Faces Servlet</servlet-name>
    <url-pattern>*.xhtml</url-pattern>
  </servlet-mapping>
  <context-param>
```

[109]

```xml
    <param-name>javax.servlet.jsp.jstl.fmt.localizationContext
</param-name>
      <param-value>resources.application</param-value>
   </context-param>
   <listener>
     <listener-class>com.sun.faces.config.ConfigureListener
</listener-class>
   </listener>
</web-app>
```

Next, you see a minimal JSF configuration file named `faces-config.xml`, which will be placed in the `WEB-INF` folder of your application. This file declares the JSF release that we are going to use, which in our case, is 2.2:

```xml
<?xml version="1.0" encoding="UTF-8"?>
<faces-config xmlns="http://xmlns.jcp.org/xml/ns/javaee"
   xmlns:xsi="http://www.w3.org/2001/XMLSchema-instance"
   xsi:schemaLocation="http://xmlns.jcp.org/xml/ns/javaee
   http://xmlns.jcp.org/xml/ns/javaee/web-facesconfig_2_2.xsd"
   version="2.2">
</faces-config>
```

Eclipse can create these configuration files for you. To do this, you will need to activate the **JavaServer Faces Facets**. Right-click on your project and select **Project Properties**. Here, you will find a set of configuration options that can be automatically added to your project under the **Project Facets** option. You may need to modify the files to ensure that the correct namespaces are used, and update the content of the `web.xml` file.

Next, we will need to add the project dependencies to the Maven configuration file, the `pom.xml` file. Maven will then download and manage all your dependencies for you upon a project build. The complete content of `pom.xml` is shown in the following code:

```xml
<project xmlns="http://maven.apache.org/POM/4.0.0" xmlns:xsi="http://www.w3.org/2001/XMLSchema-instance"
    xsi:schemaLocation="http://maven.apache.org/POM/4.0.0 http://maven.apache.org/xsd/maven-4.0.0.xsd">
    <modelVersion>4.0.0</modelVersion>
    <groupId>com.packtpub</groupId>
    <artifactId>chapter4</artifactId>
    <version>0.0.1-SNAPSHOT</version>
    <packaging>war</packaging>
    <description>Simple Java EE 7 example using WildFly</description>

    <repositories>
```

```xml
            <repository>
                <id>JBoss Repository</id>
                <url>https://repository.jboss.org/nexus/content/groups/
                    public/</url>
            </repository>
        </repositories>

        <dependencies>
            <dependency>
                <groupId>org.jboss.spec</groupId>
                <artifactId>jboss-javaee-7.0</artifactId>
                <version>1.0.1.Final</version>
                <type>pom</type>
                <scope>provided</scope>
            </dependency>
        </dependencies>
        <!-- build plugins removed for brevity -->
</project>
```

> You will notice that the JBoss Nexus repository is being used rather than Maven Central. This is because since Java EE 6, JBoss has hosted its own EE API. The motivation for this was the unimplemented methods in Java EE 6. To understand the full motivation, navigate to `https://developer.jboss.org/blogs/donnamishelly/2011/04/29/jboss-java-ee-api-specs-project`. I would recommend that you use the version hosted by JBoss, as it is identical to the code shipped with WildFly.

Adding JSF components

For the purpose of learning how to package a Java EE 7 application, we will show you how to combine JSF components, such as JSF views with Enterprise components like CDI and EJBs.

In this example, we will create a simple caching system that uses an EJB singleton to handle the cache in memory. Then, we show you how to persist data to a database. Let's start by adding a page named `index.xhtml` to your dynamic web project:

```
<!DOCTYPE html>
<html xmlns="http://www.w3.org/1999/xhtml"
    xmlns:h="http://xmlns.jcp.org/jsf/html"
    xmlns:f="http://xmlns.jcp.org/jsf/core">

<h:head>
```

The Undertow Web Server

```xml
            <link href="main.css" rel="stylesheet" type="text/css" />
    </h:head>
    <h:body>
        <h2>JSF 2 example on WildFly 8</h2>
        <h:form id="jsfexample">
            <h:messages />
            <h:panelGrid columns="2" styleClass="default">
                <h:outputText value="Enter key:" />
                <h:inputText value="#{manager.key}" />

                <h:outputText value="Enter value:" />
                <h:inputText value="#{manager.value}" />

                <h:commandButton actionListener="#{manager.save}"
                    styleClass="buttons" value="Save key/value" />
                <h:commandButton actionListener="#{manager.clear}"
                    styleClass="buttons" value="Clear cache" />
            </h:panelGrid>

            <h:dataTable value="#{manager.cacheList}" var="item"
                styleClass="table" headerClass="table-header"
                rowClasses="table-odd-row,table-even-row">
                <h:column>
                    <f:facet name="header">Key</f:facet>
                    <h:outputText value="#{item.key}" />
                </h:column>
                <h:column>
                    <f:facet name="header">Value</f:facet>
                    <h:outputText value="#{item.value}" />
                </h:column>
            </h:dataTable>
        </h:form>
    </h:body>
</html>
```

> To learn about JSF, please refer to the online tutorial at http://docs.oracle.com/javaee/7/tutorial/doc/jsf-intro.htm.

The following code references a backing bean named manager, which is used to store and retrieve key/value pairs. Backing beans are simple Java classes which are used as models for UI components. You will also notice the @RequestScoped annotation in the PropertyManager class.

Chapter 4

> When defining the scope of a backing bean, you should only use the `javax.faces.bean.RequestScoped` annotation if you are not using CDI, which is highly unlikely. Instead, you should use the annotations found in the `javax.enterprise.context.*` package, which is part of the Context and Dependency Injection framework.

Now, let's see how to code the `PropertyManager` managed bean:

```
package com.packtpub.chapter4.bean;
import java.util.List;
import javax.ejb.EJB;
import javax.enterprise.context.RequestScoped;
import javax.faces.application.FacesMessage;
import javax.faces.context.FacesContext;
import javax.faces.event.ActionEvent;
import javax.inject.Named;
import org.jboss.logging.Logger;
import com.packtpub.chapter4.ejb.SingletonBean;
import com.packtpub.chapter4.entity.Property;

@Named("manager")
@RequestScoped
public class PropertyManager {

    private Logger logger = Logger.getLogger(getClass());

    @EJB
    private SingletonBean ejb;
    private String key;
    private String value;

    public void save(ActionEvent e) {
        try {
            ejb.save(key, value);
            FacesContext.getCurrentInstance().addMessage(
                    null,
                    new FacesMessage(FacesMessage.SEVERITY_INFO,
                            "Property Saved!", null));
        } catch (Exception ex) {
            logger.error("Error saving property", ex);
            FacesContext.getCurrentInstance().addMessage(
                    null,
                    new FacesMessage(FacesMessage.SEVERITY_ERROR,
```

[113]

```
                        "Error Saving!", ex.getMessage()));
        }
    }
    public void clear(ActionEvent e) {
        logger.info("Called clear");
        ejb.deleteAll();
    }
    public List<Property> getCacheList() {
        return ejb.getProperties();
    }
// getters and setters removed for brevity
}
```

The most important part of this class is the `@Named` annotation. Annotating the class with `@Named` allows this class to be picked up as a CDI managed bean. The name passed into the annotation defines how this bean can be referenced via the Expression Language (EL). Next, the `@EJB` annotation is used to inject the `SingletonBean` into the class.

> You can find out more about JSF managed beans at the Java EE tutorial here: http://docs.oracle.com/javaee/7/tutorial/doc/jsf-develop.htm.

Adding the EJB layer

The `SingletonBean` is an EJB, which is marked with the special `@javax.ejb.Singleton` annotation. A class with such an annotation is guaranteed to be instantiated only once per application, and exists for the life cycle of the application. In the Java EE context, singleton beans are primarily used to store application-wide shared data. Now, we need to create a new class named `SingletonBean`. The aim of this class will be to save and retrieve key/value pairs:

```
package com.packtpub.chapter4.ejb;

import java.util.ArrayList;
import java.util.List;

import javax.annotation.PostConstruct;
import javax.ejb.LocalBean;
import javax.ejb.Remote;
import javax.ejb.Singleton;
import javax.persistence.EntityManager;
import javax.persistence.PersistenceContext;
```

```java
import javax.persistence.Query;
import javax.persistence.TypedQuery;

import com.packtpub.chapter4.entity.Property;

@Singleton
@LocalBean
public class SingletonBean {

    private List<Property> cache = new ArrayList<>();

    @PostConstruct
    public void initCache() {
        this.cache = queryCache();
        if (cache == null) {
            cache = new ArrayList<Property>();
        }
    }

    public void deleteAll() {
        this.cache.clear();
    }

    public void save(String key, String value) {
        Property property = new Property(key, value);
        this.cache.add(property);
    }

    public List<Property> getProperties() {
        return cache;
    }
}
```

The last class we need to add is `Property`, which is a plain `JavaBean` class:

```java
package com.packtpub.chapter4.entity;

public class Property {
    private String key;
    private String value;
    // GETTERS & SETTERS omitted for brevity
}
```

Once you reach this point, you should have a project containing the items shown in the following screenshot:

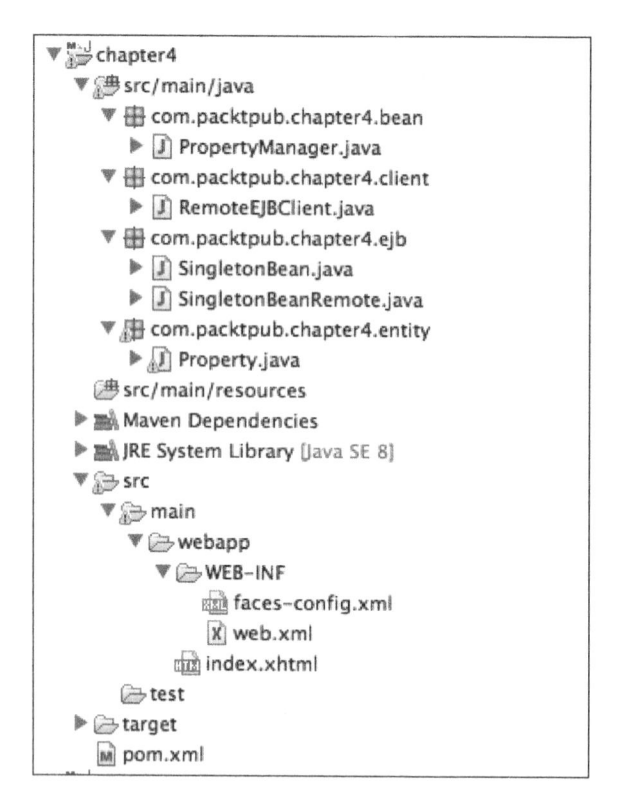

```
▼ chapter4
    ▼ src/main/java
        ▼ com.packtpub.chapter4.bean
            ▶ PropertyManager.java
        ▼ com.packtpub.chapter4.client
            ▶ RemoteEJBClient.java
        ▼ com.packtpub.chapter4.ejb
            ▶ SingletonBean.java
            ▶ SingletonBeanRemote.java
        ▼ com.packtpub.chapter4.entity
            ▶ Property.java
    src/main/resources
    ▶ Maven Dependencies
    ▶ JRE System Library [Java SE 8]
    ▼ src
        ▼ main
            ▼ webapp
                ▼ WEB-INF
                    faces-config.xml
                    web.xml
                index.xhtml
        test
    ▶ target
    pom.xml
```

Choosing the web context of the application

By default, a web application inherits the web context name from the archive name, which is deployed on the application server. Maven uses the artifact ID, followed by the version to name the archive. So, in our example, if we deploy an archive named `chapter4-0.0.1-SNAPSHOT.war`, it will be accessible using the web context name `chapter4-0.0.1-SNAPSHOT`, as shown by the following image:

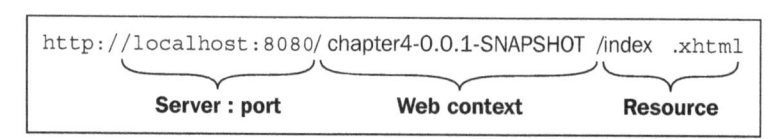

```
http://localhost:8080/ chapter4-0.0.1-SNAPSHOT /index .xhtml
    Server : port           Web context         Resource
```

The context name can be modified to something more meaningful. The simplest way to achieve this (without changing the archive name) is by adding a `jboss-web.xml` file to the `WEB-INF` folder of your project:

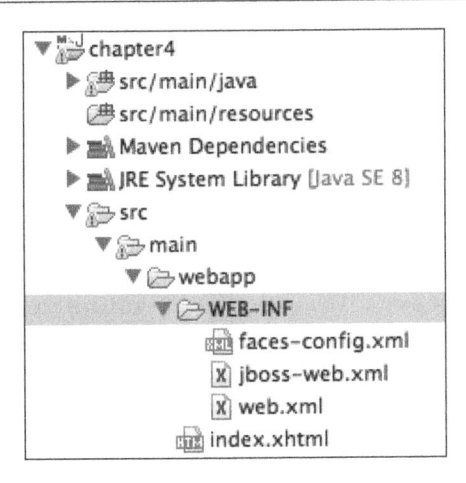

```
▼ chapter4
   ▶ src/main/java
      src/main/resources
   ▶ Maven Dependencies
   ▶ JRE System Library [Java SE 8]
   ▼ src
      ▼ main
         ▼ webapp
            ▼ WEB-INF
               faces-config.xml
               jboss-web.xml
               web.xml
            index.xhtml
```

The content of this file will include the custom web context, as specified by the `context-root` element:

```
<jboss-web>
  <context-root>chapter4</context-root>
</jboss-web>
```

Deploying the web application

Once you are happy with your settings, you can deploy and verify your application. If you are deploying your application from within Eclipse, just right-click on the WildFly Runtime Server and choose the **Add and Remove** option (assuming you installed the WildFly runtime as shown in *Chapter 1, Installing WildFly*). Next, add the web project to the list of deployed projects.

You can then deploy the application by right-clicking on the project and choosing **Full Publish**:

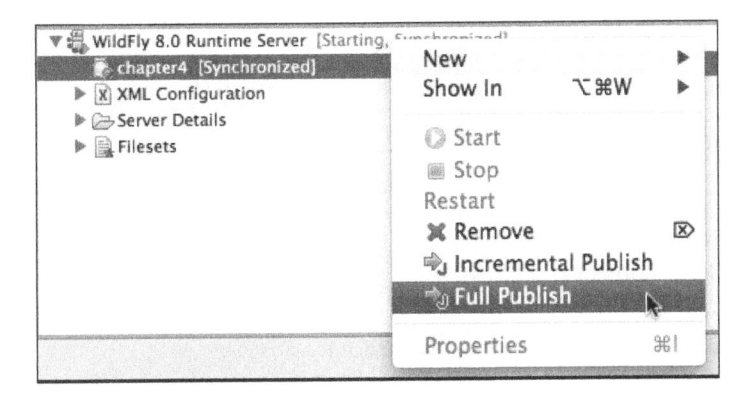

```
▼ WildFly 8.0 Runtime Server [Starting, Synchronized]
     chapter4 [Synchronized]        New                    ▶
  ▶ XML Configuration               Show In        ⌥⌘W     ▶
  ▶ Server Details
  ▶ Filesets                        ⊙ Start
                                    ■ Stop
                                    Restart
                                    ✖ Remove               ⌦
                                    ⇨ Incremental Publish
                                    ⇨ Full Publish

                                    Properties            ⌘I
```

After publishing your application, you will notice that Eclipse will copy your web application archive (`chapter4-0.0.1-SNAPSHOT.war`) to the server. It will also create a file named `chapter4-0.0.1-SNAPSHOT.war.dodeploy`. As you will learn in *Chapter 6, Application Structure and Deployment*, expanded archives, by default, require a marker file in WildFly to trigger the deployment. Eclipse is aware of this and creates the file for you.

Upon successful deployment, the `chapter4-0.0.1-SNAPSHOT.war.dodeploy` file will be replaced by a `chapter4-0.0.1-SNAPSHOT.war.deployed` marker file, which indicates that you have successfully deployed the web application. You can verify that your application works correctly by pointing to the `index.xhtml` page at `http://localhost:8080/chapter4/index.xhtml`, as shown in the following screenshot:

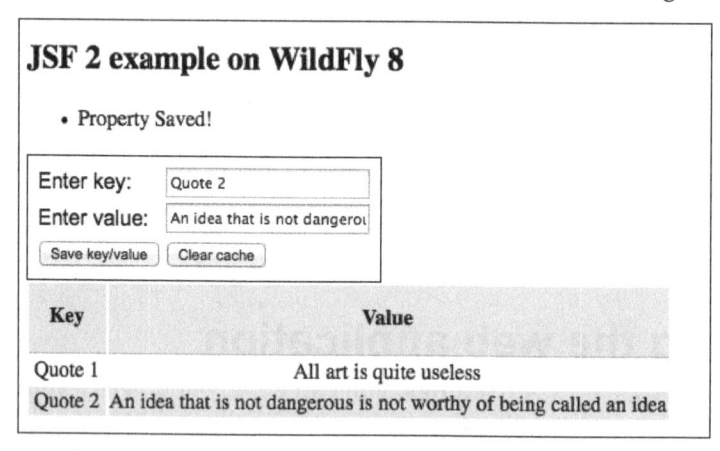

Deploying a web application to the root context

In our example, we have shown how to deploy the web application to a custom context using `jboss-web.xml`. One particular case of web context is the `root` context. This typically resolves to `http://localhost:8080` and is used to provide some welcome context by the web server. By default, WildFly has a root context that is mapped in the `JBOSS_HOME/welcome-content` folder. You can, however, override it by deploying one of your applications to the `root` context. This requires two simple steps:

1. First, you need to remove the following line from your Undertow subsystem:

   `<location name="/" handler="welcome-content"/>`

2. Then, in your application, add a `jboss-web.xml` file that contains the `root` context for your application:

   ```
   <jboss-web>
       <context-root>/</context-root>
   </jboss-web>
   ```

Adding a remote EJB client

Before adding any code for the remote EJB client, we need to add two dependencies to `pom.xml`. This ensures that our code will compile and run without errors:

```xml
<!-- this is required for a security -->
<dependency>
    <groupId>org.jboss.sasl</groupId>
    <artifactId>jboss-sasl</artifactId>
    <version>1.0.4.Final</version>
    <scope>provided</scope>
</dependency>
<!-- this is required for the RemoteEJBClient.java to compile -->
<dependency>
    <groupId>org.jboss</groupId>
    <artifactId>jboss-ejb-client</artifactId>
    <version>2.0.2.Final</version>
    <scope>provided</scope>
</dependency>
```

In order to test our application with a remote client, we need to create a remote interface to the EJB:

```java
package com.packtpub.chapter4.ejb;

import java.util.List;
import com.packtpub.chapter4.entity.Property;

public interface SingletonBeanRemote {
    public void deleteAll();
    public void save(String key, String value);
    public List<Property> getProperties();
}
```

The concrete implementation of this interface is the `SingletonBeanRemoteImpl` class, which has the same Java method implementations as the `SingletonBean` class that we showed in the earlier section:

```java
@Singleton
@LocalBean
@Remote(SingletonBeanRemote.class)
public class  SingletonBean implements SingletonBeanRemote {
// Bean class unchanged
}
```

[119]

EJB remote invocation happens through the **Remoting** framework, which uses **Simple Authentication and Security Layer** (**SASL**) for client-server authentication. You need to explicitly set the security provider by adding the following specification to the test client:

```
static {
   Security.addProvider(new JBossSaslProvider());
}
```

The next part is quite tricky. We need to determine the **Java Naming and Directory Interface** (**JNDI**) name of the EJB, for which we will need to look up the remote EJB. The JNDI name varies depending on whether the EJB is stateful or stateless. The following table outlines the syntax for both SLSBs and SFSBs:

EJB type	JNDI syntax
Stateless EJB	`ejb:<app-name>/<module-name>/<distinct-name>/<bean-name>!<fully-qualified-classname-of-the-remote-interface>`
Stateful EJB	`ejb:<app-name>/<module-name>/<distinct-name>/<bean-name>!<fully-qualified-classname-of-the-remote-interface>?stateful`

The following table bisects each of these properties:

Parameter	Description
`app-name`	This is the application name and is used in the event that the application has been deployed as an Enterprise archive. It typically corresponds to the Enterprise archive name without `.ear`. Since we packed our application in a web archive, this parameter will not be used.
`module-name`	This is the module within which the EJBs are contained. Since we deployed the application in a file named `chapter4-0.0.1-SNAPSHOT.war`, it corresponds to `chapter4-0.0.1-SNAPSHOT`.
`distinct-name`	This is an optional name that can be assigned to distinguish between different EJB implementations. It's not used in our example.
`bean-name`	This is the EJB name, which, by default, is the class name of the bean implementation class, in our case, `SingletonBeanRemoteImpl`.
`fully-qualified-classname-of-the-remote-interface`	This obviously corresponds to the fully qualified class name of the interface you are looking up, in our case, `com.packtpub.chapter4.ejb.SingletonBeanRemote`.

> Please notice that stateful EJBs require an additional `?stateful` parameter to be added to the JNDI lookup name.

With this information on the JNDI namespace, you will be ready to understand the client code:

```java
package com.packtpub.chapter4.client;

import java.security.Security;
import java.util.*;
import javax.naming.*;
import org.jboss.ejb.client.*;
import org.jboss.sasl.JBossSaslProvider;
import com.packtpub.chapter4.ejb.SingletonBean;
import com.packtpub.chapter4.ejb.SingletonBeanRemote;
import com.packtpub.chapter4.entity.Property;

public class RemoteEJBClient {
    static {
        Security.addProvider(new JBossSaslProvider());
    }
    public static void main(String[] args) throws Exception {
        testRemoteEJB();
    }
    private static void testRemoteEJB() throws NamingException {
        final SingletonBeanRemote ejb = lookupEJB();
        ejb.save("entry", "value");
        List<Property> list = ejb.getProperties();
        System.out.println(list);
    }
    private static SingletonBeanRemote lookupEJB()
      throws NamingException {

        Properties clientProperties = new Properties();
        clientProperties.put("endpoint.name", "client-endpoint");
        clientProperties.put("remote.connections", "default");
        clientProperties.put("remote.connection.default.port",
           "8080");
        clientProperties.put("remote.connection.default.host",
           "localhost");
        clientProperties.put("remote.connectionprovider.
           create.options.org.xnio.Options.SSL_ENABLED", "false");
```

```java
        clientProperties.put("remote.connection.default.connect.
          options.org.xnio.Options.SASL_POLICY_NOANONYMOUS",
          "false");

        EJBClientConfiguration ejbClientConfiguration =
          new PropertiesBasedEJBClientConfiguration(
          clientProperties);
        ContextSelector<EJBClientContext> ejbContextSelector =
          new ConfigBasedEJBClientContextSelector(
          ejbClientConfiguration);

        EJBClientContext.setSelector(ejbContextSelector);

        final Hashtable<String, String> jndiProperties =
          new Hashtable<>();
        jndiProperties.put(Context.URL_PKG_PREFIXES,
          "org.jboss.ejb.client.naming");
        final Context context = new InitialContext(jndiProperties);
        final String appName = "";
        final String moduleName =
          "chapter4-webapp-example-0.0.1-SNAPSHOT";
        final String distinctName = "";

        final String beanName =
          SingletonBean.class.getSimpleName();
        final String viewClassName =
          SingletonBeanRemote.class.getName();
        return (SingletonBeanRemote) context.lookup("ejb:" +
          appName + "/" + moduleName + "/" + distinctName +
          "/" + beanName + "!" + viewClassName);
    }
}
```

As you can see, the major complexity of the remote EJB client code is related to the JNDI lookup section. You might have noticed that in the highlighted section, we initialized the JNDI context with a property named `Context.URL_PKG_PREFIXES` to specify the list of package prefixes to be used when loading URL context factories. In our case, we set it to `org.jboss.ejb.client.naming` so that the JNDI API knows which classes are in charge of handling the `ejb:` namespace.

Configuring the client using a properties file

Finally, you might wonder how the client actually knows the server location where the remote EJBs are hosted. This can be solved by adding the following client-side property file named `jboss-ejb-client.properties` to the client classpath:

```
remote.connectionprovider.create.options.org.xnio.Options.
  SSL_ENABLED=false
```

```
remote.connections=default
remote.connection.default.host=localhost
remote.connection.default.port = 8080
remote.connection.default.connect.options.org.xnio.Options.
   SASL_POLICY_NOANONYMOUS=false
```

Within this file, you can specify a set of properties prefixed by `remote.connectionprovider.create.options`, which will be used during the remote connection. In our example, we just set the `org.xnio.Options.SSL_ENABLED` property to `false`, which means that a clear text transmission will be used to connect the client and server.

The `remote.connections` property is used to specify a set of one or more connections that map to an EJB receiver. In our case, there is a single remote connection named `default`, which maps to the `localhost` and the remoting port `8080`.

Finally, we need to specify that an SASL anonymous connection will be used; otherwise, without an authentication, our connection will be refused.

Configuring the client programmatically

Another way to configure the client's connection properties is to configure them programmatically. Here, we create a `Properties` object and populate it with the same key/value pairs that are in the `jboss-ejb-client.properties` configuration file. The important parts of the code are highlighted in bold:

```
private static SingletonBeanRemote lookupEJB()
  throws NamingException {
    Properties clientProperties = new Properties();
    clientProperties.put("endpoint.name", "client-endpoint");
    clientProperties.put("remote.connections", "default");
    clientProperties.put("remote.connection.default.port",
      "8080");
    clientProperties.put("remote.connection.default.host",
      "localhost");
    clientProperties.put("remote.connectionprovider.
      create.options.org.xnio.Options.SSL_ENABLED", "false");
    clientProperties.put("remote.connection.default.
      connect.options.org.xnio.Options.SASL_POLICY_NOANONYMOUS",
      "false");

    EJBClientConfiguration ejbClientConfiguration =
      new PropertiesBasedEJBClientConfiguration(clientProperties);
        ContextSelector<EJBClientContext> ejbContextSelector =
      new ConfigBasedEJBClientContextSelector(
        ejbClientConfiguration);
```

```java
EJBClientContext.setSelector(ejbContextSelector);

final Hashtable<String, String> jndiProperties =
  new Hashtable<>();
jndiProperties.put(Context.URL_PKG_PREFIXES,
  "org.jboss.ejb.client.naming");
final Context context = new InitialContext(jndiProperties);
final String appName = "";
final String moduleName =
  "chapter4-webapp-example-0.0.1-SNAPSHOT";
final String distinctName = "";

final String beanName = SingletonBean.class.getSimpleName();
final String viewClassName =
  SingletonBeanRemote.class.getName();
return (SingletonBeanRemote) context.lookup("ejb:" +
  appName + "/" + moduleName + "/" + distinctName + "/" +
  beanName + "!" + viewClassName);
}
```

Configuring data persistence

We will now further enhance our application by storing the key/value pairs in a relational database instead of keeping them in memory. To do this, we will need to create a **persistence context**. Again, let me remind you that its purpose is not to teach the theory behind data persistence, but rather to show how to configure it within your applications.

The persistence subsystem is included, by default, within all server configurations:

```xml
<extension module="org.jboss.as.jpa"/>
<subsystem xmlns="urn:jboss:domain:jpa:1.1"></subsystem>
```

The JPA module is not loaded by default in the application server. However, as soon as the application server detects that your application has `persistence.xml` or persistence annotations, the JPA module will be automatically started.

So, let's add the JPA `persistence.xml` configuration file to our project, which will reference the data source used to map our entities to the database:

```xml
<?xml version="1.0" encoding="UTF-8"?>
<persistence xmlns="http://xmlns.jcp.org/xml/ns/javaee/persistence"
    xmlns:xsi="http://www.w3.org/2001/XMLSchema-instance"
    xsi:schemaLocation="http://xmlns.jcp.org/xml/ns/javaee http://
        xmlns.jcp.org/xml/ns/javaee/persistence/persistence_2_1.xsd"
    version="2.1">
```

```xml
<persistence-unit name="persistenceUnit" transaction-type="JTA">
    <provider>org.hibernate.jpa.HibernatePersistenceProvider
    </provider>
    <jta-data-source>java:jboss/datasources/MySqlDS</jta-data-
       source>
    <properties>
        <property name="hibernate.dialect" value="org.hibernate.
           dialect.MySQLDialect" />
    </properties>
</persistence-unit>
</persistence>
```

The key attributes of this file are the persistence unit's name, which will identify its unique name, and the jta-data-source, which must match a valid datasource definition. In the earlier chapter, we defined this datasource bound to a MySQL database.

> The persistence.xml file can specify either a JTA datasource or a non-JTA datasource. Within a Java EE environment, you have to use a JTA datasource (even when reading data without an active transaction).

Finally, the properties element can contain any configuration property for the underlying persistence provider. Since WildFly uses Hibernate as the EJB persistence provider, you can pass any Hibernate options here.

Once created, this file needs to be placed in the META-INF folder of your source/main/resources folder, as shown in the following screenshot:

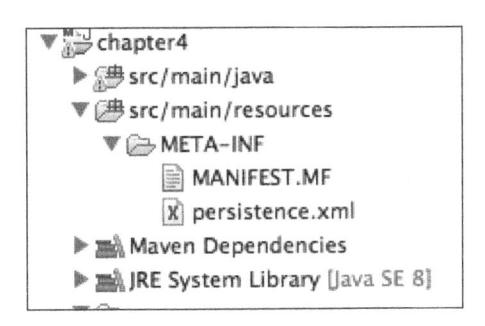

```
▼ chapter4
  ▶ src/main/java
  ▼ src/main/resources
     ▼ META-INF
        MANIFEST.MF
        persistence.xml
  ▶ Maven Dependencies
  ▶ JRE System Library [Java SE 8]
```

> **The real path of the persistence.xml file**
>
> Please note that the content of the Eclipse src/main/resources directory will be placed in the WEB-INF/classes directory of your web application when Maven builds it.

Using a default datasource for the JPA subsystem

In this example, we are referencing the datasource from within the `persistence.xml` file, thus following a canonical approach well-known to many developers.

You can, however, choose a default datasource for all your JPA applications by adding the `default-datasource` element into the JPA subsystem:

```
<subsystem xmlns="urn:jboss:domain:jpa:1.0">
  <jpa default-datasource="java:jboss/datasources/MySqlDS"/>
</subsystem>
```

This way, all JPA applications that haven't defined the `jta-data-source` element in `persistence.xml` will use the default datasource configured in the main server configuration file.

Configuring entities

Once your persistence configuration is defined, the only change we need to make in our application is to add the `javax.persistence` annotations to our entity class. The `@Entity` annotation means that the class will be registered as a JPA entity:

```
package com.packtpub.chapter4.entity;
import java.io.Serializable;
import javax.persistence.Column;
import javax.persistence.Entity;
import javax.persistence.Id;

@Entity
public class Property implements Serializable {
    @Id
    @Column(name = "id")
    private String key;
    @Column(name = "value")
    private String value;
    //getters and setters omitted for brevity
}
```

Our session bean needs to be changed, as well. Instead of reading and writing to the in-memory cache, we will write to both the cache and the database, and read only from the in-memory cache. When the application is restarted, the in-memory cache will be populated with data queried from the database. Although this is nothing fancy, for the sake of this demonstration, it is just fine:

```java
import java.util.ArrayList;
import java.util.List;
import javax.annotation.PostConstruct;
import javax.ejb.Singleton;
import javax.persistence.*;
import com.packtpub.chapter4.entity.Property;

@Singleton
public class SingletonBean  {
  private  List<Property> cache;
  @PersistenceContext(unitName = "persistenceUnit")
  private EntityManager em;

  @PostConstruct
  public void initCache(){
    this.cache = queryCache();
    if (cache == null) cache = new ArrayList<Property>();
  }

  public void delete(){
    Query query = em.createQuery("delete FROM
      com.packtpub.chapter4.entity.Property");
    query.executeUpdate();
    this.cache.clear();
  }

  public void put(String key,String value){
    Property p = new Property();
    p.setKey(key);
    p.setValue(value);
    em.persist(p);
```

```java
        this.cache.add(p);
    }
```

```java
package com.packtpub.chapter4.ejb;

import java.util.ArrayList;
import java.util.List;

import javax.annotation.PostConstruct;
import javax.ejb.LocalBean;
import javax.ejb.Remote;
import javax.ejb.Singleton;
import javax.persistence.EntityManager;
import javax.persistence.PersistenceContext;
import javax.persistence.Query;
import javax.persistence.TypedQuery;

import com.packtpub.chapter4.entity.Property;

@Singleton
@LocalBean
public class SingletonBean {

    private List<Property> cache = new ArrayList<>();

    @PersistenceContext(unitName = "persistenceUnit")
    private EntityManager em;

    @PostConstruct
    public void initCache() {
        this.cache = queryCache();
        if (cache == null) {
            cache = new ArrayList<Property>();
        }
    }

    public void deleteAll() {
        Query query = em.createQuery("DELETE FROM Property");
        query.executeUpdate();
    }

    public void save(String key, String value) {
```

```
            Property property = new Property(key, value);
            em.persist(property);
            this.cache.add(property);
        }

        private List<Property> queryCache() {
            TypedQuery<Property> query =
              em.createQuery("FROM Property", Property.class);
            List<Property> list = query.getResultList();
            return list;
        }

        public List<Property> getProperties() {
            return cache;
        }
    }
```

Sections of the preceding code have been highlighted to show you where the code has been modified to use data persistence. The most relevant section is the `@javax.persistence.PersistenceContext` annotation, which references a JPA context defined in the `persistence.xml` file.

Once deployed, this application will persist data to your MySQL database.

Configuring persistence in other application archives

In our example, we created a Java EE 7 application that is made of web components and EJBs using a single web application archive. This is absolutely fine and expected, as Java EE allows the mixing and matching of frontend components and server-side components within a single web archive.

You can, however, deploy an application where the web layer is separated from the business service layer. For example, suppose you were to deploy your entities in a separate JAR file; the correct place for the `persistence.xml` file would be beneath the `META-INF` folder of your JAR archive.

> To confirm, if you are placing your JPA entities inside a WAR file, the `persistence.xml` file should be placed in the `WEB-INF/classes/META-INF` folder. If you package your JPA entities within a JAR file inside a web application, you should place the `persistence.xml` file in the `META-INF` folder.

Technically speaking, if you have multiple JAR files in your application, you can deploy the `persistence.xml` file in a single archive and refer to the persistence unit using the `jarName#unitName` notation. For example, this application's persistence unit could be referenced from another JAR file using the following annotation:

```
@PersistenceContext(unitName="wildflyapp.jar#unitName")
```

Switching to a different provider

By default, WildFly 8.1 uses Hibernate 4.3.5 as a persistence provider. The Hibernate JARs are included under the `modules` folder in the `org.hibernate` path. If, however, your application requires a different version of Hibernate, such as 3.5, you can still bundle the JARs into your application by adding the dependency to your `pom.xml` file and setting the scope to `runtime`:

```
<dependency>
    <groupId>org.hibernate</groupId>
    <artifactId>hibernate-core</artifactId>
    <version>3.5.0-Final</version>
    <scope>runtime</scope>
</dependency>
```

Besides this, you need to set the `jboss.as.jpa.providerModule` property to `hibernate3-bundled` in your `persistence.xml` configuration file. The JPA deployer will detect the presence of a different version of the persistence provider and activate that version:

```
<persistence-unit>
    <properties>
        <property name="jboss.as.jpa.providerModule" value="hibernate3-bundled" />
    </properties>
</persistence-unit>
```

Using Jipijapa

You can also use the Jipijapa project to simplify switching to a different JPA provider. If you use Jipijapa, you will need to ensure that your persistence provider is included as a runtime dependency in your `pom.xml` file, and you will also need to include the correct Jipijapa integration JAR file. To use Hibernate 3, you will need to add the following dependency in `pom.xml`:

```
<dependency>
    <groupId>org.jipijapa</groupId>
    <artifactId>jipijapa-hibernate3</artifactId>
```

```
    <version>1.0.1.Final</version>
</dependency>
```

With Jipijapa, you can easily switch to a different version of Hibernate, or to a different ORM provider such as EclipseLink or OpenJPA. For more details on using the Jipijapa project, you can refer to the WildFly docs at https://docs.jboss.org/author/display/WFLY8/JPA+Reference+Guide#JPAReferenceGuide-BackgroundontheJipijapaproject.

Summary

In this chapter, we discussed the Undertow subsystem configuration, which is found within the main configuration file.

The Undertow server configuration is broken into two main parts: server configuration, which is used to configure static resources, such as HTML pages, images, listeners, and hosts, and the servlet container configuration, which is used to configure dynamic resources such as JSPs.

We then went through an example application that demonstrated how to package and deploy a Java EE 7 web module on the application server.

Then, we discussed the JPA subsystem and showed you how to add data persistence to the initial example. We outlined the correct location of the persistence.xml file, which is required to be placed in the WEB-INF/classes/META-INF folder of your web application or in the META-INF folder of your JAR file.

Having completed the application server standalone configuration, we will now move on to the next chapter and look at how to configure application server domains.

5
Configuring a WildFly Domain

Now that we have looked at the core configuration of the server, we can move on to the domain configuration. Shaping a server domain is a key task for administrators who want to efficiently coordinate a set of application servers. In this chapter, we will describe all the steps necessary to create and configure a domain of WildFly instances.

As we will see shortly, the configuration of subsystems does not vary between standalone and domain configuration. To work with domains, we also need to learn about the domain controller and host controller configurations. These are responsible for handling and coordinating the lifecycle of applications across several servers.

So, in this chapter, we will cover the following topics:

- Introduction to the WildFly domain
- How to configure the domain components
- The criteria to choose between a domain and a standalone server
- Introducing WildFly domain mode

Introducing the WildFly domain

The concept of a domain mode might be perceived as a little difficult to understand. The reason for this is that in the Java EE paradigm, one is used to dealing with servers rather than domains.

Basically, a domain is a group of WildFly servers managed by one of the servers. The server managing the domain is called the domain controller. This group is under one administration—it is the administrative unit. It's important to understand that the concept of a domain does not interfere with the capabilities delivered by the managed servers. For example, you might set up a domain of application server nodes running in a cluster, providing load balancing and high availability. However, you can also achieve the same outcome with a set of standalone application servers.

What differentiates these two scenarios is that when running in a domain, you can efficiently manage your set of servers from a single, centralized unit. On the other hand, managing a set of standalone instances often requires sophisticated multiserver management capabilities that are significantly more complex, error-prone, and time-consuming.

From the process point of view, a domain is made up of four elements:

- **Domain controller**: The domain controller is the management control point of your domain. An AS instance running in the domain mode has, at the most, one process instance acting as a domain controller. The domain controller holds a centralized configuration that is shared by the node instances belonging to the domain.
- **Host controller**: This is a process responsible for coordinating the life cycle of server processes and the distribution of deployments, from the domain controller to the server instances, with the domain controller.
- **Process controller**: This is a very lightweight process whose primary function is to spawn server and host controller processes, and manage their input/output streams. This also allows the host controller to be patched and restarted without impacting the associated servers.
- **Application server nodes**: These are regular Java processes that map to instances of the application server. Each server node, in turn, belongs to a domain group. Domain groups will be explained in detail when we discuss the domain configuration file.

In order to understand how to configure these components, we will first look at the basic domain configuration. This configuration is provided with the application server default distribution.

Understanding the default domain configuration

Out of the box, the default domain configuration (domain.xml) includes a basic configuration made up of the following elements:

- One process controller that starts the other JVM processes
- One host controller that acts as the domain controller
- Three server nodes, with the first two being part of the main server group and the third one (inactive) as part of the other server group

> A server group is a group of servers that have the same configuration and are managed as one.

The following image reinforces these concepts:

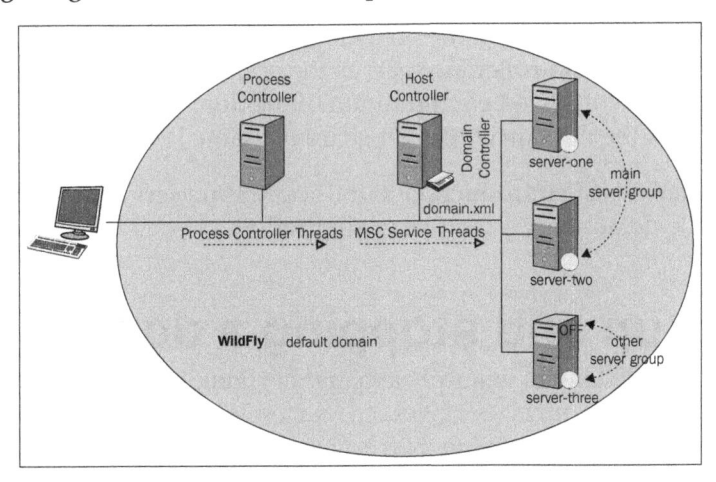

You can use the `VisualVM` utility to have a look at the low-level details of your domain from the point of view of the JVM. You can see from the following screenshot that four JVM processes are spawned. The process controller is started first, which, in turn, launches the host controller process and the two server nodes.

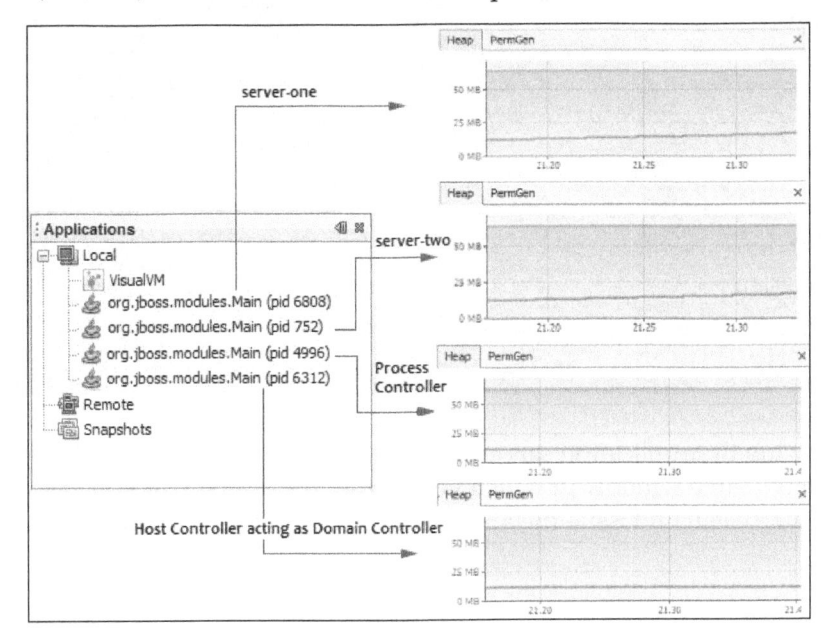

Configuring a WildFly Domain

> **VisualVM** is a Java Virtual Machine monitoring tool that is included in the default Java SE distribution. You can find it in your `JAVA_HOME/bin` folder. Simply launch `jvisualvm.exe` if you are on Windows, or `jvisualvm` if you are on Linux.

The important thing to note from the preceding screenshot is that with the basic domain setup, the host controller also acts as the domain controller, that is, the host controller holds the centralized configuration of the domain. This means that the host controller and the domain controller share the same JVM process.

Having completed a basic introduction to the application server domain, we will now cover all the details concerning its configuration.

Starting up and stopping a domain

Starting up a WildFly domain is simply a matter of running the `JBOSS_HOME\bin\domain.sh` script (`JBOSS_HOME\bin\domain.bat` on Windows). In a matter of seconds, your domain will be up and running. Have a look at the following screenshot:

In order to stop the application server domain, you can either use the *Ctrl + C* shortcut in the same window in which you started the domain, or you can use the command-line client and issue the `shutdown` command to the host controller.

Unix/Linux users can issue the following command:

```
./jboss-cli.sh --connect command=/host=master:shutdown
```

Windows users can issue the following command:

```
jboss-cli.bat --connect command=/host=master:shutdown
```

> The default host name is master, and it is defined in the host.xml, file which is located in the JBOSS_HOME\domain\configuration folder. We will learn more about it in the next section.

Once the domain starts, several log files are created within the JBOSS_HOME\domain\log directory. The host controller activity is written to the host-controller.log file, while the process controller logs are written to the process-controller.log file.

Configuring the domain

One of the main advantages of setting up a WildFly domain is the control over, and management of, the server configurations and deployments from a single centralized point. The main domain configuration consists of the following two files found in the JBOSS_HOME\domain\configuration folder, which are as follows:

- domain.xml: This file describes the capabilities of your domain servers and defines the server groups that are part of the domain. While this file can be found on each host, only the domain.xml file found on the domain controller is used.
- host.xml: This file is present on each host where the domain is installed and specifies the elements specific to the servers running on the host.

Overriding the default configuration files

It is possible to use configuration files other than the default files that are provided in a vanilla install. You can use your own custom configuration files by adding the following parameter to your shell command:

```
./domain.sh --domain-config=custom_domain.xml
./domain.sh -host-config=custom_host.xml
```

Windows users use the same parameter, but obviously use the domain.bat file.

Note also that if you don't provide any path to your custom configuration file, it's assumed to be relative to the jboss.server.config.dir directory. Otherwise, you need to provide an absolute path to your file.

Configuring the domain.xml file

The `domain.xml` file contains the domain subsystems' configuration that is shared by all the servers in the domain. The content of the file follows the structure of the standalone file, with an obvious and important difference—a domain can have several profiles defined in it. By default, four profiles are defined: a default profile, a full profile, a ha profile, and lastly, a full-ha profile, with the last two being used for clustered domains. You could also, however, define your own custom profile, such as a messaging profile, as shown in the following image:

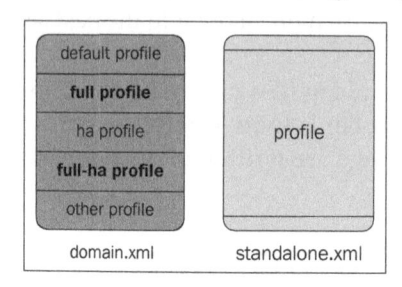

> Changing from one profile to another is the recommended way to expand or narrow the capabilities of the servers running in your domain.

Each WildFly domain can be further split into server groups, with each one bound to a different profile. The concept of server groups can be seen as a set of servers managed as a single unit by the domain. You can actually use server groups for fine-grained configuration of nodes; for example, each server group is able to define its own settings, such as customized JVM settings, socket bindings interfaces, and deployed applications. The following figure illustrates some common attributes that can be applied to servers within a server group:

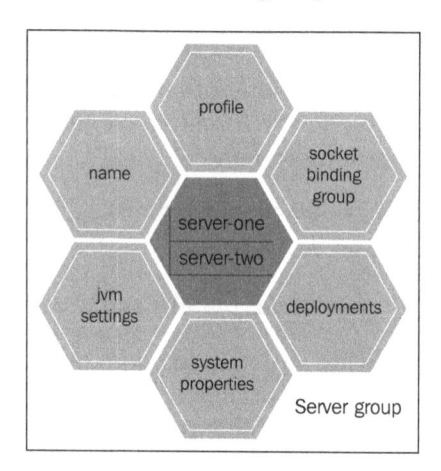

For example, here is a more complete server group definition that is bound to the `default` profile. This server group defines a web application named `sample.war`, which is made available to all servers within the group. It also defines a customized JVM configuration and some system properties (loaded at boot time), and binds its services to the `standard-sockets` definition, as follows:

```
<server-group name="custom-server-group" profile="default">
  <deployments>
    <deployment name="sample.war_v1" runtime-name="sample.war" />
  </deployments>
  <jvm name="default">
    <heap size="512m" max-size="1g"/>
  </jvm>
  <socket-binding-group ref="standard-sockets"/>
  <system-properties>
    <property name="foo" value="bar" boot-time="true"/>
    <property name="key" value="value" boot-time="true"/>
  </system-properties>
</server-group>
```

Configuring the host.xml file

The other domain configuration file is named `host.xml`, which is found in the `JBOSS_HOME\domain\configuration` folder. This file basically defines and configures the server nodes that are running on a host as part of a domain. The term "host" used here denotes a physical or virtual host. Within each host is a portion of the servers from the domain. Each host can have zero or more server instances. The following figure clarifies these details:

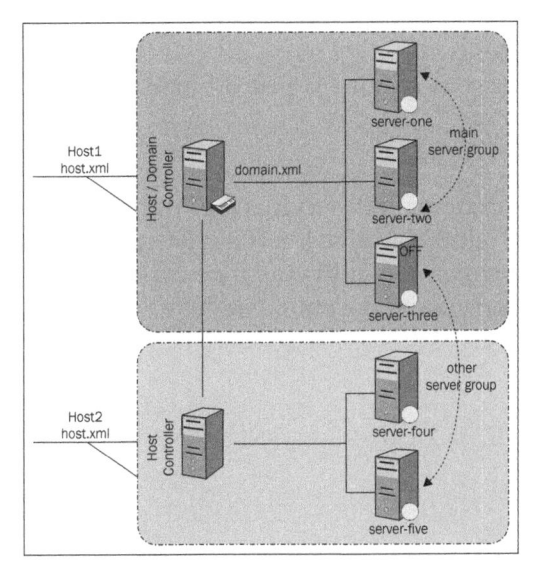

As you can see, a domain can contain several hosts (**host1, host2**) and also several groups (**main server group, other server group**). However, while a **server group** is a logical association of server nodes (which can be located anywhere), a **host** refers to a set of nodes that are located on the same physical or virtual machine. Having provided our definition of hosts, we now look into the host configuration file, which allows you to shape the following set of core domain elements:

- The management interfaces used to control the domain
- The domain controller definition
- The network interfaces where services are bound
- The defined JVM's configurations
- The servers that are part of the domain

In the next section, we will see each element of the `host.xml` file in detail and learn how to configure it appropriately.

Configuring the management interfaces

The management interface includes the definition of the native **command-line interface** (CLI) and `http` interface that are used to manage the domain. The following example has been taken from the `host.xml` file:

```
<management-interfaces>
    <native-interface security-realm="ManagementRealm">
        <socket interface="management" port="9999"/>
    </native-interface>
    <http-interface security-realm="ManagementRealm"
      http-upgrade-enabled="true">
        <socket interface="management" port="9990"/>
    </http-interface>
</management-interfaces>
```

With the default configuration, both services are bound to the `management` network interfaces. The CLI and administrative interface listen on port `9990`. The `native` interface configuration remains should you, for some reason, want to revert back to JBoss AS 7 settings and run on port number `9999`.

Configuring the network interfaces

We have just mentioned `network` interfaces. As you can guess from its name, a **network interface** refers to one network address or a set of network addresses. By default, the server contains three network interface definitions, namely, **management**, **public**, and **unsecure**, all of which are bound to the loopback address (127.0.0.1).

By changing the `inet-address` value of your network interface, you can configure the listening addresses of your application server. For example, if we want to bind the `management` interfaces to the loopback address (127.0.0.1), and the `public` interface to the address 192.168.1.1, you can simply use the following configuration:

```xml
<interfaces>
    <interface name="management">
        <inet-address value="127.0.0.1"/>
    </interface>
    <interface name="public">
        <inet-address value="192.168.1.1"/>
    </interface>
</interfaces>
```

You can also update these properties via the command line by running the following commands:

```
[standalone@localhost:9990 /] /interface=management:write-attribute(name=inet-address,value=127.0.0.1)
```

```
[standalone@localhost:9990 /] /interface=public:write-attribute(name=inet-address,value=192.168.1.1)
```

In practice, this means that the `management` interfaces (the `http` admin console and the CLI) will be bound to the loopback address, while application-related services (bound to the `public` interface) will be bound to the IP address 192.168.1.1. The following configuration is taken from the `domain.xml` file. Here, you can see how it uses the `public` interface defined previously:

```xml
<socket-binding-group name="standard-sockets"
  default-interface="public">
  <socket-binding name="http" port="8080"/>
  <socket-binding name="https" port="8443"/>
  ...
</socket-binding-group>
```

Configuring the domain controller

By default, the domain controller is located on the same machine where you started your domain. Have a look at the following commands:

```
<domain-controller>
    <local/>
</domain-controller>
```

You can, however, configure your host to use a domain controller located on a remote host in the following way:

```
<domain-controller>
    <remote host="192.168.100.1" port="9999"
        security-realm="ManagementRealm"/>
</domain-controller>
```

> This doesn't work if the management interface is bound to `localhost`. Ensure that you update the management interface correctly.

Configuring the domain controller on a remote host means that the local configuration (`domain.xml`) will not be used, and that all server nodes on that host will use the centralized remote configuration. You need authorization to access the domain controller. We will cover the details of this in the domain example toward the end of the chapter.

Configuring the JVM

One of the key aspects of the domain configuration is the definition of JVM arguments for a given host. The JVM's elements are defined in the `host.xml` file. Here, you can define JVM settings and associate them with a name:

```
<jvms>
    <permgen size="256m" max-size="256m"/>
    <jvm-options>
        <option value="-server"/>
    </jvm-options>
</jvms>
```

> Currently, there is no element available to configure Java 8 Metaspace properties. To configure these, you need to add them as `option` elements. To set the initial size, use `-XX:MetaspaceSize=256m`, and to set the maximum size, use `-XX:MaxMetaspaceSize=256m`.

This JVM definition can then be used as part of your server group configuration by referencing the `jvm` name property in your `server-group` configuration. Also note that any JVM definitions within the `server-group` overrides those in the `jvms` definition. For example, the `main-server-group` (`domain.xml`) server group uses the `default` JVM for all server nodes, but redefines the `heap max-size` and `size` values. Have a look at the following code:

```xml
<server-group name="main-server-group" profile="full">
  <jvm name="default">
    <heap size="64m" max-size="512m"/>
  </jvm>
  <socket-binding-group ref="full-sockets"/>
</server-group>
```

The defined JVMs can be also be associated with a single server, thus overriding the server group definition. For example, here, `server-one` (defined in `host.xml`) inherits the `default` JVM configuration but then overrides the minimum (512 MB) and maximum heap size (1 GB):

```xml
<server name="server-one" group="main-server-group" auto-start="true">
  <jvm name="default">
    <heap size="512m" max-size="1G"/>
  </jvm>
</server>
```

Adding JVM options to a server definition

If you want to further specialize your JVM configuration, for example, by adding nonstandard options to the virtual machine, you can use the `jvm-options` element (`host.xml`). In this example, we add the concurrent, low-pause garbage collector to the `default` JVM options:

```xml
<jvms>
    <jvm name="default">
        <heap size="64m" max-size="128m"/>
        <jvm-options>
            <jvm-option value="-XX:+UseConcMarkSweepGC"/>
        </jvm-options>
    </jvm>
</jvms>
```

Order of precedence between elements

In the previous section, we showed you how to use the default JVM definition in the different configuration files (host.xml and domain.xml). As a matter of fact, the JVM definition is a typical example of a configuration that overlaps between files, which means that the JVM can be configured at any one of the following levels:

- **Host level**: This configuration will apply to all servers that are defined in host.xml
- **Server-group level**: This configuration applies to all servers that are part of the group
- **Server level**: This configuration is used just for a single host

So far, so good. However, what happens if we define an element with the same name at multiple levels? The application server resolves this by letting most specific elements override their parent configuration. In other words, if you define a generic JVM at the host level, it is overridden by the same JVM at the server-group level. Have a look at the following code:

```xml
<!-- host.xml -->
<jvms>
  <jvm name="default">
    <heap size="64m" max-size="256m"/>
  </jvm>
</jvms>

<!-- domain.xml -->

<!-- Here the "default" jvm will be overridden by the server group jvm
definition -->

<server-group name="other-server-group" profile="default">
  <jvm name="default">
    <heap size="64m" max-size="512m"/>
  </jvm>
  <socket-binding-group ref="standard-sockets"/>
</server-group>
```

If you also define it at the server level, then that is the final choice for that server. Have a look at the following code:

```xml
<!- Here, the server definition overrides any other host/group
  definition -->
```

```
<server name="server-one" group="main-server-group">
  <jvm name="default">
    <heap size="256m" max-size="768m"/>
  </jvm>
</server>
```

The following figure describes the elements that can be defined (and possibly overridden) at different configuration levels:

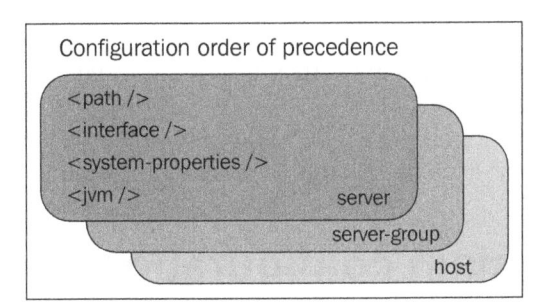

Configuration order of precedence
- `<path />`
- `<interface />`
- `<system-properties />`
- `<jvm />`

server
server-group
host

As you can see, this list also includes some elements, such as the `<path>` element, the `<interface>` element, and the `<system-properties>` element, which we have discussed in *Chapter 2, Configuring the Core WildFly Subsystems*.

Configuring server nodes

The last element of the host configuration includes the list of server nodes that are part of the domain. Configuring a server requires, at minimum, the name of the server and the group to which the server belongs. Have a look at the following code:

```
<!-- host.xml configuration file -->
<servers>
  <server name="server-one" group="main-server-group" />
</servers>
```

This server definition relies largely on default attributes for the application server nodes. You can, however, highly customize your servers by adding specific paths, socket-binding interfaces, system properties, and JVMs. Have a look at the following code:

```
<server auto-start="true" name="sample" group="sample-group" >
  <paths>
    <path name="example" path="example"
      relative-to="jboss.server.log.dir"/>
  </paths>
```

```xml
    <socket-bindings port-offset="259"
      socket-binding-group="standard-sockets" />
    <system-properties>
      <property boot-time="true" name="envVar" value="12345"/>
    </system-properties>
    <jvm name="default">
      <heap size="256m" max-size="512m"/>
    </jvm>
</server>
```

If you want to know all the applicable attributes of the server nodes' configuration, we suggest that you have a look at the `jboss-as-config_2_1.xsd` schema, which is located in the `JBOSS_HOME/docs/schema` folder of your server distribution. In Eclipse, you can right-click on the schema file and then click on **Generate | XML File**.

Applying domain configuration

A common misconception among users who are new to the concept of a domain is that a domain is pretty much the equivalent of a cluster of nodes, so it can be used to achieve important features, such as load balancing and high availability.

It's important to understand that a domain is not pertinent to the functionalities that your application delivers—a domain is designed around the concept of server management. Thus, you can use it to manage both clustered applications and applications that are not intended to run in a cluster.

To understand it better, let's give an example. Let's consider that your server topology consists of multiple servers, and that you have defined a datasource that will be used by your application. So, whether or not you use a cluster, you need to configure your datasource across all your standalone servers' configurations (this means adding the definition of the datasource in every `standalone.xml`) file. In this case, the advantage of using a domain is evident: the datasource definition is contained just in the domain controller that provides a central point through which users can keep configurations consistent. It also has the benefit of being able to roll out configuration changes to the servers in a coordinated fashion. One other important aspect of a domain is the ability to provide a more fine-grained configuration than clustering is able to. For example, you can define server groups, each one with its own custom configuration. In order to achieve the same thing with a clustered configuration, you have to manage each machine's standalone configuration and adapt it to your needs.

However, domain and clustering are not mutually exclusive scenarios, but are often part of a larger picture. For example, using a domain can further enhance the efficiency of a cluster in advanced configurations where you need to manage starting and stopping multiple AS instances. At the same time, clustering provides typical load balancing and high-availability features, which are not integrated into domain management.

On the other hand, there are situations where using a domain may not prove to be that useful. For example, it's possible that your system administrators have bought or developed their own sophisticated multiserver management tools that can do more or less the same things that a domain configuration is able to do. In this situation, it may not be desirable to switch out what is already configured ad hoc.

Another classic example where a domain is not needed is the development phase, where you don't gain anything from a domain installation. Rather, it may add an unneeded additional complexity to your architecture.

Furthermore, the standalone mode is the only choice available in some scenarios. For example, if you are running the application server in the embedded mode, then the choice of a domain is incompatible. For example, when using an Arquillian project, you can test your Enterprise projects using an embedded container, which is managed by Arquillian using a standalone configuration.

Summing it up, since the individual server configuration does not vary when running the domain mode or the standalone mode, you can easily develop your application in the standalone mode and then switch to the domain mode when you are about to roll out the production application.

Creating our very own domain configuration

We will now provide a detailed example of a domain configuration. In this example, we include two separate host controller configurations, each one with a list of three nodes. You need two separate installations of WildFly 8, which can be executed on either two different machines or on the same machine. When running on the same machine, it's practical to assign a virtual IP address to your machines so that you don't have any port conflict in your domain.

The following figure shows our domain project:

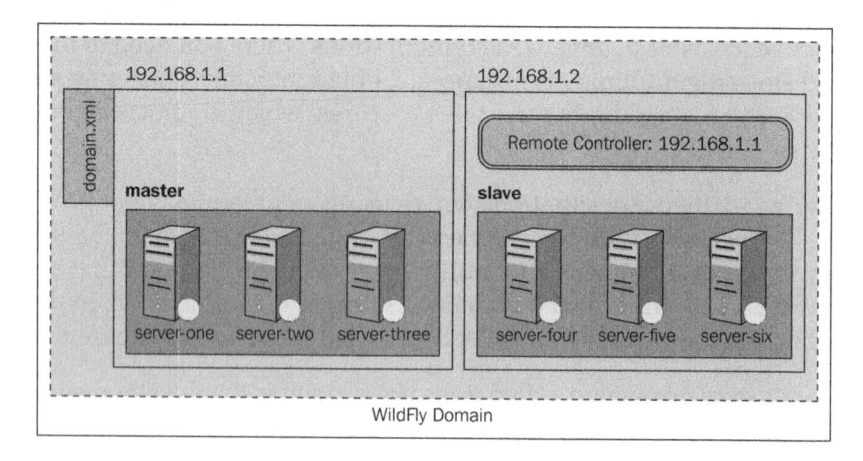

The first thing we need to do is bind the network interfaces to a valid inet address, both for the public and management interfaces. So, assuming that the first domain installation (master) will be bound to the inet address 192.168.1.1, open the host.xml file and change it accordingly, as follows:

```xml
<interfaces>
    <interface name="management">
        <inet-address value="192.168.1.1"/>
    </interface>
    <interface name="public">
        <inet-address value="192.168.1.1"/>
    </interface>
</interfaces>
```

In the second domain installation (slave), change the inet address to 192.168.1.2 in host.xml, as follows:

```xml
<interfaces>
    <interface name="management">
        <inet-address value="192.168.1.2"/>
    </interface>
    <interface name="public">
        <inet-address value="192.168.1.2"/>
    </interface>
</interfaces>
```

The next thing to do is define a unique host name for each installation. So, for the first `host.xml` file, use the following code:

```
<host name="master"/>
```

For the second file, simply use:

```
<host name="slave"/>
```

Next, the most important step is to choose where the domain controller is located. As we have shown earlier in the image, the domain controller will be located in the first installation (master), so in the `host.xml` file, you should contain the default content:

```
<domain-controller>
  <local/>
</domain-controller>
```

Now, looking at the other installation (slave), point to the domain controller that is running on host `192.168.1.1` (master), as follows:

```
<domain-controller>
  <remote host="192.168.1.1" port="9999"/>
</domain-controller>
```

Authentication is required for the slave to connect to the domain controller, so next we will add a user to the installation housing the master domain. To do this, you need to run the `add-user` script in the `bin` directory of your WildFly installation, as follows:

```
JBOSS_HOME/bin/add-user.sh
```

Perform the following steps:

1. When asked **What type of user do you wish to add?**, enter a (management user).
2. When asked for a username, enter `slave`.
3. When asked for a password, enter `password`.
4. When asked **What groups do you want this user to belong to?**, leave it blank.
5. Next, you will be asked if this is correct. Type `yes`.

6. Lastly, and most importantly, you will be asked if you want this new user to be used for one AS process to connect to another AS process. You need to type yes again. This will cause XML to be printed out, which we will use in the slave configuration:

```
Is this new user going to be used for one AS process to connect to another AS process?
e.g. for a slave host controller connecting to the master or for a Remoting connection for server to server EJB calls.
yes/no? yes
To represent the user add the following to the server-identities definition <secret value="YXNkZg==" />
root@host1:~#
```

Lastly, on the slave server, we need to add the `secret value` (printed out to the console) within the `server-identities` element in the `host.xml` file, as follows:

```xml
<security-realm name="ManagementRealm">
    <server-identities>
        <secret value="YXNkZg==" />
    </server-identities>
    ...
</security-realm>
```

The domain configuration is now complete. Let's start up the installation containing the domain controller (master) and then the second installation (slave) using the `domain.bat`/`domain.sh` scripts.

If everything is correctly configured, you will see the slave host registered on the domain controller (master), as follows:

```
JBAS011601: Bound messaging object to jndi name java:jboss/exported/jms/RemoteConnectionFactory
[Server:server-two] 15:27:17,888 INFO  [org.jboss.as.messaging] (ServerService Thread Pool -- 57)
JBAS011601: Bound messaging object to jndi name java:/ConnectionFactory
[Server:server-two] 15:27:17,889 INFO  [org.hornetq.core.server] (ServerService Thread Pool -- 56
) HQ221003: trying to deploy queue jms.queue.ExpiryQueue
[Server:server-two] 15:27:17,890 INFO  [org.jboss.as.messaging] (ServerService Thread Pool -- 56)
JBAS011601: Bound messaging object to jndi name java:/jms/queue/ExpiryQueue
[Server:server-two] 15:27:17,988 INFO  [org.jboss.as.connector.deployment] (MSC service thread 1-
1) JBAS010406: Registered connection factory java:/JmsXA
[Server:server-two] 15:27:18,142 INFO  [org.hornetq.ra] (MSC service thread 1-1) HornetQ resource
 adaptor started
[Server:server-two] 15:27:18,143 INFO  [org.jboss.as.connector.services.resourceadapters.Resource
AdapterActivatorService$ResourceAdapterActivator] (MSC service thread 1-1) IJ020002: Deployed: fi
le://RaActivatorhornetq-ra
[Server:server-two] 15:27:18,149 INFO  [org.jboss.as.connector.deployment] (MSC service thread 1-
2) JBAS010401: Bound JCA ConnectionFactory [java:/JmsXA]
[Server:server-two] 15:27:18,150 INFO  [org.jboss.as.messaging] (MSC service thread 1-2) JBAS0116
01: Bound messaging object to jndi name java:jboss/DefaultJMSConnectionFactory
[Server:server-two] 15:27:18,282 INFO  [org.jboss.as] (Controller Boot Thread) JBAS015874: WildFl
y 8.1.0.Final "Kenny" started in 21611ms - Started 210 of 258 services (89 services are lazy, pas

[Host Controller] 15:27:36,843 INFO  [org.jboss.as.domain] (Host Controller Service Threads - 30)
 JBAS010918: Registered remote slave host "slave", WildFly 8.1.0.Final "Kenny"
```

Now, let's have a look at the domain from the management console. The management interfaces are discussed in detail in the next chapter, but we need to briefly look at them for the purpose of showing our domain example.

> By default, you need to create one management user to be able to log in to the management console. For now, you can just use the username and password you created for the slave server, but in production, you would most likely create a different management user.

If you point the browser to the management interface of your master server (http://192.168.1.1:9990), you will not be able to access the management interface of your slave servers.

From the main page of the management console, there are a couple of options in which to look at your domain configuration. At this point, we are interested in looking at the host controllers that make up the domain. So, in the top menu bar, select the **Domain** menu. From here, you can select the host you are interested in from the combobox located on the left-hand side.

As you can see, you can find all servers grouped by the host, as follows:

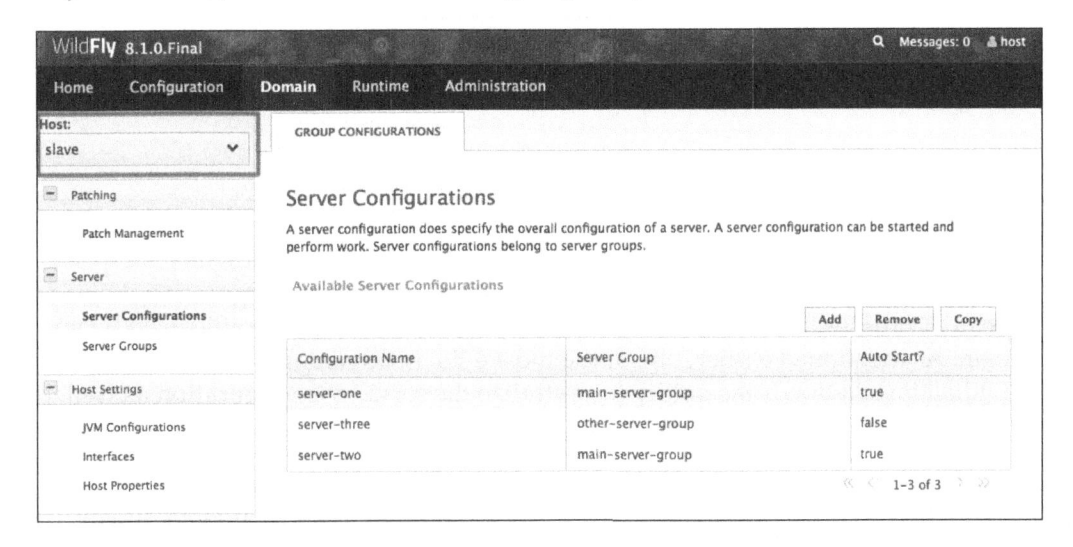

Configuration Name	Server Group	Auto Start?
server-one	main-server-group	true
server-three	other-server-group	false
server-two	main-server-group	true

Configuring a WildFly Domain

Now, select **Runtime** from the menu. From here, you can view the status of each server, group them by server-group, and start/stop each node. For example, as per the default configuration, each distribution contains three nodes: two are activated at startup, while the third one is started on demand. Hover your mouse over each node, and options will appear allowing you to start/stop the single node. You can also start/stop an entire server-group. Also, note that there is an option to change the host currently being viewed, as shown in the following screenshot:

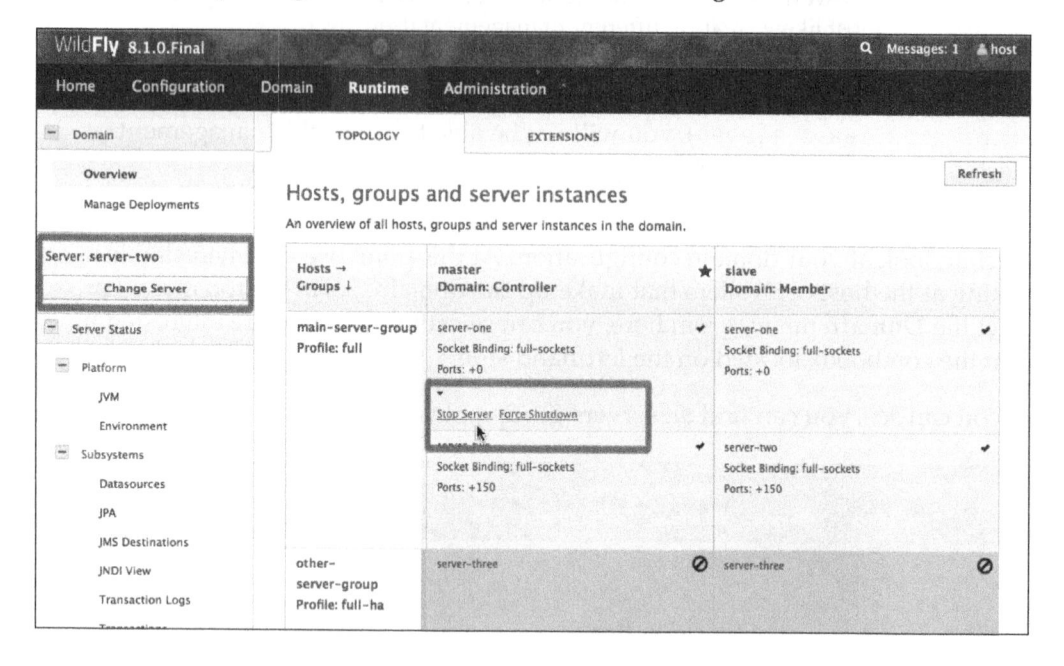

It should be clear now that each host has its own list of nodes, all of which are part of the domain. Also, remember that each host depends on the configuration defined in the `profiles` section of `domain.xml` that contains the domain profile used by your domain. As mentioned earlier, one of the most evident advantages of a domain over individual installation is the ability to centralize the services' configuration as well as the deployed resources.

From within the web console, you can also deploy applications or install modules such as JDBC drivers. In the next chapter, we will discuss in depth how to deploy and install a module to a domain. The main difference between the domain mode and the standalone mode is that once the datasource is added to the domain controller (`master`), its definition becomes part of the default profile, and every host that connects to the domain inherits its configuration.

Have a look at the following screenshot:

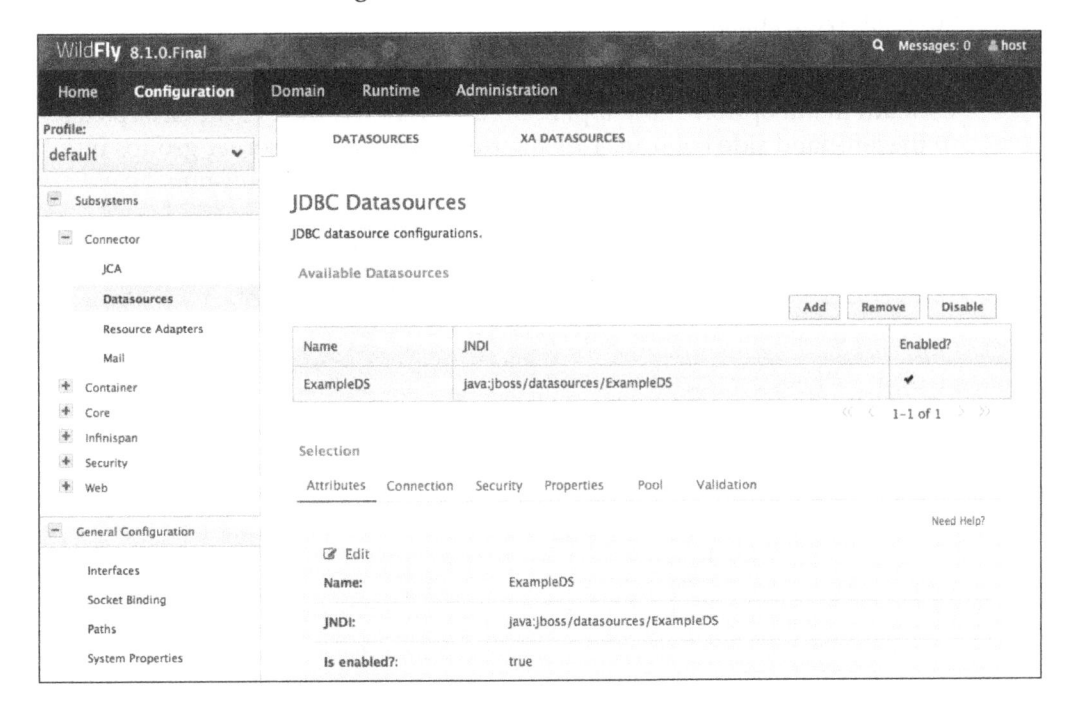

Changing the domain configuration at runtime

So far, we have modified the configuration files before starting the domain, but it is also possible to change the configuration on the fly while the domain is running. These changes will be made active without the need to restart the server, as they are done via the management console. For example, you may need to create, on the fly, a new server group and associate some servers and applications with it. It could be that one of your production applications has an issue that needs to be fixed. You could try to reproduce the issue on a development environment, but your results may not always be accurate since development and production often use different database and class versions.

So, one way you can quickly resolve the issue is by creating a new server group, associating one or more servers with it, and then deploying and testing the application on it.

Configuring a WildFly Domain

This can be done using the admin console (or the CLI) in a matter of minutes. Perform the following steps:

1. Open your browser, and navigate to the admin console. Then, select the **Domain** menu option at the top. From there, choose the **Server Groups** tab in the left-hand side column. This interface lets you add server groups by clicking on the **Add** button, as shown in the following screenshot:

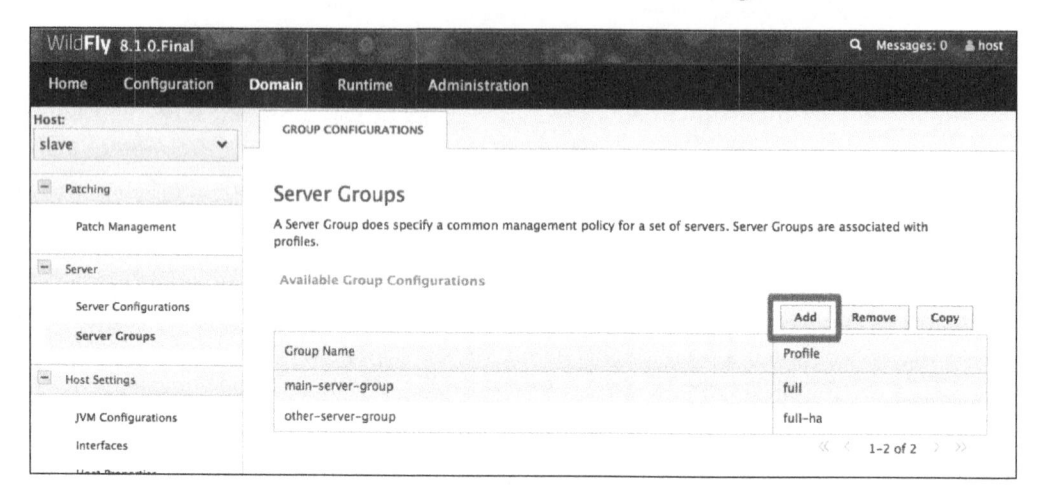

2. Then, choose a meaningful name for your group, for example, `staging-server-group`, and select a **Profile** and **Socket Binding** configuration on which the new group will be based, as follows:

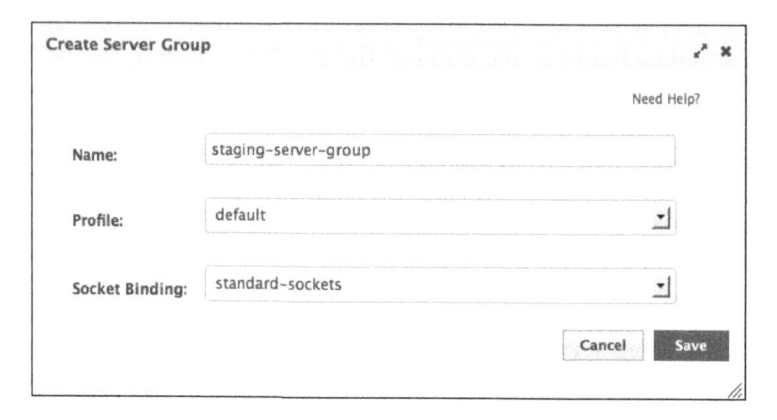

3. Now, it's time to associate one or more servers with the new group. Click on the **Server Configuration** menu on the left-hand side, and then click the **Add** button. Have a look at the following screenshot:

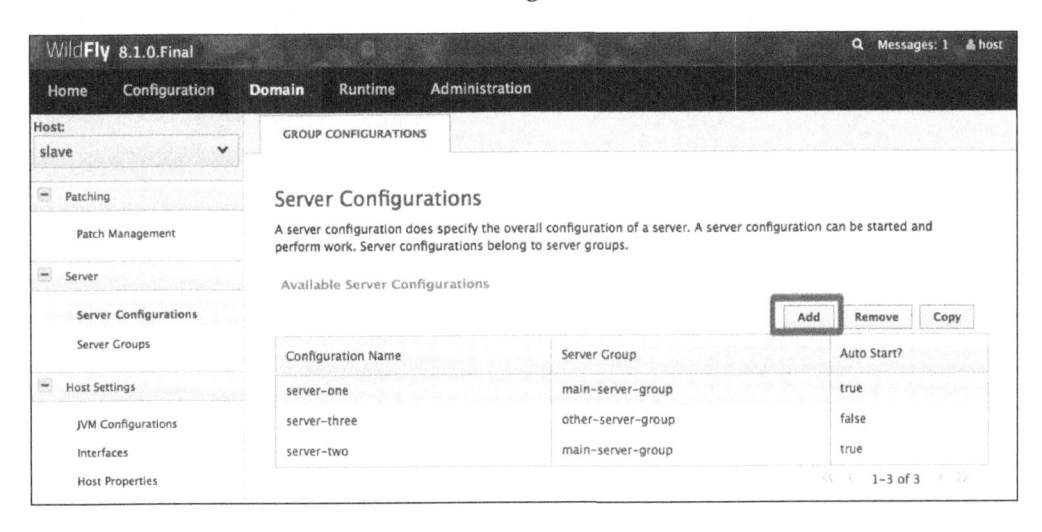

4. This pops up a dialog box that asks you for the new server name and the associated server group. In this example, we are going to call it `testServer`. Then, associate it with the `staging-server-group` with a port offset of `750` (in practice, every service is bound to a port of default port address (+ `750`)). Have a look at the following screenshot:

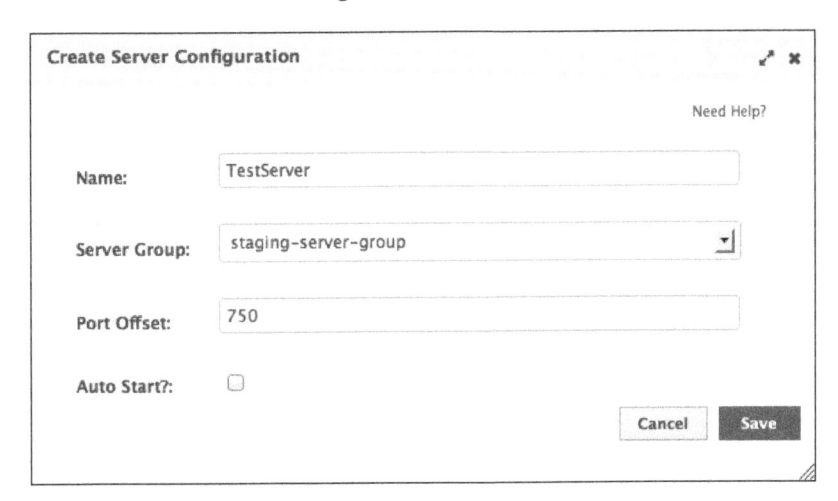

Configuring a WildFly Domain

Once you have set up a new server group and assigned one or more servers to it, you can deploy your applications to the server group. Deployment of applications can be done from the **Runtime** page. Click on **Manage Deployments** on the left-hand side, which shows you what applications, if any, are deployed. Have a look at the following screenshot:

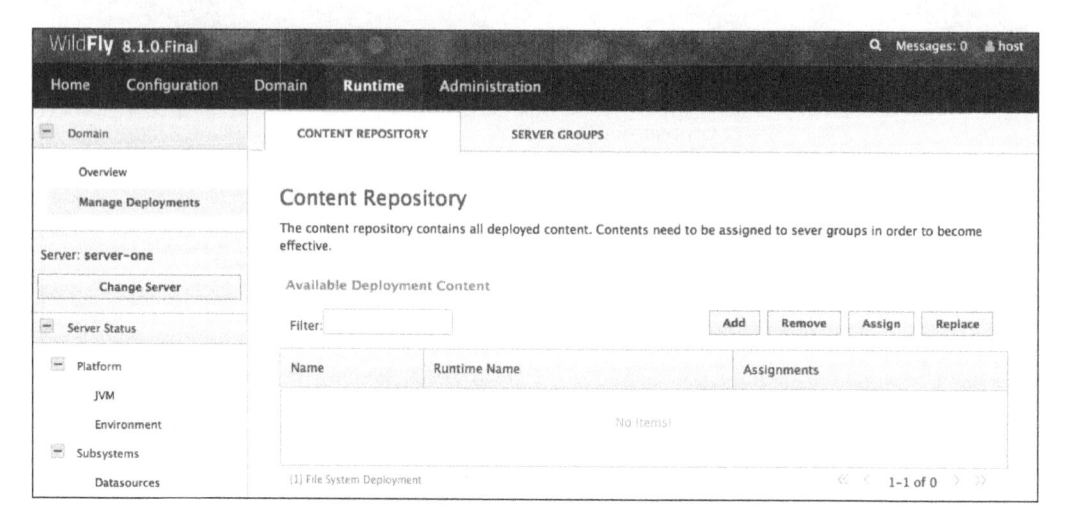

From here, you can add and remove deployments to your groups, which we will cover in the next chapter.

Summary

In this chapter, we went through the WildFly domain setup and configuration. By configuring a server domain, you can manage your servers from a single centralized point, which is desirable when you have to administer a large set of server nodes.

Every domain is composed of four main elements: the domain controller, the host controller, the process controller, and the server.

The domain controller handles the domain configuration, while the host controller coordinates the life cycle of server processes and the distribution of deployments. The process controller handles the domain server processes and manages their I/O streams.

Every domain is made up of one or more server groups, which allows fine-grained configuration of the domain. Each server group can define its own JVM attributes, socket binding interfaces, and system properties, which are loaded at startup. You can also deploy applications to each of the nodes within the domain.

Server groups are defined in the `domain.xml` configuration file, along with the enterprise services enabled for the domain.

The composition of server groups is contained in the `host.xml` file. This file also contains the location of the domain controller, the default JVMs, and `network` and `management` interfaces.

We are going to cover application deployment in detail in the next chapter, *Application Structure and Deployment*.

6
Application Structure and Deployment

Deployment is the process of uploading resources or applications on the application server. During the software development life cycle, it is the step that logically follows the development phase and can be performed either manually or in an automated fashion.

In this chapter, we will explore both approaches using the tools that are provided by the server distribution. We will also cover how to deploy resources on the application server using the WildFly plugin for Eclipse. This is the preferred choice for Java developers due to the quick deployment time.

In the last part of this chapter, we cover the details of the WildFly classloader architecture. In short, our agenda for this chapter includes the following topics:

- The type of resources that can be deployed on WildFly
- Deploying applications on a WildFly standalone instance
- Deploying applications on a WildFly domain
- Understanding WildFly's classloading architecture

Deploying resources on the application server

There are basically three file types that we work with in Java Enterprise applications, which are as follows:

- **JAR**: This is the most basic package, which can be used for both application and common resources

- **WAR**: This is used to package web applications
- **EAR**: This packages multiple WAR files or contains a set of modules

Besides these, WildFly is able to process the following archives, which provide the application server with additional functionality:

- **RAR**: This is the resource adapter file, which is used to define a resource adapter component (the resource adapter subsystem is provided by the `IronJacamar` project; for more information, visit http://www.jboss.org/ironjacamar)
- **SAR**: This file enables the deployment of service archives containing the `MBean` services, as supported by previous versions of the application server

In this chapter, we will discuss the first three kinds of archives, all of which constitute the typical packaging solution for Java Enterprise applications. Before discussing application deployment, let's look at the single archives in a little more detail.

The JAR file

A **Java Archive (JAR)** file is used to package multiple files into a single archive. Its internal physical layout is similar to a ZIP file, and as a matter of fact, it uses the same algorithm as the zip utility for compressing files.

A JAR file is generally used to distribute Java classes and associated metadata. In Java EE applications, the JAR file often contains utility code, shared libraries, and Enterprise JavaBeans (EJBs).

The WAR file

A **Web Application Archive (WAR)** file is essentially an archive used to encapsulate a web application. The web application usually includes a collection of web-related resources, such as **Java Server Pages (JSP)**, servlets, XHTML/HTML files, and so on. It also includes Java class files, and possibly other file types, depending on the technology used. Since Java EE 6, EJBs can be packaged within a WAR archive using the same packaging guidelines that apply to web application classes. This means that you can place EJB classes, along with the other class files, under the `classes` directory under `WEB-INF`. Alternatively, you can package your EJBs within a JAR file and then place this JAR file in the `WEB-INF\lib` directory of WAR.

Because of this, it's more common for developers to use the WAR file to distribute Java EE applications.

The EAR file

An **Enterprise Archive (EAR)** file represents an application archive, which acts as a container for a set of modules or WAR files. An EAR file can contain any of the following:

- One or more web modules packaged in WAR files
- One or more EJB modules packaged in JAR files
- One or more application client modules
- Any additional JAR files required by the application
- JBoss-specific archives such as the SAR file

> There are two distinct advantages of using an Enterprise Archive file. First, it helps to distribute all application components using a single archive instead of distributing every single module. Second, and most important, is the fact that applications within an EAR file are loaded by a single classloader. This means that each module has visibility on other modules packed within the same archive.

The isolation level of application modules contained in the EAR file can be modified by adding the `ear-subdeployments-isolated` element to the main configuration file (`domain.xml` or `standalone.xml`). The default value is `false`, which means that the classes in the WAR file can access the classes in the `ejb.jar` file. Likewise, the classes in the `ejb.jar` file can access each other. If, for some reason, you do not want this behavior and want to restrict the visibility of your classes, add the following lines to your configuration file:

```
<subsystem xmlns="urn:jboss:domain:ee:2.0">
    <ear-subdeployments-isolated>true</ear-subdeployments-isolated>
</subsystem>
```

In the *Explaining WildFly classloading* section, we will discuss the application server classloading architecture in depth. We will also show you how to override this configuration setting at the application level.

Deploying applications on a standalone WildFly server

Deploying applications on JBoss has traditionally been a fairly simple task, so you might wonder why a full chapter has been dedicated to it. The answer to this is that deploying applications on WildFly can be achieved in several ways, each of which we are going to look at.

First of all, we are going to look at automatic deployment of applications via the `deployments` folder, but before we do this, we need to explain the two modes available when deploying applications:

- **Automatic deployment mode**: This mode is triggered by the deployment scanner when a resource within the `deployments` folder is modified
- **Manual deployment mode**: This mode does not rely on the deployment scanner to trigger a deployment, but rather on a set of marker files to decide if the application needs to be deployed/redeployed

Automatic application deployment

Automatic application deployment consists of placing your application in the `deployments` folder, which is located at the following path:

JBOSS_HOME\standalone\deployments

By default, every application archive (WAR, JAR, EAR, and SAR) that is placed in this folder is automatically deployed on the server, as shown in the following screenshot:

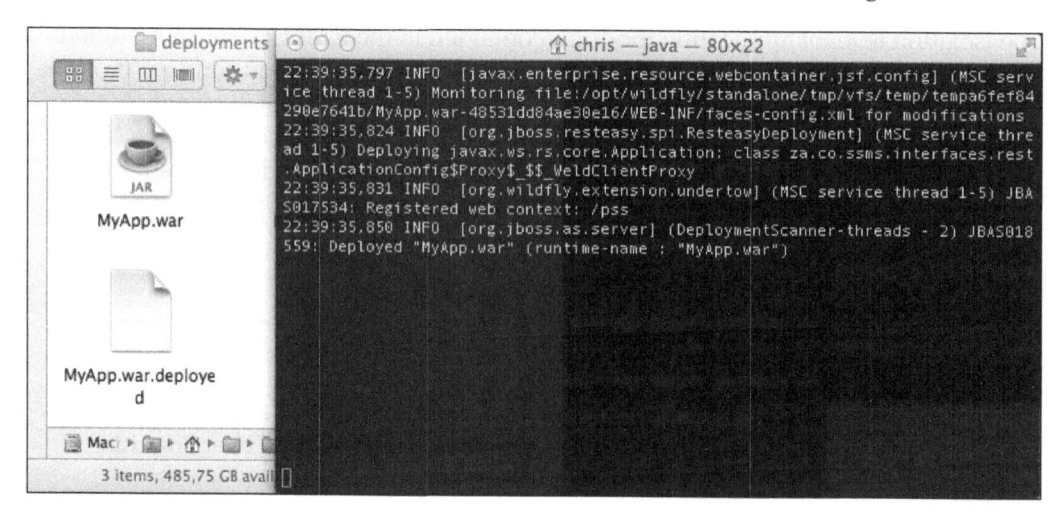

The service that scans for deployed resources is called the **deployment scanner**, and it is configured within the `standalone.xml` configuration file. You can find it by searching for the `deployment-scanner` domain. The following snippet shows the default deployment scanner configuration:

```
<subsystem xmlns="urn:jboss:domain:deployment-scanner:2.0">
    <deployment-scanner path="deployments"
       relative-to="jboss.server.base.dir" scan-interval="5000"
       runtime-failure-causes-rollback="false"/></subsystem>
```

As you can see, by default, the server scans in the `deployments` folder every `5000` ms. This service can be customized in many ways. Next, we will look at how we can further configure the deployment scanner.

Deploying applications to a custom folder

If you want to change the location of the deployment folder, you need to modify the `relative-to` and `path` properties. If you provide both properties, the `deployments` folder is a sum of both properties. For example, considering that you have defined the `wildfly8deployments` path, you can later reference it as a relative path for your deployments, as follows:

```
<paths>
  <path name="wildfly8deployments" path="/opt/applications" />
</paths>

<subsystem xmlns="urn:jboss:domain:deployment-scanner:2.0">
    <deployment-scanner path="deployments"
       relative-to="wildfly8deployments" scan-interval="5000"
       runtime-failure-causes-rollback="false"/>
</subsystem>
```

In this configuration, the deployment scanner looks for applications within the `deployments` folder under `/opt/applications`.

The same effect can be achieved using an absolute path for your deployments, leaving out the `relative-to` property and configuring the `path` element, as shown in the following example:

```
<deployment-scanner scan-interval="5000"
  runtime-failure-causes-rollback="false"
  path="/opt/applications/deployments" />
```

Changing the behavior of the deployment scanner

By default, every packaged archive that is placed in the `deployments` folder is automatically deployed. On the other hand, exploded applications need one more step to be deployed (see the *Manual application deployment* section).

We can easily change this behavior of the deployment scanner. The properties that control the `auto-deploy` feature are `auto-deploy-zipped` and `auto-deploy-exploded`, respectively, as shown in the following code:

```
<deployment-scanner scan-interval="5000"
  relative-to="jboss.server.base.dir"
  path="deployments"
  auto-deploy-zipped="true" auto-deploy-exploded="false"/>
```

You can set the `auto-deploy-exploded` property to `true` to achieve automatic deployment of exploded archives, as follows:

```
<deployment-scanner scan-interval="5000"
  relative-to="jboss.server.base.dir"
  path="deployments"
  auto-deploy-zipped="true" auto-deploy-exploded="true"/>
```

Deployment rollback

WildFly 8 introduces a new option to roll back a failed deployment. To do this, simply update the `runtime-failure-causes-rollback` property to `true`, as shown in the following code snippet. The default behavior is `false`:

```
<subsystem xmlns="urn:jboss:domain:deployment-scanner:2.0">
    <deployment-scanner path="deployments"
      relative-to="jboss.server.base.dir" scan-interval="5000"
      runtime-failure-causes-rollback="true"/></subsystem>
```

> If the `failure-causes-rollback` property is set to `true`, a deployment failure also triggers the rollback of any other deployment that was processed as part of the same scan.

Deploying an application using the CLI

Copying the application archives is often favored by many developers, as it can be performed automatically by the development environment. However, we lay stress on the advantages of using the CLI interface, which offers a wide choice of additional options when deploying and also allows you to deploy applications remotely.

All it takes to deploy an application archive is to log in to the CLI, either a local or remote instance, and issue the `deploy` command. When used without arguments, the `deploy` command prints a list of applications that are currently deployed. Take a look at the following command:

```
[disconnected /] connect
[standalone@localhost:9990 /] deploy MyApp.war
```

To deploy your application to the standalone server, pass through the relative (or absolute) path of your archive. This path obviously relates to the client machine if you are connected to a remote server. This immediately deploys your application to the server. Take a look at the following screenshot:

```
[standalone@localhost:9990 /] deploy ./target/MyApp.war
```

When you specify a relative path, it is relative to the location you started the CLI utility from. You can, however, use absolute paths when specifying the location of your archives. The CLI auto-complete functionality (using the *Tab* key) makes light work of this. Have a look at the following command:

```
[standalone@localhost:9990 /] deploy /opt/workspace/my-app/target/MyApp.war
```

By default, when you deploy via the CLI, the application is deployed and enabled so that the user can access it. If you want to just perform the deployment of the application and enable it at a later time, you can add the `--disabled` switch, as follows:

```
[standalone@localhost:9990 /] deploy ./target/MyApp.war --disabled
```

In order to enable the application, simply issue another `deploy` command without the `--disabled` switch, as follows:

```
[standalone@localhost:9990 /] deploy --name=MyApp.war
```

> Did you notice the optional `--name` switch that has been added? When using this switch, you are able to use the **tab completion** feature so that you can automatically find the inactive deployment unit.

Redeploying the application requires an additional flag to the `deploy` command. You will get an error if you try to deploy the same application twice without using this flag. The `-f` argument forces the redeployment of the application, as shown here:

```
[standalone@localhost:9990 /] deploy -f ./target/MyApp.war
```

Undeploying the application can be done through the `undeploy` command, which takes the name of the deployment as an argument, as shown here:

```
[standalone@localhost:9990 /] undeploy MyApp.war
```

Upon checking the configuration file, `standalone.xml`, you notice that the `deployment` element for your application has been removed.

Deploying an application using the web admin console

Application deployment can also be completed using the web admin console:

1. Start the console hyperlink, `http://localhost:9990/console`, in your browser.

Application Structure and Deployment

2. You need to add at least one management user to access the web console. To add a new user, execute the `add-user.bat` or `add-user.sh` script within the `bin` folder of your WildFly installation, and enter the requested information. See *Chapter 10, Securing WildFly*, for more details.

3. Server deployment is managed by the application server by selecting **Runtime** in the top menu and then choosing the **Manage Deployments** option. If you want to add a new application to WildFly, just click on the **Add** button of your console, as shown in the following screenshot:

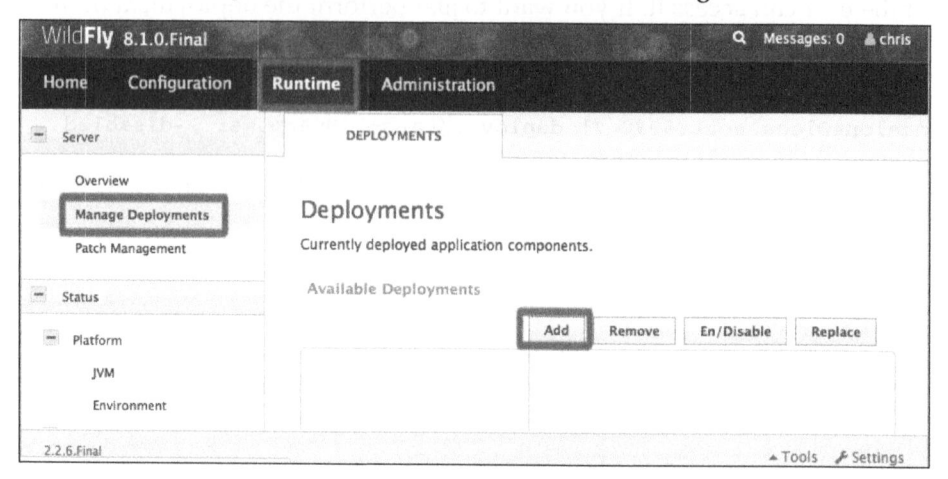

An intuitive wizard guides you through selecting your application and providing a runtime name for it, as shown in the following screenshot:

[166]

There are two properties shown in the wizard that may cause some confusion:

- The **Name** property is the name by which the deployment should be known within a server's runtime, for example, MyApp-1.0.0.war. This is used as the basis for the module names and is usually the name of the archive.
- The **Runtime Name** is typically the same as the **Name**, but there may be instances where you wish to have two deployments with the same runtime name. For example, you may have MyApp-1.0.0.war and MyApp-1.0.1.war within the content repository but have the runtime name of MyApp.war for both archives. They cannot be deployed at the same time, and one of them would need to be disabled.

The admin console, by default, deploys the application but does not enable it. By clicking on the **Enable** button, the application can now be accessed, as shown in the following screenshot:

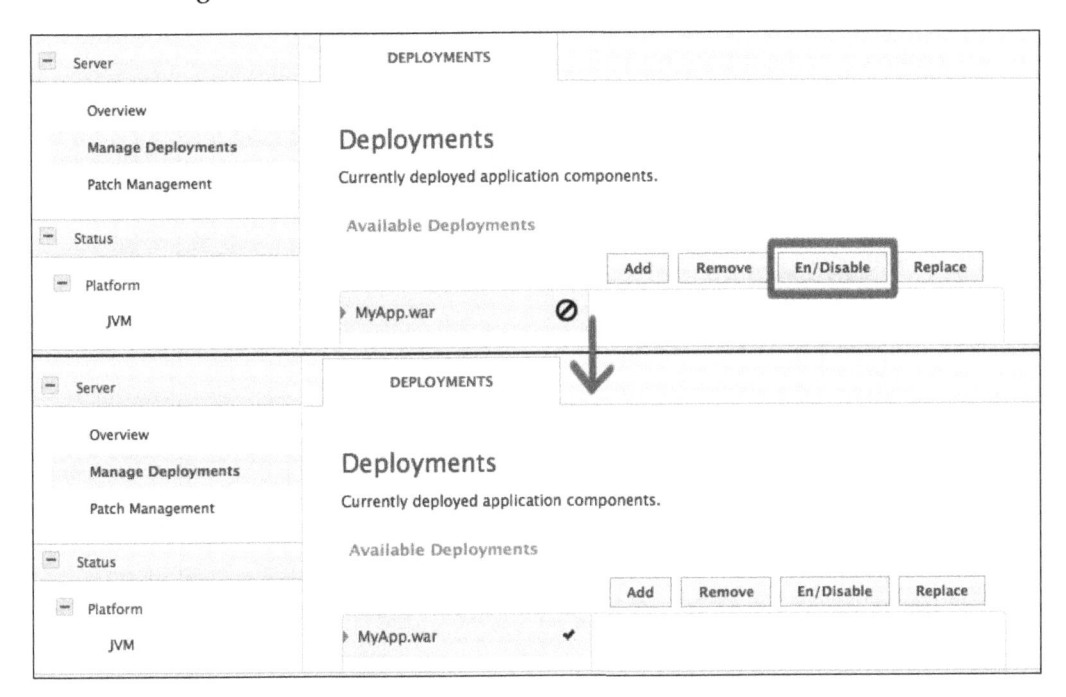

Deploying an application using the WildFly Eclipse plugin

Eclipse is the most widely used application development environment for Java developers, and it's also the favorite IDE for JBoss developers, as the JBoss Tools project (http://www.jboss.org/tools) supports the Eclipse environment by providing a set of plugins for JBoss projects.

In the first chapter of this book, we outlined the installation steps for Eclipse, along with JBoss tools. We also set up the WildFly server adapter, which allows you to start, stop, debug, and deploy applications on WildFly using the standalone mode.

Deploying applications to WildFly is easy once you have your WildFly Eclipse plugin installed:

1. Simply navigate to the **Server** tab, right-click on the **WildFly Runtime Server**, and select **Add and Remove**. You are presented with a window, as shown in the following screenshot:

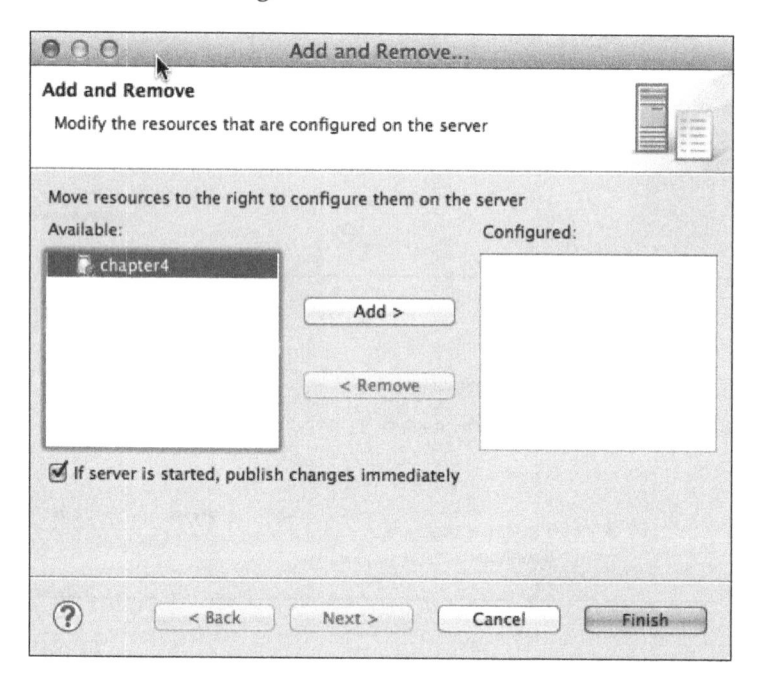

2. Next, click on your application, select **Add**, and then click on **Finish**. The project now publishes to the server. If you ever need to redeploy, click on the project you want to deploy, and choose **Full Publish**, as shown in the following screenshot:

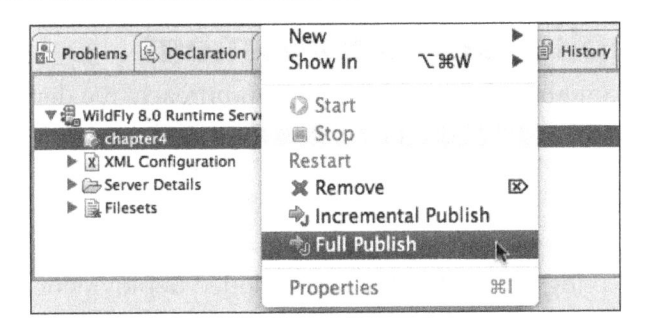

Configuring Eclipse deployments

By double-clicking on the WildFly Runtime, you have access to a tabbed menu, which contains two options: **Overview** and **Deployment**. The **Deployment** option is specific to JBoss tools and lets you choose the deployment location and packaging style of deployment. Take a look at the following screenshot:

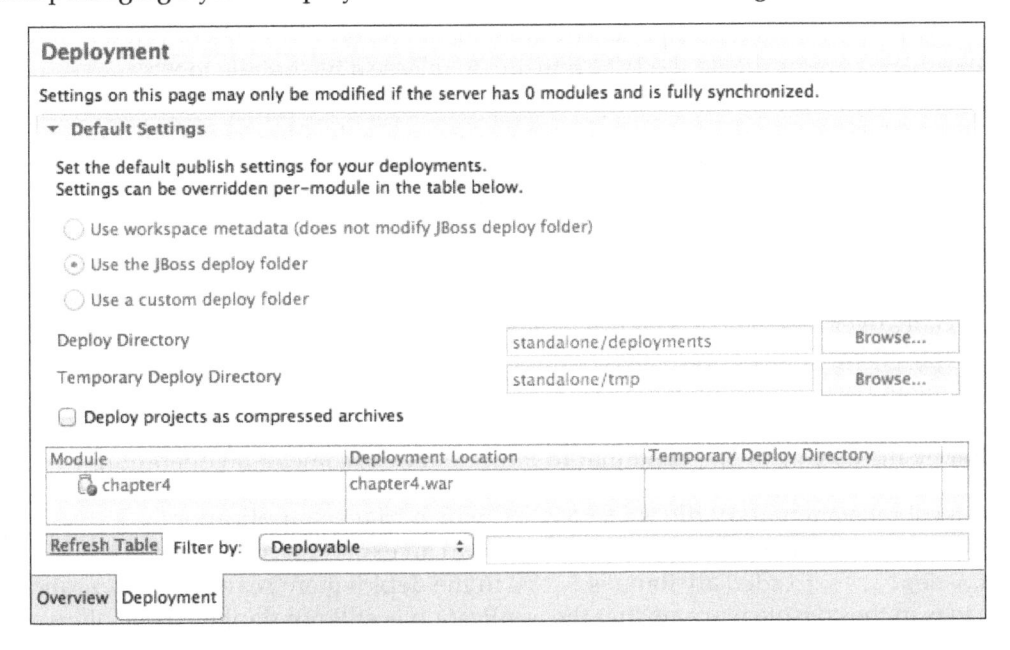

Upon checking the **Deploy projects as compressed archives** option, your application is compressed and packaged.

> If you choose to deploy your application as an exploded archive, Eclipse adds a `.dodeploy` marker file once the application has been copied to the `deployments` folder. This triggers immediate application deployment. See the next section for more information about marker files.

Manual application deployment

When using the manual application deployment approach, the deployment scanner does not automatically deploy the applications that are placed in the `deployments` folder. Rather, it uses a set of marker files, which are used to trigger application redeployment and capture the result of the operation.

You might wonder why marker files are used by the application server and why the default server configuration is set to use exploded deployments.

Actually, there are several reasons for this choice, and all of them are related to how the operating system's filesystem works. Exploded archives involve moving/replacing files in your filesystem, which should be performed automatically. By atomic operation, we mean that a filesystem operation needs to be performed as a single operation. Unfortunately, some operating systems like Windows don't treat complex filesystem operations such as a file moving as atomic operations.

Most Windows users often experience deployment issues on releases of WildFly prior to JBoss AS 7. This is due to the JVM refusing to release a file handle to `META-INF/application.xml` or an EJB descriptor file. That's because Windows uses a mandatory file lock, which prevents any application from accessing the file. On the other hand, operating systems such as UNIX use an advisory file lock, which means that unless an application checks for a file lock, it is not prevented from accessing the file.

Also, using marker files, the application server is able to solve a common issue related to large deployment files. If you've ever tried to deploy a large package unit (especially over a network), you might have experienced deployment errors because the deployment scanner starts deploying before the copy operation is completed, resulting in partially-completed deployments. Marker files are used by default for exploded deployments. They consist of empty files with a suffix, which are added either by the user or by the container to indicate the outcome of an operation.

The most relevant marker file is `.dodeploy`, which triggers application redeployment. As a matter of fact, when we add an exploded deployment and the `auto-deploy-exploded` attribute is `false` in the deployment scanner configuration, the logs in the console warn us that the application is still not deployed, as follows:

```
21:51:54,915 INFO  [org.jboss.as.server.deployment.scanner]
(DeploymentScanner-threads - 1) JBAS015003: Found MyApp.war in deployment
directory. To trigger deployment create a file called MyApp.war.dodeploy
```

Both Windows and Unix users can trigger deployment by simply running the following command:

```
echo "" > MyApp.war.dodeploy
```

Once you have started the deployment process, the application server replies with two possible outcomes. A deployed marker file (for example, `MyApp.war.deployed`) is placed in the `deployments` directory by the deployment scanner service to indicate that the given content has been deployed to the server, and your logs should confirm the outcome, as follows:

```
22:23:18,887 INFO  [org.jboss.as.server] (ServerService Thread Pool --
28) JBAS018559: Deployed "MyApp.war" (runtime-name : "MyApp.war")
```

> If you remove the `.deployed` file, the application is undeployed, and an `.undeployed` marker file is added to the `deployments` folder (for example, `MyApp.war.undeployed`). If you try to remove the `.undeployed` file, the application is deployed again. This is a useful shortcut to quickly undeploy (or redeploy) the application without deleting it on the filesystem.

The other possible outcome is a deployment failure, which is indicated by a `.failed` marker. The content of the file includes some information about the cause of the failure; however, you should check the server logs for more detailed information regarding the cause of the error.

When using the autodeploy mode, you can remove the `.failed` marker file, which redeploys the application when the folder is rescanned by the deployment scanner. Additionally, the user can place the `.skipdeploy` marker file (for example, `MyApp.war.skipdeploy`), which disables `auto-deploy` of the content for as long as this marker file is present. Use this if you rely on automatic deployment and want to ensure that no deploy is triggered when updates are still incomplete.

Let's see a sample script, which can be used to perform a safe redeployment of a web application named `MyApp.war`, when using the Linux operating system:

```
touch $JBOSS_HOME/standalone/deployments/MyApp.war.skipdeploy
cp -r MyApp.war/  $JBOSS_HOME/standalone/deployments
rm $JBOSS_HOME/standalone/deployments/MyApp.war.skipdeploy
```

Application Structure and Deployment

The Windows equivalent is defined as follows:

```
echo "" > "%JBOSS_HOME%\standalone\deployments\MyApp.war.skipdeploy"
xcopy MyApp.war %JBOSS_HOME%\standalone\deployments\MyApp.war /E /I
del %JBOSS_HOME%\standalone\deployments\MyApp.war.skipdeploy
```

Finally, the application server provides some additional temporary marker files, such as `.isdeploying`, `.isundeploying`, or `.pending`, that are placed by the deployment scanner to indicate the transition to the deployment or undeployment of a resource. Full details of marker files are provided in the `README.txt` file placed in the `deployments` folder of the server distribution. The following table displays a short summary of the available marker files used by the application server:

Marker	Created by	Description
`.dodeploy`	User	Creating this file triggers application deployment. Touching this file causes application redeployment.
`.skipdeploy`	User	Application autodeployment is disabled as long as this file exists.
`.deployed`	WildFly	The application is deployed. Removing it causes undeployment of the application.
`.undeployed`	WildFly	The application has been undeployed. Removing it causes redeployment of the application.
`.failed`	WildFly	The application deployment has failed.
`.isdeploying`	WildFly	The application deployment is in progress.
`.isundeploying`	WildFly	The application undeployment is in progress.
`.pending`	WildFly	One condition is preventing application deployment (for example, file copying in progress).

Deploying applications on a WildFly domain

Deploying applications on a WildFly domain is not as simple as deploying to a standalone server. There is no predefined `deployments` folder in the domain installation. The reason for this is that in the `domain` mode, there can be many servers belonging to different server groups, each one running different profiles. In this situation, a single `deployments` folder raises the obvious question: which server groups will use that folder?

Next, we are going to look at the options available when deploying applications to a WildFly domain. These two options are as follows:

- The **command-line interface (CLI)**
- The admin web interface

Deploying to a domain using the CLI

Let's see how to deploy an application using the CLI. Start by launching the CLI, and connect to the domain controller, as follows:

```
[disconnected /] connect
domain@localhost:9990 /]
```

When you deploy an application using the domain mode, you have to specify to which server group the deployment is associated. The CLI lets you choose between the following two options:

- Deploy to all server groups
- Deploy to a single server group

Deploying to all server groups

When choosing the option to deploy to all server groups, the application is deployed to all the available server groups. The --all-server-groups flag can be used to deploy to all the available server groups. For example, use the following command:

```
[domain@localhost:9990 /] deploy ../application.ear --all-server-groups
```

If, on the other hand, you want to undeploy an application from all server groups belonging to a domain, you have to issue the undeploy command, as follows:

```
[domain@localhost:9990 /] undeploy application.ear --all-relevant-server-groups
```

You might have noticed that the undeploy command uses --all-relevant-server-groups instead of --all-server-groups. The reason for this difference is that the deployment may not be enabled on all server groups, so by using this option, you actually undeploy it just from all those server groups in which the deployment is enabled.

Application Structure and Deployment

> Deploying an application as `disabled` can be useful if you have some startup beans (which are activated when the application is enabled) and you want to load them, but don't want to trigger their execution, for example, if the database or any other enterprise information system is temporarily unavailable.

Deploying to a single server group

The option of deploying to a single server group lets you perform a selective deployment of your application just on the server groups you have indicated, as follows:

```
[domain@localhost:9990 /] deploy application.ear --server-groups=main-server-group
```

You are not limited to a single server group. To deploy to multiple server groups, separate them with a comma, as follows:

```
[domain@localhost:9990 /] deploy application.ear --server-groups=main-server-group,other-server-group
```

Remember, you can use the autocomplete functionality (the *Tab* key) to display the list of available `--server-groups`.

Now, suppose we want to undeploy the application from just one server group. There can be two possible outcomes. If the application is available just on that server group, you successfully complete the undeployment:

```
[domain@localhost:9990 /] undeploy MyApp.war --server-groups=main-server-group
```

On the other hand, if your application is available on other server groups, the following error is returned by the CLI:

```
chris-macbook:target chris$ /opt/wildfly/bin/jboss-cli.sh
You are disconnected at the moment. Type 'connect' to connect to the server or 'help' f
or the list of supported commands.
[disconnected /] connect
[domain@localhost:9990 /] undeploy -
--headers=    --help        --path=       -l
[domain@localhost:9990 /] deploy MyApp.war --server-groups=main-server-group,other-serv
er-group
[domain@localhost:9990 /] undeploy MyApp.war --server-groups=main-server-group
Undeploy failed: {"JBAS014653: Composite operation failed and was rolled back. Steps th
at failed:" => {"Operation step-3" => "JBAS010861: Cannot remove deployment MyApp.war f
rom the domain as it is still used by server groups [other-server-group]"}}
[domain@localhost:9990 /]
```

This error occurs because when you are removing an application from a server group, the domain controller verifies that the application is not referenced by any other server group. If it is, the `undeploy` command fails.

If you wish to remove your application from a single server group, you need to issue the `-keep-content` argument. This causes the domain controller to undeploy the application from the server group while retaining the content:

```
[domain@localhost:9990 /] undeploy application.ear --server-groups=main-server-group --keep-content
```

We have covered many of the available options to deploy applications to a domain. Before moving to the admin console, let's review the CLI deployment options, as shown in the following table:

Command	Options	Effect
deploy	--all-server-groups	This deploys an application to all server groups.
undeploy	--server-groups	This deploys an application to one or more server groups.
undeploy	--all-relevant-server-groups	This undeploys and removes an application from all server groups.
undeploy	--server-groups	This undeploys an application from one server group. This fails if it's referenced in another server group.
undeploy	--server-groups -keep-content	This undeploys an application from one server group without deleting it.

Deploying to a domain using the Admin console

Deploying applications using the **Admin** console is pretty intuitive and requires just a few simple steps:

1. Start by logging in to the web application via the default address, `http://localhost:9990`.

[175]

Application Structure and Deployment

2. Then, select the **Runtime** tab in the top menu and select **Manage Deployments** in the left-hand side panel of the screen, as shown in the following screenshot:

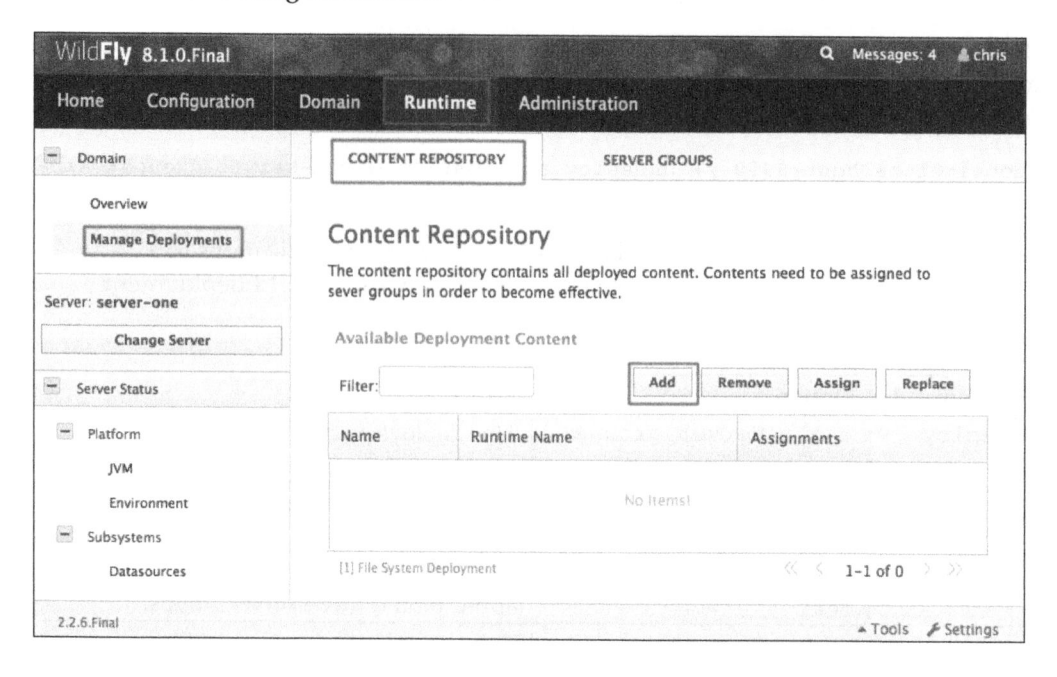

3. Before you can deploy your application to a server group, you need to upload it to the server, where it is stored in a content repository. To do this, click on **CONTENT REPOSITORY**, and then click on **Add**.

   This displays the following dialog, which allows you to upload your application:

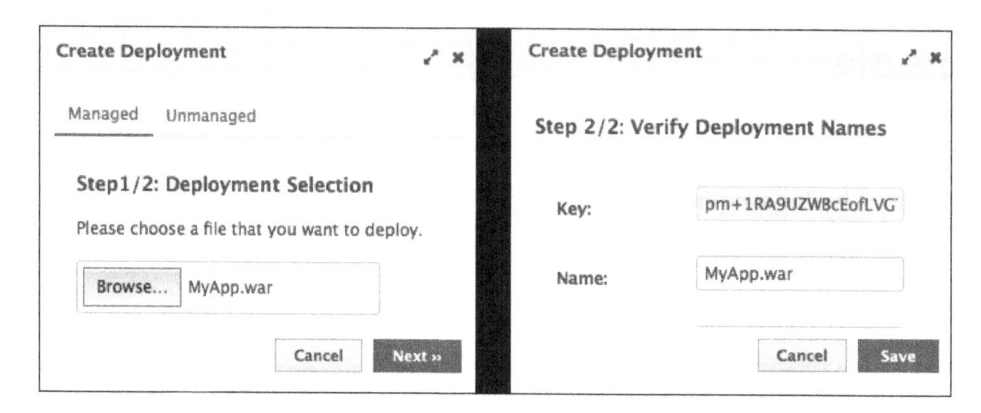

4. Once you are finished with the upload wizard, the application is uploaded to the domain repository. In order to deploy/undeploy it to the single server groups, you need to select the **SERVER GROUPS** tab, and then click on the **View** button on the server group you wish to deploy to, as shown in the following screenshot:

5. The next screen shows you all the deployments for this server group. Now, click on the **Assign** button. This allows you to select from the applications that are currently stored within the content repository. Select the checkbox for your application and then click on **Save**, as shown in the following screenshot:

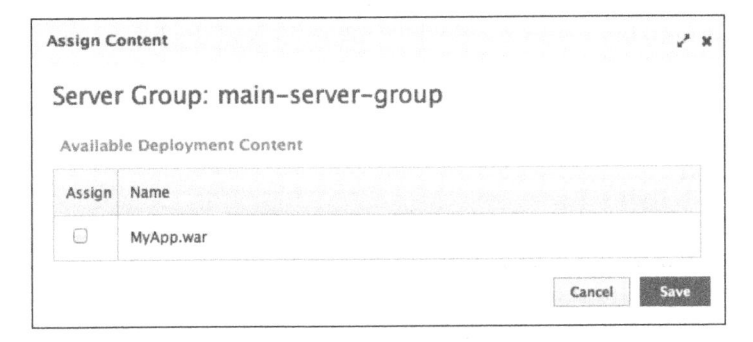

6. At this point, the application is deployed but still not enabled. Choose the **En/Disable** button to complete the deployment of the application, as shown in the following screenshot:

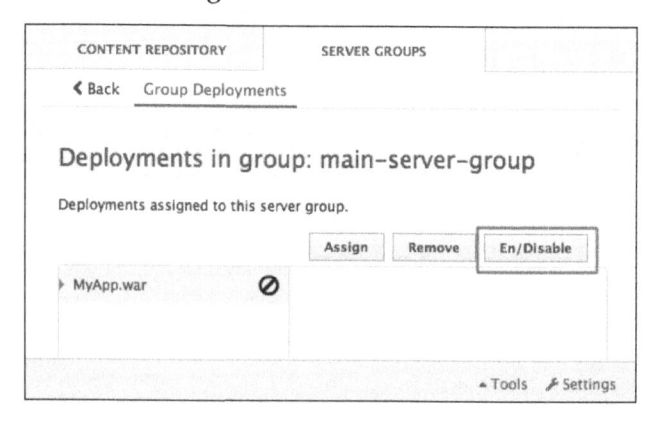

Clicking on the **Remove** button within the **SERVER GROUPS** tab removes the deployment from the server group selected, while the other **Remove** button within the **CONTENT REPOSITORY** tab actually deletes the deployment from the temporary domain repository where uploaded applications are bundled.

Explaining WildFly classloading

There are two approaches to managing dependencies, the first being the **Class-Path** approach and the second, the **Dependencies** approach. We will cover both of these topics in this section, but before we do, let's take a look at the history of classloading in WildFly in order to understand why classloading works the way it does. As mandated by the Java EE specification, an application server needs to provide an environment where any deployed application can access any class, or library of classes, of a particular version.

This is also known as **Class Namespace Isolation** (Java EE 5 specification, section EE.8.4). However, loading classes from different namespaces can raise some issues that are not easy to solve. For example, what happens if you pack a newer version of a utility library with your application, while an older version of the same library was loaded by the application server? Or, how do you simultaneously use two different versions of the same utility library within the same instance of the application server?

The JBoss AS classloading strategy has changed sensibly through the years. The 4.x releases of the application server used `UnifiedClassLoader`, which aimed to reduce communications overhead between running applications, as class data could be shared by reference or simple copies.

One of the major issues not resolved with `UnifiedClassLoader` is **classloading dependencies**. The idea is that if one application (A) uses the classes of another application (B), the system should know how to redeploy A when B gets redeployed; otherwise, it references stale classes. There were actually two different attempts to try to make this work without the user having to configure anything. Neither attempt really worked and both were dropped.

With JBoss AS 5.0, a new classloader was based on the new **Virtual File System (VFS)**. The VFS was implemented to simplify and unify file handling within the application server. The new classloader, named the VFS classloader, uses VFS to locate JAR and class files. Even though this represented a significant change in how classes were loaded in JBoss AS 5.0, the resulting behavior is much the same as that of prior versions of JBoss AS.

A common source of errors was including API classes in a deployment that was also provided by the container. This could result in multiple versions of the class being created and the deployment failing to deploy properly.

Since JBoss AS 7, classloading marks a radical departure from previous attempts. Classloading is now based on the JBoss modules project, and any application that is deployed is, in effect, a module. This fact may raise some questions, such as what module name is to be assigned to a deployed application, and how dependencies between modules are handled by the application server.

These questions will be answered in the next few sections.

Getting to know module names

Getting to know module names is not an academic exercise. We can even go so far as establishing dependencies between modules. So, in many cases, you need to know how module names are assigned to an application.

Applications that are packaged as top-level archives (such as WAR, JAR, and SAR) are assigned the following module name:

```
deployment.[archive name]
```

For example, a web application named `WebExample1.war` is deployed with the following module name:

```
deployment.WebExample1.war
```

On the other hand, for applications that contain nested modules (such as EAR), each archive is assigned a module name using the following convention:

```
deployment.[ear archive name].[sub deployment archive name]
```

So, for example, the preceding web archive, if contained in an EAR file called `EnterpriseApp.ear`, would be deployed with the following name:

`deployment.EnterpriseApp.ear.WebExample1.war`

Finding the isolation level

A general rule in WildFly 8 is that every deployed application module is isolated from other modules, that is, by default, the application does not have visibility on the AS modules, nor do the AS modules have visibility on the application.

Using the application server modules is relatively easy and can be summarized in a single sentence: add a dependency to the required module and the AS will use it. Some dependencies are automatically added to the application server, while others need to be signaled by the user:

- The core module libraries (namely, the `Enterprise` classes) are qualified as implicit dependencies, so they are automatically added to your application when the deployer detects their usage
- Other module libraries need to be explicitly declared by the user in the application's `MANIFEST` file or in a custom JBoss deployment file named `jboss-deployment-structure.xml` (more about this file in the *Advanced deployment strategies* section)

Implicit dependencies

Repeatedly declaring commonly used dependencies for your enterprise application becomes very tedious. This is why the core modules are automatically added for you by the application server. Some of these core modules are only added when the application server detects annotations or configuration files for a particular technology. For example, adding a `beans.xml` file automatically triggers the **Weld** dependency (Weld is the Contexts and Dependency injection implementation used in WildFly).

The following table outlines the modules that are implicitly added to your application:

Subsystem	Automatic dependencies	Triggered dependencies	Trigger condition
Core server	`javax.api` `sun.jdk` `org.jboss.vfs`		
EE	`javaee.api`		

Subsystem	Automatic dependencies	Triggered dependencies	Trigger condition
EJB3		javaee.api	Presence of ejb-jar.xml or EJB annotations
JAX-RS	javax.xml.bind.api	org.jboss.resteasy	Presence of JAX-RS annotations
JPA	javax.persistence	javaee.api org.jboss.as.jpa org.hibernate	Presence of @PersistenceUnit or @PersistenceContext or equivalent XML
Logging	org.jboss.logging org.apache.commons.logging org.apache.log4j org.slf4j		
Security	org.picketbox		
Web		javaee.api com.sun.jsf-impl org.hibernate.validator org.jboss.as.web org.jboss.logging	Deployment of WEB archive; JSF added if used
Web services	org.jboss.ws.api org.jboss.ws.spi		
Weld		javax.persistence.api javaee.api org.javassist org.jboss.interceptor org.jboss.as.weld org.jboss.logging org.jboss.weld.core org.jboss.weld.api org.jboss.weld.spi	Presence of beans.xml

Application Structure and Deployment

If your application uses any of the core modules indicated, then you don't need to specify its dependency, as the application server links the module automatically. If you are using Maven, then you can mark these dependencies as provided.

Explicit dependencies

Modules that are not qualified as implicit dependencies need to be declared by the user. Let's say you want to use the log4j library, which is bundled in the application server distribution. The simplest and recommended approach to achieve this is by including the `Dependencies: [module]` declaration within `META-INF/MANIFEST.MF`. The following example code for the chapter uses Maven to populate the `MANIFEST.MF` file:

```xml
<plugin>
    <artifactId>maven-war-plugin</artifactId>
    <version>2.1.1</version>
    <configuration>
        <failOnMissingWebXml>false</failOnMissingWebXml>
        <archive>
            <manifestEntries>
                <Dependencies>org.apache.log4j</Dependencies>
            </manifestEntries>
        </archive>
    </configuration>
</plugin>
```

This has the result of adding the following to your `MANIFEST.MF` file:

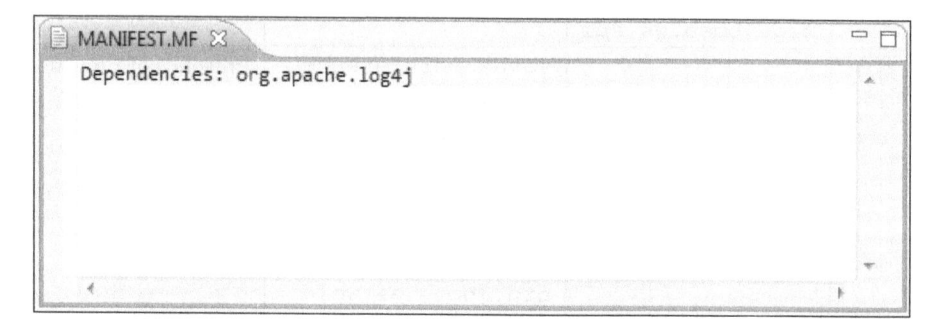

```
Dependencies: org.apache.log4j
```

> Please note that the module name does not always match the package name of the library. The actual module name is specified in the `module.xml` file by the `name` attribute of the `module` element.

You are not limited to a single dependency, as you can add multiple dependencies separated by a comma. For example, in order to add a dependency on both log4j and Apache Velocity API, use the following:

```
Dependencies: org.apache.log4j,org.apache.velocity
```

You can even export the dependencies used by one application module to other applications by adding the `export` keyword. For example, in addition to the earlier example, we're now exporting the dependencies to other modules, as follows:

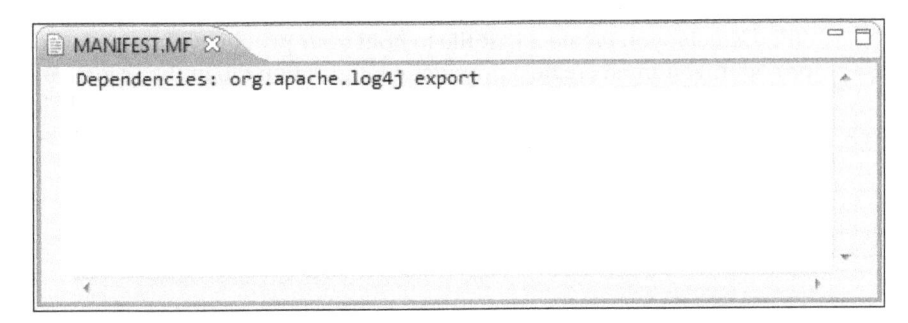

```
MANIFEST.MF
Dependencies: org.apache.log4j export
```

> The `export` parameter can also be used to export a dependency to all subdeployments contained in the EAR. Consequently, if you export a dependency from the top-level of the EAR (or by a JAR in the `ear/lib` directory), then the dependency is also available to all subdeployment units.

Applications that are marked as dependent to the `deployment.WebApp1.war` module also have access to its dependencies:

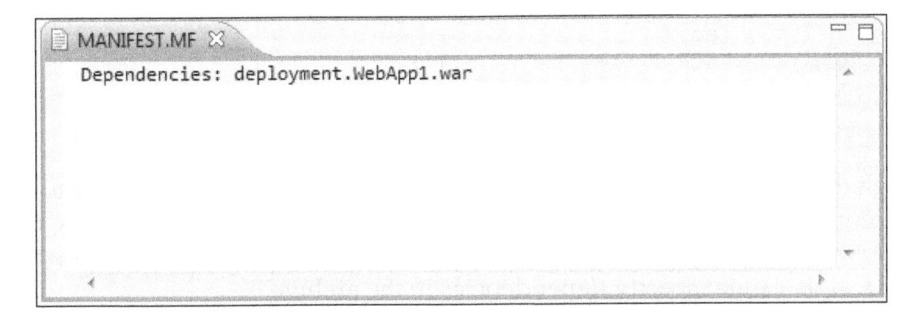

```
MANIFEST.MF
Dependencies: deployment.WebApp1.war
```

Within `META-INF/MANIFEST.MF`, you can also specify additional commands that can modify the server deployer's behavior. For example, the `optional` attribute can be added to specify that the deployment does not fail if the module is not found at the deployment time.

Application Structure and Deployment

Finally, when the `services` keyword is specified, the deployer tries to load services that are placed within the `META-INF/services` directory of the archive.

> The `service` API has become `public` in Java SE 6. A **service** can be defined as a set of programming interfaces and classes that provide access to some specific application functionality or feature. A **Service Provider Interface (SPI)** is the set of `public` interfaces and `abstract` classes that a service defines.
>
> You can define a service provider by implementing the service provider API. Usually, you create a JAR file to hold your provider. To register your provider, you must create a provider configuration file in the JAR file's `META-INF/services` directory. When adding the `services` attribute to your `META-INF/MANIFEST.MF` file, you are actually able to load the services contained in the `META-INF/services` directory.
>
> One excellent introduction to the SPI API is available at http://www.oracle.com/technetwork/articles/javase/extensible-137159.html.

Setting up global modules

Setting up global modules resembles the old AS approach to loading common libraries, where you used to place them in the `lib` folder under `JBOSS_HOME/common`.

If you define a section named `global-modules` within `standalone.xml/domain.xml`, then you make the module accessible to other AS modules. For example, instead of declaring a dependency on log4j, you can alternatively use the following section:

```xml
<subsystem xmlns="urn:jboss:domain:ee:1.0">
  <global-modules>
    <module name="org.apache.log4j" />
  </global-modules>
</subsystem>
```

Although this approach is not generally recommended, as it brings us back to the concept of a monolithic application server, it can still yield some benefits, for example, when you migrate some older applications, and also when you don't want or simply cannot specify dependencies to the archive.

Advanced deployment strategies

The topics covered so far are sufficient for the vast majority of applications. If you are using a complex archive configuration, such as an EAR archive with several modules and dependencies, it might be useful to define your classloading strategy in a single file. The configuration file, `jboss-deployment-structure.xml`, does exactly this. Some of the advantages of using this file are outlined as follows:

- You can define the dependencies of all application modules in a single file
- You can load the module classes in a fine-grained manner by including/excluding all or some parts of modules
- You can define the classloading isolation policy for your applications packaged in an enterprise archive

Let's see what `jboss-deployment-structure.xml` can do for you by taking a look at some practical examples.

Setting up a single module dependency

We have already learned how to activate a `log4j` dependency using the `Dependencies` attribute in the archive's `MANIFEST` file. The same effect can be achieved using the `jboss-deployment-structure.xml` file. Let's recap the archive structure, which is basically made up of a web application named `WebApp.war`.

As you can see in the following diagram, the `jboss-deployment-structure.xml` file needs to be placed within the `META-INF` folder of the EAR:

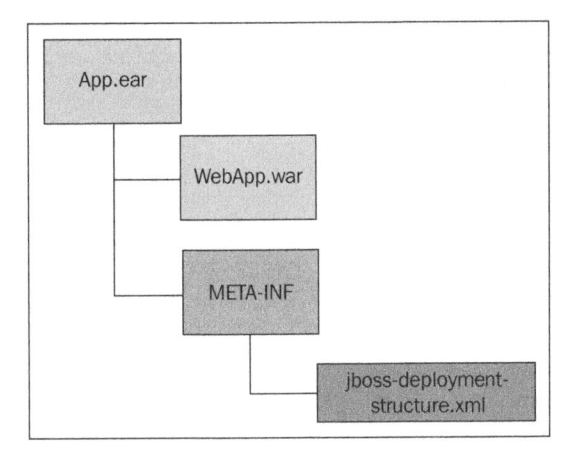

Application Structure and Deployment

The following is the content of `jboss-deployment-structure.xml`:

```
<jboss-deployment-structure>
  <sub-deployment name="WebApp.war">
    <dependencies>
      <module name="org.apache.log4j" />
    </dependencies>
  </sub-deployment>
</jboss-deployment-structure>
```

The `jboss-deployment-structure` file is not for the exclusive use of EARs and can be used within a WAR archive by placing it within the `WEB-INF` folder. It is, however, applicable only as a top-level archive. Thus, if a `jboss-deployment-structure.xml` file is placed in the WAR's `WEB-INF` folder and the WAR is packaged in an EAR file, then the `jboss-deployment-structure.xml` file is ignored. The relevant part of this file is the subdeployment element, which references the web application, including the `dependencies` element. The expected outcome is that the application server triggers the dependency to the Log4J API, which is, therefore, visible by our web application.

Excluding the server's automatic dependencies

Earlier in this chapter, we discussed how the application server can automatically trigger dependencies when certain conditions are met. For example, if you deploy a JSF application (containing the `faces-config.xml` file), then the JSF 2.2 API implementation is automatically added.

This might not always be the desired option, as you may want to provide another release implementation for that module. You can easily achieve this using the `exclusion` element in the `jboss-deployment-structure.xml` file, as shown in the following code snippet:

```
<jboss-deployment-structure>
  <deployment>
    <exclusions>
      <module name="javax.faces.api" />
      <module name="com.sun.jsf-impl" />
    </exclusions>
    <dependencies>
      <module name="javax.faces.api" slot="2.1"/>
      <module name="com.sun.jsf-impl" slot="2.1"/>
    </dependencies>
  </deployment>
</jboss-deployment-structure>
```

Notice that in the `dependencies` section, we added our alternate JSF 2.1 implementation, which is used by your application. You need to install these two modules shown in the preceding code, as explained in *Chapter 2, Configuring the Core WildFly Subsystems*. They can be placed alongside the implementations provided by WildFly by creating a folder named `2.1`. The new folder for the JSF 2.1 archive is highlighted in bold in the following command lines:

`$JBOSS_HOME/modules/system/layers/base/javax/faces/api/main`

`$JBOSS_HOME/modules/system/layers/base/javax/faces/api/main/jboss-jsf-api_2.2_spec-2.2.6.jar`

`$JBOSS_HOME/modules/system/layers/base/javax/faces/api/main/module.xml`

`$JBOSS_HOME/modules/system/layers/base/javax/faces/api/`**`2.1`**

`$JBOSS_HOME/modules/system/layers/base/javax/faces/api/`**`2.1`**`/jsf-api-2.1.jar`

`$JBOSS_HOME/modules/system/layers/base/javax/faces/api/`**`2.1`**`/module.xml`

You also need to add the `slot` attribute to the `module.xml` file, as highlighted in the following code snippet:

```
<module xmlns="urn:jboss:module:1.3" name="javax.faces.api"
  slot="2.1" >
    ...
</module>
```

Isolating sub-deployments

Considering that you have an EAR application that is made up of a web application, an EJB module, and a JAR file containing utility classes, all subdeployments are placed at the root of the archive so that they can see each other. However, let's suppose your web application contains some implementations of the same EJB. That's absolutely possible since Java EE allows your web application to include EJB classes within the `WEB-INF/classes` or `WEB-INF/lib` folder, as the following diagram depicts:

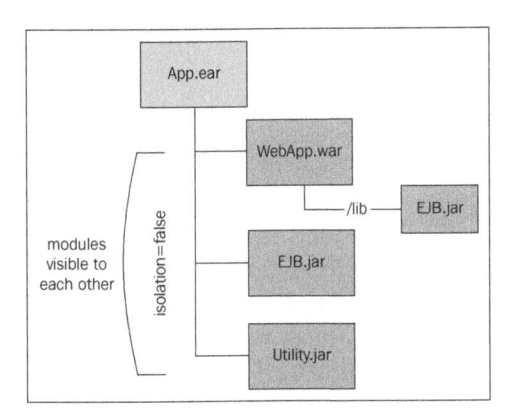

[187]

Application Structure and Deployment

How does the classloader resolve this conflict? The application server classloader has a priority list when loading classes, thus reducing any conflict between loaded classes, as follows:

- The highest priority is automatically given to modules by the container, including the Java EE APIs. Libraries contained in the `modules` folder are included in this category.
- The next priority goes to libraries that are indicated by the user within `MANIFEST.MF` of the packaged archive as dependencies (or in the `jboss-deployment-structure.xml` file).
- The penultimate priority is given to libraries that are packed within the application itself, such as classes contained in `WEB-INF/lib` or `WEB-INF/classes`.
- Finally, the last priority goes to libraries that are packed within the same EAR archive (in the EAR's `lib` folder).

So, in this example, the EJB libraries located in the `WEB-INF` folder hides the implementations of `EJB.jar` top-level deployment. If this is not the desired result, you can simply override it, as follows:

```
<jboss-deployment-structure>
  <ear-subdeployments-isolated>false</ear-subdeployments-isolated>
  <sub-deployment name="WebApp.war">
    <dependencies>
      <module name="deployment.App.ear.EJB.jar" />
    </dependencies>
  </sub-deployment>
</jboss-deployment-structure>
```

In the preceding code snippet, we added a dependency to the `EJB.jar` deployment, which is placed at the root of the EAR and which overrides the implementation packed within the web application.

> Note the `ear-subdeployments-isolated` element placed at the top of the file. By setting the EAR isolation level, you will be able to indicate if the subdeployment modules are visible to each other.

The default value of the `ear-subdeployments-isolated` element is `false`, which means that the subdeployment modules can see each other. If you are setting isolation to `true`, each module is then picked up by a different classloader, which means that the web application is unable to find the classes contained in the `EJB.jar` and `Utility.jar` libraries).

If you want to keep the deployment isolated but allow visibility between some of your dependencies, then you have two choices available:

- Move the library to the `EAR/lib` folder so that it is picked up as a separate module
- Specify a dependency using Dependencies or Class-Path in the `MANIFEST.MF` file of the calling application

In the following diagram, you can see how to correctly set up your EAR, by placing common libraries in the `lib` folder and adding a dependency to the EJB classes:

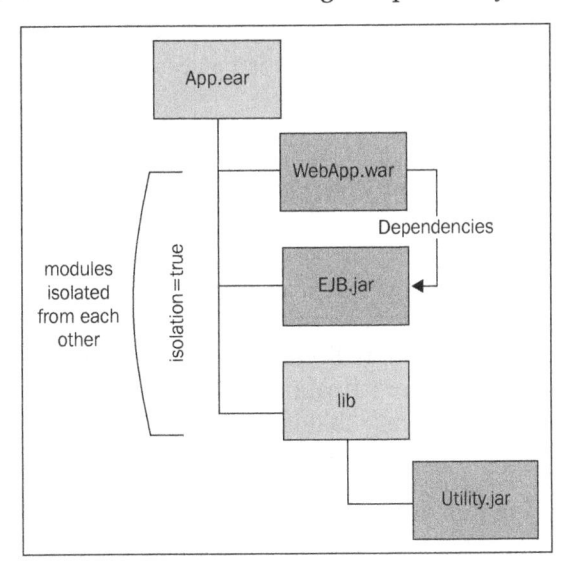

The following is the corresponding configuration required in `jboss-deployment-structure.xml`:

```xml
<jboss-deployment-structure>
  <ear-subdeployments-isolated>true</ear-subdeployments-isolated>
  <sub-deployment name="WebApp.war">
    <dependencies>
      <module name="deployment.App.ear.EJB.jar" />
    </dependencies>
  </sub-deployment>
</jboss-deployment-structure>
```

Application Structure and Deployment

> Packaging libraries in a shared library within your EAR is an option. With Java EE 5 onward, it has been possible to place these files in a shared library folder called `lib`. You can override this default folder name using the `library-directory` element in the `META-INF/application.xml` file. For example, suppose you want to use the `common` folder to hold your shared libraries, in which case you can add the following line to your `application.xml`:
>
> `<library-directory>common</library-directory>`
>
> As a side note, you should avoid placing component-declaring annotations (such as EJB3) in the shared folder, as it can have unintended consequences on the deployment process. For this reason, it is strongly recommended that you place your utility classes in the shared library folder.

Using the Class-Path declaration to solve dependencies

Until now, we have configured dependencies between modules using the JBoss way, which is the recommended choice. Nevertheless, we should also account for Java's portable way to reference one or more libraries included in the EAR file. This can be achieved by adding the `Class-Path` attribute to the `MANIFEST.MF` file. This allows a module to reference another library that is not otherwise visible to the application (think back to the earlier example of a deployment unit with the isolation set to `true`).

For example, considering that you need to reference the `Utility.jar` application from within your web application, you can simply add the following to your `META-INF/MANIFEST.MF` file directly inside your EAR:

```
Manifest-Version: 1.0
Class-Path: Utility.jar
```

You can actually include more than one library to the `Class-Path` attribute, separating them by a comma.

> Unlike the `Dependencies` attribute, the `Class-Path` attribute points to the actual JAR filename (and not the module name) to reference the dependent libraries.

Choosing between the Class-Path approach and JBoss's Dependencies approach depends on how your application is structured: using JBoss's Dependencies approach buys you a richer set of options, in particular, the ability to export the dependencies to other deployments, as we have illustrated earlier. One more point in favor of JBoss's Dependencies approach is the ability to reference modules that are not actually packaged within the application.

On the other hand, the main advantage of the Class-Path approach relies on application portability. Thus, if a fully portable solution is a priority for you, you can consider switching to the `Class-Path` manifest attribute.

Summary

In this chapter, we covered a wide variety of functionalities related to the deployment of applications. Applications are deployed differently, depending on whether they are deployed to a standalone server or to a domain of servers.

As far as standalone servers are concerned, an application can be deployed either automatically or manually. By default, packaged archives are deployed automatically. This means that all you need to do is place the archive within the `standalone/deployments` folder of the application server. Applications that are deployed manually (by default, exploded archives) need marker files to activate the deployment.

As far as domain servers are concerned, since the application server cannot determine which server group you want to target the deployment to, you need to specify this information when using either the command-line interface or the web admin interface.

One of the great advantages of using a domain of servers is the ability to deploy applications on single or multiple server groups, which can even be created and equipped at runtime.

In the later part of this chapter, we covered the classloading mechanism used by the application server. Every application deployed to WildFly is treated as a module, all of which are isolated from other modules contained in the application server distribution. Modules representing Java EE API classes are implicitly added to your application's classpath as dependencies, which means that you don't need any special configuration to deploy a Java EE application.

If you want to reference other modules contained in the application server, you simply need to add a Dependencies property within the META-INF/MANIFEST.MF file of the application. Enterprise archives can also specify dependencies on other modules by setting the Class-Path attribute within the META-INF/MANIFEST.MF file.

If you want to maintain all your dependencies in a single file, you can use the jboss-deployment-structure.xml file. This allows you to define all dependencies within an archive, including the ability to override the default EAR isolation level and filter in/out classes, which are part of the application server deployment.

In the next chapter, we will cover the management of the application server by taking a close look at the command-line interface and the web admin console.

7
Using the Management Interfaces

In this chapter, we will describe the management tools available with WildFly, which can be used to control your application server instances.

WildFly provides several administration channels. One of them is the CLI, which contains many unique features that make it convenient for daily system administration and for monitoring application server resources.

The management tools also include a web admin console that offers an elegant view of the application server subsystems, allowing you to perform administrative tasks in a simple way.

Within this chapter, we will describe the following management tools:

- The command-line interface (CLI)
- The web admin console

We will also cover the following topics:

- Creating and modifying datasources
- Getting help from the CLI
- Batch scripting
- Configuring server profiles
- Adding JMS destinations
- Configuring JMS destinations
- Configuring socket-binding groups
- Choosing between the CLI and web console

Using the Management Interfaces

The command-line interface (CLI)

Terminals and consoles were one of the earliest types of communication interfaces between a system administrator and the machine. Due to this long-time presence, most system administrators prefer to use the raw power of the command line to perform management tasks. One of the most evident advantages of using a low-level interface, such as a shell, is that tasks can often be executed as a part of batch processing or macros for repetitive actions.

> As we indicated at the beginning of this book, the CLI is located in the JBOSS_HOME/bin folder and wrapped by jboss-cli.sh (for Windows users, it's jboss-cli.bat).

By launching the shell script, you will start with a disconnected session. You can connect at any time with the connect [standalone/domain controller] command, which, by default, connects to a server controller located at localhost on port 9990:

```
You are disconnected at the moment. Type 'connect' to connect to the
server or 'help' for the list of supported commands.
[disconnected /] connect
[standalone@localhost:9990 /]
```

You can adjust the default port where the native interface is running by modifying the line highlighted in the following code snippet, which is found within the standalone.xml or domain.xml configuration file:

```
<management-interfaces>

    <http-interface security-realm="ManagementRealm" http-upgrade-
enabled="true">
        <socket-binding http="management-http"/>
    </http-interface>
</management-interfaces>

<socket-binding-group name="standard-sockets"
default-interface="public" port-offset="0">
...

<socket-binding name="management-http" interface=
"management" port="9990"/>
```

```
<socket-binding name="management-https" interface=
"management" port="9993"/>
...
</socket-binding-group>
```

As you can see from the preceding code snippet, the socket management alias is defined within the `management-interfaces` section, while the corresponding port is contained in the `socket-binding` section.

A handy switch is `--connect`, which can be used to automatically connect to your standalone/domain controller when starting the CLI, as follows:

`$JBOSS_HOME/bin/jboss-cli.sh --connect`

On a Windows machine, use the following command:

`$JBOSS_HOME/bin/jboss-cli.bat --connect`

The corresponding command for exiting the CLI is either `quit` or `exit`, which closes the connection to the main controller:

`[standalone@localhost:9990 /] quit`

Reloading the server configuration

While most changes made to the configuration via the command line take effect immediately, some changes do not and require a reload of the server configuration, for example, changing the socket-binding groups. To reload the server configuration, you need to issue the `:reload` command, as follows:

```
[standalone@localhost:9990 /] :reload
{
    "outcome" => "success",
    "result" => undefined
}
```

Employing the CLI

One of the most interesting features of the CLI is its ability to autocomplete, which helps you find the correct spelling of resources and commands. This can be achieved by simply pressing the *Tab* key. You can even use it to find out the parameters needed for a particular command, without the need to go through the reference manual.

Using the Management Interfaces

This guides us to the first part of our journey, where we will learn the available commands. So, once you have successfully connected, press the *Tab* key, and it will list the options available to you. The following screenshot shows the output:

```
You are disconnected at the moment. Type 'connect' to connect to the server or 'help' for the list of supported commands.
[disconnected /] connect
[standalone@localhost:9990 /]
alias               deployment-overlay    patch              try
batch               echo                  pwd                undeploy
cd                  echo-dmr              quit               unset
clear               help                  read-attribute     version
command             history               read-operation     xa-data-source
connect             if                    reload             :
data-source         jdbc-driver-info      run-batch
deploy              ls                    set
deployment-info     module                shutdown
[standalone@localhost:9990 /]
```

As you can see, there are over 30 options available. We can, however, group all the interactions that occur with the CLI into two broad categories:

- **Operations**: These include the resource paths (addresses) on which they are executed.
- **Commands**: These execute an action independently from the path of the current resource. These don't include the resource path.

Navigating through the resources and executing operations

Operations are strictly bound to an application server resource path. The path along the tree of resources is represented by the / character, which, as it is, represents the root of the tree, as it does in Unix filesystems.

When executing operations on the server's resources, you have to use a well-defined syntax:

```
[node-type=node-name (,node-type=node-name)*] :
  operation-name [( [parameter-name=parameter-value
  (,parameter-name=parameter-value)*] )]
```

It looks a bit awkward at first glance; however, we will try to demystify it with the following example:

```
[standalone@localhost:9990 /] /subsystem=
  deployment-scanner/scanner=default:write-attribute(name=
  scan-interval,value=2500)
{"outcome" => "success"}
```

Here, we tell the CLI to navigate to the `deployment-scanner` subsystem under the default scanner resource and set the `scan-interval` attribute to `2500` ms using the `write-attribute` operation.

This example also shows the distinction between resources, attributes, and operations.

A resource is an element of the configuration that is located under a path. All elements that are classified as resources can be managed through WildFly's interfaces. For example, `deployment-scanner` is a resource located under the `subsystem` path. It has a child element named `default` scanner (when no name attribute is specified, the name defaults to `default`). On a single resource or on child resources, you can invoke some operations, such as reading or writing the value of an attribute (`scan-interval`).

Finally, note that operations are introduced by the `:` prefix, while resources are introduced by the `/` character. The following is a screenshot that helps you consolidate the basic concepts:

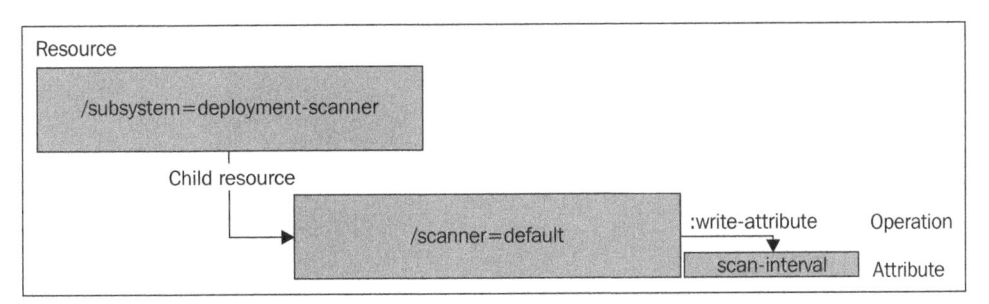

In order to move through the resource path, you can either state the full tree path (as in the earlier example) or use the `cd` command or the equivalent `cn` (change node) command to navigate to the path and then issue the desired command. For example, the previous code snippet can also be rewritten as:

```
[standalone@localhost:9990 /] cd /subsystem=deployment-scanner/
scanner=default

[standalone@localhost:9990 scanner=default] :write-attribute(name=scan-
interval,value=2500)

{"outcome" => "success"}
```

> **Do attributes modified by the CLI survive a server restart?**
> When using CLI, every change is persisted into the server configuration file. This means you must be careful when changing the server's configuration via the CLI. To play it safe, it would be wise to take a snapshot of your server configuration before making large changes. See the *Taking snapshots of the configuration* section.

As it does for the operating system shell, issuing `cd ..` will move the resource pointer to the parent resource:

```
[standalone@localhost:9990 scanner=default] cd ..
[standalone@localhost:9990 subsystem=deployment-scanner]
```

You can, at any time, check the resource path where you are located by issuing either an empty `cd` command or just `pwd`, as you do for an Unix shell, as follows:

```
[standalone@localhost:9990 scanner=default] pwd
/subsystem=deployment-scanner/scanner=default
```

Finally, in order to simplify your navigation, we'll close this section by providing you with a bird's-eye view of the application server's tree or resources, as follows:

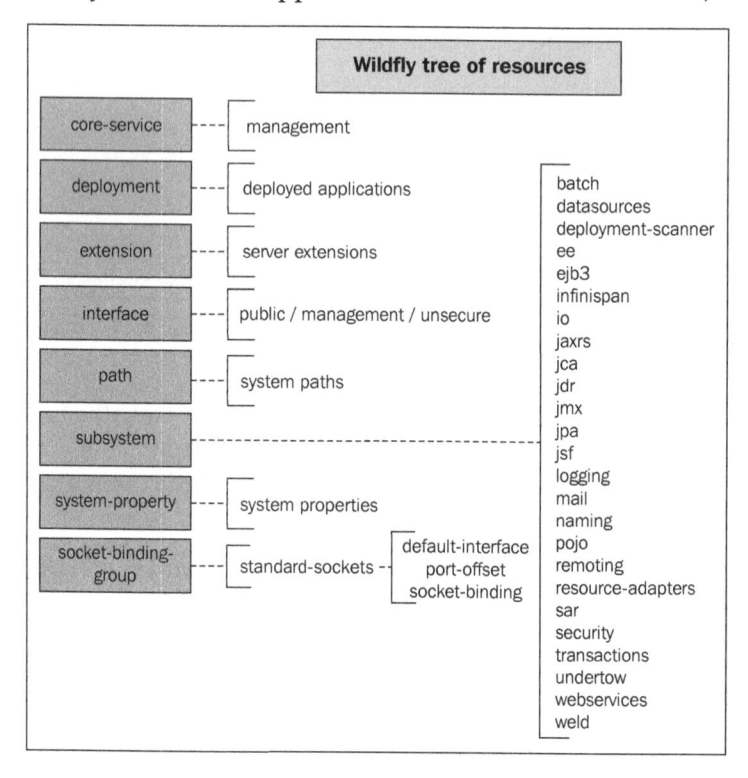

Wildfly tree of resources

- core-service ---- management
- deployment ---- deployed applications
- extension ---- server extensions
- interface ---- public / management / unsecure
- path ---- system paths
- subsystem ----
  - batch
  - datasources
  - deployment-scanner
  - ee
  - ejb3
  - infinispan
  - io
  - jaxrs
  - jca
  - jdr
  - jmx
  - jpa
  - jsf
  - logging
  - mail
  - naming
  - pojo
  - remoting
  - resource-adapters
  - sar
  - security
  - transactions
  - undertow
  - webservices
  - weld
- system-property ---- system properties
- socket-binding-group ---- standard-sockets --
  - default-interface
  - port-offset
  - socket-binding

As you can see, the tree of resources includes eight child resources, each one handling one core aspect of the application server. In *Appendix, CLI References*, you will find a handy list of useful commands that can be used for your daily system administration. Most of the time, you will navigate to the subsystem resources that contain all the application server core modules. Other resources that you might want to learn more about are the core-service, which handles management interfaces (such as the CLI itself), the deployment resource, which can be used to manipulate deployed artifacts, and the `socket-binding-group`, which is the resource you will need to change the ports used by the application server.

Operations that can be issued on a resource

Having learned the basics of navigation through the resources, let's see the commands that can be issued on a resource. Operations are triggered by the : character. You can get a list of them by using the `auto-completion` feature (the *Tab* key). The following is a list of the commands:

Command	Meaning
read-resource	This command reads a model resource's attribute values along with either basic or complete information about any child resources.
read-resource-description	This command outputs a description for the selected resource.
read-operation-names	This command reads the available operation names on the node.
read-operation-description	This command outputs a description for the available operations.
read-children-names	This command gets the name of all children under the selected resource.
read-children-resources	This command reads information about all of a resource's children that are of a given type.
read-children-types	This command provides the list of the children located under the selected resource.
read-attribute	This command gets the value of an attribute for the selected resource.
write-attribute	This command writes an attribute for the selected resource.

The `read-resource` command deserves some more explanation. Without any extra arguments, it provides information about the resource's attribute and the direct child nodes.

For example, the following is the resource scanning of the datasource subsystem, which includes the default datasource named `ExampleDS`:

```
[standalone@localhost:9990 /] /subsystem=datasources:read-resource()
{
  "outcome" => "success",
  "result" => {
    "xa-data-source" => undefined,
    "data-source" => {"java:jboss/datasources/ExampleDS" =>
      undefined},
    "jdbc-driver" => {"h2" => undefined}
  }
}
```

You might have noticed the `undefined` attribute for some elements. The information provided by the `read-resource` command is limited to listing the name of child resources. If you want to read information about all child resources, including their corresponding attributes, you have to issue the command with an additional (`recursive=true`) parameter, as follows:

```
[standalone@localhost:9990 /] /subsystem=datasources:read-
resource(recursive=true)
{
    "outcome" => "success",
    "result" => {
        "data-source" => {
            "ExampleDS" => {
                "connection-properties" => undefined,
                "connection-url" => "jdbc:h2:mem:test;
                  DB_CLOSE_DELAY=-1;DB_CLOSE_ON_EXIT=FALSE",
                "datasource-class" => undefined,
                "driver-name" => "h2",
                "enabled" => true,
            ...
            }
        },
        "jdbc-driver" => {
            "h2" => {
                "driver-module-name" => "com.h2database.h2",
```

```
                "driver-name" => "h2",
                "driver-xa-datasource-class-name" =>
                   "org.h2.jdbcx.JdbcDataSource",
                ...
            }
        },
        "xa-data-source" => undefined
    }
}
```

As you can see, by adding the `recursive=true` parameter, the CLI has also included the list of configuration parameters, which are stored as children of the datasource element. For the sake of brevity, we have intentionally included just the first few datasource parameters.

Additionally, some resources can produce metrics, which are collected as runtime attributes. These attributes are not shown by default unless you provide the `include-runtime=true` parameter. For example, within the datasource subsystem, you can view statistics related to the database connection pool:

```
[standalone@localhost:9990 statistics=pool] :read-resource(include-runtime=true)
{
    "outcome" => "success",
    "result" => {
        "ActiveCount" => "0",
        "AvailableCount" => "20",
        "AverageBlockingTime" => "0",
        "AverageCreationTime" => "0",
        "AverageGetTime" => "0",
        "BlockingFailureCount" => "0",
        "CreatedCount" => "0",
        "DestroyedCount" => "0",
        "IdleCount" => "0",
        "InUseCount" => "0",
        "MaxCreationTime" => "0",
        "MaxGetTime" => "0",
        "MaxUsedCount" => "0",
        "MaxWaitCount" => "0",
```

Using the Management Interfaces

```
            "MaxWaitTime" => "0",
            "TimedOut" => "0",
            "TotalBlockingTime" => "0",
            "TotalCreationTime" => "0",
            "TotalGetTime" => "0",
            "WaitCount" => "0"
        }
    }
```

If you want to learn more about a resource, you can use the `read-resource-description` command, which provides a short description. It also includes a description of the resource's runtime attributes. The output can be quite verbose, so here we will just include its head section:

```
[standalone@localhost:9990 statistics=pool] :read-resource-description
{
    "outcome" => "success",
    "result" => {
        "description" =>
            "Runtime statistics provided by the resource adapter.",
        "attributes" => {
            "DestroyedCount" => {
                "description" => "The destroyed count",
                "type" => INT,
                "required" => false,
                "access-type" => "metric",
                "storage" => "runtime"
            },
            "WaitCount" => {
                "description" => "The number of requests that had
                    to wait to obtain a physical connection",
                "type" => INT,
                "required" => false,
                "access-type" => "metric",
                "storage" => "runtime"
            }
        }
    }
}
```

The `read-operation-names` and `read-operation-description` commands provide the list of available operations on a certain resource and their description. These produce the information outlined in the previous table, so we will not repeat the description here.

Next, the `read-children` operations can be used to collect information about child nodes. The `read-children-types` command provides information about the child resources and is pretty similar to a simple `ls` command. For example, on the `root` resource, it will produce the following:

```
[standalone@localhost:9990 /] :read-children-types()
{
  "outcome" => "success",
  "result" => [

    "core-service",
    "deployment",
    "deployment-overlay",
    "extension",
    "interface",
    "path",
    "socket-binding-group",
    "subsystem",
    "system-property"
  ]
}
```

The `read-children-names` delivers information about a single child resource, and it's pretty much the same as issuing a `cd` resource followed by an `ls` command. For example, if we want to know the list of deployed resources on the AS, we will type in the following:

```
[standalone@localhost:9990 /] :read-children-names(child-type=deployment)
{
    "outcome" => "success",
    "result" => [
        "Enterprise.ear",
        "EJB.jar",
        "Utility.jar"
    ]
}
```

Finally, the `read-children-resources` command returns information about a child node of a certain type, which needs to be provided as an argument. This command is equivalent to executing a `read-resource` operation on each child resource. In the previous example, when we issue this command on a hypothetical `Enterprise.ear` deployment resource, it will provide the subdeployment information, as follows:

```
[standalone@localhost:9990 deployment=Enterprise.ear] :
  read-children-resources(child-type=subdeployment)
{
  "outcome" => "success",
  "result" => {
    "WebApp.war" => {
      "subdeployment" => undefined,
      "subsystem" => {"web" => undefined}
    },
    "Utility.jar" => {
      "subdeployment" => undefined,
      "subsystem" => undefined
    }
  }
}
```

Optionally, you can also add `include-runtime=true` as an argument to include runtime attributes, as well as `recursive=true` which provides information about all child resources recursively.

Executing commands with the CLI

As mentioned earlier, the CLI also includes a set of actions that are not bound to your navigation path across the AS tree, but can be issued anywhere to create and modify resources.

For example, the `version` command can be issued to retrieve some basic information about the application server and the environment when WildFly is running:

```
[standalone@localhost:9990 /] version
JBoss Admin Command-line Interface
JBOSS_HOME: /opt/wildfly-8.1.0.Final
JBoss AS release: 8.1.0.Final "Kenny"
JAVA_HOME: /Library/Java/JavaVirtualMachines/jdk1.8.0_05.jdk/Contents/Home
```

```
java.version: 1.8.0_05
java.vm.vendor: Oracle Corporation
java.vm.version: 25.5-b02
os.name: Mac OS X
os.version: 10.8.5
```

In most cases, commands are used as an alias for quickly creating some resources, such as JMS destinations and datasources.

Let's see in the following sections how this can be achieved.

Adding a JMS destination

You can add a JMS queue with the `jms-queue add` command.

> As you can see, one important difference between operations and commands is also the style used to pass parameters. Operations use brackets to pass parameters (for example, `recursive=true`). Commands pass parameters using the format (`--parameter`), as you do in a Unix shell.

The following is the synopsis of the `jms-queue add` command:

```
jms-queue add --queue-address=queue_name
  --entries=jndi-name(,jndi-name)* [--profile=profile_name]
  [--selector=selector_name] [--durable=(true|false)]
```

The only mandatory element here is `queue-address`, which specifies the queue name and the entries with the JNDI names to which the queue will be bound. The optional entries include the `selector` parameter, which can be added to specify a selector on the queue to filter messages, and the `durable` parameter, which specifies whether the queue should be durable or not (the default is `true`). Finally, note the optional `profile` element, which can be used on domain configurations to specify on which `profile` the `queue` will be created.

> Remember to start the server with the `-c standalone-full.xml` arguments in order to have a server configuration that includes the messaging subsystem. If you don't, these commands will result in errors.

The following command creates a new JMS queue (`queue1`), which is bound under the JNDI `queues/queue1` namespace:

```
jms-queue add [--profile=profile_name] --queue-address=queue1
  --entries=java:/jms/queues/queue1
```

The equivalent command to add a JMS topic is `jms-topic add`, which has the following syntax:

```
jms-topic add [--profile=profile_name] --topic-address=topic_name
   [--entries=entry(,entry)*] [--profile=profile_name]
```

This is very similar to the JMS queue, except that the JMS topic has a smaller number of parameters. Neither the `selector` nor the `durable` parameters are required here. Have a look at the following command:

```
jms-topic add [--profile=profile_name]  --topic-address=topic1
   --entries=topics/topic1
```

Creating and modifying datasources

The CLI provides a useful `data-source` command to create datasources. As the syntax of this command is quite lengthy, you may find it useful to save it as a CLI script and adapt it to your needs.

The following is the synopsis of the `data-source` command:

```
data-source [--profile=<profile_name>] add/remove
   --jndi-name=<jndi_name> --driver-name=<driver_name>
   --name=<pool_name>   --connection-url=<connection_url>
```

Except for `profile_name`, all the other parameters shown in the preceding code snippet are mandatory. That is, you need to specify them if you want to add or remove a datasource. As far as parameters are concerned, you need to state, at least, the JNDI name for the datasource (`jndi-name`), the driver name (`driver-name`), the name of the connection pool (`name`), and the connection URL (`connection-url`).

You can further customize the datasource, just as you would do in your `standalone.xml` file, by adding some optional parameters. Let's see a concrete example where we create a MySQL datasource. The first thing we need to do is to provide a JDBC-compliant driver by deploying the JAR archive. Considering you are using standalone mode, just copy the JDBC JAR file into the `deployments` folder. Take a look at the following screenshot:

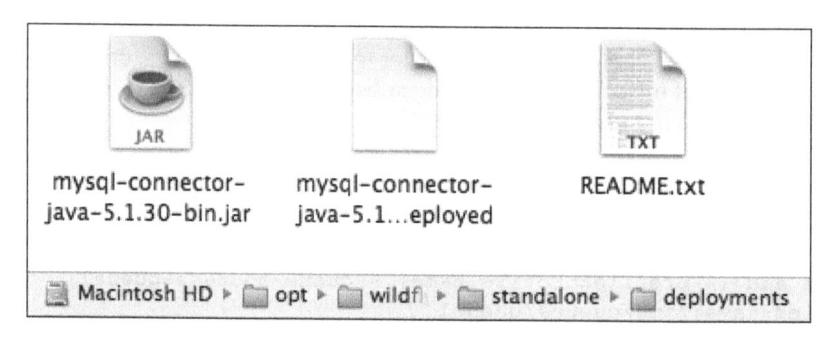

A simpler approach is to deploy the JDBC driver via the command line. Assuming you start the command-line interface from the folder where your driver is housed, you will run the following command:

```
[standalone@localhost:9990 /] deploy ./mysql-connector-java-5.1.30-bin.jar
```

> You can alternatively choose to install the JDBC driver as a module, which is the preferred way. This procedure is shown in *Chapter 3, Configuring Enterprise Services*. For the purpose of this example, we simply deploy the driver, as this expedites the installation procedure.

Now, let's verify that the driver has been correctly installed on the datasource subsystem. We can do this by means of the `installed-drivers-list` command on the datasources subsystem, as follows:

```
[standalone@localhost:9990 /] /subsystem=datasources:installed-drivers-list
{
    "outcome" => "success",
    "result" => [
        {
            "driver-name" =>
              "mysql-connector-java-5.1.30-bin.jar_com.mysql.
              jdbc.Driver_5_1",
            "deployment-name" =>
              "mysql-connector-java-5.1.30-bin.jar_com.
              mysql.jdbc.Driver_5_1",
            "driver-module-name" => undefined,
            "module-slot" => undefined,
            "driver-datasource-class-name" => undefined,
            "driver-xa-datasource-class-name" => undefined,
            "driver-class-name" => "com.mysql.jdbc.Driver",
            "driver-major-version" => 5,
            "driver-minor-version" => 1,
            "jdbc-compliant" => false
        },
        {
            "driver-name" => "h2",
            "deployment-name" => undefined,
```

```
                "driver-module-name" => "com.h2database.h2",
                "module-slot" => "main",
                "driver-datasource-class-name" => "",
                "driver-xa-datasource-class-name" =>
                    "org.h2.jdbcx.JdbcDataSource",
                "driver-class-name" => "org.h2.Driver",
                "driver-major-version" => 1,
                "driver-minor-version" => 3,
                "jdbc-compliant" => true
            }
        ]
    }
```

As you can see, there are now two drivers installed: the default H2 driver and the MySQL driver that we installed previously.

Now, we are ready to create a new datasource using the MySQL JDBC driver:

```
[standalone@localhost:9990 /] data-source
  add --jndi-name=java:/MySqlDS --name=MySQLPool
  --connection-url=jdbc:mysql://localhost:3306/MyDB
  --driver-name=mysql-connector-java-5.1.30-bin.jar_com
  .mysql.jdbc.Driver_5_1 --user-name=myuser --password=password
  --max-pool-size=30
```

In this example, we just created a MySQL-bound datasource using a custom pool size of a maximum of 30 connections.

> You don't have to remember all datasource parameter names. Just use the *Tab* key to autocomplete the parameter name. Also, take care that your driver name matches with that of the output created when you ran the `installed-drivers-list` command.

The `data-source` command can also be used to remove a datasource from the configuration. This can be done by passing the `remove` parameter and the `name` of the `datasource`, as follows:

```
[standalone@localhost:9990 /] data-source remove --name=MySQLPool
```

> You can also add and remove datasources using operations executed on the datasource system resource. See *Appendix, CLI References*, which contains a compendium of the most useful CLI commands.

Creating and modifying XA datasources

Modifying an XA datasource class for your connections is similar to that of a `data-source`. The main difference is that you will use the `xa-data-source` command, as follows:

```
[standalone@localhost:9990 /] xa-data-source add --name=MySQLPoolXA
  --jndi-name=java:/MySqlDSXA --driver-name=
  mysql-connector-java-5.1.30-bin.jar_com.mysql.jdbc.Driver_5_1
  --xa-datasource-properties=[{ServerName=localhost}{PortNumber=3306}]
```

There are three arguments required to create an XA datasource. You need a unique `name`, the `jndi-name`, and finally, the `driver-name`.

This will result in the following code snippet being added to your configuration file:

```
<xa-datasource jndi-name="java:/MySqlDSXA"
    pool-name="MySQLPoolXA" enabled="true">
  <xa-datasource-property name="ServerName">
      localhost
  </xa-datasource-property>
  <xa-datasource-property name="PortNumber">
      3306
  </xa-datasource-property>
  <driver>mysql-connector-java-5.1.30-bin.jar_com.mysql
      .jdbc.Driver_5_1</driver>
</xa-datasource>
```

Getting help from the CLI

If the syntax of CLI commands seem a bit overwhelming to you, don't despair! Besides the tab autocompletion functionality, the CLI has also has a main page for each command, just as the Unix shell does.

If you issue a generic `help` command, the CLI will return a generic quick-start guide to the interface. On the other hand, when passed as an argument to a command, it provides a helpful description of the command synopsis and their arguments. Take a look at the following code snippet:

```
[standalone@localhost:9990 /] cd --help
SYNOPSIS

    cn [node_path]
    cd [node_path]


DESCRIPTION
```

```
      Changes the current node path to the argument.

    The current node path is used as the address for operation requests
that don't contains the address part. If an operation request does
include the address, the included address is considered relative to the
current node path. The current node path may end on a node-type. In that
case, to execute an operation specifying a node-name would be sufficient
(e.g. logging:read-resource).
ARGUMENTS


    node_path       - the new value for the current node path following
                      the format

                    [node-type [=node-name (,node-type[=node-name])*]].

The following navigation signs are supported in the node-path:
  /       - the root node (e.g. 'cd /' or 'cd /some=thing');
  ..      - parent node (e.g. 'cd ..');
  .type   - node type of the current node (e.g. 'cd .type').
```

Executing CLI scripts in batch

The `batch` mode allows the execution of multiple CLI commands as an atomic unit. Just as you would expect from an ordinary transaction, if any of the commands or operations fail, the changes are rolled back. On the other hand, if the execution ends without any error, the changes are committed.

Not every command can be part of a batch. For example, navigation commands such as `cd`, `pwd`, or `help` are excluded because they do not reflect any change to the server configuration.

You can mark the beginning of a batch with the `batch` command. You will know when you are in the `batch` mode because the prompt will be marked by the # sign.

In order to mark the end of a batch sequence, you have to use the `run-batch` command. Once completed, the executed batch will be discarded and the CLI will exit the `batch` mode. Take a look at the following example:

```
[standalone@localhost:9990 /] batch
```

```
[standalone@localhost:9990 /#] jms-queue
  add --queue-address=queue1 --entries=queues/queue1
[standalone@localhost:9990 /#] deploy MDBApplication.jar
[standalone@localhost:9990 /#] run-batch
```

Before executing the batch by typing `run-batch`, you can get the list of all `batch` commands entered so far by issuing the `list-batch` command:

```
[standalone@localhost:9990 /] batch
[standalone@localhost:9990 /#] jms-queue
  add --queue-address=queue1 --entries=queues/queue1
[standalone@localhost:9990 /#] deploy MDBApplication.jar
[standalone@localhost:9990 /] list-batch
#1 jms-queue add --queue-address=queue1 --entries=queues/queue1
#2 deploy MDBApplication.jar
```

Advanced batch commands

Script batching can indeed be more complex than just starting and executing a list of commands. As a matter of fact, by pressing the *Tab* completion key when you are in the `batch` mode, you should see several additional commands available. One of the most useful ones is the `holdback-batch` command, which can be used to temporarily pause the batch of commands, as follows:

```
[standalone@localhost:9990 /# ] holdback-batch
```

In order to continue your batch of commands, just issue the `batch` command again, as follows:

```
[standalone@localhost:9990 /] batch
```

It's even possible to save the batch by assigning a unique name so that you can have multiple save points in your scripts, as follows:

```
[standalone@localhost:9990 /# ] holdback-batch step1
```

Later on, you can continue the execution by specifying the holdback name, as follows:

```
[standalone@localhost:9990 /] batch step1
```

When executed with the `-l` parameter, the `batch` command provides the list of batch files that are held:

```
[standalone@localhost:9990 /] batch -l
step1
```

The following table lists all batch-related commands:

Command	Description
`batch`	This command starts a batch of commands. When the batch is paused, it reactivates the batch.
`list-batch`	This command lists the commands that have been added to the batch.
`run-batch`	This command executes the currently active batch of commands and exits the `batch` mode.
`holdback-batch`	This command saves the currently active batch and exits the `batch` mode, without executing the batch. The held-back batch can later be re-activated by invoking batch commands.
`clear-batch`	This command removes all the existing command lines from the currently active batch. The CLI stays in the `batch` mode after the command is executed.
`discard-batch`	This command discards the currently active batch. All the commands added to the batch will be removed, the batch will be discarded, and the CLI will exit the batch mode.
`edit-batch-line`	This command replaces the existing command line from the currently active batch with the specified line number with the new command line.
`remove-batch-line`	This command removes an existing command line specified with a line number argument from the currently active batch.
`move-batch-line`	This command moves the existing line from the specified position to the new position.

Executing scripts in a file

Until now, we have seen CLI commands as part of an interactive session. You can, however, execute commands in a non-interactive fashion, adding them in a file, just as a shell script. Suppose you created a sample `test.cli` file used to issue a redeploy command:

```
connect
deploy Utility.jar --force
```

Then launch the CLI with the `-file` parameter, as follows:

```
./jboss-cli.sh --file=test.cli
```

Windows users can use the following equivalent:

`jboss-cli.bat --file=test.cli`

> You can pass the `--user` and `--password` arguments to the `jboss-cli.sh` or `jboss-cli.bat` call if you need an authentication on the management interface.

Another way to execute commands in a non-interactive way is by passing the `--commands` parameter to the CLI containing the list of command lines separated by a comma. For example, the previous script can be also be executed this way (Unix users):

`./jboss-xli.sh --commands="connect,deploy Utility.jar --force"`

The equivalent script for Windows users will be as follows:

`jboss-cli.bat --commands="connect,deploy Utility.jar --force"`

We will get the following output:

`'Utility.jar' re-deployed successfully.`

Redirecting non-interactive output

When you execute the CLI in a non-interactive way, you can redirect the output to a file, which would otherwise be printed on the screen. Just as you would do for a shell command, use the > operator to redirect the output:

```
./jboss-cli.sh --file=test.cli > out.log    # Linux
jboss-cli.bat --file=test.cli > out.log     # Windows
```

Taking snapshots of the configuration

Everyone makes mistakes, but many of them are preventable. Whenever you are performing many changes to your configuration, it's always a good idea to save copies of your work. That's where snapshots come in; one of the advantages of using the CLI is the ability to create snapshots of the configuration, which are stored in its `history` folder.

The `history` folder is located just one step under the `configuration` folder. Standalone servers have a `history` folder named `standalone_xml_history` that, at start up, contains the following files:

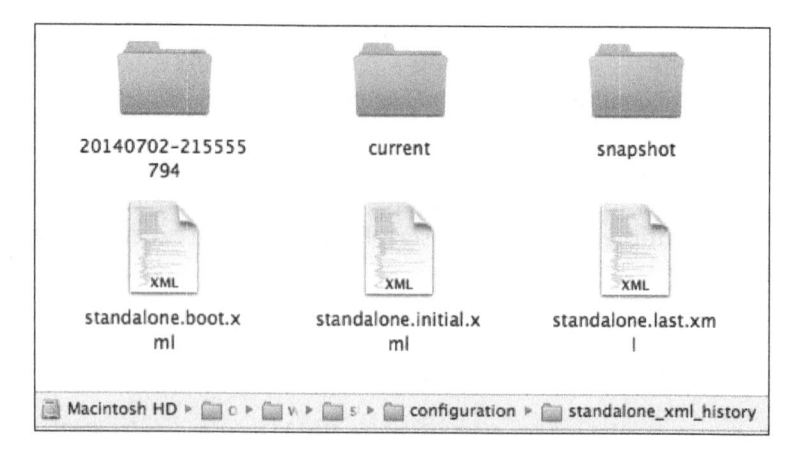

![Screenshot of standalone_xml_history folder showing folders 20140702-215555794, current, snapshot, and files standalone.boot.xml, standalone.initial.xml, standalone.last.xml]

The domain configuration, on the other hand, provides two backup directories both for the domain configuration file and the host configuration file. These folders are named `domain_xml_history` and `host_xml_history`, respectively. To make the reading less verbose, we will describe the snapshot mechanisms using a standalone server. The same rules also apply to domain servers, bearing in mind that the AS takes snapshots of both the `domain.xml` and `host.xml` files.

Let's see now what the history files are about. The `standalone.initial.xml` file contains the original application server's configuration file. This file is never overwritten by WildFly.

> If you need to restore the initial configuration, do not throw away your application server installation! Just replace the `standalone.xml` file with `standalone_xml_history/standalone.initial.xml`.

The `standalone.boot.xml` file contains the AS configuration that was used for the last successful boot of the server. This gets overwritten every time we boot the server successfully.

> If you want to undo all changes in the current session, just replace the `standalone.xml` file with `standalone_xml_history/standalone.boot.xml`.

Finally, the `standalone.last.xml` file contains the last successful configuration committed by the application server.

What the application server saves for you

The `current` folder is used as a temporary folder to store changes in the configuration that happened in the current session. Each change in the application server configuration model will result in the creation of a file named `standalone.v[n].xml`. Here, n is the number of the change that is applied (`standalone.v1.xml` for the initial configuration, `standalone.v2.xml` for the first change, and so on).

When the application server is restarted, these files are moved into a timestamped folder within the `standalone_xml_history` folder. As you can see in the following screenshot, the changes during the last session are moved at reboot into the `20140702-215555794` folder:

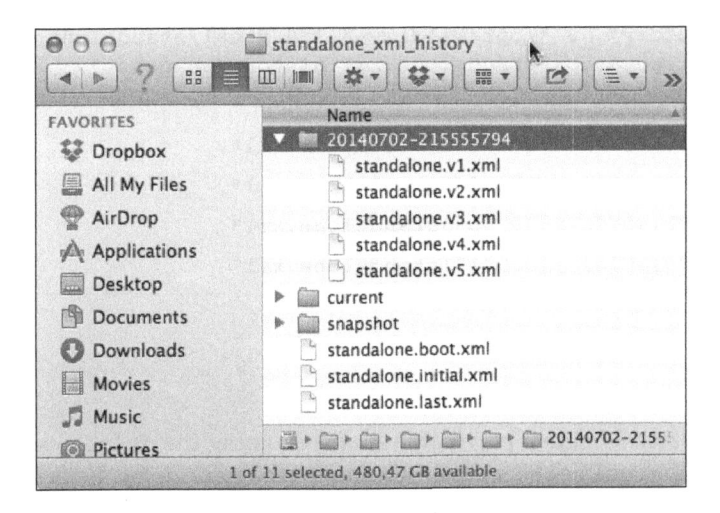

> The timestamped folders are rotated by the application server every 30 days. If you need to store a core view of the application server configuration, you should take snapshots of the application server model. The next section shows how to do this.

Taking your own snapshots

As suggested by the earlier warning, you can also take snapshots on demand, whenever you need it. Snapshots created by the user are stored directly in the `snapshot` folder. In order to take a snapshot of the configuration, just issue the `take-snapshot` command, and the CLI will back up your configuration. Take a look at the following block of code:

```
[standalone@localhost:9990 /] :take-snapshot
{
```

```
    "outcome" => "success",
    "result" => "/opt/wildfly-8.1.0.Final/standalone/configuration/
      standalone_xml_history/snapshot/
      20140702-230647552standalone.xml"
}
```

You can check the list of available snapshots using the `list-snapshots` command:

```
[standalone@localhost:9990 /] :list-snapshots
{
    "outcome" => "success",
    "result" => {
        "directory" => "/opt/wildfly-8.1.0.Final/standalone/
          configuration/standalone_xml_history/snapshot",
        "names" => [
            "20140702-230647552standalone.xml",
            "20140702-230817640standalone.xml",
            "20140702-230825599standalone.xml",
            "20140702-230828191standalone.xml"
        ]
    }
}
```

You can, at any time, delete a particular snapshot using the `delete-snapshot` command, which requires the snapshot name as the parameter. Let's suppose we need to delete the snapshot we just created:

```
[standalone@localhost:9990 /] :delete-snapshot
  (name=20140702-230828191standalone.xml)
{"outcome" => "success"}
```

History of CLI

All commands executed within a CLI session are stored in history, much like shell commands for Unix systems. CLI commands are kept in memory and also persisted on the filesystem in a file named `.jboss-cli-history` in the user's home directory. You will notice that the latest 500 commands (default history size) entered in previous sessions are part of the history.

If you want to have a look at the CLI history, just issue the `history` command:

```
[standalone@localhost:9990 /] history
```

You can also use the arrow keys to navigate back and forth through the history of commands and operations, much like what you do with a Linux bash shell.

The `history` command supports three optional arguments, which can be used to temporarily disable/enable or clear the history. In the following table, we mention their outcome:

Argument	Effect
`disable`	This command disables history expansion (but will not clear the previously recorded history).
`enable`	This command re-enables history expansion (starting from the last recorded command before the history expansion was disabled).
`clear`	This command clears the in-memory history (but not the file one).

The web admin console

Historically, the JBoss AS has always provided a web-based application to perform some administration and management tasks. Versions 4.x and earlier used the `jmx-console` to read/write and display the value of `MBeans`, which were the backbone of the application server. The `jmx-console` was indeed a useful tool; however, it also required some degree of experience to get started with. Besides this, the information contained in this application was fragmented across many `MBeans`. For example, the datasource information was contained in four `MBeans`, thus making it cumbersome to manage this resource.

The 5.x and 6.x release proposed a simpler-to-use approach made up of the admin console, which was built as a seam-based web application. Although the new admin console was a neat and simple application, some criticized it due to the fact that it consumed a good amount of memory and startup time.

WildFly continues to use the web console introduced in JBoss AS 7, which you already saw in a previous chapter. It is built using **Google Web Toolkit** (**GWT**) and uses the HTTP management API to configure a management domain or a standalone server.

Like many GWT applications, the web console uses a JSON-encoded protocol and a de-typed RPC style API to describe and execute management operations against a managed domain or standalone server.

Using the Management Interfaces

Accessing the admin console

WildFly, by default, uses port 9990 to serve the admin console. You can access it at `http://localhost:9990` as configured in your `standalone.xml/domain.xml`:

```
<socket-binding name="management-http" interface="management" port="9990"/>
```

Once you have logged in to the web admin console, you will land on the application home page. In standalone mode, you will see four main tabs: **Home**, **Configuration**, **Runtime**, and **Administration**. These tabs are explained as follows:

- **Home**: This tab contains a brief description of each tab, a variety of quick links to achieve common tasks, and lots of links for other useful resources, as shown in the following screenshot:

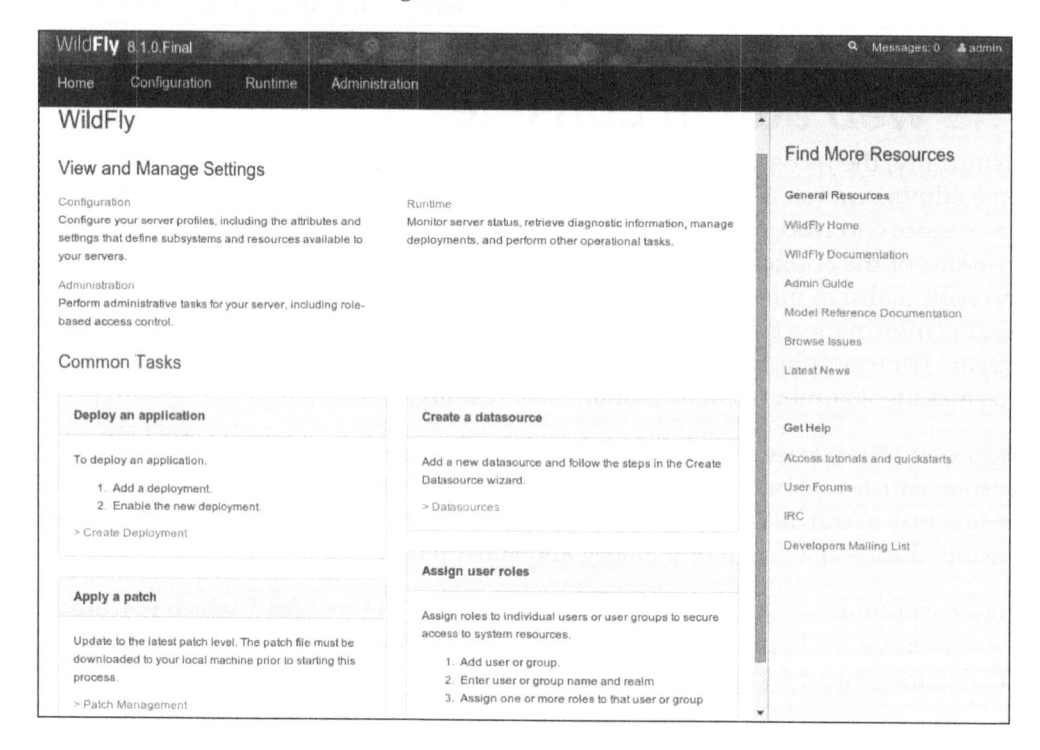

- **Configuration**: This tab can be used to model the application server configuration, as illustrated in the following screenshot:

[218]

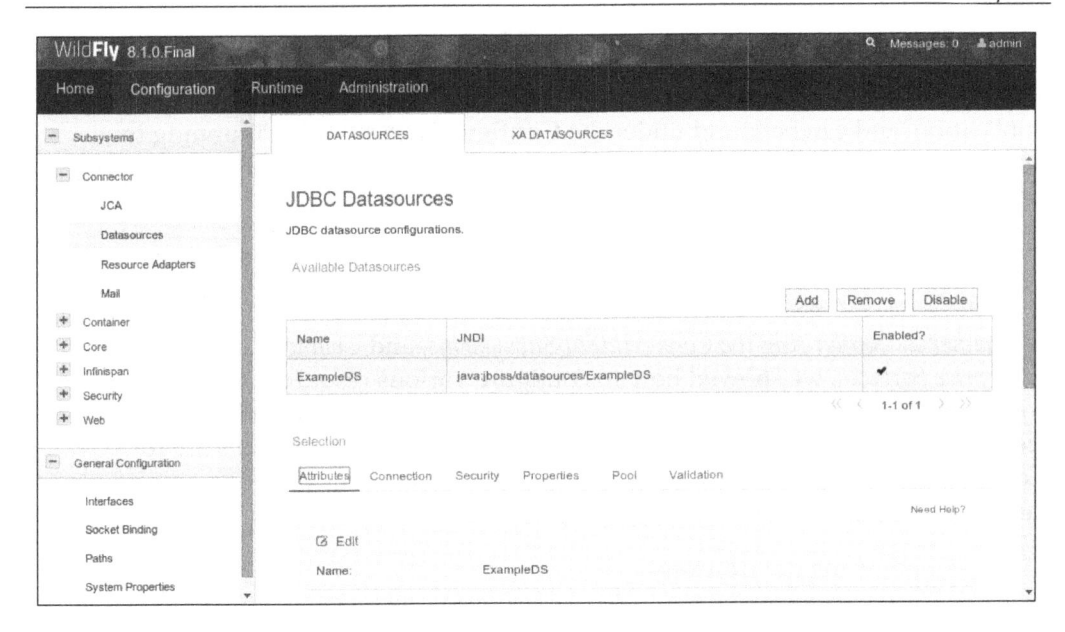

- **Runtime**: This tab can be used to manage deployments, as we learned in *Chapter 6, Application Structure and Deployment*. In the next section, we will show how easy configuring server profiles can be using the web admin console:

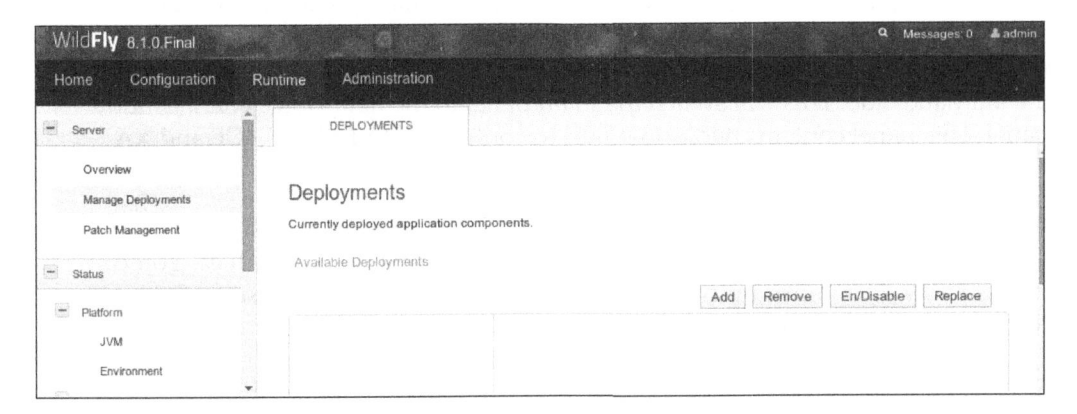

- **Administration**: This tab is used to configure users, groups, and roles. We will cover this section in greater detail in *Chapter 10, Securing WildFly*.

Configuring server profiles

The server profile configuration is located in the left-hand side of the web application, and can be found under the **Configuration** tab. When running the domain mode, you can switch between profiles by choosing the relevant profile from the combobox in the top left-hand corner of the page.

As soon as you open the **Configuration** tab, you will see the set of subsystems that can be configured through the web interface.

In *Chapter 2, Configuring the Core WildFly Subsystems*, and *Chapter 3, Configuring Enterprise Services*, we showed how to configure various resources using the main configuration file. If you are the kind of system administrator who prefers **windows, icons, menus, and pointers (WIMP)** interfaces, then the next sections are for you. Configuring the resources via the web console is pretty intuitive, so to give you a taste, we will just cover the following topics:

- Configuring datasources
- Configuring JMS resources
- Configuring socket-binding groups

Configuring datasources

You can navigate directly to the datasources configuration panel from the list of **Common Tasks** on the homepage. Otherwise, you will need to click on the **Configuration** tab, followed by the **Subsystems | Connector | Datasources** link on the left-hand side. This will switch the main panel to the datasource configuration panel. This panel contains two upper tabs to configure **DATASOURCE** and **XA DATASOURCE**. Let's see what the first tab contains.

In the middle of the panel, you can find the list of configured datasources. The actions that can be applied are located just above the list of datasources. You can create a new datasource by clicking on the **Add** button. You can also find the **Remove** and **Disable** buttons next to the **Add** button.

Editing or deleting an existing datasource is a straightforward task that can be executed with the click of a button. The same can be said about enabling and disabling the selected datasource.

Chapter 7

Here, we will show how to add a new datasource to your standalone configuration, which requires a few simple steps to be completed. Once you click on the **Add** button, a three-step wizard will guide you through the creation of the datasource. Let's configure a sample MySQL datasource for this purpose by performing the following steps:

1. The first information required will be the datasource name and its JNDI binding, as shown in the following screenshot:

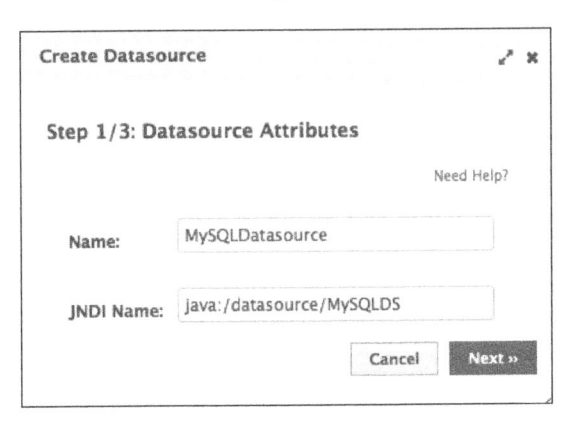

    Create Datasource

    Step 1/3: Datasource Attributes

    Need Help?

    Name: MySQLDatasource

    JNDI Name: java:/datasource/MySQLDS

    Cancel | Next »

2. The next step will be selecting the proper JDBC driver for your datasource. Provided that you have successfully installed a JDBC driver on your AS, you should have it listed as an available driver:

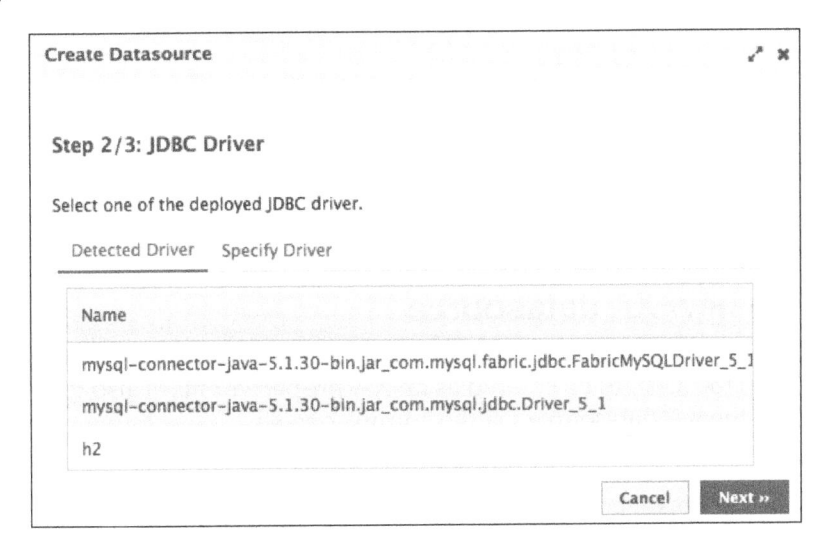

    Create Datasource

    Step 2/3: JDBC Driver

    Select one of the deployed JDBC driver.

    Detected Driver | Specify Driver

Name
mysql-connector-java-5.1.30-bin.jar_com.mysql.fabric.jdbc.FabricMySQLDriver_5_1
mysql-connector-java-5.1.30-bin.jar_com.mysql.jdbc.Driver_5_1
h2

    Cancel | Next »

[221]

3. Choose the MySQL JDBC driver, and in the next (last) step, you will be required to enter the JDBC URL of the datasource along with the **Username** and **Password** credentials, as shown in the following screenshot:

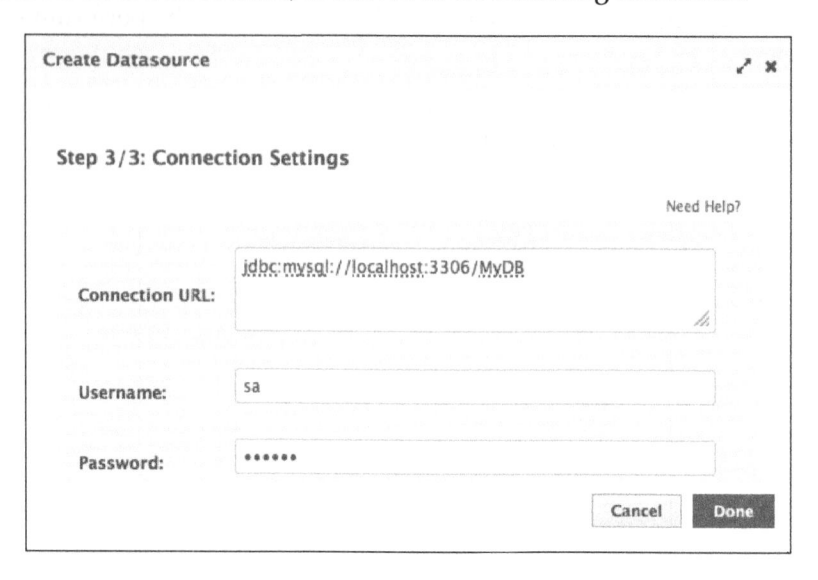

4. Clicking on **Done** completes the wizard, and you will be redirected to the main panel, where the new datasource is now listed in the datasource list. Finally, you will need to enable the new datasource by clicking on it and then clicking on **Enable**:

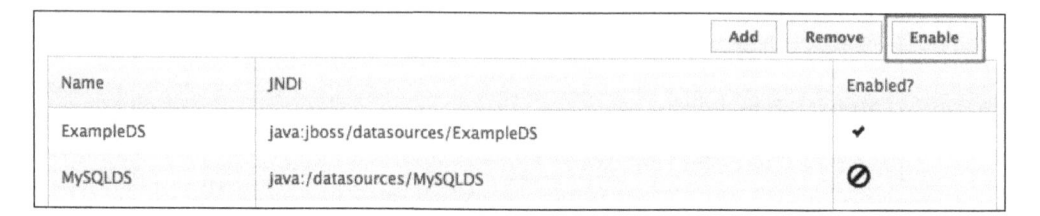

Creating a new XA datasource

As we have shown in the *The command-line interface (CLI)* section, an XA datasource requires your JDBC URL to be entered as an XA property. This is also the case when creating the XA datasource via the admin console.

Thus, the datasource JNDI naming and driver selection stays the same as for non-XA datasources. In the following screenshot, we illustrate the last two steps needed to complete the XA datasource creation:

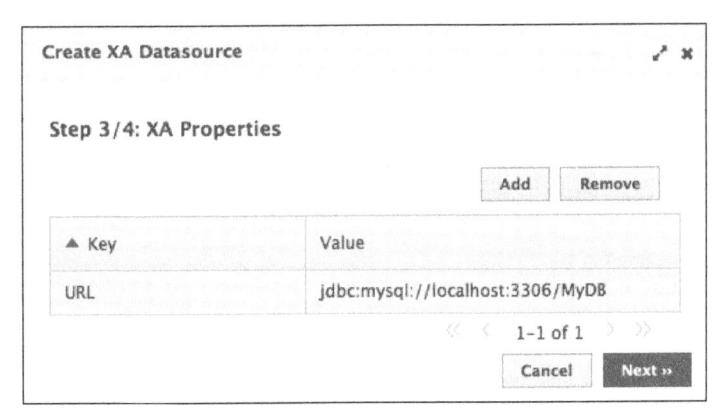

Create XA Datasource

Step 3/4: XA Properties

▲ Key	Value
URL	jdbc:mysql://localhost:3306/MyDB

1-1 of 1

In the fourth step, as shown in the following screenshot, underneath **Username** and **Password**, you will notice the option of adding a security domain. You can leave this blank for now. We will discuss security domains in *Chapter 10, Securing WildFly*.

Create XA Datasource

Step 4/4: Connection Settings

Username: sa

Password: ••••••

Security Domain:

Test Connection

Configuring JMS destinations

Creating new **Queues** and **Topics** using the web console is even more simple. Perform the following steps:

1. From the **Configuration** menu, select the **Messaging** option in the subsystems menu. The main panel will switch to display the **Messaging** providers. Now, select the required provider, and click on **View**:

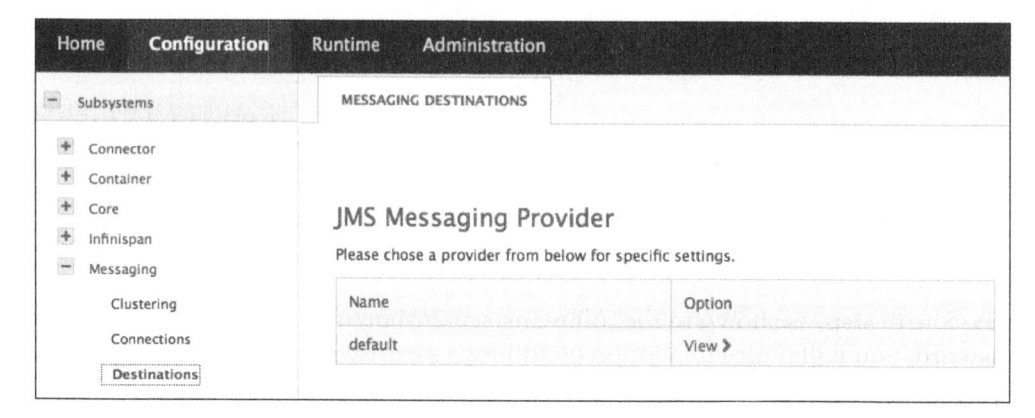

2. From there, select the resource you want to create (**Queue** or **Topic**). Then, click on the **Add** button to create a new one:

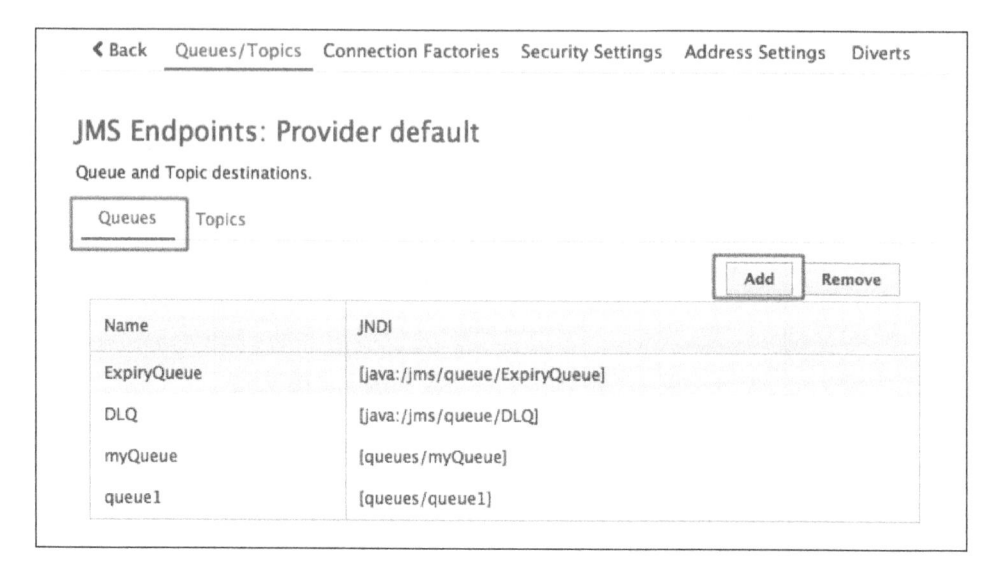

3. If you need to create a new **Queue**, all you have to do is complete the next simple dialog box, which is shown in the following screenshot:

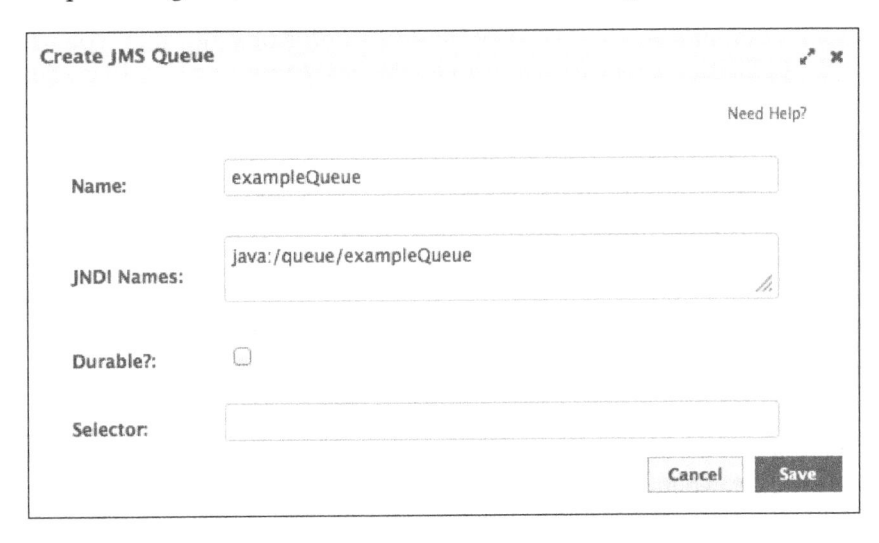

Create JMS Queue

Need Help?

Name: exampleQueue

JNDI Names: java:/queue/exampleQueue

Durable?: ☐

Selector:

Cancel Save

4. When you click on **Save**, the new JMS resource will be enlisted in the JMS subsystem panel (and also be persisted in the main configuration file), as shown in the following screenshot:

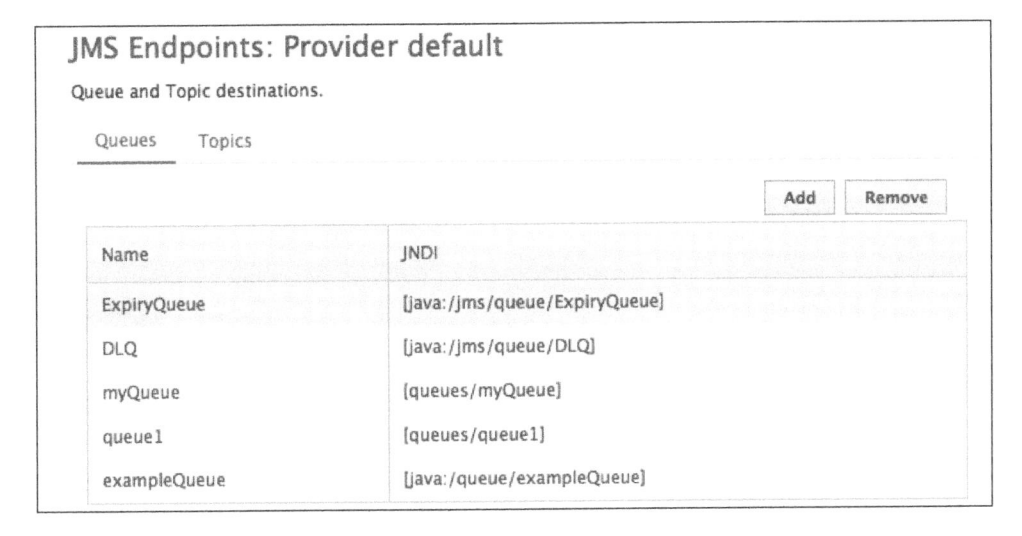

JMS Endpoints: Provider default

Queue and Topic destinations.

Queues Topics

Add Remove

Name	JNDI
ExpiryQueue	[java:/jms/queue/ExpiryQueue]
DLQ	[java:/jms/queue/DLQ]
myQueue	[queues/myQueue]
queue1	[queues/queue1]
exampleQueue	[java:/queue/exampleQueue]

Configuring socket-binding groups

Changing the socket bindings of the application server can be used to solve port conflicts with other applications or even other instances of WildFly. If you are running the application in the `domain` mode, the best thing you can do is specify a port offset for your servers, as pointed out in *Chapter 4, The Undertow Web Server*, which is all about domain servers.

If, however, you are running in the `standalone` mode, and you have to change just one or more port addresses, then it will probably be more easily achievable via the web console.

To reach the **Socket Binding groups** option, perform the following steps:

1. Click on **Socket Binding** on the left-hand side, and then click on **View** for the socket-binding group you want to modify.
2. Then, select the socket binding you want to change, for example, the **http** server port. Then, scroll down to reveal the edit options. Click on the **Edit** button and update the port value, as shown in the following screenshot:

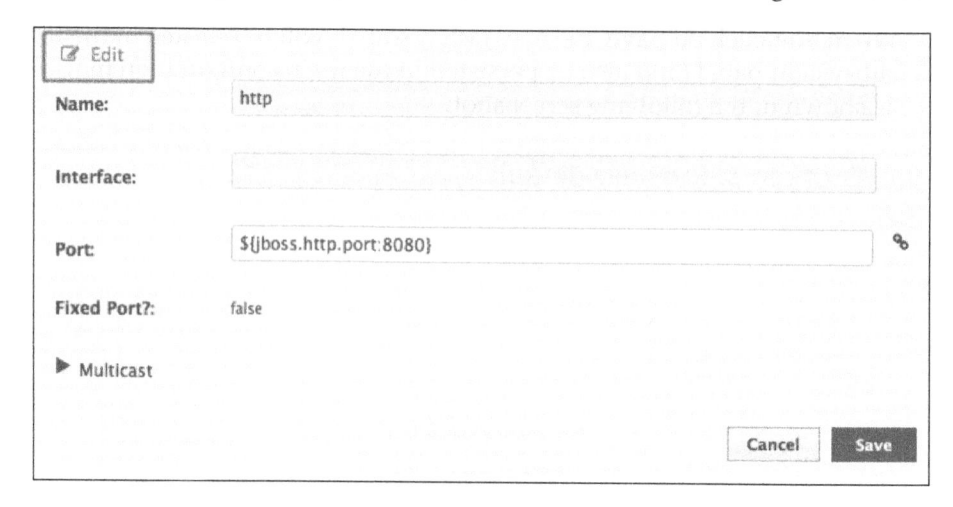

Edit	
Name:	http
Interface:	
Port:	${jboss.http.port:8080}
Fixed Port?:	false
▶ Multicast	

Cancel   Save

3. When you are done, click on the **Save** button.

> **Server restart needed?**
> Changing the socket binding groups does not produce the immediate effect of changing the server port. The updated configuration must be reloaded by the AS. You can simply restart the application server by issuing the `restart` command or, even better, by issuing the `reload` command from the CLI.

The CLI or web console?

Both management interfaces are powerful tools, and in some circumstances, one might be a better choice than another.

For example, the CLI provides a huge addition to the application server, and in a relatively short amount of time, it will let you configure its every resource, including runtime metrics, in fine detail.

On the other hand, the web console provides a simple and elegant way to manage your AS resources with little or no learning curve. In particular, we have shown in *Chapter 3*, *Configuring Enterprise Services*, how it can be easily used to manage the basic domain functionalities, such as configuring, starting, and stopping server groups and hosts.

The following table shows a summary of the main benefits of each interface:

Tool	Best for
CLI	Being an invaluable instrument for an expert system administrator
	Reaching in-depth server attributes, such as metrics
	Performing operations such as macros or batches
Web console	Being a handy tool to perform most basic administration tasks
	Managing top-level domain resources

Summary

In this chapter, you learned how to manage the application server using the tools that are part of the AS distribution.

You became acquainted with the CLI, which allows you to traverse the tree of AS resources and issue commands that can read/modify or display attributes.

One of the advantages of the CLI is that you can easily build complex management operations, thanks to its autocomplete functionality. The CLI also allows you to enlist commands in a batch so that you can execute them in an all-or-nothing fashion, which is typical of transactional systems.

The other management tool is the web interface, which allows you to operate on the server configuration using an intuitive and simple interface. For system administrators that need to perform basic administration tasks, it's an ideal tool, as it requires little or no experience to use it.

At this point, you have enough expertise to handle more complex topics. So, in the next chapter, we will discuss application server clustering, which allows you to provide scalability and high availability to your applications.

8
Clustering

This chapter will cover WildFly's clustering capabilities. The term cluster is used to describe a system split over several machines. Having the components of a system synchronize over multiple machines generally improves performance and availability.

Clustering serves as an essential component to providing scalability and high availability to your applications. One major benefit of using clustering is that you can spread the traffic load across several AS instances via **load balancing**.

Load balancing is an orthogonal aspect of your enterprise application and is generally achieved by using a properly configured web server in front of the application server. For this reason, load balancing is discussed in the next chapter while, in this chapter, we will discuss the following topics:

- All available options to set up a WildFly cluster either using a standalone configuration or a domain of servers
- How to effectively configure the various components required for clustering
- The **JGroups** subsystem, which is used for the underlying communication between nodes
- The **Infinispan** subsystem, which handles the cluster consistency using its advanced data grid platform
- The **Messaging** subsystem, which uses the HornetQ clusterable implementation

Setting up a WildFly cluster

For the benefit of impatient readers, we will immediately show you how to get a cluster of WildFly nodes up and running.

All you have to do to shape a new server profile is create a new XML configuration file. As the standalone server holds just a single profile, you will likely want to use either the configuration file named `standalone-ha.xml` or `standalone-full-ha.xml`. Both of these ship with WildFly. This configuration file contains all the clustering subsystems.

On the other hand, a domain server is able to store multiple profiles in the core `domain.xml` configuration file, hence you can use this file both for clustered domains and for nonclustered domain servers.

> Clustering and domains are two separate concepts, the functionality of each does not overlap. While the aim of clustering is to provide scalability, load balancing, and high availability, a domain is a logical grouping of servers that share a centralized domain configuration and can be managed as a single unit.

We will now describe the different ways to assemble and start a cluster of standalone servers and domain servers.

Setting up a cluster of standalone servers

Configuring WildFly clusters for standalone servers can be broken down into two main possibilities:

- A cluster of WildFly nodes running on different machines
- A cluster of WildFly nodes running on the same machine

We will look at each of these in turn.

A cluster of nodes running on different machines

If you decide to install each WildFly server on a dedicated machine, you are *horizontally scaling* your cluster. In terms of configuration, this requires the least effort—all you have to do is bind the server to its IP address in the configuration file, and start the server using the `standalone-ha.xml` configuration. Let's build an example with a simple, two-node cluster as illustrated in the following figure:

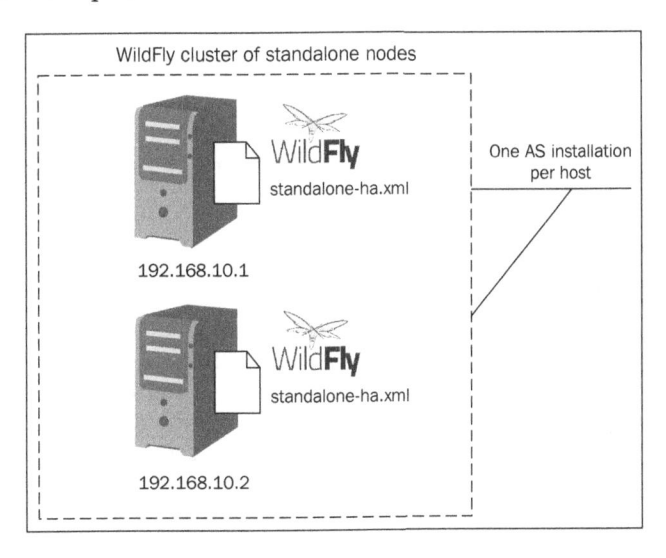

Open the `standalone-ha.xml` file on each WildFly distribution, and navigate to the `interfaces` section. Within the nested interface element, insert the IP address of the standalone server. For the first machine (`192.168.10.1`), we will define the following:

```xml
<interfaces>
        <interface name="management">
            <inet-address value="192.168.10.1"/>
        </interface>
        <interface name="public">
            <inet-address value="192.168.10.1"/>
        </interface>
</interfaces>
```

On the second machine (`192.168.10.2`), we will bind to the other IP address:

```xml
<interfaces>
        <interface name="management">
            <inet-address value="192.168.10.2"/>
        </interface>
        <interface name="public">
            <inet-address value="192.168.10.2"/>
        </interface>
</interfaces>
```

This is the only thing you need to change in your configuration. To start the cluster, you have to start your standalone server using the `standalone-ha.xml` configuration file as follows:

./standalone.sh -c standalone-ha.xml

> Rather than updating the `standalone-ha.xml` file with the IP address of each server, you can use the `-b` option, which allows you to provide the binding IP address on server startup. In addition, you can use the `-bmanagement` flag to specify the management-interface address. Using these options, the previous configuration for the first server can be rewritten as:
>
> standalone.sh -c standalone-ha.xml -b 192.168.10.1
>   -bmanagement 192.168.10.1
>
> For the second server, it can be rewritten as:
>
> standalone.sh -c standalone-ha.xml -b 192.168.10.2
>   -bmanagement 192.168.10.2

Within a few seconds, your servers will be running; however, we have not mentioned any details relating to clustering nodes in the console. This is because, in WildFly, the core services are only started on demand. This means the clustering services are started only when the server detects that they are required and are stopped when no longer required. Hence, simply starting the server with a configuration that includes the clustering subsystems will not initiate the clustering services. To do this, we will need to deploy a cluster-enabled application.

So, in order to verify our installation, we will deploy a bare-bones, cluster-enabled, web application named `Example.war`. To enable clustering of your web applications, you must mark them as *distributable* in the `web.xml` descriptor:

```xml
<web-app>
   <distributable/>
</web-app>
```

When you have deployed the application to both machines, you will see that the clustering services are now started and that each machine is able to find other members within the cluster, as follows:

```
15:33:40,526 INFO  [org.hibernate.hql.internal.ast.ASTQueryTranslatorFactory] (ServerService Thread Pool -- 54) HHH000397: Using ASTQueryTranslatorFactory
15:33:42,094 INFO  [org.infinispan.remoting.transport.jgroups.JGroupsTransport] (ServerService Thread Pool -- 55) ISPN000094: Received new cluster view: [packtpub-server2/web|0] (1) [packtpub-server2/web]
15:33:42,118 INFO  [org.infinispan.remoting.transport.jgroups.JGroupsTransport] (ServerService Thread Pool -- 55) ISPN000079: Cache local address is packtpub-server2/web, physical addresses are [188.226.238.227:55200]
15:33:42,136 INFO  [org.infinispan.factories.GlobalComponentRegistry] (ServerService Thread Pool -- 55) ISPN000128: Infinispan version: Infinispan 'Infinium' 6.0.2.Final
15:33:42,798 INFO  [org.infinispan.jmx.CacheJmxRegistration] (ServerService Thread Pool -- 56) ISPN000031: MBeans were successfully registered to the platform MBean server.
15:33:42,803 INFO  [org.infinispan.jmx.CacheJmxRegistration] (ServerService Thread Pool -- 54) ISPN000031: MBeans were successfully registered to the platform MBean server.
15:33:42,858 INFO  [org.jboss.as.clustering.infinispan] (ServerService Thread Pool -- 54) JBAS010281: Started default-host/chapter4 cache from web container
15:33:42,866 INFO  [org.jboss.as.clustering.infinispan] (ServerService Thread Pool -- 56) JBAS010281: Started dist cache from web container
15:33:43,167 INFO  [javax.enterprise.resource.webcontainer.jsf.config] (MSC service thread 1-2) Initializing Mojarra 2.2.6-jbossorg-4 20140501-1134 for context '/chapter4'
15:33:44,354 INFO  [org.wildfly.extension.undertow] (MSC service thread 1-2) JBAS017534: Registered web context: /chapter4
```

A cluster of nodes running on the same machine

The second variant of the standalone configuration comes into play when your server nodes are located (all or some of them) on the same machine. This scenario generally applies when you are scaling your architecture *vertically* by adding more hardware resources to your computer.

Configuring server nodes on the same machine obviously requires duplicating your WildFly distribution on your filesystem. In order to avoid port conflicts between server distributions, you have to choose between the following two options:

- Define multiple IP address on the same machine
- Define a port offset for each server distribution

Setting up a cluster on the same machine using multiple IP addresses

This is also known as **multihoming** and requires a small amount of configuration to get working. Each operating system uses a different approach to achieve this. Illustrating the possible ways to configure multihoming is outside the scope of this book but, if you are interested in multihoming, we have provided links with detailed instructions on how to set up multihoming on Linux and Windows.

If you are using Linux, this tutorial describes in detail how to assign multiple IPs to a single network interface, also known as **IP aliasing**:

http://www.tecmint.com/create-multiple-ip-addresses-to-one-single-network-interface/

Windows users can refer to the following blog that details how to set up multihoming in Windows 7:

http://shaheerart.blogspot.com/2011/05/how-to-configure-multihomed-server-in.html

Once you have set up your network interface correctly, you will need to update your `standalone-ha.xml` file. You need to bind each IP to a different WildFly instance, just as we did when setting up the multiple-host cluster. Within the configuration file, navigate to the `interfaces` section and, within the nested `interface` element, insert the IP address to be bound to that standalone server:

```xml
<interfaces>
    <interface name="management">
        <inet-address value="192.168.10.2"/>
    </interface>
    <interface name="public">
        <inet-address value="192.168.10.2"/>
    </interface>
</interfaces>
```

In this example, the first server distribution is bound to the IP Address `192.168.10.1` and the second one to `192.168.10.2`. (remember that you can also use the `-b` and `-bmanagement` switches described earlier).

The following figure depicts this scenario:

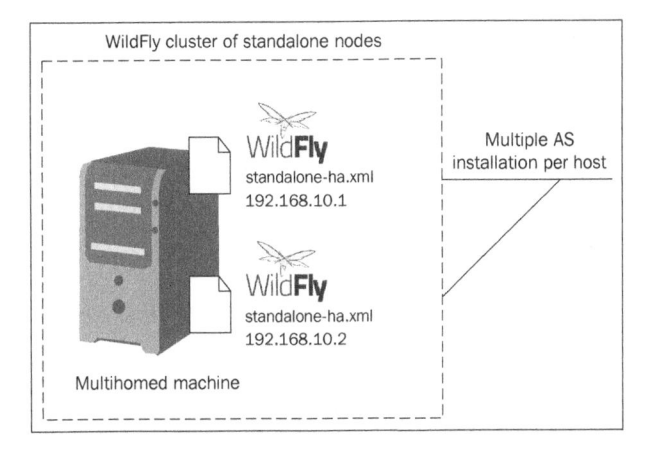

Setting up a cluster on the same machine using port offset

Configuring multihoming is not always a viable choice, as it requires a relative amount of network administration experience. A simpler and more straightforward option is to define a port offset for each of your cluster members. By defining a port offset for each server, all the default-server binding interfaces will shift by a fixed number, hence you will not have two servers running on the same ports, causing port conflicts.

When using port offset, you will bind each server to the same IP address. So, for all your server distributions, you will configure the `standalone-ha.xml` file as follows:

```
<interfaces>
        <interface name="management">
            <inet-address value="192.168.10.1"/>
        </interface>
        <interface name="public">
            <inet-address value="192.168.10.1"/>
        </interface>
</interfaces>
```

You will then leave the first server configuration unchanged. It will use the default socket-binding ports:

```
<socket-binding-group name="standard-sockets" default-
interface="public" port-offset="0">
...
</socket-binding-group>
```

Clustering

For the second server configuration, you will specify a `port-offset` value of `150`:

```
<socket-binding-group name="standard-sockets" default-
interface="public" port-offset="150"
...
</socket-binding-group>
```

Your cluster configuration is now complete. You can verify this by starting each server distribution by passing it as an argument to the configuration file as follows:

`standalone.sh -c standalone-ha.xml`

From the following screenshot, you can see that a port offset of 150 has been applied:

```
21:31:29,232 INFO  [org.wildfly.extension.undertow] (MSC service thread 1-4) JBAS017531: Host de
fault-host starting
21:31:29,308 INFO  [org.wildfly.extension.undertow] (MSC service thread 1-5) JBAS017519: Underto
w AJP listener ajp listening on /127.0.0.1:8159
21:31:29,308 INFO  [org.wildfly.extension.undertow] (MSC service thread 1-6) JBAS017519: Underto
w HTTP listener default listening on /127.0.0.1:8230
21:31:29,327 INFO  [org.jboss.modcluster] (ServerService Thread Pool -- 54) MODCLUSTER000001: In
itializing mod_cluster version 1.3.0.Final
21:31:29,413 INFO  [org.jboss.modcluster] (ServerService Thread Pool -- 54) MODCLUSTER000032: Li
stening to proxy advertisements on /224.0.1.105:23364
```

Setting up a cluster of domain servers

When you are configuring a domain cluster, you will find that the clustering subsystems are already included within the main configuration file `domain.xml`.

As a matter of fact, the WildFly domain deals with clustering just as another profile used by the application server. Opening the `domain.xml` file, you will see that the application server ships with the following four profiles:

- The `default` profile for nonclustered environments
- The `ha` profile for clustered environments
- The `full` profile with all the subsystems for nonclustered environments
- The `full-ha` profile with all the subsystems for clustered environments

So, in order to use clustering on a domain, you have to first configure your server groups to point to one of the `ha` profiles.

Let's look at an example configuration that uses two server groups. The following code snippet is from `domain.xml`:

```xml
<server-groups>
    <server-group name="main-server-group" profile="ha">
        <jvm name="default">
            <heap size="64m" max-size="512m"/>
        </jvm>
            <socket-binding-group ref="ha-sockets"/>
    </server-group>
    <server-group name="other-server-group" profile="ha">
        <jvm name="default">
            <heap size="64m" max-size="512m"/>
        </jvm>
        <socket-binding-group ref="ha-sockets"/>
    </server-group>
</server-groups>
```

As highlighted in the `socket-binding-group` element, we are referencing the `ha-sockets` group, which contains all socket bindings used for the cluster. Have a look at the following code:

```xml
<socket-binding-group name="ha-sockets" default-interface="public">
    <socket-binding name="ajp" port="8009"/>
    <socket-binding name="http" port="8080"/>
    <socket-binding name="https" port="8443"/>
    <socket-binding name="jgroups-mping" port="0" multicast-
        address="230.0.0.4" multicast-port="45700"/>
    <socket-binding name="jgroups-tcp" port="7600"/>
    <socket-binding name="jgroups-tcp-fd" port="57600"/>
    <socket-binding name="jgroups-udp" port="55200" multicast-
        address="230.0.0.4" multicast-port="45688"/>
    <socket-binding name="jgroups-udp-fd" port="54200"/>
    <socket-binding name="modcluster" port="0" multicast-
        address="224.0.1.105" multicast-port="23364"/>
    <socket-binding name="txn-recovery-environment" port="4712"/>
    <socket-binding name="txn-status-manager" port="4713"/>
    <outbound-socket-binding name="mail-smtp">
        <remote-destination host="localhost" port="25"/>
    </outbound-socket-binding>
</socket-binding-group>
```

Clustering

Next, we need to define the servers that are part of the domain (and of the cluster). To keep things simple, we will reuse the domain server list that is found in the default `host.xml` file, as shown in the following code snippet:

```xml
<servers>
    <server name="server-one" group="main-server-group">
        <jvm name="default">
    </server>
    <server name="server-two" group="main-server-group" auto-start="true">
        <socket-bindings port-offset="150"/>
    </server>
    <server name="server-three" group="other-server-group" auto-start="false">
        <socket-bindings port-offset="250"/>
    </server>
</servers>
```

We do not need to specify the socket-binding group for each server, as this was configured in the `domain.xml` file. If we want to override the socket-binding group, then we can add the following to the `host.xml` file:

```xml
<servers>
    ...
    <server name="server-one" group="other-server-group" auto-start="false">
        <socket-bindings socket-binding-group="ha-sockets"/>
    </server>
</servers>
```

The following figure shows an overview of this configuration:

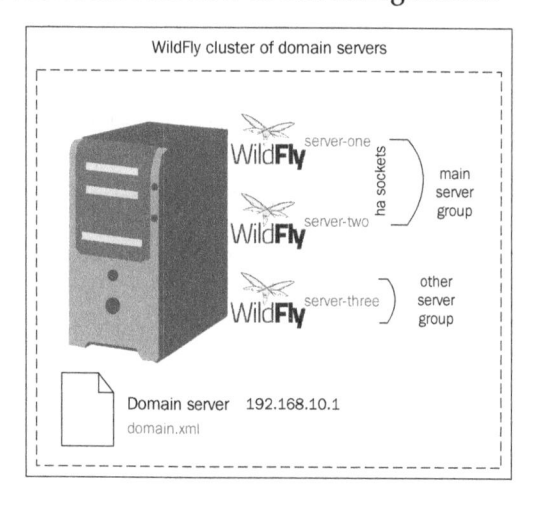

Your clustered domain can now be started using the standard batch script (`domain.sh` or `domain.bat`). The server groups will now point to the ha profile and form a cluster of two nodes.

Troubleshooting the cluster

Communication via nodes in a cluster is achieved via UDP and multicasts.

> A multicast is a protocol by which data is transmitted simultaneously to all hosts that are part of the multicast group. You can think about multicast as a radio channel where only those tuned to a particular frequency receive the data.

If you are having problems, typically it is due to one of the following reasons:

- The nodes are behind a firewall. If your nodes are on different machines, then it is possible that the firewall is blocking the multicasts. you can test this by disabling the firewall for each node or adding the appropriate rules.
- You are using a home network or are behind a gateway. Typically, home networks will redirect any UDP traffic to the **Internet Service Provider (ISP)**, which is then either dropped by the ISP or just lost. To fix this, you will need to add a route to the firewall/gateway that will redirect any multicast traffic back on to the local network instead.

> **Mac OS X**
>
> If you are using a Mac, you may get a **java.io.IOException: Network is unreachable** error when trying to start a domain in the ha mode. To get around this, you will need to create a proper network route to use UDP as follows:
>
> `sudo route add 224.0.0.0 127.0.0.1 -netmask 240.0.0.0`

To allow you to check whether your machine is set up correctly for multicast, JGroups ships with two test applications that can be used to test IP multicast communication. The test classes are `McastReceiverTest` and `McastSenderTest`.

In order to test multicast communication on your server, you should first navigate to the location of the jgroups JAR within the modules directory, shown here:

`JBOSS_HOME/modules/system/layers/base/org/jgroups/main`

Within this directory, you will find `jgroups-3.4.3.Final.jar`, which contains the test programs.

Clustering

Now, run the `McastReceiverTest` by running the following command:

```
java -classpath jgroups-3.4.3.Final.jar org.jgroups.tests.
McastReceiverTest -mcast_addr 224.10.10.10 -port 5555
```

On the same machine, but in a different terminal, run the `McastSenderTest` command, as follows:

```
java -classpath jgroups-3.4.3.Final.jar org.jgroups.tests.McastSenderTest
-mcast_addr 224.10.10.10 -port 5555
```

If multicast works correctly, you should be able to type in the `McastSenderTest` window and see the output in the `McastReceiverTest` window, as shown in the following screenshot:

You should perform this test on each machine in the cluster. Once you have done this, you need to ensure that UDP communication works between each machine in the cluster by running `McastSenderTest` on one machine and `McastReceiverTest` on the other.

Finally, if you are experiencing issues with the default multicast address or port, you can change it by modifying the `jgroups-udp` socket-binding group within the `domain.xml` file:

```
<socket-binding-groups>
    ...
    <socket-binding-group name="ha-sockets"
      default-interface="public">
        ...
        <socket-binding name="jgroups-udp" port="55200"
            multicast-address="${jboss.default.multicast.
              address:230.0.0.4}"
            multicast-port="45688"/>
        ...
    </socket-binding-group>
</socket-binding-groups>
```

Configuring the WildFly cluster

WildFly supports clustering out of the box. There are several libraries that work together to provide support for clustering. The following figure shows the basic clustering architecture adopted by WildFly:

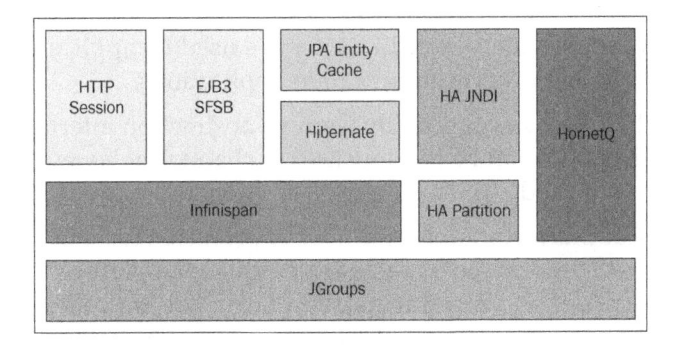

The JGroups library is core to WildFly clustering. It provides the communication channels between nodes of the cluster using a multicast transmission. These channels are created upon deployment of a clustered application and are used to transmit sessions and contexts around the cluster.

Another important component of clustering is **Infinispan**. Infinispan handles the replication of your application data across the cluster by means of a distributed cache.

Configuring the JGroups subsystem

Within the realm of JGroups, nodes are commonly referred to as **members**, and clusters are referred to as **groups**.

A node is a process running on a host. JGroups keeps track of all processes within a group. When a node joins a group, the system sends a message to all existing members of that group. Likewise, when a node leaves or crashes, all the other nodes of that group are notified.

As we outlined earlier in the chapter, the processes (nodes) of a group can be located on the same host, or on different machines on a network. A member can also be part of multiple groups. The following figure illustrates a detailed view of JGroups architecture:

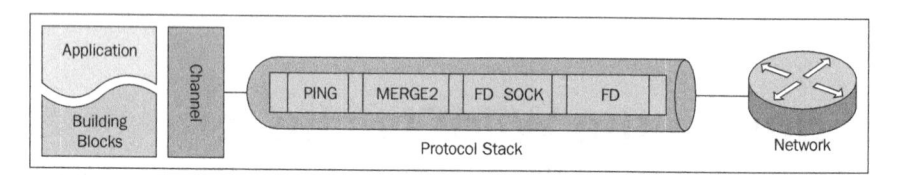

A JGroups process broadly consists of three parts, namely a **Channel**, the **Building Blocks**, and the **Protocol Stack**.

- A **Channel** is a simple socket-like interface used by application programmers to build reliable group communication applications.
- The **Building Blocks** collectively form an abstraction interface layered on top of channels, which can be used instead of channels whenever a higher level interface is required.
- The **Protocol Stack** contains a number of protocol layers in a bidirectional list. All messages sent have to pass through all the protocols. A layer does not *necessarily* correspond to a transport protocol. For example, a fragmentation layer might break up a message into several smaller messages, adding a header with an ID to each fragment, and reassemble the fragments on the receiver's side.

In the previous figure, when sending a message, the PING protocol is executed first, then MERGE2, followed by FD_SOCK, and finally, the FD protocol. When the message is received, this order would be reversed, which means that it would meet the FD protocol first, then FD_SOCK, followed by MERGE2, and finally up to PING. In WildFly, the JGroups configuration is found within the JGroups subsystem in the main standalone-ha.xml/domain.xml configuration file.

Within the JGroups subsystem, you can find the list of configured transport stacks. The following code snippet shows the default UDP stack used for communication between nodes:

```
<subsystem xmlns="urn:jboss:domain:jgroups:2.0" default-stack="udp">
    <stack name="udp">
        <transport type="UDP" socket-binding="jgroups-udp"/>
        <protocol type="PING"/>
        <protocol type="MERGE3"/>
        <protocol type="FD_SOCK" socket-binding="jgroups-udp-fd"/>
        <protocol type="FD_ALL"/>
        <protocol type="VERIFY_SUSPECT"/>
        <protocol type="pbcast.NAKACK2"/>
        <protocol type="UNICAST3"/>
        <protocol type="pbcast.STABLE"/>
        <protocol type="pbcast.GMS"/>
        <protocol type="UFC"/>
        <protocol type="MFC"/>
        <protocol type="FRAG2"/>
        <protocol type="RSVP"/>
    </stack>
    ...
</subsystem>
```

UDP is the default protocol for JGroups and uses multicast (or, if not available, multiple unicast messages) to send and receive messages. A multicast UDP socket can send and receive datagrams from multiple clients. Another feature of multicast is that a client can contact multiple servers with a single packet, without knowing the specific IP address of any of the hosts.

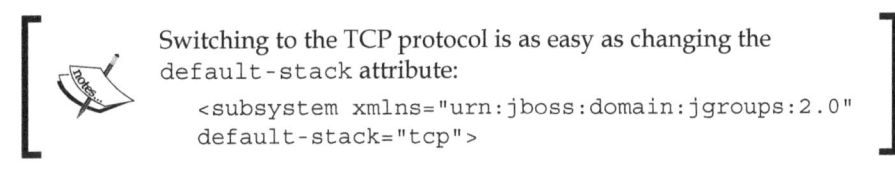

> Switching to the TCP protocol is as easy as changing the `default-stack` attribute:
> ```
> <subsystem xmlns="urn:jboss:domain:jgroups:2.0"
> default-stack="tcp">
> ```

TCP stacks are typically used when IP multicasting cannot be used for some reason. For example, when you want to create a network over a WAN. We will cover TCP configuration later in this chapter.

Clustering

A detailed description of all JGroups protocols is beyond the scope of this book but, for convenience, you can find a short description of each in the following table. To find out more about these protocols, or about JGroups, you can refer to the JGroups site at `http://jgroups.org/manual/html/index.html`.

Category	Usage	Protocols
Transport	This is responsible for sending and receiving messages across the network	`IDP`, `TCP`, and `TUNNEL`
Discovery	This is used to discover active nodes in the cluster and determine who the coordinator is	`PING`, `MPING`, `TCPPING`, and `TCPGOSSIP`
Failure detection	This one is used to poll cluster nodes to detect node failures	`FD`, `FD_SIMPLE`, `FD_PING`, `FD_ICMP`, `FD_SOCK`, and `VERIFY_SUSPECT`
Reliable delivery	This ensures that messages are actually delivered in the right order (FIFO) to the destination node	`CAUSAL`, `NAKACK`, `pbcast.NAKACK`, `SMACK`, `UNICAST`, and `PBCAST`
Group membership	This is used to notify the cluster when a node joins, leaves, or crashes	`pbcast.GMS`, `MERGE`, `MERGE2`, and `VIEW_SYNC`
Flow control	This is used to adapt the data-sending rate to the data-receipt rate among the nodes	`FC`
Fragmentation	This fragments messages larger than a certain size and unfragments them at the receiver's side	`FRAG2`
State transfer	This one synchronizes the application state (serialized as a byte array) from an existing node with a newly-joining node	`pbcast.STATE_TRANSFER` and `pbcast.STREAMING_STATE_TRANSFER`

Customizing the protocol stack

If you want to customize your transport configuration at a lower level, then you can override the default properties used by JGroups or even the single protocol properties. For example, the following configuration can be used to change the default send or receive buffer used by the JGroups UDP stack:

```
<subsystem xmlns="urn:jboss:domain:jgroups:2.0"
  default-stack="udp">
```

```xml
<stack name="udp">
  <transport type="UDP" socket-binding="jgroups-udp"
    diagnostics-socket-binding="jgroups-diagnostics">
    <property name="ucast_recv_buf_size">50000000</property>
    <property name="ucast_send_buf_size">1280000</property>
    <property name="mcast_recv_buf_size">50000000</property>
    <property name="mcast_send_buf_size">1280000</property>
  </transport>
  ...
</stack>
</subsystem>
```

If you want to have a look at all the properties available within the JGroups subsystem, either at transport level or at the protocol level, you can consult the JGroups XSD file, `jboss-as-jgroups_2_0.xsd`, found in the `JBOSS_HOME/docs/schema` folder of your server distribution.

Configuring the Infinispan subsystem

One of the requirements of a cluster is that data is synchronized across its members. This is because, should there be a failure of a node, the application and its session can continue on other members of the cluster. This is known as **High Availability**.

WildFly uses Infinispan as the distributed caching solution behind its clustering functionality. Although Infinispan is embedded within the application server, it can also be used as a standalone data-grid platform.

We will now quickly look at Infinispan's configuration, which is found in the Infinispan subsystem within the main `standalone-ha.xml` or `domain.xml` configuration file.

The following is the backbone of the Infinispan configuration:

```xml
<subsystem xmlns="urn:jboss:domain:infinispan:2.0">
  <cache-container name="server" aliases=
    "singleton cluster" default-cache="default" module=
    "org.wildfly.clustering.server">
  <transport lock-timeout="60000"/>
  <replicated-cache name="default" mode="SYNC" batching="true">
      <locking isolation="REPEATABLE_READ"/>
  </replicated-cache>
  </cache-container>
```

```
<cache-container name="web" default-cache="dist"
  module="org.wildfly.clustering.web.infinispan">
    ...
</cache-container>
<cache-container name="ejb" aliases="sfsb" default-cache=
  "dist" module="org.wildfly.clustering.ejb.infinispan">
    ...
</cache-container>
<cache-container name="hibernate" default-cache=
  "local-query" module="org.hibernate">
    ...
</cache-container>
</subsystem>
```

One of the key differences between the standalone Infinispan configuration and the Infinispan subsystem within WildFly is that the WildFly configuration exposes multiple `cache-container` elements, while the native configuration file contains configurations for a single cache container.

Each `cache-container` element contains one or more caching policies, which define how data is synchronized for that specific cache container. The following caching strategies can be used by cache containers:

- **Local**: In this caching mode, the entries are stored on the local node only, regardless of whether a cluster has formed. Infinispan typically operates as a local cache.
- **Replication**: In this caching mode, all entries are replicated to all nodes. Infinispan typically operates as a temporary data store and doesn't offer increased heap space.
- **Distribution**: In this caching mode, the entries are distributed to a subset of the nodes only. Infinispan typically operates as a data grid providing increased heap space.
- **Invalidation**: In this caching mode, the entries are stored in a cache store only (such as a database) and invalidated from all nodes. When a node needs the entry, it will load it from a cache store. In this mode, Infinispan operates as a distributed cache, backed by a canonical data store, such as a database.

In the following sections, we will have a more detailed look at some of the cache configurations, such as `session` caches (the `web` cache and the `SFSB` cache) and the `hibernate` cache. Understanding these is essential if you are to configure your clustered applications properly.

Configuring session cache containers

In this section, we will look at the caching configuration for the HTTP session and for stateful and singleton-session beans. The way the caches are configured for these three is very similar. For this reason, we will discuss them together and show the similarities between them. So, here is the `cache-container` configuration for the `web` cache, the `ejb` cache, and the `server` cache. The `web` cache refers to the HTTP session cache, the `ejb` cache relates to stateful session beans (SFSBs), and the `server` cache relates to the singleton-session beans:

```xml
<subsystem xmlns="urn:jboss:domain:infinispan:2.0">

    <cache-container name="server" aliases=
      "singleton cluster" default-cache="default" module=
      "org.wildfly.clustering.server">
        <transport lock-timeout="60000" />
        <replicated-cache name="default" mode="SYNC"
          batching="true">
            <locking isolation="REPEATABLE_READ" />
        </replicated-cache>
    </cache-container>

    <cache-container name="web" default-cache="dist"
       module="org.wildfly.clustering.web.infinispan">
        <transport lock-timeout="60000" />
        <distributed-cache name="dist" mode="ASYNC"
          batching="true" l1-lifespan="0" owners="2">
            <file-store />
        </distributed-cache>
    </cache-container>

    <cache-container name="ejb" aliases=
      "sfsb" default-cache="dist" module=
      "org.wildfly.clustering.ejb.infinispan">
        <transport lock-timeout="60000" />
        <distributed-cache name="dist" mode="ASYNC"
          batching="true" l1-lifespan="0" owners="2">
            <file-store />
        </distributed-cache>
    </cache-container>
</subsystem>
```

The configuration for each container can contain one or more caching strategy elements. These elements are as follows:

- `replicated-cache`
- `distributed-cache`
- `invalidation-cache`
- `local-cache`

Each of these cache elements can be defined zero or more times. To specify which cache element to use for the cache container, simply reference the name of the cache as the property of the `default-cache` attribute. In the next section, we will explore in detail the differences between these cache modes. Within each cache definition, you may have noticed the `locking` attribute that corresponds to the equivalent database isolation levels. Infinispan supports the following isolation levels:

- `NONE`: No isolation level means no transactional support.
- `READ_UNCOMMITTED`: The lowest isolation level, dirty reads are allowed, which means one transaction may see uncommitted data from another transaction. Rows are only locked during the writing of data, not for reads.
- `READ_COMMITTED`: The transaction acquires read and write locks on all retrieved data. Write locks are released at the end of the transaction, and read locks are released as soon as the data is selected.
- `REPEATABLE_READ`: This is the default isolation level used by Infinispan. The transaction acquires read and write locks on all retrieved data and is kept until the end of the transaction. Phantom reads can occur. Phantom reads are when you execute the same query in the same transaction and get a different number of results.
- `SERIALIZABLE`: The strictest isolation level. All transactions occur in an isolated fashion as if they are being executed serially (one after the other), as opposed to concurrently.

Another element nested within the cache configuration is `file-store`. This element configures the path in which to store the cached data. The default data is written in the `jboss.server.data.dir` directory under a folder with the same name as the cache container.

For example, the following figure shows the default `file-store` path for the standalone `web` cache container:

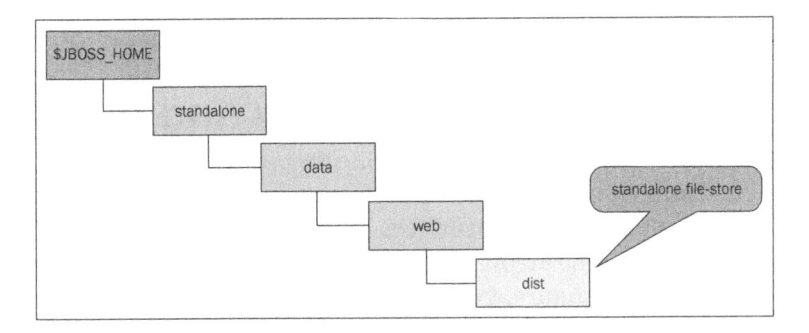

If you wish, you can customize the `file-store` path using the `relative-to` and `path` elements, just as we did in *Chapter 2, Configuring the Core WildFly Subsystems*, for the path element:

```
<cache-container name="web" default-cache="dist"
  module="org.wildfly.clustering.web.infinispan">
    <distributed-cache name="dist" mode="ASYNC"
      batching="true" l1-lifespan="0" owners="2">
        <file-store relative-to="jboss.server.data.dir"
          path="my-cache"/>
    </distributed-cache>
</cache-container>
```

Before moving on, let's briefly look at the way messages are sent between each node.

Data synchronization across members can be done via synchronous messages (`SYNC`) or asynchronous messages (`ASYNC`), which are defined as follows:

- **Synchronous** messaging is the least efficient of the two, as each node needs to wait for a message acknowledgement from other cluster members. However, synchronous mode is useful if you have a need for high consistency.
- **Asynchronous** messaging is the quicker of the two, the flip side being that consistency suffers. Asynchronous messaging is particularly useful when HTTP session replication and sticky sessions are enabled. In this scenario, a session is always accessed from the same cluster node. Only when a node fails is the data accessed from a different node.

The SYNC and ASYNC properties are set in the `mode` attribute of the cache element:

```
<distributed-cache name="dist" mode="ASYNC"    batching="true"
  l1-lifespan="0" owners="2">
```

Choosing between replication and distribution

When using **replicated** caching, Infinispan will store every entry on every node in the cluster grid. This means that entries added to any one of these cache instances will be replicated to all other cache instances in the cluster, and any entry can be retrieved from any cache. The arrows indicate the direction in which data is being replicated. In the following figure, you can see that session data from Node 1 is being copied to Nodes 2, 3, and 4:

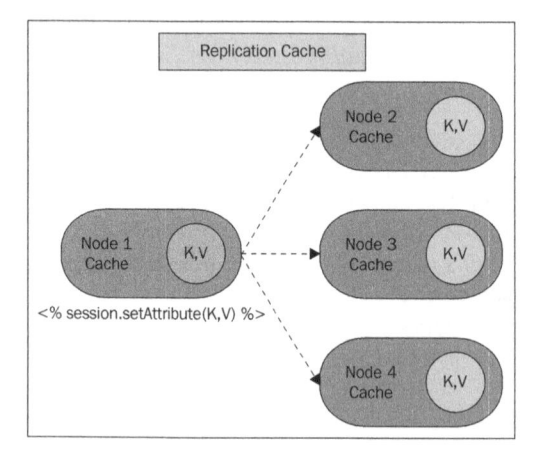

The scalability of replication is a function of cluster size and average data size. If we have many nodes and/or large data sets, we hit a scalability ceiling.

> If `DATA_SIZE * NUMBER_OF_HOSTS` is smaller than the memory available to each host, then replication is a viable choice.

On the other hand, when using **distributed** caching, Infinispan will store every cluster entry on a subset of the nodes in the grid.

Distribution makes use of a consistent-hash algorithm to determine where entries should be stored within the cluster. You can configure how many copies of a cache entry are maintained across the cluster. The value you choose here is a balance between performance and durability of data. The more copies you maintain, the lower the performance, but the lower the risk of losing data due to server outages.

> You can use the `owners` parameter (with a default value of 2) to define the number of cluster-wide copies for each cache entry:
>
> ```
> <distributed-cache name="dist" mode="ASYNC"
>     batching="true" l1-lifespan="0" owners="2">
>   <file-store/>
> </distributed-cache>
> ```

The following figure shows how the session data will be replicated across the nodes when the `owners` parameter is set to 2. Each node replicates its session data to two other nodes:

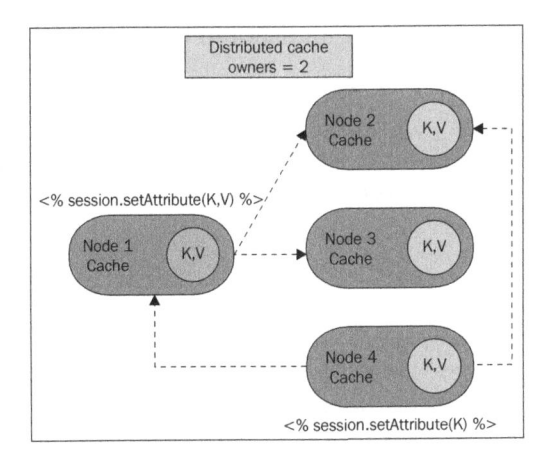

The choice between replication and distribution depends largely on the cluster size. For example, replication provides a quick and easy way to share states across a cluster; however, it only performs well in small clusters (fewer than ten servers). This is due to the increased number of replication messages that need to be sent as cluster size increases. In a distributed cache, several copies of an entry are maintained across nodes in order to provide redundancy and fault tolerance. The number of copies saved is typically far fewer than the number of nodes in the cluster. This means a distributed cache provides a far greater degree of scalability than a replicated cache.

Configuring the hibernate cache

The hibernate cache container is a key part of your configuration as it handles the caching of your data tier. WildFly uses hibernate as the default JPA implementation, so the concepts described in this chapter apply both to hibernate applications and to JPA-based applications. Hibernate caches are conceptually different from session-based caches. They are based on the assumption that you have a permanent storage for your data (the database) This means that it is not necessary to replicate or distribute copies of the entities across the cluster in order to achieve high availability. You just need to inform your nodes when data has been modified so that the entry in the cache can be invalidated. If a cache is configured for invalidation rather than replication, every time data is changed in a cache, other caches in the cluster receive a message that their data is now stale and should be evicted from memory.

The benefit of this is twofold. First, network traffic is minimized as invalidation messages are very small compared to replicating updated data. Second, caches in the cluster will only need to do database lookups when data is stale. Whenever a new entity or collection is read from database, it's only cached **locally** in order to reduce traffic between nodes:

```
<cache-container name="hibernate" default-cache="local-query"
module="org.hibernate">
    <transport lock-timeout="60000"/>
    <local-cache name="local-query">
        <transaction mode="NONE"/>
        <eviction strategy="LRU" max-entries="10000"/>
        <expiration max-idle="100000"/>
    </local-cache>
    ...
</cache-container>
```

The `local-query` cache is configured by default to store up to 10,000 entries in an LRU vector. Each entry will be evicted from the cache automatically if it has been idle for 100,000 milliseconds, as per the `max-idle` attribute.

The following is a summary of the eviction strategies supported by Infinispan:

- NONE: This value disables the eviction thread
- UNORDERED: This is now deprecated. Using this value will cause the LRU to be used

- `LRU`: This value causes evictions to occur based on a **least-recently-used** pattern
- `LIRS`: This value addresses shortcomings of LRU. Eviction relies on inter-reference recency of cache entries

> To read more about how LIRS works, see the Infinispan documentation at http://infinispan.org/docs/6.0.x/user_guide/user_guide.html#_eviction_strategies.

Once the local cache entity is updated, the cache will send a message to other members of the cluster, telling them that the entity has been modified. This is when the `invalidation-cache` comes into play. Take a look at the following code:

```
<invalidation-cache name="entity" mode="SYNC">
    <transaction mode="NON_XA"/>
    <eviction strategy="LRU" max-entries="10000"/>
    <expiration max-idle="100000"/>
</invalidation-cache>
```

The default configuration for the invalidation cache uses the same eviction and expiration settings as for local query cache. The maximum number of entries is set to 10,000 and the idle time before expiration to 100,000 milliseconds. The invalidation cache can also be configured to be synchronous (`SYNC`) or asynchronous (`ASYNC`). If you configure your invalidation cache to be synchronous, then your cache will be blocked until all caches in the cluster receive responses to invalidation messages. On the other hand, an asynchronous invalidation cache does not block and wait for a response, which results in increased performance. By default, hibernate is configured to use `REPEATABLE_READ` as the cache isolation level. For most cases, the default isolation level of `REPEATABLE_READ` will suffice. If you want to update it to, say, `READ_COMMITTED`, then you will need to add the following to your configuration:

```
<invalidation-cache mode="SYNC" name="entity">
    ...
    <locking isolation="READ_COMMITTED"/>
</invalidation-cache>
```

The last bit of configuration we are going to look at within the Infinispan subsystem is the `timestamp` cache. The `timestamp` cache keeps track of the last time each database table was updated.

The `timestamp` cache is strictly related to the query cache. It is used to store the result set of a query run against the database. If the query cache is enabled, before a query run, the query cache is checked. If the timestamp of the last update on a table is greater than the time the query results were cached, the entry is evicted from the cache and a fresh database lookup is made. This is referred to as a cache miss. Have a look at the following code:

```
<replicated-cache name="timestamps" mode="ASYNC">
        <transaction mode="NONE"/>
        <eviction strategy="NONE"/>
</replicated-cache>
```

By default, the `timestamps` cache is configured with asynchronous replication as the clustering mode. Since all cluster nodes must store all timestamps, local or invalidated cache types are not allowed, and no eviction/expiration is allowed either.

Using replication for the hibernate cache

There may be situations when you want to replicate your entity cache across other cluster nodes, instead of using local caches and invalidation. This may be the case when:

- Queries executed are quite expensive
- Queries are likely to be repeated in different cluster nodes
- Queries are unlikely to be invalidated out of the cache (Hibernate invalidates query results from the cache when one of the entity classes involved in the query's WHERE clause changes)

In order to switch to a replicated cache, you have to configure your `default-cache` attribute, as shown in the following code snippet, as well as add the relevant `replicated-cache` configuration:

```
<cache-container name="hibernate" default-cache="replicated-cache"
module="org.hibernate">
    <replicated-cache name="replicated-cache" mode="SYNC">
        <locking isolation="REPEATABLE_READ"/>
    </replicated-cache>
</cache-container>
```

Advanced Infinispan configuration

Until now, we looked at the essential components required to get working with a clustered application. Infinispan has a wealth of options available to further customize your cache.

> For more information on advanced configuration of Infinispan via the Infinispan subsystem, you can check out the documentation at http://infinispan.org/docs/6.0.x/infinispan_server_guide/infinispan_server_guide.html

Configuring the Infinispan transport

The Infinispan subsystem relies on the JGroups subsystem to transport cached data between nodes. JGroups uses UDP as the default transport protocol as defined by the `default-stack` attribute in the JGroups subsystem:

```
<subsystem xmlns="urn:jboss:domain:jgroups:2.0" default-stack="udp">
    ...
</subsystem>
```

You can, however, configure a different transport for each cache container. If you want to use TCP as the transport protocol for the web cache container, then you can add the `stack` attribute and set it to `tcp`:

```
<cache-container name="web" default-cache="dist">
   <transport lock-timeout="60000" stack="tcp"/>
</cache-container>
```

The default UDP transport is usually suitable for large clusters. It may also be suitable if you are using replication or invalidation, as it minimizes opening too many sockets.

To learn about the differences between TCP and UDP, please refer to this external link at http://www.skullbox.net/tcpudp.php.

Configuring the Infinispan threads

It is important to note that the thread-pool subsystem has been deprecated in WildFly 8. It is quite likely that it will be removed completely in WildFly 9. The configuration in this section can still be used in WildFly 8, but you will need to add the threads subsystem to your configuration file. Take a look at the following code:

```
<extensions>
    ...
    <extension module="org.jboss.as.threads"/>
</extensions>
```

Clustering

Just as you can for JGroups transport, you can externalize your Infinispan thread configuration, moving it into the thread-pool subsystem. The following thread pools can be configured per cache-container:

Thread pool	Description
transport	This gives the size of the bounded thread pool whose threads are responsible for transporting data across the network
listener-executor	This gives the size of the thread pool used for registering and getting notified when some cache events take place
replication-queue-executor	This gives the size of the scheduled replication executor used for replicating cache data
eviction-executor	This gives the size of the scheduled executor service used to periodically run eviction cleanup tasks

Customizing the thread pool may be required in some cases, for example, you may want to apply a cache replication algorithm. You may then need to choose the number of threads used for replicating data. In the following example, we are externalizing the thread pools of the web `cache-container` by defining a maximum of 25 threads for the bounded-queue-thread-pool and five threads for replicating data:

```
<subsystem xmlns="urn:jboss:domain:infinispan:2.0">

  <cache-container name="web" default-cache="repl"
    listener-executor="infinispan-listener"
    eviction-executor="infinispan-eviction"
    replication-queue-executor="infinispan-repl-queue">
    <transport executor="infinispan-transport"/>
  </cache-container>
</subsystem>
...
<subsystem xmlns="urn:jboss:domain:threads:1.1">
  <thread-factory name="infinispan-factory" priority="1"/>
  <bounded-queue-thread-pool name="infinispan-transport"/>
    <core-threads count="1"/>
    <queue-length count="100000"/>
    <max-threads count="25"/>
    <thread-factory name="infinispan-factory"/>
  </bounded-queue-thread-pool>
  <bounded-queue-thread-pool name="infinispan-listener"/>
    <core-threads count="1"/>
    <queue-length count="100000"/>
    <max-threads count="1"/>
```

```
      <thread-factory name="infinispan-factory"/>
    </bounded-queue-thread-pool>
    <scheduled-thread-pool name="infinispan-eviction"/>
      <max-threads count="1"/>
      <thread-factory name="infinispan-factory"/>
    </scheduled-thread-pool>
    <scheduled-thread-pool name="infinispan-repl-queue"/>
      <max-threads count="5"/>
      <thread-factory name="infinispan-factory"/>
    </scheduled-thread-pool>
</subsystem>
```

Clustering the messaging subsystem

We will conclude this chapter by discussing the messaging subsystem.

The JMS provider used in WildFly is **HornetQ**. In order to share the message processing load, HornetQ servers can be grouped together in a cluster. Each active node in the cluster contains an active HornetQ server. HornetQ manages its own messages and handles its own connections. Behind the scenes, when a node forms a cluster connection to another node, a core bridge connection is created between them. Once the connection has been established, messages can flow between each of the nodes.

Clustering is automatically enabled in HornetQ if one or more `cluster-connection` elements are defined. The following example is taken from the default `full-ha` profile:

```
<subsystem xmlns="urn:jboss:domain:messaging:2.0">
    <hornetq-server>
        ...
        <cluster-connections>
            <cluster-connection name="my-cluster">
                <address>jms</address>
                <connector-ref>http-connector</connector-ref>
                <discovery-group-ref discovery-group-name=
                   "dg-group1"/>
            </cluster-connection>
        </cluster-connections>
    </hornetq-server>
</subsystem>
```

Clustering

Now, let's look at how to configure the `cluster-connection`. The following is a typical cluster connection configuration. You can either update the default `cluster-connection`, or you can add your own `cluster-connection` element within your `<hornetq-server>` definition.

```
<subsystem xmlns="urn:jboss:domain:messaging:2.0">
    <hornetq-server>
        ...
        <cluster-connections>
            <cluster-connection name="my-cluster">
                <address>jms</address>
                <connector-ref>http-connector</connector-ref>
                <discovery-group-ref discovery-group-name=
                  "dg-group1"/>
                <retry-interval>500</retry-interval>
                <forward-when-no-consumers>false
                  </forward-when-no-consumers>
                <max-hops>1</max-hops>
            </cluster-connection>
        </cluster-connections>
    </hornetq-server>
</subsystem>
```

The `cluster-connection name` attribute obviously defines the cluster connection name, which we are going to configure. There can be zero or more cluster connections configured in your messaging subsystem.

The `address` element is a mandatory parameter and determines how messages are distributed across the cluster. In this example, the cluster connection will only load balance the messages that are sent to addresses that start with `jms`. This cluster connection will, in effect, apply to all JMS queue and topic subscriptions. This is because they map to core queues that start with the substring `jms`.

The `connector-ref` element references the connector, which has been defined in the `connectors` section of the messaging subsystem. In this case, we are using the http connector (see *Chapter 3, Configuring Enterprise Services*, for more information about the available connectors).The `retry-interval` element determines the interval in milliseconds between the message retry attempts. If a cluster connection is attempted and the target node has not been started, or is in the process of being rebooted, then connection attempts from other nodes commence only once the time period defined in the `retry-interval` has elapsed.

The `forward-when-no-consumers` element, when set to `true`, will ensure that each incoming message is distributed round robin even though there may not be a consumer on the receiving node.

> You can actually specify the connection load-balancing policy within the `connection-factory` element. The out-of-the-box policies are **Round-Robin** (`org.hornetq.api.core.client.loadbalance.RoundRobinConnectionLoadBalancingPolicy`) and **Random** (`org.hornetq.api.core.client.loadbalance.RandomConnectionLoadBalancingPolicy`). You can also add your own policy by implementing the `org.hornetq.api.core.client.loadbalance.ConnectionLoadBalancingPolicy` interface.
>
> The following example shows how to use the random policy for a connection factory:
>
> ```
> <connection-factory name="InVmConnectionFactory">
>     ...
>     <connection-load-balancing-policy-class-name>
>       org.hornetq.api.core.client.loadbalance.
>       RandomConnectionLoadBalancingPolicy
>     </connection-load-balancing-policy-class-name>
> </connection-factory>
> ```

Finally, the optional `max-hops` value is set to 1 (default), which is the maximum number of times a message can be forwarded between nodes. A value of 1 means messages are only load balanced to other HornetQ serves, which are directly connected to this server. HornetQ can also be configured to load-balance messages to nodes that are indirectly connected to it, that is, the other HornetQ servers are intermediaries in a chain.

> You can also refer to `jboss-as-messaging_2_0.xsd` for the full list of available parameters. This can be found in the `JBOSS_HOME/docs/schema` folder of your server distribution.

Configuring messaging credentials

If you try to start a cluster where nodes use the `full-ha` profile, you will get an error logged to the console, as follows:

```
ERROR [org.hornetq.core.server] (default I/O-1) HQ224018: Failed to create session: HornetQClusterSecurityException[errorType=CLUSTER_SECURITY_EXCEPTION message=HQ119099: Unable to authenticate cluster user: HORNETQ.CLUSTER.ADMIN.USER]
```

Clustering

This is because, when attempting to create connections between nodes, HornetQ uses a cluster user and cluster password. As you can see in the default configuration, you are required to update the password value:

```xml
<subsystem xmlns="urn:jboss:domain:messaging:2.0">
    <hornetq-server>
        <cluster-password>
            ${jboss.messaging.cluster.password:CHANGE ME!!}
        </cluster-password>
        <journal-file-size>102400</journal-file-size>
        ...
    </hornetq-server>
</subsystem>
```

Once you have changed this password, start your cluster, and you should see a successful bridge between nodes:

Configuring clustering in your applications

We will now complete our journey through the clustering system by looking at how to cluster the following:

- Session beans

- Entities
- Web applications

Clustering session beans

In *Chapter 3, Configuring Enterprise Services*, we discussed the difference between **Stateless Session Beans (SLSBs)**, **Stateful Session Beans (SFSBs)**, and **Singleton Session Beans**.

SLSBs are not able to retain state between invocations, so the main benefit of clustering an SLSB is to balance the load between an array of servers:

```
@Stateless
@Clustered
public class ClusteredBean {
   public void doSomething() {
   // Do something
   }
}
```

If you want to further specialize your SLSB, then you can choose the load-balancing algorithm used to distribute the load between your EJBs. The following are the available load-balancing policies for your SLSB:

Load-balancing policy	Description
RoundRobin	It is the default load-balancing policy. The smart proxy cycles through a list of WildFly Server instances in a fixed order.
RandomRobin	Under this policy, each request is redirected by the smart proxy to a random node in the cluster.
FirstAvailable	It implies a random selection of the node, but subsequent calls will stick to that node until the node fails. The next node will again be selected randomly.
FirstAvailableIdenticalAllProxies	This is the same as FirstAvailable, except that the random node selection will then be shared by all dynamic proxies.

Clustering

Then, you can apply the load-balancing policy as in the following example:

```
@Clustered(loadBalancePolicy="FirstAvailable")
```

In JBoss AS 7, you were required to annotate your SFSB with `@Clustered` in order to replicate the state of the SFSB. In WildFly, this is not the case, as SFSB are configured to have passivation enabled by default. This means that as long as you annotate your bean with `@Stateful`, and you are using a server profile that supports high availability, your SFSB will have its state replicated across servers. Have a look at the following code:

```
@Stateful
public class ClusteredBean {
    public void doSomething() {
    // Do something
    }
}
```

To disable passivation/replication, you can simply set `passivationCapable` to `false`, as shown here:

```
@Stateful(passivationCapable=false)
public class ClusteredBean {
    public void doSomething() {
    // Do something
    }
}
```

By default, SFSBs use the cache container named `ejb`, which replicates sessions across all nodes. Should your application server node fail while sessions are running, the EJB proxy will detect it and choose another node where session data has been replicated. You can, however, reference a custom cache container used by your SFSB with the `@org.jboss.ejb3.annotation.CacheConfig` annotation. Have a look at the following code:

```
@Stateful
@CacheConfig(name="custom-ejb")
public class ClusteredBean {
    ...
}
```

The following is the corresponding cache container that uses a distributed cache:

```
<cache-container name="custom-ejb" default-cache="dist" module="org.
wildfly.clustering.ejb.infinispan" aliases="sfsb">
    <distributed-cache name="dist" batching="true" mode="ASYNC"
        owners="3">
        <locking isolation="REPEATABLE_READ"/>
        <file-store/>
```

```
        </distributed-cache>
    </cache-container>
```

Clustering entities

As entities sit deep in the backend, they do not need to be considered with regard to load-balancing logic or session replication. However, it is useful to cache your entities to avoid roundtrips to the database. The EJB3 persistence layer implementation in WildFly is Hibernate 4.3.5. The Hibernate framework includes a complex cache mechanism, which is implemented both at the Session level and at the SessionFactory level.

The cache used in the Session level is called the first-level cache and only has session scope. This cache is cleared as soon as the Hibernate session using it is closed. Hibernate uses second-level caching to store entities or collections retrieved from the database. It can also store the results of recent queries. It is the second-level cache that we need to cluster, as this cache is used across sessions.

Enabling the second-level cache for your enterprise applications is relatively straightforward. If you are using JPA, then all you need to do to enable the second-level cache is add the following to your `persistence.xml` configuration file:

```
<shared-cache-mode>ENABLE_SELECTIVE</shared-cache-mode>
<properties>
    <property name="hibernate.cache.use_second_level_cache"
       value="true"/>
    <property name="hibernate.cache.use_minimal_puts" value="true"/>
</properties>
```

The first element, `shared-cache-mode`, is the JPA 2.x way of specifying whether the entities and entity-related state of a persistence unit will be cached. The `shared-cache-mode` element has five possible values, as indicated in the following table:

Shared Cache mode	Description
ALL	This value causes all entities and entity-related states and data to be cached.
NONE	This value causes caching to be disabled for the persistence unit.
ENABLE_SELECTIVE	This value allows caching if the `@Cacheable` annotation is specified on the entity class.
DISABLE_SELECTIVE	This value enables the cache and causes all entities to be cached except those for which `@Cacheable(false)` is specified.

The property named `hibernate.cache.use_minimal_puts` performs some optimization on the second-level cache by reducing the amount of writes in the caches at the cost of some additional reads. This is beneficial when clustering your entities, as the put operation is very expensive as it activates cache replication listeners.

In addition, if you plan to use the Hibernate query cache in your applications, you need to activate it with a separate property, as follows:

```xml
<property name="hibernate.cache.use_query_cache" value="true"/>
```

For the sake of completeness, we will also include the configuration needed to use Infinispan as a caching provider for native Hibernate applications. This is the list of properties you have to add to your `hibernate.cfg.xml`:

```xml
<property name="hibernate.cache.region.factory_class" value=
   "org.hibernate.cache.infinispan.JndiInfinispanRegionFactory"/>
<property name="hibernate.cache.infinispan.cachemanager" value=
   "java:CacheManager/entity"/>
<property name="hibernate.transaction.manager_lookup_class" value=
   "org.hibernate.transaction.JBossTransactionManagerLookup"/>
<property name="hibernate.cache.use_second_level_cache" value=
   "true"/>
<property name="hibernate.cache.use_minimal_puts" value="true"/>
```

As you can see, the configuration is more verbose because you have to tell Hibernate to use Infinispan as a caching provider. This requires setting the correct Hibernate transaction factory using the `hibernate.transaction.factory_class` property.

The `hibernate.cache.infinispan.cachemanager` property exposes the cache manager used by Infinispan. By default, Infinispan binds the cache manager responsible for the second-level cache to the JNDI name `java:CacheManager/entity`.

Finally, the `hibernate.cache.region.factory_class` property tells Hibernate to use Infinispan's second-level caching integration, which uses `CacheManager`, as defined previously, as the source for the Infinispan cache's instances.

Caching entities

Unless you have set `shared-cache-mode` to `ALL`, Hibernate will not automatically cache your entities. You have to select which entities or queries need to be cached. This is definitely the safest option since indiscriminate caching can hurt performance. The following example shows how to do this for JPA entities using annotations:

```
import javax.persistence.*;
import org.hibernate.annotations.Cache;
```

```
import org.hibernate.annotations.CacheConcurrencyStrategy;

@Entity
@Cacheable
@Cache(usage = CacheConcurrencyStrategy.TRANSACTIONAL, region
="properties")

public class Property {

@Id
@Column(name="key")
private String key;

@Column(name="value")
private String value;

// Getter & setters omitted for brevity
}
```

Using JPA annotations

The `@javax.persistence.Cacheable` annotation dictates whether this entity class should be cached in the second-level cache. This is only applicable when the `shared-cache-mode` is not set to `ALL`.

Using Hibernate annotations

The `@org.hibernate.annotations.Cache` annotation is the older annotation used to achieve the same purpose as `@Cacheable`. You can still use it to define which strategy Hibernate should use to control concurrent access to cache contents.

The `CacheConcurrencyStrategy.TRANSACTIONAL` property provides support for Infinispan's fully-transactional JTA environment.

If there is a chance that your application data is read but never modified, you can apply the `CacheConcurrencyStrategy.READ_ONLY` property that does not evict data from the cache (unless performed programmatically):

```
@Cache(usage=CacheConcurrencyStrategy.READ_ONLY)
```

Finally, the last attribute is the caching region that defines where entities are placed. If you do not specify a cache region for an entity class, all instances of this class will be cached in the `_default` region. Defining a caching region can be useful if you want to perform a fine-grained management of caching areas.

Caching queries

The query cache can be used to cache the result set of a query. This means that if the same query is issued again, it will not hit the database but return the cached value.

> The query cache does not cache the state of the actual entities in the result set; it caches only the identifier values and results of the value type.

In the following example, the query result set named `listUsers` is configured to be cached using the `@QueryHint` annotation inside a `@NamedQuery` annotation:

```
@NamedQueries(
{
@NamedQuery(
name = "listUsers",
query = "FROM User c WHERE c.name = :name",
hints = { @QueryHint(name = "org.hibernate.cacheable", value = "true") }
)
})
public class User {

@Id
@Column(name="key")
private String key;

@Column(name="name")
private String name;

...
}
```

> Overuse of the query cache may reduce your application's performance, so use it wisely. First, the query cache will increase the memory requirements if your queries (stored as key in the query cache map) are made up of hundreds of characters.
>
> Second, and more important, the result of the query cache is invalidated each time there's a change in one of the tables you are querying. This can lead to a very poor hit ratio of the query cache. Therefore, it is advisable to turn off the query cache unless you are querying a table that is seldom updated.

Clustering web applications

Clustering web applications requires the least effort. As we touched upon earlier, all you need to do to switch on clustering in a web application is add the following directive in the `web.xml`:

```
<web-app>
    <distributable/>
</web-app>
```

By default, clustered web applications will use the web cache contained in the Infinispan configuration. You also have the option of setting up a specific cache per deployment unit. This can be achieved by adding the `replication-config` directive to the `jboss-web.xml` file and specifying the cache name to use:

```
<jboss-web>
  <replication-config>
    <cache-name>web.dist</cache-name>
  </replication-config>
</jboss-web>
```

The previous configuration should obviously reference a cache defined in the main configuration file:

```
<cache-container name="web" default-cache="repl">
   <alias>standard-session-cache</alias>

   <distributed-cache mode="ASYNC" name="web.dist" batching="true">
       <locking isolation="REPEATABLE_READ"/>
       <file-store/>
   </distributed-cache>
</cache-container>
```

Summary

In this chapter, we looked at a lot of configuration options around clustering. There was a lot of information to take in but, in summary, we will mention the following key points.

A WildFly cluster can be composed of either standalone nodes or as part of a domain of servers .The clustering subsystem is defined in the `standalone-ha.xml` and `standalone-full-ha.xml` configurations files.

There are three main components required for clustering: JGroups, Infinispan, and messaging. JGroups provides communication between nodes in a cluster. By default, JGroups uses UDP multicast messages to handle the cluster life cycle events.

Within enterprise applications, there are several caches that need to be configured in order to achieve consistency of data. There are four cache containers configured by default in WildFly. These are the singleton session bean cluster `cache-container`, the SLSB `cache-container`, the web `cache-container`, and the Hibernate `cache-container`.

The singleton cluster (server) `cache-container` is configured to replicate singleton session bean data across nodes in the cluster. The SFSB's (ejb) `cache-container` is configured to replicate stateful session bean data across nodes in the cluster. The web `cache-container` is configured to replicate HTTP session data across nodes in the cluster. The Hibernate `cache-container` uses a more complex approach by defining a `local-query` strategy to handle local entities. An `invalidation-cache` is used when data is updated and other cluster nodes need to be informed. Finally, a `replicated-cache` is used to replicate the query timestamps.

Lastly, we looked at the messaging subsystem, which can be easily clustered by defining one `cluster-connection` element. This will cause messages to be transparently load-balanced across your JMS servers.

In the next chapter we will look at load balancing, the other half of the story when it comes to configuring high availability.

9
Load-balancing Web Applications

In the previous chapter, we illustrated the basic concepts of how to cluster web applications. However, this is only part of the story. To further improve availability, we need to look at how to load-balance your WildFly servers.

Load balancing is the distribution of incoming traffic between servers that host the same application content. Load balancing improves application availability by ensuring that any single server does not take too much load, and that the application remains available should a single server fail.

Historically, the JBoss AS has inherited the load-balancing libraries from Tomcat, which was part of the application server's web module. The web module used mod_jk (an Apache module) to connect Tomcat to a web server, such as Apache. For those of you who are unfamiliar with Tomcat and Apache, Tomcat (also known as Apache Tomcat) is an open source servlet container, while Apache (also known as Apache2 or Apache HTTPD) is an HTTP web server.

While you can still use mod_jk to connect Undertow to a web server, you should consider using the mod_cluster API. The mod_cluster API is an HTTPD-based load balancer that has several advantages over mod_jk, such as improved performance and reliability. We will cover the installation of both mod_jk and mod_cluster in this chapter.

Having made this short introduction, next we will introduce the advantages of using a web server in front of your web applications. We will then continue by covering the following topics:

- Connecting WildFly to Apache using mod_jk and mod_proxy
- Connecting WildFly to Apache using the mod_cluster API

Load-balancing Web Applications

Benefits of using the Apache web server with WildFly

In most real-world situations, it's common to find the Apache web server as an entry point to your application server. Some advantages of this are:

- **Speed**: Apache is generally faster at serving static content.
- **Security**: By placing WildFly behind Apache, you only need to worry about connections from a single point of entry. WildFly can be configured to accept connections from a single IP (the server hosting Apache) and will not be accessible directly from the Internet. Essentially, Apache becomes a smart proxy server.
- **Load balancing and clustering**: Using Apache as a frontend, you can distribute traffic to multiple WildFly server instances. If one of your servers fails, the communication transparently continues to another node in the cluster.

As stated previously, connecting Apache and WildFly can be done in one of two ways: by either using Tomcat's `mod_jk` library or Apache's `mod_proxy` libraries. As the installation of both `mod_jk` and `mod_proxy` does not differ from earlier AS releases, we will just include a quick setup guide for your reference.

If, however, you are planning to set up a high-performance, dynamic cluster of web servers, you should consider migrating to the newer `mod_cluster` API, which is discussed in the following sections of this chapter.

Using the mod_jk library

The `mod_jk` library is a common solution to front WildFly with the Apache web server. All requests first arrive at the Apache web server. Apache then accepts and processes any static resource requests, such as requests for HTML pages or graphical images. Then, with the help of `mod_jk`, Apache requests dynamic resources, such as JSPs or Servlets, to Undertow. The communication between Apache and Undertow is sent over the network using the AJP protocol, as shown in the following screenshot:

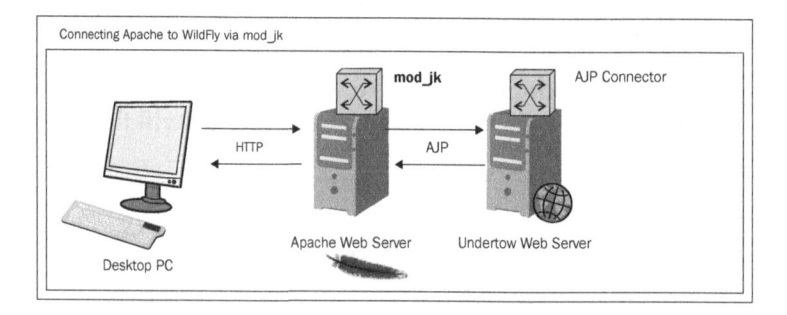

Installing Apache

The most common operating system for live environments is Linux. For this reason, we will demonstrate how to install mod_jk in Ubuntu. Bear in mind that the configuration may differ slightly depending on the flavor of Linux you use. These instructions work for Ubuntu Server.

You need to install Apache before attempting to install mod_jk. You can install Apache by issuing the following commands in the terminal:

```
sudo apt-get update
sudo apt-get install -y apache2
```

Make sure that you can view the Apache welcome page after completing the installation. Simply enter the IP of the server as the URL of your browser. Take a look at the following screenshot:

Installing mod_jk

Next, we need to install mod_jk. The following command will install the module, enable it, and restart Apache:

```
sudo apt-get install libapache2-mod-jk
```

You can then confirm that the module has been enabled by typing the following command. This will list all currently enabled modules:

```
sudo apache2ctl -M
```

Load-balancing Web Applications

Then, you need to modify the virtual host within for the default configuration file, `default`, which can be found in the `/etc/apache2/sites-enabled` directory. The configuration shows the updated default configuration of the file. The line you need to add is highlighted in the following code:

```
<VirtualHost *:80>
    ServerAdmin webmaster@localhost

    JkMount /* loadbalancer
    <Directory />
        Options FollowSymLinks
        AllowOverride None
    </Directory>

    ErrorLog ${APACHE_LOG_DIR}/error.log
    CustomLog ${APACHE_LOG_DIR}/access.log combined
</VirtualHost>
```

The `JkMount` directive tells Apache which URLs it should forward to the `mod_jk` module, which in turn forwards them to the Undertow web container. In the preceding example, all requests with the URL path `/*` are sent to the `mod_jk` connector. This means that all requests are sent. You can also forward specific URLs to `mod_jk`, for example, `/website*`.

If you forward all URLs, you may want to unmount one or two URLs so that static data can be served from Apache. This can be achieved using the `JkUmount` directive. For example, if you want Apache to serve static media files in the `images` directory, you will have a configuration like this:

```
<VirtualHost *:80>
    ServerAdmin webmaster@localhost

    JkMount /* loadbalancer
    JkUmount /images/* loadbalancer

    <Directory />
        Options FollowSymLinks
        AllowOverride None
    </Directory>

    ErrorLog ${APACHE_LOG_DIR}/error.log
    CustomLog ${APACHE_LOG_DIR}/access.log combined
</VirtualHost>
```

Next, you need to configure the mod_jk workers file, workers.properties, which is found in the /etc/libapache2-mod-jk folder. This file specifies the IP addresses of the Undertow web servers, between which the load is balanced. Optionally, you can add a configuration that specifies how calls should be load-balanced across each of the servers. For a two-node setup, the file will look like this:

```
# Define worker list
worker.list=loadbalancer,jkstatus
# Set properties for worker1 (ajp13)
worker.worker1.type=ajp13
worker.worker1.host=192.168.0.1
worker.worker1.port=8009

# Set properties for worker2 (ajp13)
worker.worker2.type=ajp13
worker.worker1worker12.host=192.168.0.2
worker.worker1worker12.port=8009
worker.worker1.lbfactor=1
worker.loadbalancer.type=lb
worker.loadbalancer.balance_workers=worker1,worker2
```

In the workers.properties file, each node is defined using the worker.[n] naming convention, where n represents an arbitrary name you choose for each web server container. For each worker, you must specify the hostname (or IP address) and the port number of the AJP13 connector running in the web server.

The load balancer type lb means that workers perform weighted round-robin load balancing with sticky sessions.

You will need to restart Apache after modifying the worker.properties file. Take a look at the following command:

sudo /etc/init.d/apache2 restart

In WildFly, the default configuration in the ha profiles already defines the AJP connector. If you are not using one of the ha profiles, for example, you are using standalone.xml, you need to add the following highlighted line:

```
<subsystem xmlns="urn:jboss:domain:undertow:1.1">
    <buffer-cache name="default"/>
    <server name="default-server">
        <ajp-listener name="ajp" socket-binding="ajp"/>
        <http-listener name="default" socket-binding="http"/>
        ....
    </server>
</subsystem>
```

The AJP connector is also already defined in the `socket-binding-group` element in the ha profiles. Again, for the non-ha profiles, you will need the AJP configuration. In the following code snippet, you can see that the AJP connector is listening on port number 8009. Have a look at the following code:

```xml
<socket-binding-group name="standard-sockets"
  default-interface="public" port-offset="0">
    <socket-binding name="management-http"
       interface="management" port="9990"/>
    <socket-binding name="management-https"
       interface="management" port="9993"/>
    <socket-binding name="ajp" port="8009"/>
    ...
</socket-binding-group>
```

Once you set up this configuration, you should refresh the page showing you the Apache welcome page. It will now show the WildFly welcome page. This proves that Apache is directing the requests to WildFly. Stop one of the WildFly servers and refresh the page once more. You will continue to see the WildFly welcome page, as all requests are now being directed to the other WildFly server.

Configuring mod_proxy

In WildFly, there is support for an optional module named mod_proxy. When installed, it can be configured so that Apache acts as a proxy server. This can be used to forward requests to a particular web application server, such as WildFly, without having to configure a web connector, such as mod_jk.

To install and enable mod_proxy, you need to run the following commands:

```
sudo apt-get install libapache2-mod-proxy-html
sudo a2enmod proxy-http
```

Then, you need to include these two directives in your default site file. You need to do this for each web application that you wish to forward to WildFly for example, to forward an application with a context path of /app. Have a look at the following code:

```
ProxyPass          /app  http://localhost:8080/app
ProxyPassReverse   /app  http://localhost:8080/app
```

This tells Apache to forward URLs matching `http://localhost/app/*` to the WildFly HTTP connector listening on port number 8080.

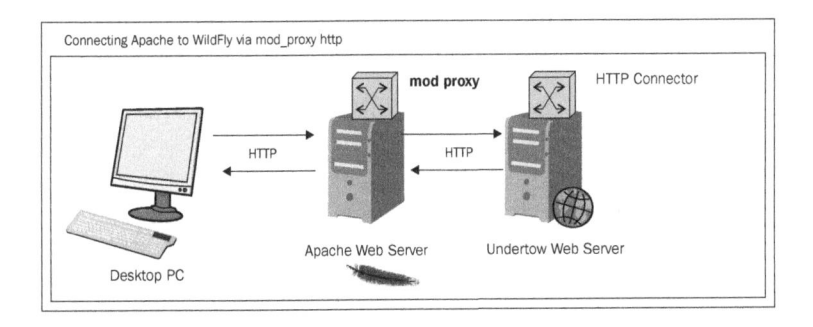

[Diagram: Connecting Apache to WildFly via mod_proxy http — Desktop PC ↔ HTTP ↔ Apache Web Server (mod proxy) ↔ HTTP ↔ Undertow Web Server (HTTP Connector)]

As shown in the preceding diagram, Apache's `mod_proxy` is TCP-based and uses HTTP, so you don't need to add anything else within your WildFly configuration. On top of this, there is also support for another module, `mod_proxy_ajp`. This module can be used in much the same way as `mod_proxy` except that it uses the AJP protocol to proxy Apache requests to WildFly. Before you can use it, you will need to enable it as follows:

`sudo a2enmod proxy-ajp`

Then, add the highlighted lines to your virtual host in the default site file:

```
<VirtualHost *:80>
        ServerAdmin webmaster@localhost
        DocumentRoot /var/www/html

        ProxyPass / ajp://localhost:8009/
        ProxyPassReverse / ajp://localhost:8009/

        ErrorLog ${APACHE_LOG_DIR}/error.log
        CustomLog ${APACHE_LOG_DIR}/access.log combined
</VirtualHost>
```

Here, we simply redirect all traffic (/) to the web server listening on localhost at port number 8009. Take a look at the following screenshot:

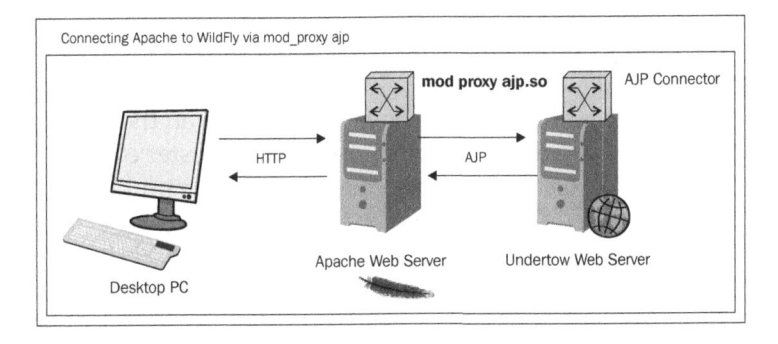

[Diagram: Connecting Apache to WildFly via mod_proxy ajp — Desktop PC ↔ HTTP ↔ Apache Web Server (mod proxy ajp.so) ↔ AJP ↔ Undertow Web Server (AJP Connector)]

Again, if you use a non-ha profile, you need to add the AJP listener to your Undertow configuration, as follows:

```xml
<subsystem xmlns="urn:jboss:domain:undertow:1.1">
    <buffer-cache name="default"/>
    <server name="default-server">
        <ajp-listener name="ajp" socket-binding="ajp"/>
        <http-listener name="default" socket-binding="http"/>
        ....
    </server>
</subsystem>
```

Then, you need to add the AJP port as a socket-binding element, as follows:

```xml
<socket-binding-group name="standard-sockets" default-interface="public" port-offset="0">
    <socket-binding name="management-http" interface="management"
        port="9990"/>
    <socket-binding name="management-https" interface="management"
        port="9993"/>
    <socket-binding name="ajp" port="8009"/>
    ....
</socket-binding-group>
```

Load-balancing with mod_cluster

The `mod_cluster` is an HTTP-based load balancer, which, like `mod_jk`, can be used to forward requests to a set of application server instances. There are several advantages of using `mod_cluster` over `mod_jk` or `mod_proxy`:

- Dynamic clustering configuration
- Better load balancing due to the ability to use server-side load metrics
- Better integration with the application life cycle
- AJP is optional

When using a standard load balancer, such as `mod_jk`, you have to provide a static list of nodes that are used to spread load. This process is inconvenient, especially if you want to dynamically add or remove nodes depending on the amount of traffic around your application. In addition to this, using a flat cluster configuration can be tedious and prone to error, especially if you have a high number of nodes in your cluster.

When using `mod_cluster`, nodes are dynamically added to, or removed from, your cluster. To achieve this, each WildFly server communicates its life cycle state to Apache.

Apache sends UDP messages, the so-called advertisements, on a multicast group. Each of the WildFly servers in the cluster subscribes to this group. It is via this group that WildFly is informed about HTTP proxies (Apache in this case). Then, each WildFly instance notifies the HTTP proxies about their availability, and then the proxy adds them to a list of nodes. Should a WildFly server be removed, the other WildFly servers in the group will be notified.

The following diagram helps illustrate this concept:

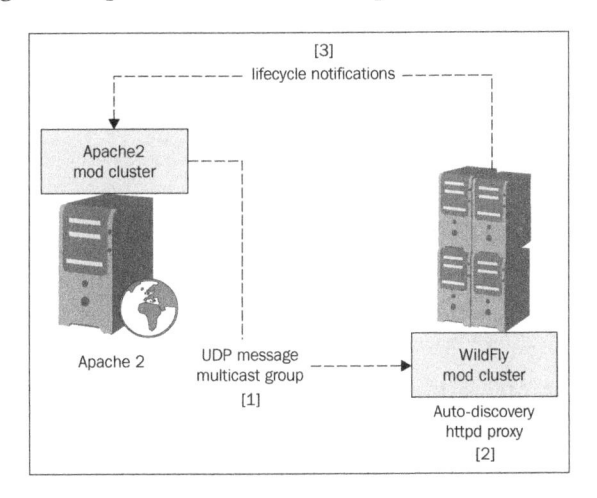

Another key feature of `mod_cluster` resides in the load metrics. Load metrics are determined on the server side and are then sent to the Apache side as circumstances change. As a consequence, `mod_cluster` provides a far more robust architecture than traditional HTTPD-based load balancers, where metrics are statically held on the proxy.

> For more information on how server-side load metrics are calculated, refer to the `mod_cluster` documentation at http://docs.jboss.org/mod_cluster/1.2.0/html/java.load.html.

Another advantage of using `mod_cluster` is the ability to intercept life cycle events, such as undeployment and redeployment. As mentioned previously in this section, these are synchronized between Apache and the nodes in the cluster.

Installing mod_cluster libraries

There are two things to consider when installing and configuring `mod_cluster`. The first involves the WildFly configuration, and the second involves downloading and installing the `mod_cluster` libraries to Apache. We will look at WildFly first, as it is preconfigured, and then move on to the installation of `mod_cluster`.

Bundled in your WildFly installation, you will find the mod_cluster 1.3.0 module. This subsystem is included as part of the clustering configuration in both the `standalone-ha.xml` and `domain.xml` configuration files, as follows:

```xml
<subsystem xmlns="urn:jboss:domain:modcluster:1.2">
    <mod-cluster-config advertise-socket="modcluster" connector="ajp">
        <dynamic-load-provider>
            <load-metric type="cpu"/>
        </dynamic-load-provider>
    </mod-cluster-config>
</subsystem>
```

The preceding default configuration references its `socket-binding` through the `advertise-socket` element:

```xml
<socket-binding name="modcluster" port="0" multicast-
address="224.0.1.105" multicast-port="23364"/>
```

Also, note that the default configuration uses the AJP protocol. The `connector` property references the name of the Undertow listener that the `mod_cluster` reverse proxy will connect to. The following is the Undertow configuration with the `ajp-listener` highlighted:

```xml
<subsystem xmlns="urn:jboss:domain:undertow:1.1">
    <buffer-cache name="default"/>
    <server name="default-server">
        <ajp-listener name="ajp" socket-binding="ajp"/>
        <http-listener name="default" socket-binding="http"/>
        ....
    </server>
</subsystem>
```

You will also need to ensure that your interfaces are correctly configured to the IP of the server your WildFly server(s) is/are running on. Update your `hosts.xml` or `standalone-ha.xml` file, replacing the IP with the your server's IP:

```
<interfaces>
    <interface name="management">
        <inet-address value="178.62.50.168"/>
    </interface>
    <interface name="public">
        <inet-address value="178.62.50.168"/>
    </interface>
</interfaces>
```

Let's now move on to the second part—the installation and configuration of `mod_cluster` within Apache.

If you do not have Apache installed, you should follow the instructions from earlier in this chapter (see the *Installing Apache* section). We first need to install the required Apache modules. These modules are used to interact with `mod_cluster` on WildFly.

In this example, we are using Apache 2.2, which requires Version 1.2.x of `mod_cluster`. If you are using Apache 2.4, then you can use a later version of `mod_cluster`, namely Version 1.3.x. You can also use Version 1.2.x, but it will need to be compiled for Apache 2.4. To see your version of Apache, run the following command:

apache2ctl -V

> At the time of writing, 1.3.x binaries were not available from the download site, so you might need to compile them from the source (`https://github.com/modcluster/mod_cluster/tree/master`)..
>
> Please check the download site before deciding to go down the route of compiling the source. If you wish to compile the module, you should check `http://www.openlogic.com/blog/bid/247607/JBoss-AS7-Clustering-Using-mod_cluster-and-http-2-4-Part-1`.

Go to the download site (`http://mod-cluster.jboss.org/downloads`), and select the binaries for your platform. Select **mod_cluster modules for httpd**:

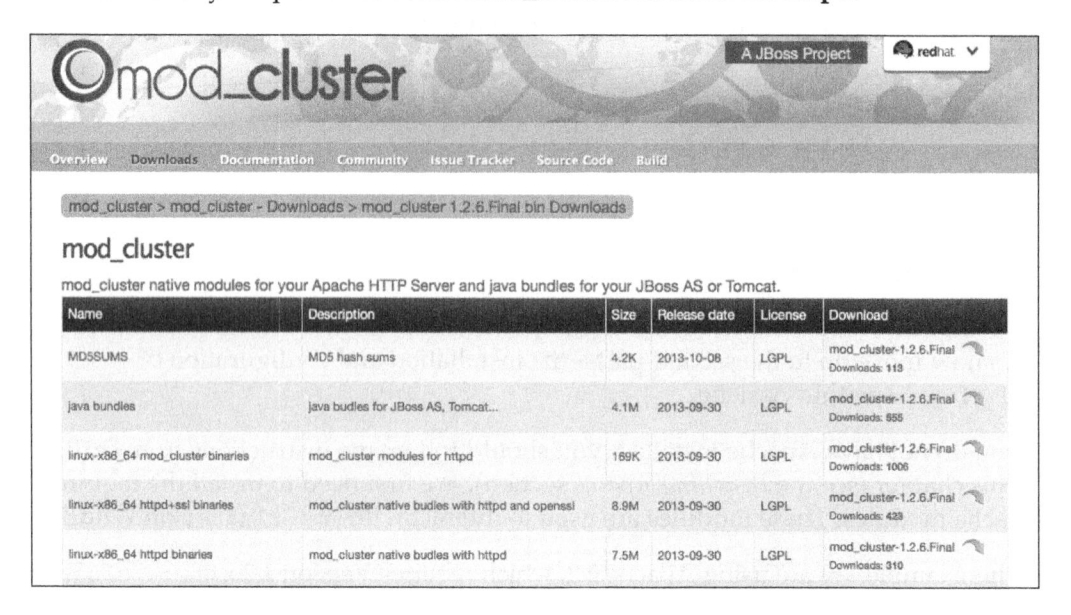

Once the binaries have been downloaded, you need to extract the archive to the `module` directory in Apache. When you extract the downloaded archive, you should see the following files:

- `mod_advertise.so`
- `mod_manager.so`
- `mod_proxy_cluster.so`
- `mod_slotmem.so`

You can run the following commands to achieve this. The first one downloads the file from the `mod_cluster` website using the URL from the download page. The second one extracts the TAR file, and the final command copies the libraries to the `modules` directory.

```
wget -c http://downloads.jboss.org/mod_cluster/1.2.6.Final/linux-x86_64/mod_cluster-1.2.6.Final-linux2-x64-so.tar.gz
tar -xzvf mod_cluster-1.2.6.Final-linux2-x64-so.tar.gz
cp ./*.so /usr/lib/apache2/modules
```

The mod_cluster configuration

Next, we need to create two files within the `/etc/apache2/mods-available` directory. The first one is called `mod_cluster.load` and contains the list of libraries this module depends on. The following is the complete content of the file:

```
LoadModule proxy_module
   /usr/lib/apache2/modules/mod_proxy.so
LoadModule proxy_http_module
   /usr/lib/apache2/modules/mod_proxy_http.so
LoadModule proxy_ajp_module
   /usr/lib/apache2/modules/mod_proxy_ajp.so
LoadModule slotmem_module
   /usr/lib/apache2/modules/mod_slotmen.so

LoadModule manager_module
   /usr/lib/apache2/modules/mod_manager.so
LoadModule proxy_cluster_module
   /usr/lib/apache2/modules/mod_proxy_cluster.so
LoadModule advertise_module
   /usr/lib/apache2/modules/mod_advertise.so
```

> The slotmen module name has changed from `mod_slotmen.so` to `mod_cluster_slotmen.so` in Version 1.3.x.

This list contains the four libraries we just copied to the `module` folder, and the pre-existing `mod_proxy` libraries.

Each of these modules performs a specific role within the load-balancing functionality. The core modules are `mod_proxy`, `mod_proxy_ajp`, and `mod_proxy_http`. They forward requests to cluster nodes using either the HTTP/HTTPS protocol or the AJP protocol.

Next, `mod_manager` is a module that reads information from WildFly and updates the shared memory information in conjunction with `mod_slotmem`. The `mod_proxy_cluster` is the module that contains the balancer for `mod_proxy`. Finally, `mod_advertise` is an additional module that allows HTTPD to advertise via multicast packets, the IP, and port number where the `mod_cluster` is listening.

The next file we need to create is called `mod_cluster.conf`. This file is placed alongside `mod_cluster.load` within the `/etc/apache2/mods-available` directory, as follows:

```
CreateBalancers 1

<IfModule manager_module>
    Listen 127.0.1.1:6666
    ManagerBalancerName mycluster

    <VirtualHost 127.0.1.1:6666>
        KeepAliveTimeout 300
        MaxKeepAliveRequests 0
        AdvertiseFrequency 5
        ServerAdvertise On
        EnableMCPMReceive

        <Location />
            Order deny,allow
            Allow from 127.0.1
        </Location>

    </VirtualHost>
</IfModule>
```

You have to replace the `127.0.1.1` IP address with the IP address that WildFly uses to connect to Apache. If your Apache and WildFly are on different servers, then it will be the IP of your Apache server. You also need to update the port value of 6666 with the one you want to use for communicating with WildFly.

As the configuration currently stands, the Apache virtual host allows incoming requests from:

- IP addresses with prefix `127.0.1`
- The sub-network `127.0.1.0/24`

The `CreateBalancers` directive configures how the HTTP balancers are created in virtual hosts. The possible values of `CreateBalancers` are 0, 1, and 2, outlined as follows:

- `0`: Creates balancers in all virtual hosts
- `1`: Does not create any balancers
- `2`: Creates a balancer for the main server only

> Setting `CreateBalancers` to 1 means that you must configure a balancer in the `ProxyPass` directive (shown further in the chapter). For more information, please see this link: http://docs.jboss.org/mod_cluster/1.2.0/html/native.config.html#d0e485

The `KeepAliveTimeout` directive allows the same connection to be reused within 300 seconds. The number of requests per connection is unlimited since we are setting `MaxKeepAliveRequests` to `0`. The `ManagerBalancerName` directive provides the balancer name for your cluster (defaults to `mycluster`).

What is most important for us is the `ServerAdvertise` directive. It uses the advertise mechanism to tell WildFly to whom it should send the cluster information.

You can also refine the time elapsed between multicasting advertising messages with the `AdvertiseFrequency` directive, which defaults to 10 seconds.

> **Overview of the advertising mechanism**
>
> The default multicast IP address and port used for advertising is `224.0.1.105:23364`. These values match the WildFly bindings defined in the following socket-binding named `modcluster`:
>
> ```
> <socket-binding name="modcluster" port="0"
>   multicast-address="224.0.1.105"
>   multicast-port="23364"/>
> ```
>
> If you ever change these values in WildFly, you will also have to match it on the HTTPD side with the `AdvertiseGroup` directive:
>
> ```
> AdvertiseGroup 224.0.1.105:23364
> ```

The very last thing you need to configure is the virtual host in your site configuration file. Create a file called `wildfly` within the `/etc/apache2/sites-enabled` directory. Add the following highlighted code lines:

```
<VirtualHost *:80>
    ServerAdmin webmaster@localhost

    ProxyPass / balancer://mycluster stickysession=JSESSIONID|jsessionid nofailover=On
    ProxyPassReverse / balancer://mycluster

    <Location />
        Order deny,allow
        Allow from All
    </Location>
```

```
        ErrorLog ${APACHE_LOG_DIR}/error.log
        CustomLog ${APACHE_LOG_DIR}/access.log combined
</VirtualHost>
```

As a final note, if you have not already enabled `proxy_ajp` and `proxy_http`, you will need to do so in order for `mod_cluster` to work, as follows:

```
a2enmod proxy proxy_ajp proxy_http
```

You can now enable the WildFly site:

```
sudo a2ensite wildfly
```

Now, enable the `mod_cluster` module and restart Apache:

```
sudo a2enmod mod_cluster
sudo /etc/init.d/apache2 restart
```

Testing mod_cluster

To verify that everything works correctly, start your WildFly domain ensuring that your server group is using an `ha` profile. Deploy the application we used in *Chapter 4, The Undertow Web Server*, to that same server group. If all is configured correctly, you should see the application when you navigate to the context root `chapter4` at `http://178.62.50.168/chapter4`.

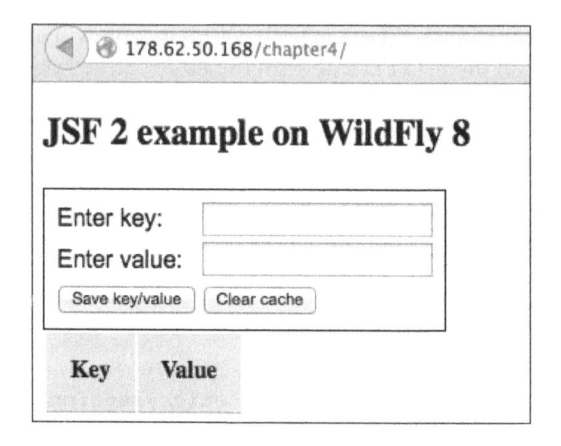

Managing mod_cluster via the CLI

There are a couple of tools that can be used to manage and retrieve runtime information from your cluster. Your first option is the command-line management interface, which allows you to investigate the `mod_cluster` subsystem.

The first command you need to learn is `list-proxies`, which returns merely the hostnames (and port) of the connected proxies:

```
[domain@localhost:9990 /] /host=master/server=server-one/
subsystem=modcluster:list-proxies
{
    "outcome" => "success",
    "result" => ["apache-wildfly:6666"]
}
```

While this can be useful for a quick inspection of your cluster members, you can get more detailed information with the `read-proxies-info` command that actually sends an information message to the HTTPD server:

```
[domain@localhost:9990 /] /host=master/server=server-one/
subsystem=modcluster:read-proxies-info
{
    "outcome" => "success",
    "result" => [
        "apache-wildfly:6666",
        "Node: [1],Name: master:server-two,Balancer: mycluster,LBGroup: ,Host: 178.62.50.168,Port: 8159,Type: ajp,Flushpackets: Off,Flushwait: 10,Ping: 10,Smax: 26,Ttl: 60,Elected: 0,Read: 0,Transfered: 0,Connected: 0,Load: 97
Node: [2],Name: master:server-one,Balancer: mycluster,LBGroup: ,Host: 178.62.50.168,Port: 8009,Type: ajp,Flushpackets: Off,Flushwait: 10,Ping: 10,Smax: 26,Ttl: 60,Elected: 0,Read: 0,Transfered: 0,Connected: 0,Load: 98
Vhost: [1:1:1], Alias: localhost
Vhost: [1:1:2], Alias: default-host
Vhost: [2:1:3], Alias: localhost
Vhost: [2:1:4], Alias: default-host
Context: [1:1:1], Context: /chapter4, Status: ENABLED
Context: [2:1:2], Context: /chapter4, Status: ENABLED
"
    ]
}
```

The `mod_cluster` subsystem also allows us to use the `read-proxies-configuration` command, which provides more verbose information about your cluster. For the sake of brevity, we will omit printing its output.

The list of proxies that are part of your cluster can also be modified with the CLI. For example, you can use the `add-proxy` command to add a proxy that has not been captured by the mod_cluster's `httpd` configuration. Have a look at the following code:

```
[domain@localhost:9990 /] /host=master/server=server-one/
subsystem=modcluster:add-proxy(host=192.168.0.11, port=9999)
{
    "outcome" => "success"
}
```

You can also remove proxies from the list using the corresponding `remove-proxy` command:

```
[domain@localhost:9990 /] /host=master/server=server-one/
subsystem=modcluster:remove-proxy(host=192.168.0.11, port=9999)
{
    "outcome" => "success"
}
```

Managing your web contexts with the CLI

You can use the CLI to manage your web contexts. For example, the `enable-context` command can be used to tell Apache that a particular web context is able to receive requests, as follows:

```
[standalone@localhost:9990 subsystem=modcluster] :enable-
context(context=/app, virtualhost=default-host)
```

`{"outcome" => "success"}`

The corresponding `disable-context` command can be used to prevent Apache from sending *new* requests:

```
[standalone@localhost:9990 subsystem=modcluster] :disable-
context(context=/app, virtualhost=default-host)
```

`{"outcome" => "success"}`

To stop Apache from sending requests from a web context, you can use the `stop-context` command, as follows:

```
[standalone@localhost:9990 subsystem=modcluster] :stop-context(context=/
app, virtualhost=default-host, waittime=50)
```

`{"outcome" => "success"}`

Adding native management capabilities

If you are not able (or simply don't want) to use the CLI, then you can also configure the Apache web server to provide a basic management interface through the browser.

In order to do that, all you need to add is the `mod_cluster_manager` application context, as follows:

```
<Location /mod_cluster_manager>
     SetHandler mod_cluster-manager
     Order deny,allow
     Deny from all
     Allow from 192.168.10
</Location>
```

You can test your `mod_cluster` manager application by navigating to `http://192.168.10.1/http://192.168.10.1/mod_cluster_manager`.

In our example, the `mod_cluster` manager displays information about all the WildFly nodes that have been discovered through multicast announcements. Take a look at the following screenshot:

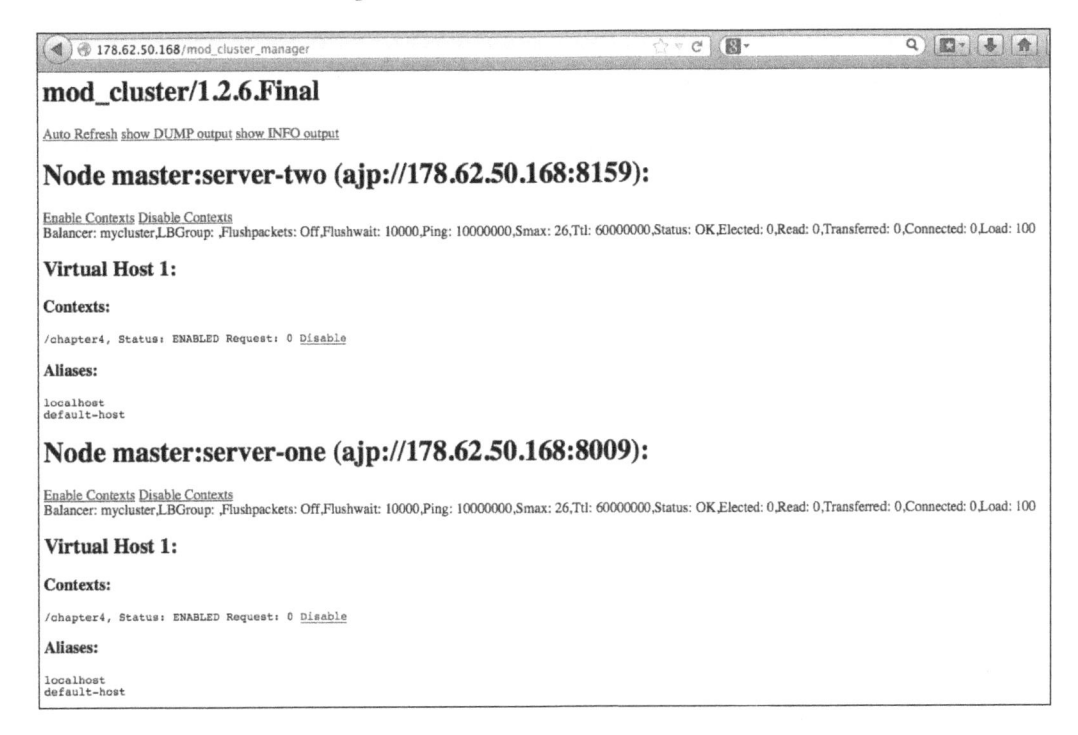

mod_cluster/1.2.6.Final

Auto Refresh show DUMP output show INFO output

Node master:server-two (ajp://178.62.50.168:8159):

Enable Contexts Disable Contexts
Balancer: mycluster,LBGroup: ,Flushpackets: Off,Flushwait: 10000,Ping: 10000000,Smax: 26,Ttl: 60000000,Status: OK,Elected: 0,Read: 0,Transferred: 0,Connected: 0,Load: 100

Virtual Host 1:

Contexts:

/chapter4, Status: ENABLED Request: 0 Disable

Aliases:

localhost
default-host

Node master:server-one (ajp://178.62.50.168:8009):

Enable Contexts Disable Contexts
Balancer: mycluster,LBGroup: ,Flushpackets: Off,Flushwait: 10000,Ping: 10000000,Smax: 26,Ttl: 60000000,Status: OK,Elected: 0,Read: 0,Transferred: 0,Connected: 0,Load: 100

Virtual Host 1:

Contexts:

/chapter4, Status: ENABLED Request: 0 Disable

Aliases:

localhost
default-host

Load-balancing Web Applications

In the `mod_cluster` manager page, you have lots of useful information, such as the number of hosts that are currently active (in our example, two nodes) and the web contexts that are available. By default, all web contexts are mounted automatically (not requiring an explicit mount as for `mod_jk`), but you can exclude or include them by clicking on the **Disable/Enable** link, which is placed next to the web context.

Managing web contexts using the configuration file

For the sake of completeness, we will add one more option that can be used to manage your web context using your application server configuration file. By default, all web contexts are enabled; however, you can exclude web contexts from the main configuration file using the `excluded-contexts` directive. Take a look at the following code:

```
<subsystem xmlns="urn:jboss:domain:modcluster:1.2">
    <mod-cluster-config excluded-contexts="ROOT, webapp1"/>
</subsystem>
```

Troubleshooting mod_cluster

Installing and enabling `mod_cluster` on Apache requires just a few steps to get working. However, should you have problems, you can allow a verbose output, which will cause an overview of your configuration to be displayed. Add the `AllowDisplay` directive to your `mod_cluster_manager` application context as highlighted as follows:

```
<Location /mod_cluster_manager>
    SetHandler mod_cluster-manager
    Order deny,allow
    Deny from all
    Allow from 192.168.10
</Location>

AllowDisplay On
```

When adding this directive, you will get further information about the modules loaded into HTTPD. This output may help you narrow down any issues, as shown in the following screenshot:

mod_cluster/1.2.6.Final

start of "httpd.conf" configuration
mod_proxy_cluster.c: OK
mod_sharedmem.c: OK
Protocol supported: http AJP
mod_advertise.c: OK
Server: 127.0.1.1
Server: 127.0.1.1 VirtualHost: *:80
Server: 127.0.1.1 VirtualHost: *:6666 Advertising on Group 224.0.1.105 Port 23364 for http://127.0.1.1:6666 every 5 seconds
end of "httpd.conf" configuration

Auto Refresh show DUMP output show INFO output

One more possible cause of errors is a firewall preventing the broadcast of advertising messages. Remember that advertisement messages use the UDP port number 23364 and the multicast address 224.0.1.105. In order to verify if advertising is an issue, you can try to turn it off by setting the following in the HTTPD side:

```
ServerAdvertise Off
```

This directive should be matched on the application server side by the `proxy-list` element. This element defines the list of HTTPD servers with which the WildFly server will initially communicate:

```
<mod-cluster-config proxy-list="192.168.10.1:6666">
    ...
</mod-cluster-config>
```

If there is more than one proxy, then the `proxy-list` will contain a comma-separated list.

You can also check that `mod_cluster` is correctly advertising messages by running a test class `Advertise`, which can be found at `https://github.com/modcluster/mod_cluster/blob/master/test/java/Advertize.java`. You will need to compile the class and then run it as follows:

```
java Advertise 224.0.1.105 23364
```

If the module, that is, advertizing, is correctly configured, you will see something like the following command lines displayed:

```
received from /192.168.0.10:23364
received: HTTP/1.0 200 OK
```

```
Date: Sat, 26 Jul 2014 20:03:12 GMT
Sequence: 121
Digest: 4dedd3761d451227f36534b63ca2a8a1
Server: b23584e2-314f-404d-8fde-05069bfe5dc7
X-Manager-Address: 127.0.1.1:6666
X-Manager-Url: /b23584e2-314f-404d-8fde-05069bfe5dc7
X-Manager-Protocol: http
X-Manager-Host: 127.0.1.1
```

Finally, don't forget to check the error log in the Apache `logs` directory for any errors.

Also, make sure that you have enabled the `mod_proxy_http` module, as `mod_cluster` will fail to work without it.

Load-balancing between nodes

We will run a couple of tests in order to investigate how `mod_cluster` distributes the load between several different clients.

For these tests, we will use a very basic web application. The application source can be found with the source code for this book; the project is called `chapter9-balancer`. It contains a simple `index.jsp` page, which dumps a message on the console:

```
<%
Integer counter = (Integer)session.getAttribute("counter");
if (counter == null) {
   session.setAttribute("counter",new Integer(1));
}
else {
   session.setAttribute("counter",new Integer(counter+1));
}
System.out.println("Counter"+session.getAttribute("counter"));
%>
```

After deploying the application, go to the URL `http://192.168.0.10/balancer/index.jsp`. After making several requests, you will see that each subsequent request is sent to the same server. This shows that `mod_cluster` follows a sticky-session policy. Have a look at the following screenshot:

```
[Server:server-one] 14:27:19,641 INFO  [stdout] (default task-2) Counter1
[Server:server-one] 14:27:29,857 INFO  [stdout] (default task-3) Counter2
[Server:server-one] 14:27:34,391 INFO  [stdout] (default task-4) Counter3
[Server:server-one] 14:27:35,817 INFO  [stdout] (default task-5) Counter4
[Server:server-one] 14:27:44,487 INFO  [stdout] (default task-6) Counter5
[Server:server-one] 14:27:45,210 INFO  [stdout] (default task-7) Counter6
[Server:server-one] 14:27:45,666 INFO  [stdout] (default task-8) Counter7
[Server:server-one] 14:27:45,986 INFO  [stdout] (default task-9) Counter8
[Server:server-one] 14:27:46,298 INFO  [stdout] (default task-10) Counter9
[Server:server-one] 14:28:11,460 INFO  [stdout] (default task-12) Counter10
root@apache-wildfly:~#
```

For the purpose of our tests, we need a software application that can be used to launch several requests to our cluster. We will use JMeter, a Java desktop application, which is generally used to test load, test functional behavior, and measure performance. JMeter can be downloaded from http://jmeter.apache.org/download_jmeter.cgi.

In short, a JMeter test plan consists of one or more thread groups, logic controllers, listeners, timers, assertions, and configuration elements.

For the purpose of our example, we will just create the following elements:

- A **Thread Group**, which is configured to run 100 subsequent requests
- An **HTTP Request** element that contains information about the web application's end point

To do this, open JMeter and navigate to **Test Plan | Add | Threads | Thread Group**, as shown in the following screenshot:

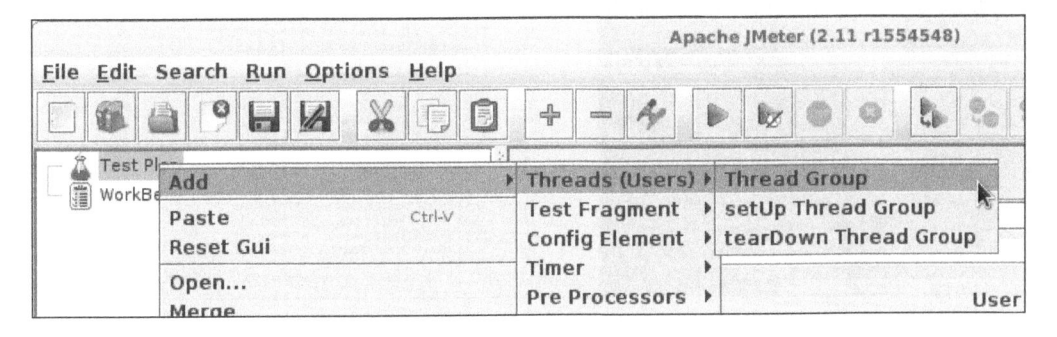

Load-balancing Web Applications

Set the number of threads (users) to 100. Now right-click on the newly created **Thread Group | Add | Sampler | HTTP Request**. In here, add the server IP and path, as shown to the right-hand side of the following screenshot. The port number can be left blank as it defaults to port number 80. Take a look at the following screenshot:

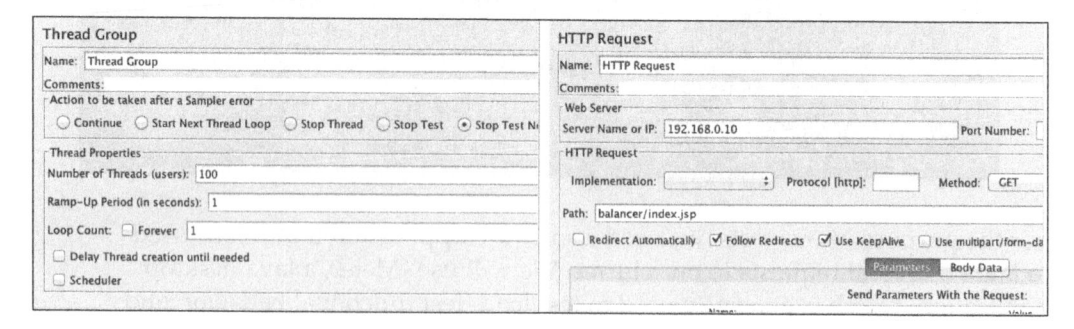

Additionally, you should add a **Listener** element that collates the test plan result into a table/graph in order for you to view the results. To do this, navigate to **HTTP Request | Add | Listener | View Results in Table**. Now, from the top menu, navigate to **Run | Start**, and the JMeter test will be executed.

Running the test shows that the requests are roughly split between the two servers. Have a look at the following screenshot:

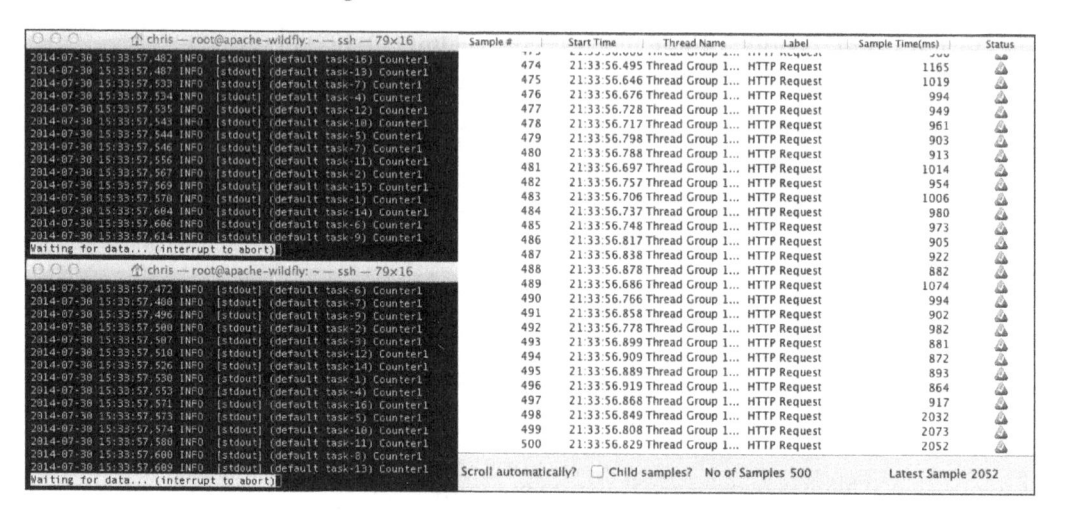

Using load metrics

Various system load metrics are collected from each server. These statistics allow a normalized load value to be calculated for each server. When the cluster is under light load, the incoming requests are evenly distributed to each server node. As the load increases, the amount of traffic sent to a given node depends on its current load, that is, more traffic will be directed to the node that has the least load.

The default `mod_cluster` configuration is configured with a dynamic load provider, as shown in the following code:

```xml
<subsystem xmlns="urn:jboss:domain:modcluster:1.2">
    <mod-cluster-config advertise-socket="modcluster" connector="ajp">
        <dynamic-load-provider>
            <load-metric type="cpu"/>
        </dynamic-load-provider>
    </mod-cluster-config>
</subsystem>
```

You can customize load balancing by adding further `load-metric` elements. For example:

```xml
<subsystem xmlns="urn:jboss:domain:modcluster:1.2">
  <mod-cluster-config advertise-socket="modcluster" connector="ajp">
    <dynamic-load-provider history="10" decay="2">
      <load-metric type="cpu" weight="2" capacity="1"/>
            <load-metric type="sessions" weight="1"
                capacity="512"/>
    </dynamic-load-provider>
  </mod-cluster-config>
</subsystem>
```

The most important factors when computing load balancing are the `weight` and `capacity` properties. The `weight` (the default is 1) indicates the impact of a metric with respect to the other metrics. In the previous example, the CPU metric will have twice the impact compared to the sessions that have a load factor metric of 1.

The `capacity` property, on the other hand, can be used for a fine-grained control over the load metrics. By setting a different capacity to each metric, you can actually favor one node over another while preserving the metric weights.

The list of supported load metrics is summarized in the following table:

Metric	Factor used to compose metric
cpu	CPU load
heap	Heap memory usage as a percentage of max heap size
sessions	Number of web sessions
requests	Number of requests/sec
send-traffic	Number of outgoing requests in traffic
receive-traffic	Number of incoming requests post traffic

The preceding metrics can also be set using the CLI, for example, supposing that you want to add a metric that is based on the amount of heap used by the proxy. Don't forget to reload the configuration when notified to do so (enter the `reload` command). Here's what you need to issue:

```
[standalone@localhost:9990 /] /subsystem=modcluster/mod-cluster-
config=configuration/dynamic-load-provider=configuration/load-
metric=heap:add(type=heap)
{
    "outcome" => "success",
    "response-headers" => {
        "operation-requires-reload" => true,
        "process-state" => "reload-required"
    }
}
[standalone@localhost:9990 /] /subsystem=modcluster/mod-cluster-
config=configuration/dynamic-load-provider=configuration:read-resource()
{
    "outcome" => "success",
    "result" => {
        "decay" => 2,
        "history" => 9,
        "custom-load-metric" => undefined,
        "load-metric" => {
            "cpu" => undefined,
            "heap" => undefined
        }
    }
}
```

You can also remove the metric using the `remove` command, as follows:

```
[standalone@localhost:9990 /] /subsystem=modcluster/mod-cluster-config=configuration/dynamic-load-provider=configuration/load-metric=heap:remove()
{
    "outcome" => "success",
    "response-headers" => {
        "operation-requires-reload" => true,
        "process-state" => "reload-required"
    }
}
```

An example for setting dynamic metrics on a cluster

In the following example, we have a very simple cluster comprising two nodes. Each node has the same JVM operating defaults, and each one is running on two identical machines.

We will, however, simulate memory-intensive operations on the first node so that the amount of heap memory used differs between each server, as shown in the following screenshot:

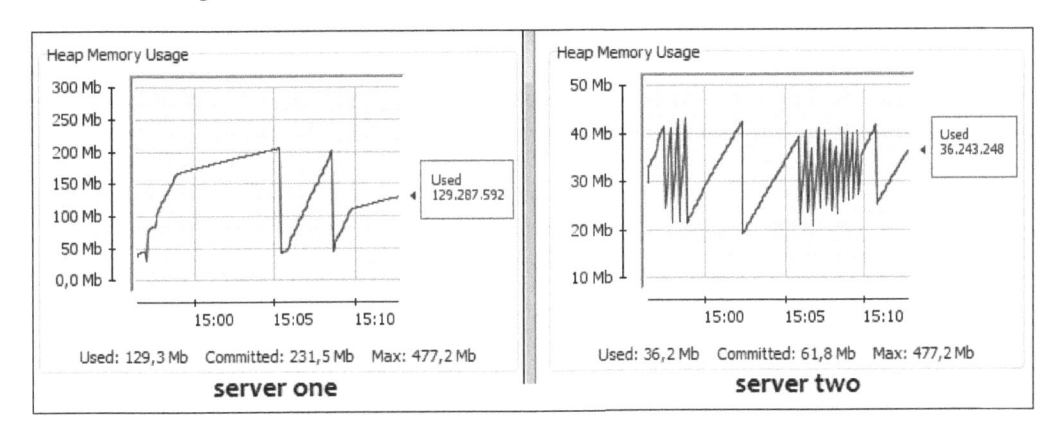

This is a common scenario in web applications where different circumstances have a different impact on each server's memory, for example, holding data temporarily in the HTTP session.

In such a case, using a round-robin approach to distribute a request may lead to an "out-of-memory" scenario on some nodes in your cluster. You can try to mitigate this by simply modifying the configuration of the loading metrics, as follows:

```xml
<subsystem xmlns="urn:jboss:domain:modcluster:1.2">
    <mod-cluster-config advertise-socket="mod_cluster">
        <dynamic-load-provider history="10" decay="2">
            <load-metric type="heap" weight="2" />
            <load-metric type="mem"  weight="1" />
            <load-metric type="cpu"  weight="1" />
        </dynamic-load-provider>
    </mod-cluster-config>
</subsystem>
```

When using this configuration on both nodes, the heap memory usage has twice the impact of other enlisted metrics (operating system memory and CPU speed).

The outcome of this is that the second server handles 55 percent of the requests, while the first server handles 45 percent.

By setting the appropriate capacity, you can further achieve a better level of granularity to node-weighting, for example, by setting a higher capacity on the first server, as follows:

```xml
<load-metric type="heap" weight="2" capacity="512"/>
```

You can set a lower capacity on the second one, as follows:

```xml
<load-metric type="heap" weight="2" capacity="1"/>
```

Then, the outcome of the test will be different, as the second server now delivers more responses than the first one, counterbalancing the weight metric.

> The capacity of each metric defaults to 512 and should be configured such that 0 <= (load / capacity) >= 1.

Summary

In this chapter, we showed various ways of distributing application load across a set of nodes. This is referred to as load balancing.

Load balancing requires a web server, such as Apache, which directs traffic to your various application servers.

In the first half of this chapter, we illustrated how to use the mod_jk and mod_proxy libraries in WildFly. The mod_jk library requires some configuration on both the HTTPD side and the AS side. The mod_proxy library is a more immediate solution and a preferred solution when using WildFly as it requires simply configuring the end points on the HTTPD side.

In the second half of the chapter, we looked at the recommended approach to load-balance calls between applications using mod_cluster.

The main advantage of using mod_cluster versus traditional load balancers is that it does not require a static list of worker nodes, rather, it registers application servers and their applications dynamically using a multicast-based advertising mechanism.

This is especially useful in a cloud environment, where you cannot rely on a flat list of nodes. It is much more beneficial to add or remove nodes on the fly.

Finally, another major benefit of mod_cluster is that you can use a dynamic set of metrics that are calculated on the server side to define the load between server nodes. For example, you can give priority to servers that have better specifications, such as higher RAM or better processing power.

In the next chapter, we are going to look at one of the most important parts of WildFly administration, that is, security.

10
Securing WildFly

Security is a key element of any enterprise application. You must be able to control and restrict who is permitted to access your applications and what operations users may perform.

The **Java Enterprise Edition (Java EE)** specification defines a simple, role-based security model for **Enterprise Java Beans (EJBs)** and web components. The implementation of JBoss security is delivered by the PicketBox framework (formerly known as the JBoss security), which provides authentication, authorization, auditing, and mapping capabilities to Java applications.

As the number of topics concerned with security requires a book in its own right, this chapter will focus on the topics that are of interest to the majority of administrators and developers. We will cover the following topics in detail:

- A short introduction to the Java security API
- The basics of the WildFly security subsystem
- Defining login modules and their integration with various enterprise components (for example, web application EJB)
- Securing the management interfaces
- Using **Secure Sockets Layer (SSL)** to encrypt network calls to web applications

Approaching Java security API

Java EE security services provide a robust and easily configurable security mechanism to authenticate users and authorize access to application functions and associated data. To better understand the topics related to security, we will first provide some basic definitions:

Authentication is the process of ensuring that a person is who he claims to be. Authentication is usually performed by checking that a user's login credentials match those stored in a datastore. Login credentials typically consist of a username and password but can also be in the form of an X.509 certificate or **one-time password** (**OTP**). The following figure demonstrates the flow of a login process. The end user provides a username and password, which is submitted to the application server. The login module checks the user's details against those stored in a datastore. If the credentials match, the user is logged in; if the credentials do not match, then the login process will fail. Have a look at the following diagram:

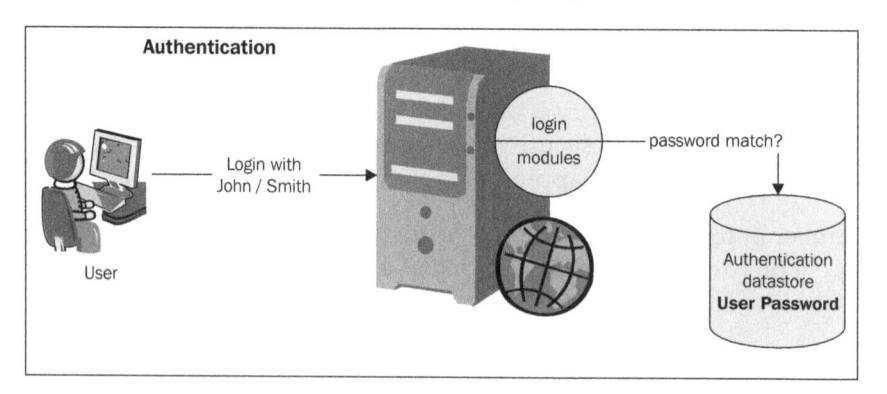

Authorization is the process by which you verify that a user has the permission to access a particular system resource. Authorization should occur after authentication has taken place. Have a look at the following diagram:

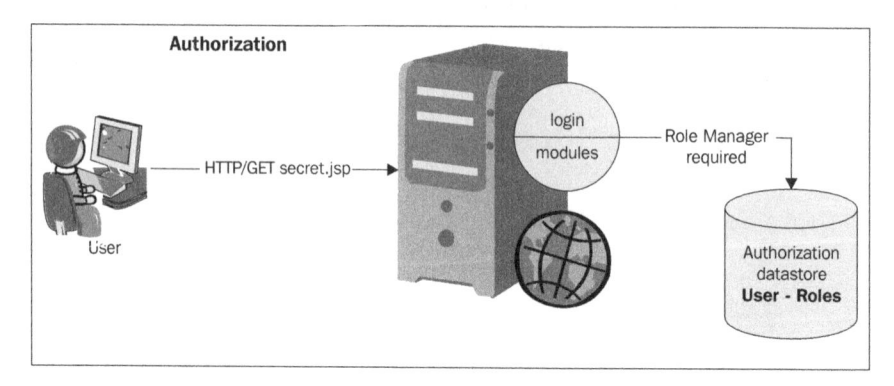

In Java EE, the component containers are responsible for providing application security. A container basically provides two types of security: **declarative** and **programmatic**.

- **Declarative security** defines an application component's security requirements by means of deployment descriptors and/or annotations. A deployment descriptor is an external file that can be modified without the need to recompile the source code.

    For example, Enterprise JavaBeans components can use an EJB deployment descriptor that must be named `ejb-jar.xml` and placed in the `META-INF` folder of the EJB JAR file.

    Web components use a web application deployment descriptor named `web.xml` located in the `WEB-INF` directory.

    Annotations are specified within a class file, which means any changes will require the code to be recompiled.

    Using annotations provides many benefits over deployment descriptors. First, it is clearer in the source code as to what is happening rather than having this information scattered over various XML files. Second, it is easier to maintain as there are fewer configuration files.

    The use of annotations also means less boilerplate code for the developer.

- **Programmatic security** comes into the picture when security checks are embedded within an application code. It can be used when declarative security alone is not sufficient to express the security model of an application. For example, the Java EE security API allows the developer to test whether or not the current user has a specific role, using the following methods:

    - `isUserInRole()`: Use this method within servlets and JSPs (adopted in `javax.servlet.http.HttpServletRequest`)
    - `isCallerInRole()`: Use this method in EJBs (adopted in `javax.ejb.SessionContext`)

    In addition, there are other API calls that provide access to the user's identity, which are as follows:

    - `getUserPrincipal()`: Use this method within servlets and JSPs (adopted in `javax.servlet.http.HttpServletRequest`)
    - `getCallerPrincipal()`: Use this method in EJBs (adopted in `javax.ejb.SessionContext`)

Using these APIs, you can develop a complex authorization model programmatically.

> While annotations themselves are programmatic, they enable a declarative style of security. For this reason, annotations are considered to encompass both the declarative and programmatic security concepts.

The Java EE security model is declarative, due to which embedding the security code into your business component is not an option. The term declarative here means that you describe the security roles and permissions in a standard XML descriptor. Declarative security allows the logic from this cross-cutting concern to be extracted away from core business logic. This results in a clearer and more readable code.

The default implementation of the declarative security model is based on **Java Authentication and Authorization Service (JAAS)** login modules and subjects. WildFly security has a security proxy layer that allows the developer to create custom security services if the default implementation does not suffice. This allows custom security to be built independently of the bean object using it, without polluting the business code.

WildFly uses the PicketBox framework, which builds on JAAS. PicketBox is used to secure all the Java EE technologies running in the application server.

The WildFly security subsystem

The WildFly security subsystem is an extension of the application server and is included by default in both the standalone servers and domain servers. Have a look at the following code:

```
<extension module="org.jboss.as.security"/>
```

The following is the default security subsystem contained in the server configuration file:

```
<subsystem xmlns="urn:jboss:domain:security:1.2">
  <security-domains>
    <security-domain name="other" cache-type="default">
      <authentication>
        <login-module code="Remoting" flag="optional">
          <module-option name="password-stacking"
              value="useFirstPass"/>
        </login-module>
```

```xml
        <login-module code="RealmDirect" flag="required">
          <module-option name="password-stacking"
             value="useFirstPass"/>
        </login-module>
      </authentication>
    </security-domain>
    <security-domain name="jboss-web-policy" cache-type="default">
      <authorization>
        <policy-module code="Delegating" flag="required"/>
      </authorization>
    </security-domain>
    <security-domain name="jboss-ejb-policy" cache-type="default">
      <authorization>
        <policy-module code="Delegating" flag="required"/>
      </authorization>
    </security-domain>
  </security-domains>
</subsystem>
```

As you can see, the configuration is pretty short, as it relies largely on default values, especially for high-level structures, such as the security management area.

> A security domain does not explicitly require an authorization policy. If a security domain does not define an authorization module, the default jboss-web-policy and jboss-ejb-policy authorizations are used. In such a case, the delegating authorization policy is applied, which simply delegates the authorization to another module declared as <module-option>.

You can override the default authentication/authorization managers with your own implementation by defining your own security management configuration. It is unlikely that you will have to override these interfaces, so we will concentrate on the security-domain element, which is a core aspect of the WildFly security subsystem.

A **security domain** can be imagined as a customs office for foreigners. Before the request crosses the WildFly borders, the security domain performs all the required authorization and authentication checks and notifies the caller whether they can proceed or not.

Security domains are generally configured at server startup or in a running server and subsequently bound to the JNDI tree under the key java:/jaas/. Within the security domain, you can configure login authentication modules so that you can easily change your authentication provider by simply changing its login module.

The following table describes all the available login modules, including a short description of them:

Login module	Description
Client	This login module is designed to establish caller identity and credentials when AS is acting as a client. It should never be used as part of a security domain for actual server authentication.
Database	This login module loads user/role information from a database.
Certificate	This login module is designed to authenticate users based on the X.509 certificates.
CertificateRoles	This login module extends the Certificate login module to add role-mapping capabilities from a properties file.
DatabaseCertificate	This login module extends the Certificate login module to add role-mapping capabilities from a database table.
DatabaseUsers	This is a JDBC-based login module that supports authentication and role mapping.
Identity	This login module simply associates the principles specified in the module options with any subject authenticated against the module.
Ldap	This login module loads user/role information from an LDAP server.
LdapExtended	This login module is an alternate LDAP login module implementation that uses searches to locate both the user as well as the associated roles to bind the authentication.
RoleMapping	This login module is used to map roles that are the end result of the authentication process to one or more declarative roles.
RunAs	This login module can be used to allow another login module to interact with a secured EJB that provides authentication services.
Simple	This login module is used to quickly set up the security for testing purposes.
ConfigureIdentity	This is a login module that associates the principles specified in the module options with any subject authenticated against the module.
PropertiesUsers	This login module uses a properties file to store the username and password for authentication. No roles are mapped.
SimpleUsers	This login module stores username and password as options.
LdapUsers	This login module authenticates users using a LDAP server.

Login module	Description
Kerberos	This login module uses Sun's `Kerberos` login module as a mechanism for authentication.
SPNEGOUsers	This login module works in conjunction with `SPNEGOAuthenticator` to handle the authentication.
AdvancedLdap	This login module is a refactoring of the `LdapExtLoginModule`, which is able to separate the login steps (find, authenticate, or map roles) so that any of the actions can be undertaken separately.
AdvancedADLdap	This login module is an extension of the `AdvancedLdap` login module, which is also able to query the primary group of the user being authenticated.
UsersRoles	This login module is a simple properties-map-based login module that consults two Java properties-formatted text files to map the username to the password (`users.properties`) and username to roles (`roles.properties`).

Activating a login module is a two-step procedure, which is as follows:

1. First, you need to define the login module within your `standalone.xml`/`domain.xml` configuration file.
2. Then, you need to tell your applications to use a login module to perform authentication and authorization.

> In earlier releases of the application server, the login module was configured in a separate file named `login-config.xml`. Porting earlier login modules into the new application server is not too complex, as the format of the login module is pretty much the same as the new application server.

We will now expand these points in more detail. Let's see first how to define some commonly-used login modules, and then we will apply them to the Java EE components, such as servlets, EJB, and web services.

Using the UsersRoles login module

The `UsersRoles` login module is one of the simplest security domains that can be implemented for testing purposes in your applications. It is based on two files, which are as follows:

- `users.properties`: This file contains the list of usernames and passwords
- `roles.properties`: This file contains the mapping between the users and the roles

Securing WildFly

Here is a sample `UsersRoles` configuration that stores the security files in the application server's configuration directory:

```
<security-domain name="basic" cache-type="default">
 <authentication>
   <login-module code="UsersRoles" flag="required">
      <module-option name="usersProperties" value="${jboss.server.
        config.dir}/users.properties"/>
      <module-option name="rolesProperties" value="${jboss.server.
        config.dir}/roles.properties"/>
   </login-module>
 </authentication>
</security-domain>
```

All you need to do to start using your security domain is add the two properties files into the specified path (for a standalone system, the default is `JBOSS_HOME/standalone/configuration`) and add your username and password within it. This login module does not support hashed passwords; only clear passwords are supported. For example, the `users.properties` file can contain something like the following:

```
myusername=mypassword
```

The `roles.properties` file contains the sets of roles for a given username. Adding a suffix to the username, as shown in the second line of the following code, allows you to assign the username roles to a group of roles:

```
myusername=myrole1,myrole2
myusername.MyRoleGroup1=myrole3,myrole4
```

This means that authenticating with the admin/admin credentials will assign the role of manager to the user.

Using the Database login module

A database security domain follows the same logic exposed in the earlier example, the difference being that it stores the credentials within the database. In order to run this example, we need to refer to the `MySqlDS` datasource that we created earlier, in *Chapter 3, Configuring Enterprise Services*. Have a look at the following code:

```
<security-domain name="mysqldomain" cache-type="default">
    <authentication>
        <login-module code="Database" flag="required">
            <module-option name="dsJndiName" value="java:/
              MySqlDS"/>
            <module-option name="principalsQuery" value="select
              passwd from USERS where user=?"/>
```

```xml
            <module-option name="rolesQuery" value="select role,
               'Roles' from USER_ROLES where user=?"/>
        </login-module>
    </authentication>
</security-domain>
```

> You will notice in the `rolesQuery` module option that there is a second select item (`Roles`). This corresponds to a `RoleGroup` column and must always be supplied with "R" (in capital letters)..

In order to start using this configuration, you first have to create the required tables and insert some sample data into it:

```
CREATE TABLE USERS(user VARCHAR(64) PRIMARY KEY, passwd VARCHAR(64));
CREATE TABLE USER_ROLES(user VARCHAR(64), role VARCHAR(32));

INSERT INTO USERS VALUES('admin', 'admin');
INSERT INTO USER_ROLES VALUES('admin', 'Manager');
```

As you can see, the admin user will map to the `Manager` role. One caveat of this configuration is that it uses clear-text passwords in the database so, before rolling this module production, you should consider additional security for your login module. Let's see how you can do this in the next section.

Encrypting passwords

Storing passwords in the database as clear-text strings is not considered a good practice. As a matter of fact, a database has even more potential security issues than a regular filesystem.

Fortunately, securing application passwords is relatively easy and can be achieved by adding a few extra options to your login module. As a minimum, you need to specify that the stored passwords are encrypted using a **message digest algorithm**. For example, in the `mysqlLogin` module, you can add the highlighted lines at the end:

```xml
<login-module code="Database" flag="required">
    <module-option name="dsJndiName" value="java:/MySqlDS"/>
    <module-option name="principalsQuery" value="SELECT passwd FROM
       USERS WHERE user=?"/>
    <module-option name="rolesQuery" value="SELECT role, 'Roles' FROM
       USER_ROLES WHERE user=?"/>
    <module-option name="hashAlgorithm" value="MD5"/>
    <module-option name="hashEncoding" value="BASE64"/>
    <module-option name="hashStorePassword" value="true"/>
</login-module>
```

Here, we specified that the password will be hashed against an MD5 hash algorithm; you can alternatively use any other algorithm allowed by your JCA provider, such as SHA.

> For a production environment, you should avoid MD5 hashing, as it is a very weak hash. Ideally, you should use something like SHA-512 with a large number of hash iterations. You should also use a single, randomly generated salt per user. At the time of writing, one of the best hashing algorithms is bcrypt, which generates the salt for you. You should do your research before making a final decision. These encryptions are not supported by the DatabaseServerLoginModule, so you will need to create your own custom login module. Refer to the following link to write a custom login module: https://docs.jboss.org/jbossas/docs/Server_Configuration_Guide/4/html/Writing_Custom_Login_Modules-A_Custom_LoginModule_Example.html.

For the sake of completeness, we include here a small application, which uses the java.security.MessageDigest and the org.jboss.security.Base64Util classes to generate the base-64 hashed password to be inserted in the database. Have a look at the following code:

```
public class Hash {

    public static void main(String[] args) throws Exception {
        String password = args[0];

        MessageDigest md = MessageDigest.getInstance("MD5");

        byte[] passwordBytes = password.getBytes();
        byte[] hash = md.digest(passwordBytes);
        String passwordHash =
           Base64.getEncoder().encodeToString(hash);
        System.out.println("password hash: "+passwordHash);
    }
}
```

Running the main program with `admin` as the argument generates the hash **X8oyfUbUbfqE9IWvAW1/3**. This hash will be the updated password for the admin user of our database. Have a look at the following screenshot:

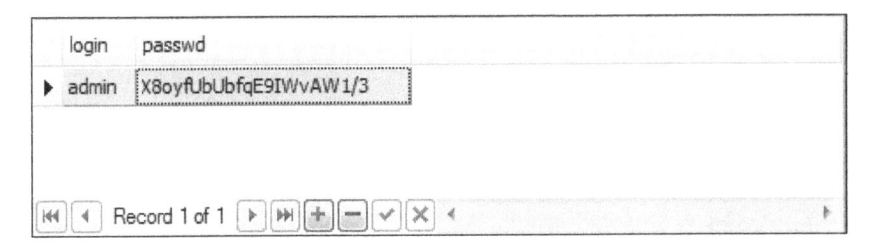

login	passwd
▶ admin	X8oyfUbUbfqE9IWvAW1/3

Record 1 of 1

> If you are not using Java 8, you can use the `org.jboss.security.Base64Utils` library instead of `Java 8` as shown in this section.

Using an LDAP login module

The **Lightweight Directory Access Protocol** (**LDAP**) is the *de facto* standard for providing directory services to applications. An LDAP server can provide central directory information for the following:

- User credentials (login and password)
- User directory information (such as names and e-mail addresses)
- Web directories

The working of LDAP revolves around a data structure known as **entry**. An entry has a set of named component parts called **attributes** that hold the data for that entry. These attributes are like the fields in a database record.

An entry's content and structure are defined by its object class. The object class (along with server and user settings) specifies which attributes must exist and which may exist in that particular entry.

All entries stored in an LDAP directory have a unique **distinguished name** or **DN**. The DN for each LDAP entry is composed of two parts: the **relative distinguished name** (**RDN**) and the location within the LDAP directory where the record resides.

In practice, the RDN is the portion of your DN that is not related to the directory tree structure and, in turn, is composed of one or several attribute names/value pairs. Let's see a concrete example of an organization, as shown in the following diagram:

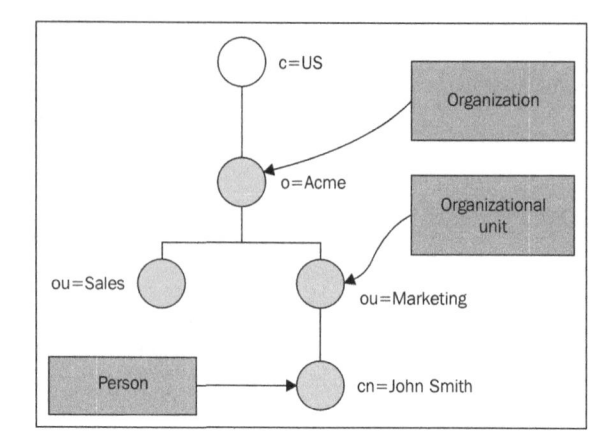

In the preceding diagram, `cn=John Smith` (where `cn` stands for "common name") could be an RDN. The attribute name is `cn`, and the value is `John Smith`.

On the other hand, the DN for `John Smith` would be `cn=John Smith, ou=Marketing, o=Acme`, and `c=US` (where `ou` is short for organizational unit, `o` is short for organization, and `c` is for country).

Connecting LDAP to WildFly

Connecting WildFly and LDAP can be done by means of several LDAP login modules. The first and obvious thing we need to do is run an instance of an LDAP server. Today, there are a huge number of LDAP servers available (both commercial and open source), and maybe you already configured one to run in your company. Just in case you don't have one, or simply don't want to add sample data to it, we suggest you have a look at the Apache Directory project (http://directory.apache.org/). It provides an excellent solution to get started with LDAP and to build complex directory infrastructures.

Once installed, we suggest that you use the Apache Directory Studio (available at the same link), as it allows you to quickly create a directory infrastructure. The simplest way to create a directory from scratch is by means of an **LDAP Data Interchange Format** (**LDIF**) file. Within this file, you can specify all entries that will be loaded by the LDAP engine.

> A quick shortcut to import an LDIF file from the Apache studio is in the file menu **File | Import | LDIF** into **LDAP**.

Here's a basic LDIF file we will use:

```
dn: dc=example,dc=com
objectclass: top
objectclass: dcObject
objectclass: organization
dc: example
o: MCC

dn: ou=People,dc=example,dc=com
objectclass: top
objectclass: organizationalUnit
ou: People

dn: uid=admin,ou=People,dc=example,dc=com
objectclass: top
objectclass: uidObject
objectclass: person
uid: admin
cn: Manager
sn: Manager
userPassword: secret

dn: ou=Roles,dc=example,dc=com
objectclass: top
objectclass: organizationalUnit
ou: Roles

dn: cn=Manager,ou=Roles,dc=example,dc=com
objectClass: top
objectClass: groupOfNames
cn: Manager
description: the JBossAS7 group
member: uid=admin,ou=People,dc=example,dc=com
```

Once you import this information into the LDAP server, you will end up with a small directory, as shown in the following screenshot:

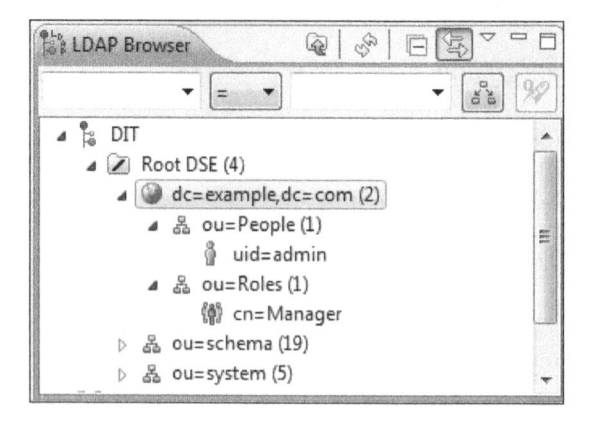

Within this directory, we have just one user registered as admin, belonging to the Manager role, as in other login modules we have seen in the earlier sections.

Now, we will configure the LDAP connection on WildFly. For our purposes, we will use the LdapExtended login module implementation, as shown in the following code. This implementation uses searches to locate both the user and the associated roles to bind as per authentication. The roles query will follow distinguished names (DNs) recursively to navigate a hierarchical role structure. Have a look at the following code:

```
<login-module code="LdapExtended" flag="required">

    <module-option name="java.naming.factory.initial"
        value="com.sun.jndi.ldap.LdapCtxFactory"/>
    <module-option name="java.naming.provider.url"
        value="ldap://localhost:10389"/>
    <module-option name="java.naming.security.authentication"
        value="simple"/>
    <module-option name="bindDN" value="uid=admin,ou=system"/>
    <module-option name="bindCredential" value="secret"/>
    <module-option name="baseCtxDN" value="ou=People,dc=example,
        dc=com"/>
    <module-option name="baseFilter" value="(uid={0})"/>
    <module-option name="rolesCtxDN" value="ou=Roles,dc=example,
        dc=com"/>
    <module-option name="roleFilter" value="(member={1})"/>
    <module-option name="roleAttributeID" value="cn"/>
    <module-option name="searchScope" value="ONELEVEL_SCOPE"/>
    <module-option name="allowEmptyPasswords" value="true"/>
</login-module>
```

Here is a brief description of the `LdapExtended` module's properties:

- `bindDN`: This is the DN used to bind against the LDAP server for the user and roles queries, which, in our case, is `"uid=admin,ou=system"`.
- `baseCtxDN`: This is the fixed DN of the context to start the user search from. In our example, it is `"ou=People,dc=example,dc=com."`.
- `baseFilter`: This is a search filter used to locate the context of the user to be authenticated. The input `username` or `userDN`, as obtained from the login module, will be substituted into the filter anywhere a `{0}` expression is seen.
- `rolesCtxDN`: This is the fixed DN of the context to search for user roles. Consider that this is not the DN of the location of the actual roles; rather, this is the DN of where the objects containing the user roles are.
- `roleFilter`: This is a search filter used to locate the roles associated with the authenticated user. An example search filter that matches on the input username is `(member={0})`. An alternative that matches on the authenticated user DN is `(member={1})`.
- `roleAttributeID`: This is the name of the role attribute of the context that corresponds to the name of the role.
- `searchScope`: This sets the search scope to one of the following strings:
    - `ONELEVEL_SCOPE`: This scope searches for users and associated roles directly under the named roles context.
    - `SUBTREE_SCOPE`: If the role's context is `DirContext`, this scope searches the subtree rooted at the named object, including the named object itself. If the role's context is not `DirContext`, this scope searches only the object.
    - `OBJECT_SCOPE`: This scope searches the named roles context only.
- `allowEmptyPasswords`: This is a flag indicating whether `empty(length==0)` passwords should be passed to the LDAP server.

Securing web applications

Okay! So, we touched upon some of the commonly used login modules. These login modules can be used by any Java EE application, so it's time to show a concrete example. In this section, we will show you how to apply a login module to a web application in order to show an implementation of basic web authentication.

> Basic access authentication is the simplest way to provide a username and password when making a request through a browser.
>
> It works by sending an encoded string containing the user credentials. This Base64-encoded string is transmitted and decoded by the receiver, resulting in a colon-separated username and password string.

The first thing we need to do is turn on web authentication. This requires you to define the `security-constraints` in the web application configuration file (`web.xml`). Have a look at the following code:

```xml
<web-app>
...
  <security-constraint>
    <web-resource-collection>
      <web-resource-name>HtmlAuth</web-resource-name>
      <description>application security constraints
      </description>
      <url-pattern>/*</url-pattern>
      <http-method>GET</http-method>
      <http-method>POST</http-method>
      <http-method>PUT</http-method>
      <http-method>DELETE</http-method>
    </web-resource-collection>
    <auth-constraint>
      <role-name>Manager</role-name>
    </auth-constraint>
  </security-constraint>
  <login-config>
    <auth-method>BASIC</auth-method>
    <realm-name>Sample Realm</realm-name>
  </login-config>

  <security-role>
    <role-name>Manager</role-name>
  </security-role>
</web-app>
```

The preceding configuration will add a security constraint to all URLs, which obviously includes all your JSP servlets. Access will be restricted to users authenticated with the `Manager` role.

> Considering that we are using the `Database` login module, the `Manager` role will be granted to users that have authenticated with the admin credentials.

The next configuration tweak needs to be performed in JBoss web deployment's descriptor `WEB-INF/jboss-web.xml`. There, you need to declare the security domain that will be used to authenticate the users. Have a look at the following code:

```
<jboss-web>
    <security-domain>java:/jboss/env/mysqldomain</security-domain>
</jboss-web>
```

Pay attention to the `security-domain` element. The value of this element must be exactly the same as the one you typed into the security domain's `name` attribute.

> For an overview of which JNDI names are valid in WildFly, please refer to the following link: https://docs.jboss.org/author/display/WFLY8/Developer+Guide#DeveloperGuide-ReviewtheJNDINamespaceRules.

The following diagram outlines the whole configuration sequence as applied to a `Database` login module. Have a look at the following diagram:

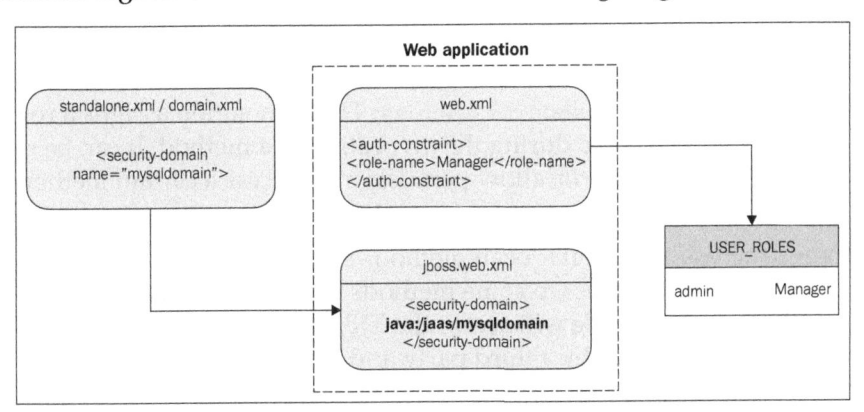

Once you deploy your application, the outcome of this action should be a popup, requesting user authentication, as shown in the following screenshot:

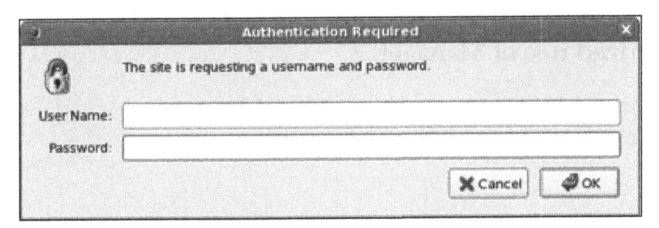

Logging in with `admin/admin` will grant access to the application with the `Manager` role.

Securing EJBs

Securing applications by means of a web login form is the most frequent option in enterprise applications. Nevertheless, the HTTP protocol is not the only choice available to access applications. For example, EJBs can be accessed by remote clients using the RMI-IIOP protocol. In such a case, you should further refine your security policies by restricting access to the EJB components, which are usually involved in the business layer of your applications.

> **How does security happen at EJB level?**
> Authentication must be performed before any EJB method is called, and authorization should be performed at the beginning of each EJB method call.

The basic security checks can be achieved using the following five annotations:

- `@org.jboss.ejb3.annotation.SecurityDomain`: This annotation specifies the security domain, which is associated with a specific class.
- `@javax.annotation.security.RolesAllowed`: This annotation specifies the list of roles permitted to access a method(s) in an EJB.
- `@javax.annotation.security.RunAs`: This annotation assigns a role dynamically to the EJB during the invocation of a method. It can be used if you need to *temporarily* allow permission to access a certain method.
- `@javax.annotation.security.PermitAll`: This annotation allows all roles to access a particular bean method. The purpose of this annotation is to widen security access to some methods in a situation where you don't exactly know what role will access the EJB. (Imagine that some modules have been developed by a third party and they access your EJB with some poorly identified roles).
- `@javax.annotation.security.DenyAll`: This annotation denies access to all roles. It has a purpose similar to that of `PermitAll`.

In the following example, we are restricting access to the EJB named `SecureEJB` only to the authorized role of Manager:

```
import org.jboss.ejb3.annotation.SecurityDomain;
import javax.annotation.security.RolesAllowed;

@Stateless
@SecurityDomain("mysqldomain")
@RolesAllowed( { "Manager" })
```

```
public class SecureEJB {
    ...
}
```

> Be careful! There is more than one `SecurityDomain` annotation available in the server's classpath. As shown here, you have to include `org.jboss.ejb3.annotation.SecurityDomain`. The `@RolesAllowed` annotation, on the other hand, calls for importing `javax.annotation.security.RolesAllowed`.

Annotations can also be applied at the method level. For example, if we need a special role named `SuperUser` to insert a new user, then we tag the method, as follows:

```
@RolesAllowed({"SuperUser"})
public void createUser(String country,String name) {
    User customer = new User ();
    customer.setCountry(country);
    customer.setName(name);
    em.persist(customer);
}
```

Securing web services

Web services authorization can be carried out in two ways, depending on whether we are dealing with a POJO-based web service or EJB-based web services.

Security changes to POJO web services are identical to those that we introduced for servlets or JSP, which include defining `security-constraints` into `web.xml` and login modules into `jboss-web.xml`.

If you are using a web client to access your web service, that's all you need to get authenticated. If you are using a standalone client, you will need to specify the credentials to the JAX-WS factory, as shown in the following code snippet:

```
JaxWsProxyFactoryBean factory = new JaxWsProxyFactoryBean();

factory.getInInterceptors().add(new LoggingInInterceptor());
factory.getOutInterceptors().add(new LoggingOutInterceptor());

factory.setServiceClass(POJOWebService.class);
factory.setAddress("http://localhost:8080/pojoService");
factory.setUsername("admin");
factory.setPassword("admin");
POJOWebService client = (POJOWebService) factory.create();

client.doSomething();
```

Securing WildFly

What about EJB-based web services? The configuration is slightly different. As the security domain is not specified in the web descriptors, we have to provide it by means of annotations:

```
@Stateless
@WebService(targetNamespace = "http://www.packtpub.com/",
    serviceName = "SecureEJBService")
@WebContext(authMethod = "BASIC",
    secureWSDLAccess = false)
@SecurityDomain(value = "mysqldomain")
public   class SecureEJB {
    ...
}
```

As you can see, the `@WebContext` annotation reflects the same configuration options as POJO-based web services, with BASIC authentication and unrestricted WSDL access.

The `@SecurityDomain` annotation should be familiar to you now, as we introduced it when showing you how to secure an EJB. As you can see in the preceding web service example, it is the equivalent of the information contained in the `jboss-web.xml` file (it references the `mysqldomain` security domain).

> If you prefer using XML deployment descriptors, the previous security configuration can also be specified by means of the `META-INF/ejb-jar.xml` and `META-INF/jboss-ejb3.xml` files.

Securing the management interfaces

One of the most important tasks for the system administrator is restricting access to the server management interfaces. Without a security policy, every user can gain access to the application server and modify its properties.

The attribute that is used to switch on security on the management interface is a security realm that needs to be defined within the `security-realms` section. Have a look at the following code:

```
<management>
    <security-realms>
        <security-realm name="ManagementRealm">
            <authentication>
                <local default-user="$local" skip-group-
                    loading="true"/>
                <properties path="mgmt-users.properties" relative-
                    to="jboss.server.config.dir"/>
```

```
            </authentication>
            <authorization map-groups-to-roles="false">
                <properties path="mgmt-groups.properties" relative-
                    to="jboss.server.config.dir"/>
            </authorization>
        </security-realm>
    </security-realms>
    ...
    <management-interfaces>
        <http-interface security-realm="ManagementRealm" http-upgrade-
            enabled="true">
            <socket-binding http="management-http"/>
        </http-interface>
    </management-interfaces>
</management>
```

With the default configuration, the user properties are stored in the `mgmt-users.properties` file and the group properties in the `mgmt-groups.properties` file. Both these files can be found in the `configuration` directory of your server.

> Users and groups can be added to these property files at any time. Any updates after the server has started are detected automatically.

By default, this management realm expects the entries to be in the following format:

```
username=HEX( MD5( username ':' realm ':' password))
```

This means that each user is associated with a hex-encoded hash that consists of the username, the name of the realm, and the password.

To add new users, you can use the utility script contained in the `bin` folder of your WildFly installation named `add-user.sh` (Linux) or `add-user.bat` (Windows). As you can see from the following screenshot, the `add-user` script requires the following pieces of information:

- **Realm**: This is the name of the realm used to secure the management interfaces. If you just press *Enter*, the user will be added in the default realm named `ManagementRealm`.
- **Username**: This is the username we are going to add (it needs to be alphanumeric).
- **Password**: This is the password field, which needs to be different from the username.
- **Groups**: This is the name of the group you want the user to be part of. If you leave this blank, you will not be added to any groups.

Securing WildFly

- **AS process**: This determines whether you want the user to be used to connect to another WildFly instance.

```
chris-macbook:bin chris$ ./add-user.sh

What type of user do you wish to add?
 a) Management User (mgmt-users.properties)
 b) Application User (application-users.properties)
(a):

Enter the details of the new user to add.
Using realm 'ManagementRealm' as discovered from the existing property files.
Username : chris
Password :
Re-enter Password :
What groups do you want this user to belong to? (Please enter a comma separated list, or leave blank for none)[ ]:
About to add user 'chris' for realm 'ManagementRealm'
Is this correct yes/no? yes
Added user 'chris' to file '/Users/chris/workspace/wildfly-8.1.0.Final/standalone/configuration/mgmt-users.properties'
Added user 'chris' to file '/Users/chris/workspace/wildfly-8.1.0.Final/domain/configuration/mgmt-users.properties'
Added user 'chris' with groups  to file '/Users/chris/workspace/wildfly-8.1.0.Final/standalone/configuration/mgmt-groups.properties'
Added user 'chris' with groups  to file '/Users/chris/workspace/wildfly-8.1.0.Final/domain/configuration/mgmt-groups.properties'
Is this new user going to be used for one AS process to connect to another AS process?
e.g. for a slave host controller connecting to the master or for a Remoting connection for server to server EJB calls.
yes/no? no
chris-macbook:bin chris$
```

Here, we have just added the user `chris` to the default realm. This resulted in the following property being added to `mgmt-users.properties` of your standalone and domain configurations:

```
chris=554dadf6fa222d6ea11a470f3dea7a94
```

You will now be able to connect to a remote WildFly management interface using this user, as shown in the following screenshot:

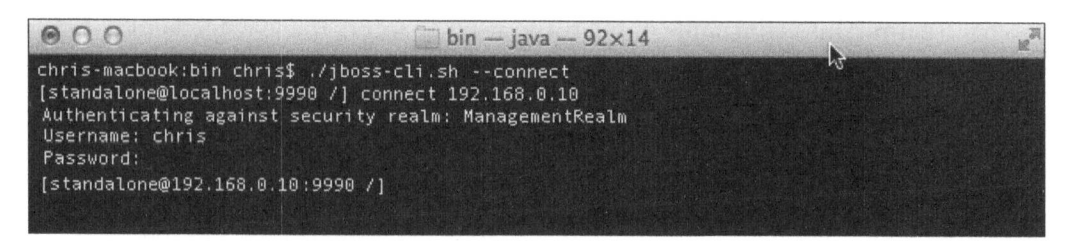

```
chris-macbook:bin chris$ ./jboss-cli.sh --connect
[standalone@localhost:9990 /] connect 192.168.0.10
Authenticating against security realm: ManagementRealm
Username: chris
Password:
[standalone@192.168.0.10:9990 /]
```

A much easier way to add users is to use a non-interactive shell. This approach works by passing the username, password, and optionally the realm name to the `add-user` script:

```
add-user.sh myuser mypassword realm1
```

Role-based access control

Role-based access control (**RBAC**) is a new feature introduced in WildFly 8. It allows system administrators to create users for the administration console but with restrictions to certain parts of the system. In JBoss AS 7, an admin console user had access to everything, which is equivalent to the SuperUser role in WildFly 8.

RBAC is not enabled by default. To enable it, run the following command:

```
jboss-cli.sh --connect --command="/core-service=management/
access=authorization:write-attribute(name=provider,value=rbac)"
```

Then, reload the server config:

```
jboss-cli.sh --connect --command=":reload"
```

If you have existing users before enabling RBAC, you need to manually configure each user by mapping that user to a role. If we had a user called Yevai and wanted to assign her the role of SuperUser, we would do the following:

```
jboss-cli.sh --connect --command="/core-service=management/access=
  authorization/role-mapping=SuperUser/include=
  user-yevai:add(name=yevai,type=USER)"
```

There are seven predefined roles in WildFly 8. Each of them is outlined in the following table. They are ordered with the most restrictive roles at the top and the least restrictive at the bottom.

Role	Permissions
Monitor	This user can read the configuration and the current runtime state
Operator	This user has all the permissions of the preceding role, and can modify the runtime state, such as restarting or reloading the server, and flushing the database connection pool
Maintainer	This user has all the permissions of all the preceding roles, and can modify the persistent state, such as deploying applications and setting up new datasources
Deployer	This user has all the permissions of all the preceding roles, but with permissions to applications only. This user cannot change the configuration of the server

Securing WildFly

Role	Permissions
Administrator	This user has all the permissions of all the preceding roles, and can view and modify sensitive data, such as the access control system
Auditor	This user has all the permissions of all the preceding roles, and can view and modify resources to administer the audit-logging system
SuperUser	This user has all permissions

Configuring groups

One of the new features in WildFly is the ability to assign users to groups. This means that you can assign a bunch of users to a group and then the group to a role. To create a new user and assign them to a group, you can run the following noninteractive command:

```
user-add.sh -u tavonga -p mypassword -g MyGroup
```

Users can be managed via the admin console by a user who has the role of either Administrator or SuperUser. To do this, log in to the admin console, and navigate to the **Administration** tab. Here, you can add users to groups, create groups, and finally view members of each role. Have a look at the following screenshot:

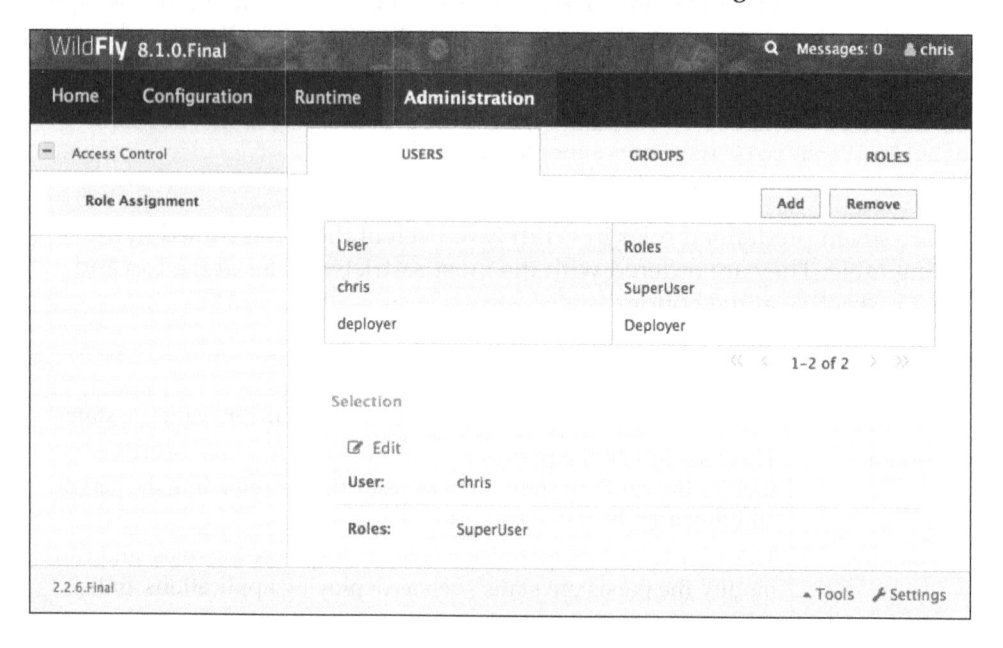

Securing the transport layer

If you create a mission-critical application with just the bare concepts we covered until now, you will not be guaranteed to be shielded from all security threats. For example, if you need to design a payment gateway, where credit card information is transmitted by means of an EJB or servlet, using just the authorization and authentication stack is really not enough.

In order to prevent disclosure of information, you have to use a protocol that provides data **encryption**. Encryption is the conversion of data into a form that cannot be understood by people or systems eavesdropping on your network. Conversely, **decryption** is the process of converting encrypted data back into its original form, so it can be understood.

The protocols used to secure communication are SSL and TLS, the latter being considered a replacement for the older SSL.

> The differences between the two protocols are minor. TLS uses *stronger* encryption algorithms and has the ability to work on different ports. For the rest of our chapter, we will refer to SSL for both protocols.

There are two basic techniques to encrypt information: **symmetric encryption** (also called **secret key** encryption) and **asymmetric encryption** (also called **public key** encryption).

Symmetric encryption is the oldest and best-known technique. It is based on a secret key, which is applied to the text of a message to change the content in a particular way. As long as both the sender and recipient know the secret key, they can encrypt and decrypt all messages that use this key. These encryption algorithms typically work fast and are well-suited to encrypting blocks of messages at once.

One significant issue with symmetric algorithms is the requirement of an organization to distribute keys to users. This generally results in more overhead from the administrative aspect, while the keys remain vulnerable to unauthorized disclosure and potential misuse.

For this reason, a mission-critical enterprise system usually relies on asymmetric encryption algorithms. These tend to be easier to employ, manage, and make the system ultimately more secure.

Asymmetric cryptography, also known as public key cryptography, is based on the concept that the key used to encrypt the message is not the one used to decrypt the message. Each user holds a couple of keys: the public key, which is distributed to other parties, and the private key, which is kept in secret. Each message is encrypted with the recipient's public key and can only be decrypted (by the recipient) with their private key. Have a look at the following diagram:

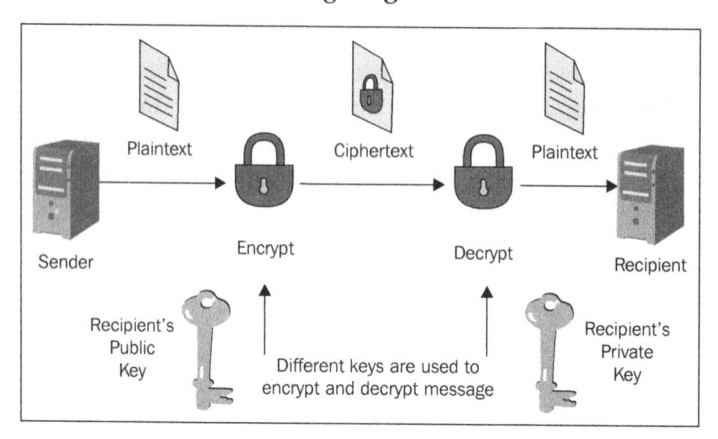

Using asymmetric encryption, you can be sure that your message cannot be disclosed by a third party. However, you *still* have one vulnerability.

Let's suppose you want to exchange information with a business partner, so you are requesting their public key by telephone or by e-mail. A fraudulent user intercepts your e-mail or simply listens to your conversation and quickly sends you a fake e-mail with their public key. Now, even if your data transmission is secured, it will be directed to the wrong person! This type of eavesdropping is called the man-in-the-middle attack.

In order to solve this issue, we need a document that verifies that the public key belongs to an individual. This document is called a **digital certificate** or the public key certificate. A digital certificate consists of a formatted block of data that contains the name of the certificate holder (which may be either a username or a system name), the holder's public key, and the digital signature of a **Certification Authority (CA)** for authentication. The certification authority attests that the sender's name is the one associated with the public key in the document.

A prototype of a digital certificate is shown here:

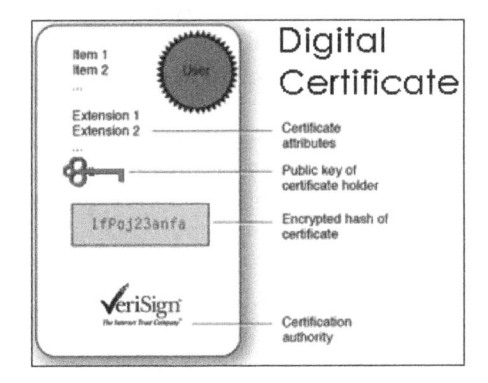

Public key certificates are commonly used for secure interaction with websites. By default, web browsers ship with a set of predefined CAs. They are used to verify that the public certificate served to the browser when you enter a secure site has been actually issued by the owner of the website. In short, if you connect your browser to https://www.abc.com and your browser doesn't give certificate warning, you can be sure that you can safely interact with the entity in charge of the site.

> **Simple authentication and client authentication**
>
> In the previous example, we depicted a simple server authentication. In this scenario, the only party that needs to prove its identity is the server.
>
> However, SSL is also able to perform a **mutual authentication** (also called client or two-way authentication) in case the server requests a client certificate during the SSL handshake over the network.
>
> The client authentication requires a client certificate in the X.509 format from a CA. The X.509 format is an industry-standard format for SSL certificates. In the next section, we will explore the available tools to generate digital certificates and also how you can have your certificates signed by a CA.

Enabling the Secure Socket Layer

WildFly uses the **Java Secure Socket Extension (JSSE)**, which is bundled in the Java Standard Edition to leverage the SSL/TLS communication.

Securing WildFly

An enterprise application can secure two protocols: HTTP and RMI. HTTP communication is handled by the Undertow subsystem within the `standalone.xml`/`domain.xml` file. Securing the RMI transport is not always a compelling requirement for your applications as, in most production environments, WildFly is placed behind a firewall.

As you can see from the following diagram, your EJBs are not directly exposed to untrusted networks and are usually connected via a web server.

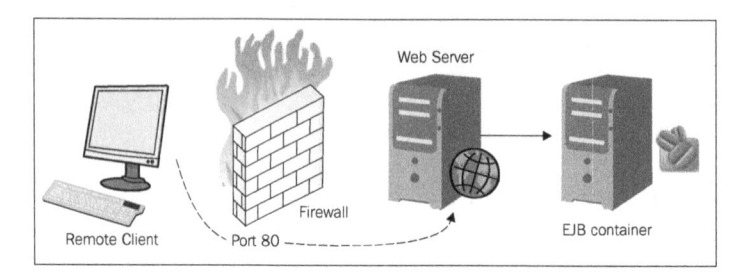

In order to configure WildFly to use SSL, we need a tool that generates a public key/private key pair in the form of an X.509 certificate for use by the SSL server sockets. This is covered in the next section.

Certificate management tools

One tool that can be used to set up a digital certificate is `keytool`, a key and certificate management utility that ships with the Java SE. It enables users to administer their own public/private key pairs and associated certificates for use in self-authentication (where the user authenticates himself or herself to other users or services) or data integrity and authentication services using digital signatures. It also allows users to cache the public keys (in the form of certificates) of their communicating peers.

The `keytool` certificate stores the keys and certificates in a file termed as `keystore`, a repository of certificates used to identify a client or a server. Typically, a `keystore` contains a single client or server's identity, which is password protected. Let's see an example of `keystore` generation:

```
keytool -genkeypair -keystore wildfly.keystore
  -storepass mypassword -keypass mypassword -keyalg RSA
  -validity 180 -alias wildfly -dname "cn=packtpub,o=PackPub,c=GB"
```

This command creates the `keystore` named `wildfly.keystore` in the working directory and assigns it the password `mypassword`. It generates a public/private key pair for the entity whose "distinguished name" has a common name `packtpub`, the organization `PacktPub`, and a two-letter country code of `GB`.

This results in a self-signed certificate (using the RSA signature algorithm) that includes the public key and the distinguished-name information. This certificate will be valid for 180 days and is associated with the private key in a `keystore` entry referred to by the alias as `wildflybook`.

> A self-signed certificate is a certificate that has not been verified by a CA and hence leaves you vulnerable to the classic man-in-the-middle attack. A self-signed certificate is only suitable for in-house use or for testing while you wait for the official certificate to arrive.

Securing HTTP communication with a self-signed certificate

Now let's see how you can use this `keystore` file to secure your WildFly web channel. Open the server configuration file (`standalone.xml/domain.xml`), and navigate to the undertow subsystem.

First, we need to add an `https-listener` element to the server configuration, as shown in bold in the following code snippet:

```xml
<subsystem xmlns="urn:jboss:domain:undertow:1.1">
    <buffer-cache name="default"/>
    <server name="default-server">
        <https-listener name="https" socket-binding="https" security-
            realm="CertificateRealm"/>
        <http-listener name="default" socket-binding="http"/>
        <host name="default-host" alias="localhost">
            <location name="/" handler="welcome-content"/>
            <filter-ref name="server-header"/>
            <filter-ref name="x-powered-by-header"/>
        </host>
    </server>
</subsystem>
```

Securing WildFly

Now, create a new security realm within the `management` element. The mandatory attributes are highlighted in bold in the following code. There is the path of the keystore, along with its password. The `keystore` element also takes `alias`, `relative-to`, and `key-password` attributes, all of which are optional:

```
<management>
    <security-realms>
        <security-realm name="CertificateRealm">
            <server-identities>
                <ssl>
                    <keystore path="wildfly.keystore"
                        relative-to="jboss.server.config.dir"
                        keystore-password="mypassword"/>
                </ssl>
            <server-identities>
        </security-realm>
    </security-realms>
</management>
```

Last of all, you will need to copy the `wildfly.keystore` file to your `JBOSS_HOME/standalone/configuration` folder.

Restart WildFly to load these changes. At the bottom of your console logs, during server startup, you should see the following printout (**Undertow HTTPS listener https listening on /127.0.0.1:8443**).

If you try to access a web application via HTTPS on your SSL-configured WildFly server, for example, if you deploy `chapter4` and access it via `https://localhost:8443/chapter4`, you will be greeted by the following screen (the screen displayed will depend on your browser):

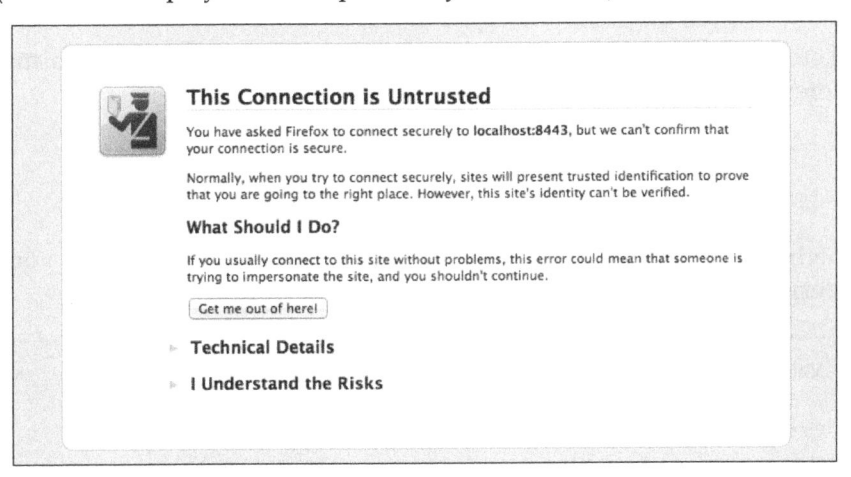

This Connection is Untrusted

You have asked Firefox to connect securely to **localhost:8443**, but we can't confirm that your connection is secure.

Normally, when you try to connect securely, sites will present trusted identification to prove that you are going to the right place. However, this site's identity can't be verified.

What Should I Do?

If you usually connect to this site without problems, this error could mean that someone is trying to impersonate the site, and you shouldn't continue.

[Get me out of here!]

▸ **Technical Details**

▸ **I Understand the Risks**

If you are unfamiliar with how certificates work, once the browser has established a secure connection with the web server, the web server sends a certificate back to the browser. Because the certificate we just installed has *not been* signed by any recognized CA, the browser security sandbox warns the user about the potential security threat.

As this is an in-house test, we can safely proceed by choosing **I Understand the Risks** | **Add Exception** | **Confirm Security Exception**. That's all you need to do in order to activate the SSL with a self-signed certificate.

Securing the HTTP communication with a certificate signed by a CA

In order to get a certificate that your browser recognizes, you need to issue a **certificate-signing request** (**CSR**) to a CA. The CA will then return a signed certificate that can be installed on your server. Most of these services are not free. The cost depends on the number of certificates you are requesting, the encryption strength, and other factors. StartSSL provides a free, low assurance certificate for servers on a public domain name.

Securing WildFly

So, to generate a CSR, you need to use the `keystore` that you created earlier and `keyentry`. Have a look at the following code:

```
keytool -certreq -keystore wildfly.keystore -alias wildfly -storepass
mypassword -keypass mypassword   -keyalg RSA  -file certreq.csr
```

This will create a new certificate request named `certreq.csr`, with the format shown here:

```
-----BEGIN NEW CERTIFICATE REQUEST-----
   ...
-----END NEW CERTIFICATE REQUEST-----
```

The following certificate needs to be sent to a CA assuming, for example, you have chosen **Verisign** (http://www.verisign.com) as the CA:

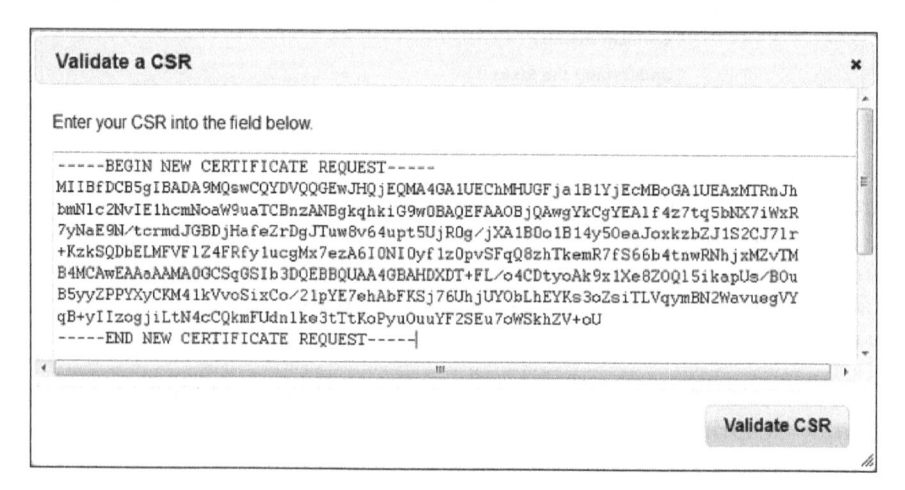

After submitting your CSR, the CA will return a signed certificate that needs to be imported into your keychain. Let's suppose that you have saved your CA certificate in a file named `signed_ca.txt`. Have a look at the following command:

```
keytool -import -keystore wildfly.keystore -alias testkey1 -storepass
mypassword -keypass mypassword -file signed_ca.txt
```

Here, the `-import` option is used to add a certificate or certificate chain to the list of trusted certificates as specified by the `-keystore` parameter and identified by the `-alias` parameter. The parameter `-storepass` specifies the password that is used to protect the `keystore`. If the `-keypass` option is not provided, and the private key password is different from the `keystore` password, you will be prompted for it.

Now, your web browser will recognize your new certificate as being signed by a CA and will no longer complain that it cannot validate the certificate.

Summary

We began this chapter discussing the basic concepts of security and the difference between authentication and authorization.

Authentication is used to verify the identity of a user, while authorization is used to check if the user has the rights to access a particular resource.

WildFly uses the PicketBox framework. PicketBox sits at the top of the Java Authentication and Authorization Service (JAAS) and secures all the Java EE technologies running in the application. The core section of the security subsystem is contained in the security-domain element, which performs all the required authorization and authentication checks.

We then took a look at some of the login modules used to check user credentials against different datastores. Each login module can be used by enterprise applications in either a programmatic or a declarative way. While programmatic security can provide a fine-grained security model, you should consider using declarative security, which allows a clean separation between the business layer and the security policies.

Later in the chapter, you saw how you can secure the management interfaces, namely, the new command-line interface, by adding a security realm to them.

In the last section of this chapter, we looked at how you can encrypt the communication channel using the Secure Socket Layer and how you can use certificates produced by the `keytool` Java utility.

In the next chapter, we will end our discussion of WildFly by showing how you can configure and distribute enterprise applications on OpenShift, a JBoss cloud solution.

11
WildFly, OpenShift, and Cloud Computing

Since the terminology used within the realm of cloud computing can be a source of confusion, the first section of this chapter will provide an overview of the basic concepts of cloud computing. We will then discuss the OpenShift project and the benefits it will bring to your organization.

Introduction to cloud computing

What is cloud computing? We hear this term everywhere, but what does it really mean? We have all used the cloud knowingly or unknowingly. If you use Gmail, Hotmail, or any other popular e-mail service, you have used the cloud. Simply put, cloud computing is a set of pooled computing resources and services delivered over the Web.

Client computing is not a new concept in the computer industry. Those of you who have been in the IT business for a decade or two will remember that the first type of client-server applications were the mainframe and terminal applications. At that time, storage and CPU was very expensive, and the mainframe pooled both types of resources and served them to thin-client terminals.

With the advent of the PC revolution, which brought mass storage and cheap CPUs to the average corporate desktop, the file server gained popularity as a way to enable document sharing and archiving. True to its name, the file server served storage resources to the clients in an enterprise, while the CPU cycles needed to do productive work were all produced and consumed within the confines of the PC client.

In the early 1990s, the budding Internet finally had enough computers attached to it that academic institutions began seriously thinking about how to connect those machines together to create massive, shared pools of storage and computational power that would be much larger than what any individual institution could ever afford to build. This is when the idea of *the grid* began to take shape.

Cloud computing versus grid computing

In general, the terms "grid" and "cloud" seem to be converging due to some similarities; however, there are a list of important differences between them that are often not understood, generating confusion and clutter within the marketplace. Grid computing requires the resources of many computers to solve a single problem, at the same time. Hence, it may or may not be in the cloud, depending on the type of use you make of it. One concern about the grid is that if one piece of the software on a node fails, other pieces of the software on other nodes may fail, too. This is alleviated if that component has a failover component on another node, but problems can still arise if the components rely on other pieces of software to accomplish one or more grid computing tasks. Have a look at the following screenshot:

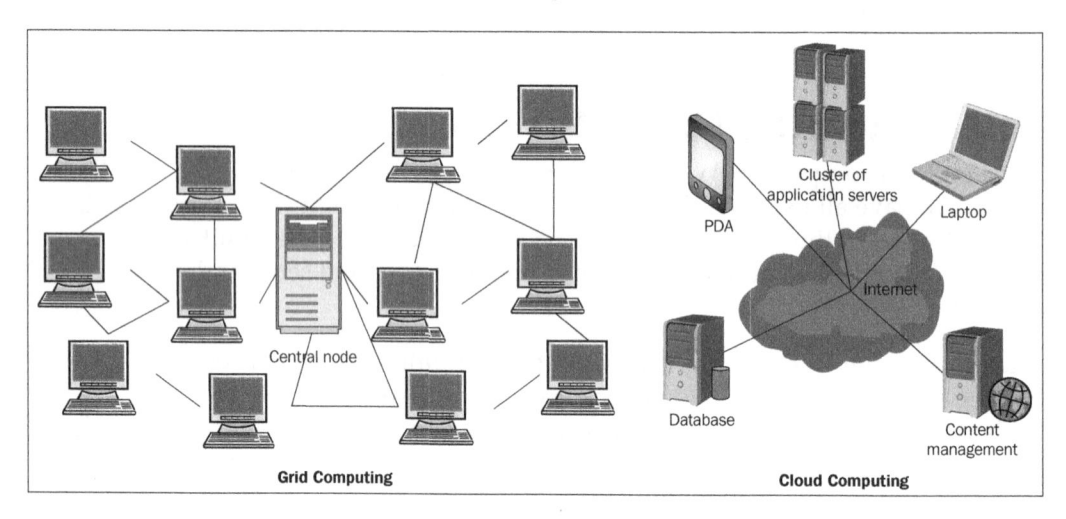

Cloud computing evolves from grid computing and allows on-demand provisioning of resources. With cloud computing, companies can scale up to massive capacities in an instant, without having to invest in a new infrastructure, train new personnel, or license new software.

> **Grid and cloud – similarities and differences**
>
> The difference between the grid and the cloud lies in the way the tasks are computed. In a computational grid, one large job is divided into many small portions and executed on multiple machines. This characteristic is fundamental to a grid.
>
> Cloud computing is intended to allow the user to avail of various services without investing in the underlying architecture. Cloud services include the delivery of software, infrastructure, and storage over the Internet either as separate components or as a complete platform.

Advantages of cloud computing

We just went through the basics of cloud computing, and now we will outline some of the benefits you may get if you move over to using the cloud services:

- **On-demand service provisioning**: Using self-service provisioning, customers can have access to cloud services quickly and easily with no hassle. The customer simply requests a number of computing, storage, software, processes, or other resources from the service provider.

- **Elasticity**: This means that customers no longer need to predict traffic but can promote their sites aggressively and spontaneously. Engineering for peak traffic becomes a thing of the past.

- **Cost reduction**: By purchasing just the right amount of IT resources on demand, an organization can avoid purchasing unnecessary equipment. For SMEs, using the cloud may also reduce the need for in-house IT administrators.

- **Application programming interfaces (APIs)**: APIs make it possible for an organization's software to interact with cloud services. This means system administrators can interact with their cloud model. Cloud computing systems typically use REST-based APIs.

Although cloud computing brings many advantages, there are some disadvantages or potential risks that you must account for. The most compelling threat is that sensitive data processed outside the enterprise brings with it an inherent level of risk. This is because outsourced services bypass the physical, logical, and personnel controls a software house exerts over in-house programs. In addition, when you use the cloud, you probably won't know exactly where your data is hosted. In fact, you might not even know what country it will be stored in, leading to potential issues with local jurisdiction.

As Gartner Group (http://www.gartner.com) suggests, you should always ask providers to supply specific information on the hiring and oversight of privileged administrators. Besides this, the cloud provider should provide evidence that encryption schemes are designed and tested by experienced specialists. It is also important to understand whether the providers will make a contractual commitment to obey local privacy requirements on behalf of their customers.

Cloud computing options

Cloud computing can be divided into the following three possible forms, depending on where the cloud is hosted, each option bringing a different level of security and management overhead:

- **Public cloud**: This option is used when services and infrastructure are provided off-site and often shared across multiple organizations. Public clouds are generally managed by an external service provider.
- **Private cloud**: This option provides IT cloud resources that are dedicated to a single organization and offered on demand. A private cloud infrastructure is maintained on a private network.
- **Hybrid cloud**: This option is a mix of private and public clouds managed as a single entity, allowing you to keep aspects of your business in the most efficient environment.

The decision to adopt one among the different kinds of cloud computing options is a matter of discussion between experts, and it generally depends on several key factors. For example, as far as security is concerned, although public clouds offer a secure environment, private clouds offer an inherent level of security that meets even the highest of standards. In addition, you can add security services, such an **Intrusion Detection System** (**IDS**) and dedicated firewalls. A private cloud might be the right choice for a large organization carrying a well-run data-center with a lot of spare capacity. It is more expensive to use a public cloud even if you have to add new software to transform that data center into a cloud.

On the other hand, as far as scalability is concerned, one negative aspect of private clouds is that their performance is limited to the number of machines in your cloud cluster. Should you max out your computing power, another physical server will need to be added. Besides this, public clouds typically deliver a *pay-as-you-go* model, where you pay by the hour for the computing resources you use. This kind of utility pricing is economical if you're spinning up and tearing down development servers on a regular basis.

So, the majority of public cloud deployments are generally used for web servers or development systems where security and compliance requirements of larger organizations and their customers are not an issue. Private clouds are generally preferred by mid-size and large enterprises because they meet the stricter security and compliance requirements. The downside of private clouds is that the organizations implementing them need dedicated, high-performance hardware. Have a look at the following diagram:

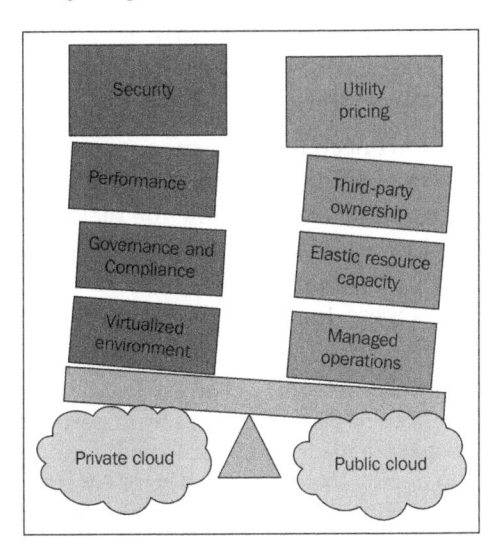

Types of cloud services

Cloud computing services can be broadly classified into the following three types. These types are also known as cloud service models or SPI service models.

- **Infrastructure as a Service (IaaS)**: This service allows you to spin up computers on demand. For each server, you will be able to select the amount of RAM, the number of processors, the amount of hard disk space, and the operating system. It allows you to do all this in a matter of minutes, making the acquisition of hardware easier, cheaper, and quicker. Well-known providers of this service include Amazon EC2, Google Compute Engine, Rackspace, and DigitalOcean.

> DigitalOcean is relatively new to the market. You can spin up a server instance in less than 60 seconds! The major selling point of DigitalOcean is the simplicity of the interface, which means there will be no more crawling through pages and pages of documentation. In addition to this, it is very reasonably priced. If you are considering an IaaS provider, DigitalOcean should definitely be added to your list.

- **Platform as a Service (PaaS)**: This service offers a development platform for developers. The end users write their own code, and the PaaS provider uploads that code and presents it on the Web.

    By using PaaS, you don't need to invest money to get that project environment ready for your developers. The PaaS provider will deliver the platform on the Web, and in most cases, you can consume the platform using your browser. There is no need to download any software. This combination of simplicity and cost-efficiency empowers small and medium-sized companies, and even individual developers, to launch their own cloud SaaS.

    > Examples of PaaS providers are Facebook and OpenShift. Facebook is a social application platform where third parties can write new applications that are made available to end users. OpenShift allows developers to deploy their WildFly web or enterprise applications to the cloud as simply as issuing a `git push` command.

- **Software as a Service (SaaS)**: This service is based on the concept of renting software from a service provider instead of buying it. The software is usually accessed via the browser. Also known as *software on demand*, it is currently the most popular type of cloud computing because of its high flexibility, great services, enhanced scalability, and low maintenance. Examples of SaaS are Zoho, Google Docs, and the SalesForce CRM application. Have a look at the following screenshot:

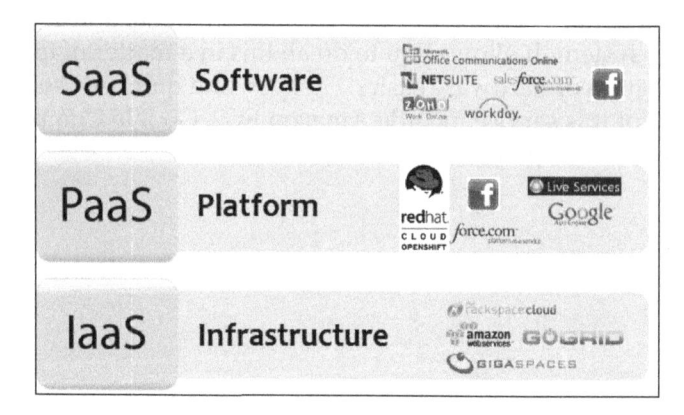

You might wonder whether it is possible for some providers to be defined both as a *platform* and as *software*. The answer is yes! For example, Facebook can be defined as both a platform (because services and applications can be can be delivered via the Facebook API) and as software (as it is used by millions of end users).

Red Hat originally developed the OpenShift platform to deploy and manage Java EE applications on JBoss/WildFly servers running on the cloud.

OpenShift offers three versions of the software, which are as follows:

- **Online**: This version is a free, cloud-based platform used to deploy new and existing Java EE, Ruby, PHP, Node.js, Perl, and Python applications on the cloud in a matter of minutes.
- **Origin**: This version is a free and open source version of the software. It only comes with community support. To run this, you need your own infrastructure. This version is beyond the scope of this book, so it will not be covered.
- **Enterprise**: This version can be downloaded and run anywhere you want, including Amazon, Rackspace, or your own infrastructure. It is packaged with Red Hat Enterprise Linux, is stable, and comes with full support from Red Hat.

Getting started with OpenShift Online

OpenShift allows you to create, deploy, and manage applications within the cloud. It provides disk space, CPU resources, memory, and network connectivity. You can choose from a range of web cartridges, including Tomcat, WildFly, Jenkins, and many more. You can also plug in database cartridges, such as MySQL. Depending on the type of application you are building, you also have access to a template filesystem layout for that type (for example, PHP, WSGI, and Rack/Rails). OpenShift also generates a limited DNS for you.

To get started with OpenShift Online, the first thing you need to do is create an account. Go to OpenShift's home page at `https://www.openshift.com/`, and select **SIGN UP**. Complete the online registration and verify your e-mail address.

Before you can create an application, you need to create a **domain**. OpenShift uses non-strict domains (that is, there is no preceding period).

Log in to your OpenShift account and navigate to the **Settings** tab. Enter your domain name and click on **Save**. Have a look at the following screenshot:

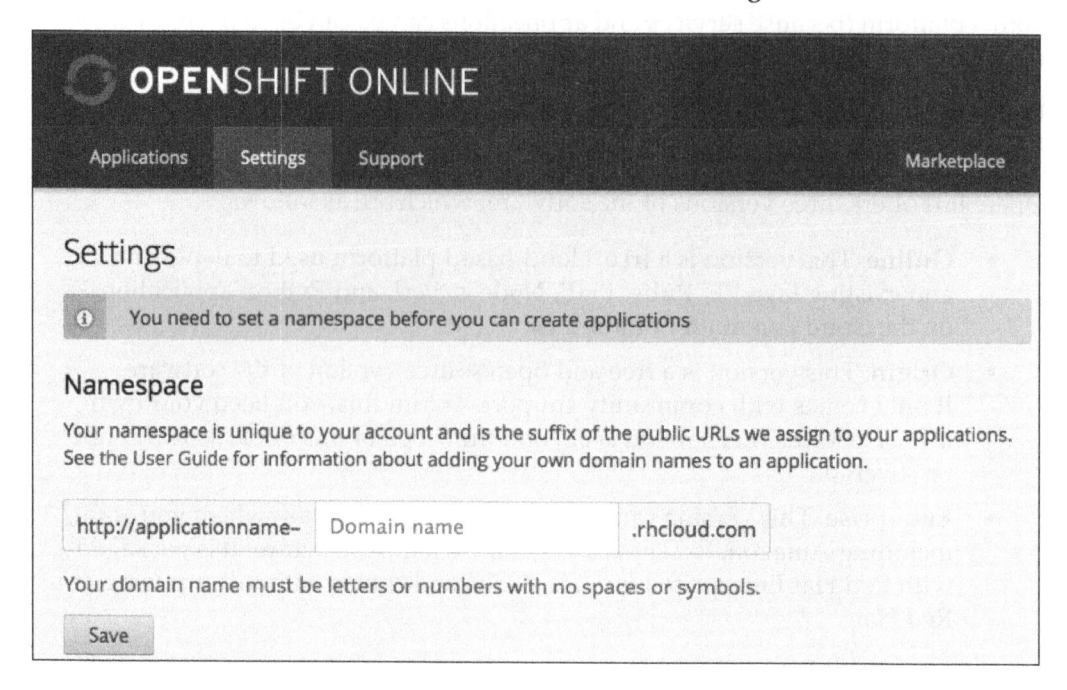

> Each account can only support a single domain. Should you wish to use more than one domain, you need to create a separate account with a different username.

Installing OpenShift client tools

Installing OpenShift client tools is a simple process. The following guide shows you how to install the tools in Ubuntu 14.04. If you want to install them in a different flavor of Linux or in a different operating system, refer to the Red Hat documentation at `https://access.redhat.com/documentation/en-US/OpenShift_Online/2.0/html/Client_Tools_Installation_Guide/chap-OpenShift_Client_Tools.html`.

1. First, ensure that you have the latest package list by executing the following command:

   ```
   $ sudo apt-get update
   ```

2. You will then need to install the required dependencies, `ruby`, `rubygems`, and `git`, by running the following command:

   ```
   $ sudo apt-get install ruby-full rubygems-integration git-core
   ```

3. We can now install the client tools by running the following command:

   ```
   $ gem install rhc
   ```

   After running this command, you should see something like the following:

   ```
   Fetching: net-ssh-2.9.1.gem (100%)
   ...
   Fetching: rhc-1.28.5.gem (100%)
   ===========================================================
   If this is your first time installing the RHC tools, please run
   'rhc setup'
   ===========================================================
   Successfully installed net-ssh-2.9.1
   ...
   Successfully installed rhc-1.28.5
   10 gems installed
   Installing ri documentation for net-ssh-2.9.1...
   ...
   Installing RDoc documentation for rhc-1.28.5...
   ```

   > It is important that you run the setup wizard before using the client tools. Failing to do so might cause problems later on.

4. To run the setup, type the following command:

   ```
   rhc setup
   ```

The setup will require you to enter data for the following queries in the order they appear onscreen:

- For **Enter the server hostname**, just press *Enter* to use the default value, which is the server used for OpenShift Online.
- For **Enter username and password**, enter your account username and password.
- If there are no SSH keys on your system, one will be generated. You will be asked if you want to upload the key to the server. Type `yes`.
- If you did not create a domain earlier, you will be prompted to add a domain now.

Accessing your OpenShift account from a different computer

Communication between your computer and OpenShift happens over SSH using secure keys. In order to use your domain from a different machine, simply download and install the OpenShift client tools to your other computer. When you run the tools setup, the key for your computer will be added to your keys on the server.

To revoke access, you will need to delete the key for that computer. You can do this by logging in to OpenShift, navigating to **Settings**, and scrolling down until you reach **Public Keys**. Now, delete the key that relates to the computer you want to revoke access from.

Creating our first OpenShift application

Before we develop an application to run on OpenShift, we should first define some OpenShift terms:

- **Application**: This is obviously the application you will deploy to OpenShift.
- **Gear**: This is the container that contains your server, along with the various resources required to run your application, such as RAM, the processor, and hard disk space.
- **Cartridge**: A cartridge is a plugin that provides a specific functionality. For example, you can select a WildFly cartridge and a database cartridge to be added to your gear.

Installing your first cartridge

To view all available cartridges, run the following command:

```
$ rhc cartridge list
```

The syntax to create an application is as follows:

```
$ rhc app create app_name cartridge_name
```

At the time of writing, there is no WildFly cartridge available in the cartridge list. For this example, I am going to use a cartridge that is available on GitHub (https://github.com/openshift-cartridges/openshift-wildfly-cartridge). Navigate to the folder where you want your code to be located. If you are using Eclipse, you may want to `cd` into your workspace folder. Using the preceding syntax, but replacing the cartridge name with the cartridge URL, we will create the application, as follows:

```
$ rhc app create wildfly https://cartreflect-claytondev.rhcloud.com/
  reflect?github=openshift-cartridges/
  openshift-wildfly-cartridge#WildFly8
```

After running this command, a significant amount of information will be printed to the console. We will deal with this output one piece at a time. The first piece of information is the detail related to the cartridge and gear. We can see the URL from where the cartridge was cloned from, the gear size, and the domain:

```
Application Options
-------------------
Domain:     chrisritchie
Cartridges: https://cartreflect-claytondev.rhcloud.com/reflect?
  github=openshift-cartridges/openshift-wildfly-cartridge#WildFly8
Gear Size:  default
Scaling:    no
```

The next part shows that the application is being created, and that an artifact is being deployed on the gear:

```
Creating application 'wildfly' ... Artifacts deployed: ./ROOT.war
done
```

Printed out next are the details for the management console, which are as follows:

```
WildFly 8 administrator added.  Please make note of these credentials:
  Username: admin6vIBvE6
  Password: B_vh3CA5v4Dc
  run 'rhc port-forward wildfly to access the web admin area on port 9990.
Waiting for your DNS name to be available ... done
```

The following part shows the remote Git repository being cloned to your local hard drive. The SSH key for the gear will be added to your `known_hosts` file once you allow it:

```
Cloning into 'wildfly'...
The authenticity of host 'wildfly-chrisritchie.rhcloud.com (50.16.172.242)' can't be established.
RSA key fingerprint is cf:ee:77:cb:0e:fc:02:d7:72:7e:ae:80:c0:90:88:a7.
Are you sure you want to continue connecting (yes/no)? yes
Warning: Permanently added 'wildfly-chrisritchie.rhcloud.com,50.16.172.242' (RSA) to the list of known hosts.
Your application 'wildfly' is now available.
```

Lastly, your application URL, remote GIT repository, and SSH location are all printed out, as follows:

```
  URL:        http://wildfly-chrisritchie.rhcloud.com/
  SSH to:     53e905324382ecc7c30001d0@wildfly-chrisritchie.rhcloud.com
  Git remote: ssh://53e905324382ecc7c30001d0@wildfly-chrisritchie.rhcloud.com/~/git/wildfly.git/
```

```
Run 'rhc show-app wildfly' for more details about your app.
```

Now, you can verify that your server is up and running, and that you can access the deployed application by pointing your browser to the URL specified in the preceding output (`http://wildfly-chrisritchie.rhcloud.com/`). Have a look at the following screenshot:

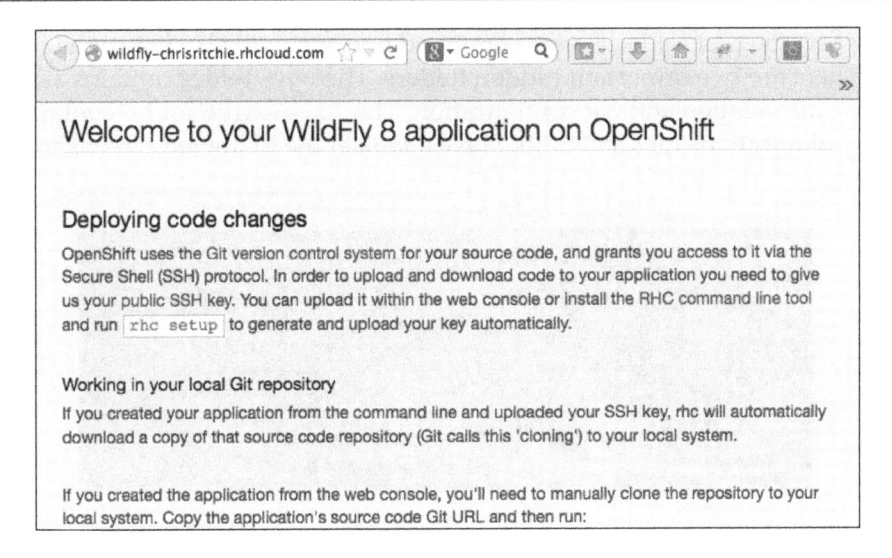

> **Welcome to your WildFly 8 application on OpenShift**
>
> **Deploying code changes**
> OpenShift uses the Git version control system for your source code, and grants you access to it via the Secure Shell (SSH) protocol. In order to upload and download code to your application you need to give us your public SSH key. You can upload it within the web console or install the RHC command line tool and run `rhc setup` to generate and upload your key automatically.
>
> **Working in your local Git repository**
> If you created your application from the command line and uploaded your SSH key, rhc will automatically download a copy of that source code repository (Git calls this 'cloning') to your local system.
>
> If you created the application from the web console, you'll need to manually clone the repository to your local system. Copy the application's source code Git URL and then run:

Now, let's turn our attention to the local repository on your computer.

> You can import the repository into Eclipse by selecting **File** | **Import** | **Projects** from **GIT** | **Existing local repository** | **Add**. Then, browse to the location of your `git` repository and import it as a new Maven project so that Eclipse can automatically generate the project configuration files for you.

If you look at the structure of the `git` repository, as shown in the following screenshot, you will see that the `src` folder follows a typical Maven project structure for a web application:

```
▶ deployments
  pom.xml
  README.md
▼ src
  ▼ main
    ▼ java
    ▼ resources
    ▼ webapp
      ▼ images
          jbosscorp_logo.png
        index.html
        snoop.jsp
      ▼ WEB-INF
          web.xml
```

If you inspect the root folder via the command line, you will also notice the hidden folders. There are two important hidden folders. The `.git` folder contains all your versioning information and Git configuration. The `.openshift` folder contains various configurations for OpenShift. Have a look at the following screenshot:

```
chris-macbook:wildfly chris$ ls -lah
total 16
drwxr-xr-x    8 chris  staff   272B Aug 11 21:21 .
drwxr-xr-x@   9 chris  staff   306B Aug 11 21:20 ..
drwxr-xr-x   13 chris  staff   442B Aug 11 21:21 .git
drwxr-xr-x    6 chris  staff   204B Aug 11 21:20 .openshift
-rw-r--r--    1 chris  staff   177B Aug 11 21:20 README.md
drwxr-xr-x    3 chris  staff   102B Aug 11 21:21 deployments
-rw-r--r--    1 chris  staff   2.1K Aug 11 21:20 pom.xml
drwxr-xr-x    3 chris  staff   102B Aug 11 21:21 src
chris-macbook:wildfly chris$
```

The `deployments` folder performs the same task as the `JBOSS_HOME/standalone/deployments` directory. Applications placed here will be automatically deployed when the repository is pushed to the remote Git repository.

Understanding the workflow

Just before we start to code the actual application, we need to understand the workflow and how the code is deployed to the server. Here are the basic steps:

1. Modify the source code in the local Git repository.
2. Add any deployments, such as JDBC connectors, to the `deployments` folder. This step is optional.
3. Stage all files to the local repository, ready for committing.
4. Commit the files to the local repository.
5. Push the changes to the remote repository. This will trigger deployment on your gear. You don't need to add your application WAR to the `deployments` folder.

Building the application

So, now we need to create our own application. For the first example, we will deploy a simple service that downloads the text within a text area as a PDF file. This application consists of a servlet that translates the request into a PDF response using the **iText** library (available at `http://itextpdf.com/download.php`). Here is the servlet:

```java
package com.packtpub.chapter11;

import java.io.IOException;

import javax.servlet.*;
import javax.servlet.annotation.WebServlet;
import javax.servlet.http.*;

import com.itextpdf.text.*;
import com.itextpdf.text.pdf.PdfWriter;

@WebServlet("/convert")
public class TextToPdf extends HttpServlet {

    public void init(ServletConfig config)
      throws ServletException{
        super.init(config);
    }

    public void doGet(HttpServletRequest request,
      HttpServletResponse response) throws ServletException,
        IOException{
        doPost(request, response);
    }

    public void doPost(HttpServletRequest request,
      HttpServletResponse response) throws ServletException,
        IOException {
        String text = request.getParameter("text");
        response.setContentType("application/pdf");
        Document document = new Document();
        try{
            PdfWriter.getInstance(document,
              response.getOutputStream());
            document.open();
            document.add(new Paragraph(text));
            document.close();
        }catch(DocumentException e){
            e.printStackTrace();
        }
    }
}

public void init(ServletConfig config) throws ServletException{
    super.init(config);
```

```java
    }

    public void doGet(HttpServletRequest request,
        HttpServletResponse response) throws ServletException,
          IOException{
        doPost(request, response);
    }

    public void doPost(HttpServletRequest request,
      HttpServletResponse response) throws ServletException,
      IOException{
        String text = request.getParameter("text");
        response.setContentType("application/pdf");
        Document document = new Document();
        try{
            PdfWriter.getInstance(document,
            response.getOutputStream());
        document.open();

        document.add(new Paragraph(text));

        document.close();
        }catch(DocumentException e){
            e.printStackTrace();
        }
    }
```

We also need to add the itextpdf library to the project's pom.xml file so that the code can compile. Have a look at the following code:

```xml
<dependency>
    <groupId>com.itextpdf</groupId>
    <artifactId>itextpdf</artifactId>
    <version>5.5.2</version>
</dependency>
```

In addition, we need an HTML/JSP page that contains a text area. This code is inside the createpdf.html file:

```html
<form action="TextToPdf" method="post">
    <textarea cols="80" rows="5" name="text">
        This text will be converted to PDF.
    </textarea>
    <input type="submit" value="Convert to PDF">
</form>
```

We have now finished the application. We need to add and commit our application to our local Git repository using the following `git add` command:

```
$ git add *
```

Then, enter the following `git commit` command:

```
$ git commit -m "Initial commit of wildfly app"
```

Lastly, you need to push your local changes to the remote repository sitting on your gear, as follows:

```
$ git push
```

This will push up your code and trigger various Git hooks that cause your code to be compiled, packaged, and deployed, as you can see from the following output. The build output has been omitted for brevity.

```
Counting objects: 19, done.
Compressing objects: 100% (8/8), done.
Writing objects: 100% (12/12), 1.58 KiB | 0 bytes/s, done.
Total 12 (delta 3), reused 0 (delta 0)
remote: Stopping wildfly cart
remote: Sending SIGTERM to wildfly:72039 ...
remote: Building git ref 'master', commit 7d63607
...
remote: [INFO] Scanning for projects...
remote: [INFO]
remote: [INFO] ------------------------------------------------------------------
remote: [INFO] Building wildfly 1.0
remote: [INFO] ------------------------------------------------------------------
...
remote: [INFO] ------------------------------------------------------------------
remote: [INFO] BUILD SUCCESS
remote: [INFO] ------------------------------------------------------------------
...
remote: Preparing build for deployment
remote: Deployment id is aed5acfd
remote: Activating deployment
remote: Deploying WildFly
remote: Starting wildfly cart
...
remote: CLIENT_MESSAGE: Artifacts deployed: ./ROOT.war
```

```
remote: ------------------------
remote: Git Post-Receive Result: success
remote: Activation status: success
remote: Deployment completed with status: success
To ssh://53e905324382ecc7c30001d0@wildfly-chrisritchie.rhcloud.com/~/
git/wildfly.git/
   76af36f..7d63607  master -> master
```

We can now finally access our application using `http://wildfly-chrisritchie.rhcloud.com/createpdf.html`. Have a look at the following screenshot:

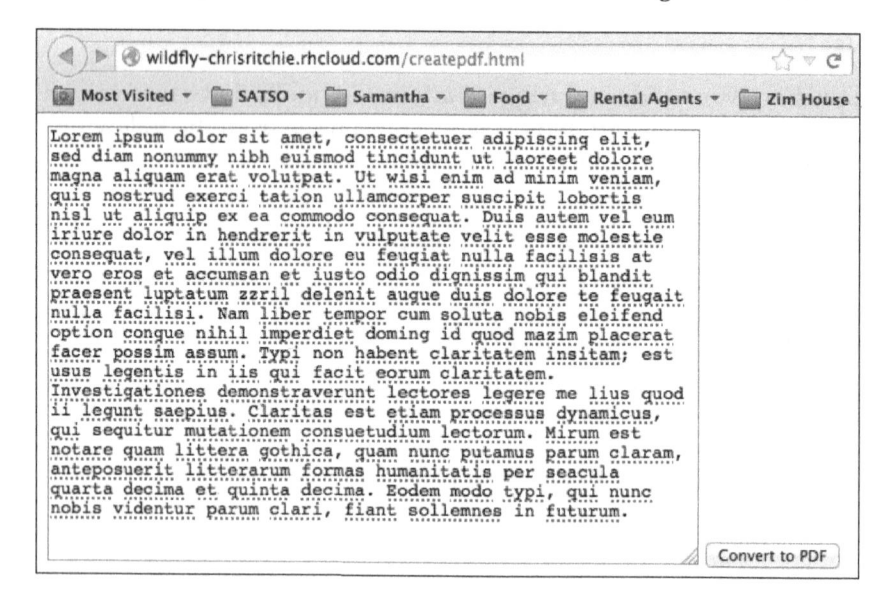

After entering some text and clicking on the **Convert to PDF** button, a PDF file is downloaded containing the text, as follows:

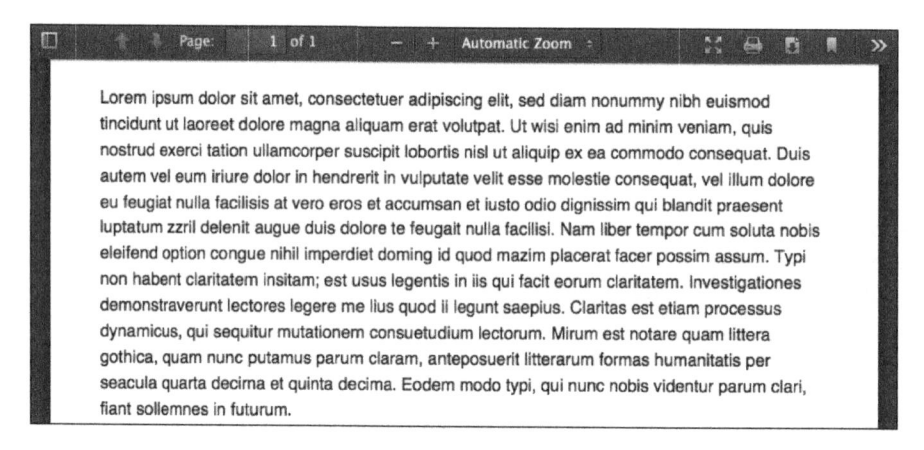

Launching our application generates a PDF file as the result—your first cloud application! Now that we have deployed a simple application to your OpenShift gear, in the next section, we will show you how to manage your OpenShift applications and introduce some advanced features.

Viewing the OpenShift server logfiles

At some point, you will need to see what is happening on the server side. Maybe your application is failing to deploy, or you need to see the logs after you encounter an error. There are a few ways you can view the OpenShift server logs:

- Tail the logfile using client tools
- Run SSH into the gear

Tailing the logfile

Tailing the application server log is simple. You just need to run the `rhc tail` command. For example, to view the log for the example application that we called `wildfly`, you need to execute the following:

```
$ rhc tail -a wildfly
```

This will print out the latest entries from the logfile, as follows:

```
2014-08-11 22:11:39,270 INFO   [org.wildfly.extension.undertow]
  (MSC service thread 1-4) JBAS017534: Registered web context: /
2014-08-11 22:11:41,411 INFO   [org.jboss.as.server]
  (ServerService Thread Pool -- 54) JBAS018559: Deployed "ROOT.war"
  (runtime-name : "ROOT.war")
2014-08-11 22:12:26,849 INFO   [org.jboss.as] (Controller Boot Thread)
  JBAS015961: Http management interface listening on
  http://127.6.97.1:9990/management
2014-08-11 22:12:26,862 INFO   [org.jboss.as]
  (Controller Boot Thread) JBAS015951: Admin console listening on
  http://127.6.97.1:9990
2014-08-11 22:12:26,864 INFO   [org.jboss.as]
  (Controller Boot Thread) JBAS015874: WildFly 8.1.0.Final "Kenny"
  started in 219903ms - Started 299 of 429 services
  (177 services are lazy, passive or on-demand)
```

To exit the log, simply press *Ctrl + C*.

Viewing logs via SSH

Using the `rhc tail` command is only useful part of the time. Most likely, you will want to view the entire log or search the log. For this, you need to SSH into the gear. We use the `-a` switch to specify the application name, as follows.

```
$ rhc ssh -a wildfly
```

By typing `ls app_name`, you can see that the directory structure is similar to that of a WildFly install. You can now view your file using the `less` command, which means you have full control over navigation and search within the file:

```
$ less wildfly/standalone/logs/server.log
...


==> example/logs/server.log <==
14:41:18,706 INFO  [org.jboss.as.connector.subsystems.datasources] (Controller Boot Thread) Deploying JDBC-compliant driver class org.h2.Driver (version 1.2)
14:41:18,712 INFO  [org.jboss.as.connector.subsystems.datasources] (Controller Boot Thread) Deploying non-JDBC-compliant driver class com.mysql.jdbc.Driver (version 5.1)
14:41:18,732 INFO  [org.jboss.as.clustering.infinispan.subsystem] (Controller Boot Thread) Activating Infinispan subsystem.
14:41:18,860 INFO  [org.jboss.as.naming] (Controller Boot Thread) Activating Naming Subsystem
14:41:18,877 INFO  [org.jboss.as.naming] (MSC service thread 1-1) Starting Naming Service
```

> Using the `less` command gives you much more control than using `tail`. Pressing *Shift + F* starts the tailing of the file, and *Ctrl + C* stops the tailing of the file. A backslash allows you to search backwards, and a question mark allows you to search forward in the file. It becomes easy to find occurrences of exceptions and errors.

Managing applications in OpenShift

At first, it might appear difficult to manage your application on a remote server. Once you have learned the commands to manage your application, this concern should be greatly reduced.

In order to control your applications, you can use the `rhc app` command, which takes the action to be performed and the `-a` command that specifies the application name. For example:

```
$rhc app restart -a app_name
```

The following table shows the list of commands available to manage your applications. You can view the list of available options via the command line, using the `--help` flag:

Option	Description
start	Starts an application
stop	Stops an application that is currently running
force-stop	Kills the application's processes
restart	Restarts an application
reload	Reloads an application
delete	Deletes an application
configure	Configures properties for an application
create	Creates an application
deploy	Deploys an application
scale-up	Scales up the application cartridge
scale-down	Scales down the application cartridge
show	Shows an application's information
tidy	Deletes an application's logfiles and temporary files

If you want to delete the application we created earlier, you will use the following command:

```
$ rhc app delete -a wildfly


This is a non-reversible action! Your application code and data will be
permanently deleted if you continue!

Are you sure you want to delete the application 'atestapp'? (yes|no): yes

Deleting application 'wildfly' ... deleted
```

Configuring your applications

When you create an application, you will have a local copy of the repository, which contains your application code and the WildFly server's `deployments` folder. Besides this, there are a couple of hidden folders in your Git repository. The first one is the `.git` folder, which contains all your Git-related configuration. The second folder is `.openshift`. The following is the content of the `.openshift` folder:

```
chris-macbook:.openshift chris$ ls -lah
drwxr-xr-x   3 chris   staff    102B Aug 11 21:20 action_hooks
drwxr-xr-x   4 chris   staff    136B Aug 11 21:20 config
drwxr-xr-x   8 chris   staff    272B Aug 11 21:20 cron
drwxr-xr-x   3 chris   staff    102B Aug 11 21:20 markers
```

The `action_hooks` folder is where developers can put action hook scripts that will be executed during the OpenShift build life cycle.

> You can create a build script to perform application initialization, such as creating tables or setting variables. For full details on supported action hooks, see the documentation at http://openshift.github.io/documentation/oo_user_guide.html#build-action-hooks.

The `cron` folder allows the developer to add cron jobs on the gear. The scripts added will be scheduled according to whether they are put in the `minutely`, `hourly`, `daily`, `weekly`, or `monthly` folders.

The `markers` folder can be used to set various settings. For example, the `skip_maven_build` marker file will instruct the Maven compiler to skip the build process. Lastly and importantly, the `config` folder has the following structure:

```
chris-macbook:.openshift chris$ ls -lah config/
drwxr-xr-x   3 chris   staff    102B Aug 11 21:20 modules
-rw-r--r--   1 chris   staff     29K Aug 11 21:20 standalone.xml
```

As you expected, the `standalone.xml` file is the WildFly configuration file for your applications. The `modules` folder is where you can add your own modules, as you would in a native install of WildFly.

We have only touched upon the basics of what OpenShift can do. For a more in-depth look, see the OpenShift user guide at http://openshift.github.io/documentation/oo_user_guide.html.

Adding a database cartridge

Every enterprise application needs some kind of storage for its data. OpenShift allows you to add database cartridges after creating your application. To view the list of possible cartridges, you can issue the following command:

```
$ rhc cartridge list
```

Within the list that outputs, you will see various database vendor cartridge options. In this example, we are going to add the MySQL database cartridge to our application. To do this, run the following command:

```
$ rhc cartridge add mysql-5.5
```

> If you configure your application to be scalable, the database cartridge will be installed into a new gear. If your application is not configured to be scalable, it will be added to the same gear as your application. This is to ensure that your database is not affected when you scale up or scale down your gears.

The output will print the information we need related to our new database, such as the root password, connection URL, and so on:

```
chris-macbook:wildfly chris$ rhc cartridge add mysql-5.5

Adding mysql-5.5 to application 'wildfly' ... done

mysql-5.5 (MySQL 5.5)
---------------------
  Gears:           Located with wildfly-wildfly-8
  Connection URL:  mysql://$OPENSHIFT_MYSQL_DB_HOST:$OPENSHIFT_MYSQL_DB_PORT/
  Database Name:   wildfly
  Password:        y-rftt5LU16j
  Username:        adminWfn4mG6

MySQL 5.5 database added.  Please make note of these credentials:

   Root User: adminWfn4mG6
   Root Password: y-rftt5LU16j
   Database Name: wildfly
```

```
Connection URL: mysql://$OPENSHIFT_MYSQL_DB_HOST:$OPENSHIFT_MYSQL_DB_
PORT/
```

You can manage your new MySQL database by also embedding phpmyadmin.

The phpmyadmin username and password will be the same as the MySQL credentials above.

RESULT:

Mysql 5.1 database added. Please make note of these credentials:

  Root User: admin

  Root Password: SH-v4VuAZ_Se

  Database Name: example

The beauty of this is that you do not need to further configure your `standalone.xml` file, as all the environment variables are set for you when you add the MySQL cartridge. You can access the datasource immediately using the JNDI namespace of `java:jboss/datasources/MysqlDS`. Take a look at the datasource configuration in the `standalone.xml` file. You will see all properties are external environment variables, as follows:

```xml
<datasource jndi-name="java:jboss/datasources/MySQLDS"
  enabled="${mysql.enabled}" use-java-context="true"
  pool-name="MySQLDS" use-ccm="true">
    <connection-url>jdbc:mysql://${env.OPENSHIFT_MYSQL_DB_HOST}:
      ${env.OPENSHIFT_MYSQL_DB_PORT}/${env.OPENSHIFT_APP_NAME}
      </connection-url>
    <driver>mysql</driver>
    <security>
        <user-name>${env.OPENSHIFT_MYSQL_DB_USERNAME}</user-name>
        <password>${env.OPENSHIFT_MYSQL_DB_PASSWORD}</password>
    </security>
    <validation>
        <check-valid-connection-sql>SELECT 1
          </check-valid-connection-sql>
        <background-validation>true</background-validation>
        <background-validation-millis>60000
          </background-validation-millis>
        <!--<validate-on-match>true</validate-on-match>-->
    </validation>
    <pool>
        <flush-strategy>IdleConnections</flush-strategy>
```

```
        </pool>
</datasource>
```

To remove the database cartridge, and thus disable it, you can simply run the following command:

```
$ rhc cartridge remove mysql-5.5
```

Using OpenShift Tools and Eclipse

Alongside the client tools, there is also a plugin for Eclipse that allows you to integrate with OpenShift. If you prefer graphical interfaces over the command line, you should consider this plugin.

Installing OpenShift Tools requires the same steps as when we installed the WildFly plugin in *Chapter 2, Configuring the Core WildFly Subsystems*. Perform the following steps to install OpenShift Tools:

1. In Eclipse, go to the marketplace by clicking on **Help | Eclipse Marketplace**.
2. Search for the version of JBoss Tools that matches your Eclipse version.
3. Click on **Install**. You will be presented with the full list of features available.
4. You can now select **JBoss OpenShift Tools** along with any other features you want, as shown in the following screenshot:

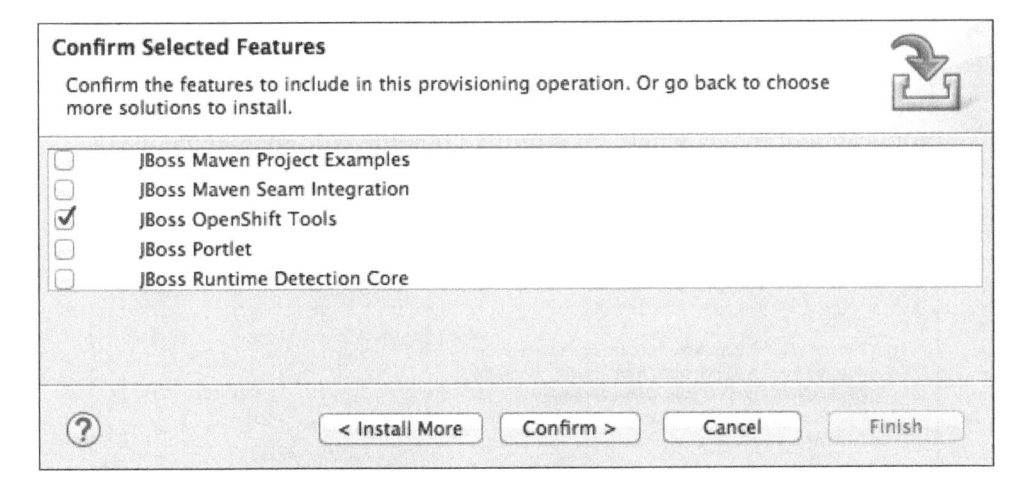

Confirm Selected Features

Confirm the features to include in this provisioning operation. Or go back to choose more solutions to install.

- ☐ JBoss Maven Project Examples
- ☐ JBoss Maven Seam Integration
- ☑ JBoss OpenShift Tools
- ☐ JBoss Portlet
- ☐ JBoss Runtime Detection Core

[< Install More] [Confirm >] [Cancel] [Finish]

5. Click on **Confirm**, accept the license terms, and click on **Finish**.

When Eclipse restarts, you will be able to create new applications or import existing applications. Creating a new application is straightforward. Perform the following steps:

1. Navigate to **File | New | OpenShift Application**. Have a look at the following screenshot:

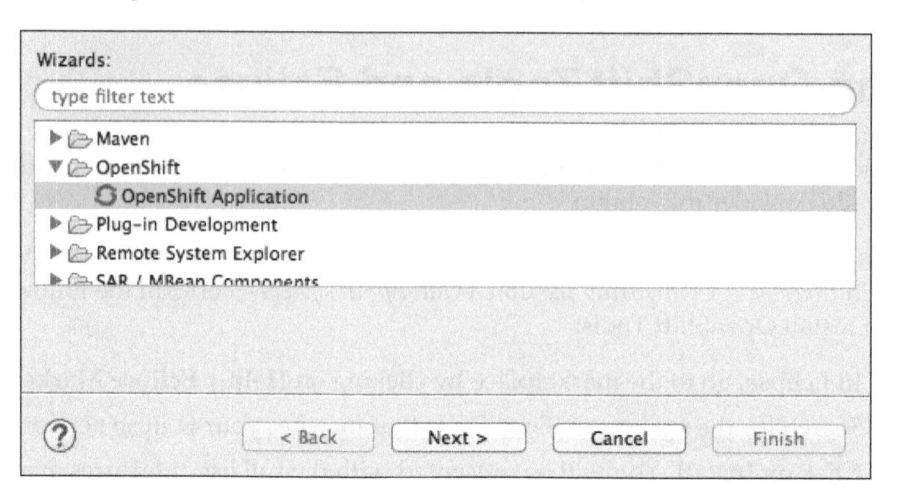

2. You will be presented with a pop up allowing you to enter your OpenShift account's username and password. Enter your details and click on **OK**.

3. The next screen will allow you to either download an existing application from the OpenShift cloud or create a new one. We will create a new one here and leave you to investigate the option of downloading an existing application if that is what you require. Look for WildFly 8 in the list of possible quickstart cartridges. Have a look at the following screenshot:

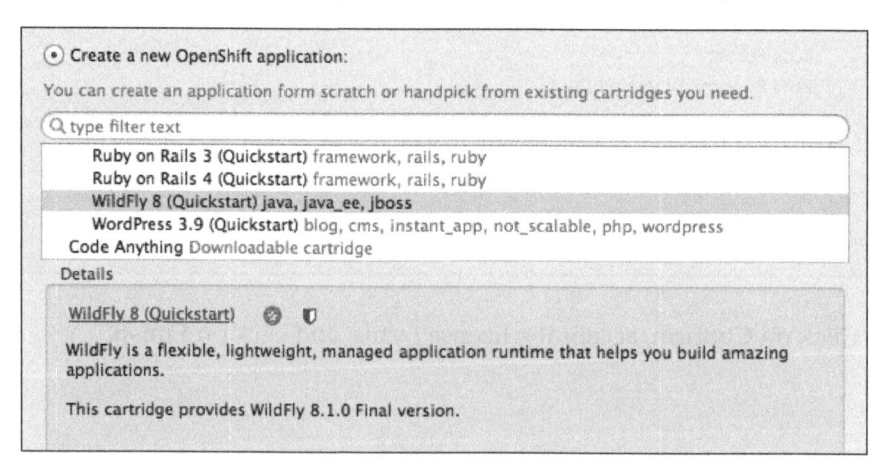

4. Click on Next, enter the name of your application, and select your gear profile. Have a look at the following screenshot:

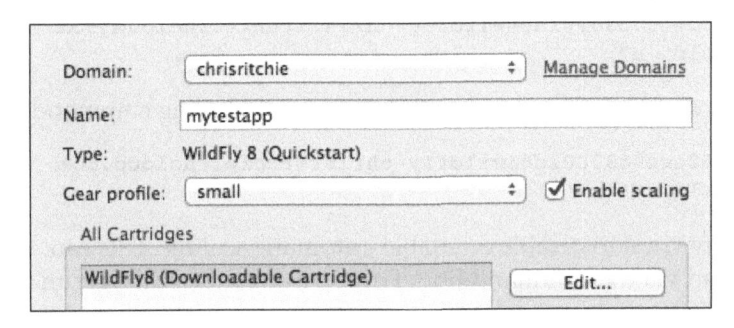

5. Click on **Next**, and **Next** again. Your new application is now complete and the gear is configured.

This tutorial is meant to be a brief introduction to the OpenShift Tools plugin. If you are interested in using OpenShift Tools, please refer to the online documentation at `http://docs.jboss.org/tools/4.1.0.Final/en/User_Guide/html_single/index.html#chap-OpenShift_Tools`.

Scaling your application

Until now, we have mentioned some of the most essential features of the OpenShift platform. Although all the available options cannot be covered within a single chapter, there is one more feature that needs to be covered, which is application scaling.

For an application to be scalable, you must pass the -s switch as you create the application with the following command:

```
$ rhc app create app_name type -s
```

> It is not possible to make a non-scalable application scalable. To do this, you need to take a snapshot of the application, spin up a new scalable application, and then push your code to it.

Once you have created a scalable application, it will automatically add nodes to the cluster when the number of concurrent requests exceed 90 percent of the maximum concurrent requests over one period. It will automatically scale down when the number of concurrent requests fall below 49.9 percent of the maximum concurrent requests over three consecutive periods.

You can also scale your application manually via the command line.
To manually scale up your application, run the following command:

```
$ 53e905324382ecc7c30001d0@wildfly-chrisritchie.rhcloud.com
  "haproxy_ctld -u"
```

To manually scale down your application, run the following command:

```
$ 53e905324382ecc7c30001d0@wildfly-chrisritchie.rhcloud.com
  "haproxy_ctld -d"
```

Lastly, you may want to disable or enable automatic scaling. This can also be achieved via the command line. To stop automatic scaling, run the following command:

```
$ 53e905324382ecc7c30001d0@wildfly-chrisritchie.rhcloud.com
  "haproxy_ctld_daemon stop"
```

To start automatic scaling, run the following command:

```
$ 53e905324382ecc7c30001d0@wildfly-chrisritchie.rhcloud.com
  "haproxy_ctld_daemon start"
```

Summary

In this chapter, we looked at an alternative to the traditional approach of hosting applications on a company's own infrastructure. The OpenShift platform offers free and paid versions of a PaaS that enables developers to deploy to the cloud without having to worry about downloading and managing the stack, writing scripts, or installing agents.

The OpenShift platform bears some similarities to other cloud solutions, such as MS Azure. Just like Azure, OpenShift is a service managed and run by the vendor. OpenShift provides the ability to quickly choose from multiple cartridges, each of which plugs in a resource required to run your application. With a single Git command, your source code is pushed to the gear, and your application is built and then deployed to the server.

There are several ways to manage your OpenShift gears. First, you can manage them via the command line. This is the best option as you have full control over your gears. Secondly, there is the web interface, which has limited functionality but is fine to quickly create a new application. Lastly, there is OpenShift Tools, which is part of JBoss Tools, a suite of plugins for Eclipse.

There are three options available when using OpenShift. OpenShift Online is a product that offers free and subscription-based services. All the gears are hosted on the public cloud. OpenShift Enterprise allows you to download a stable and supported version of OpenShift to be run on your own hardware. Finally, if you want the latest features (with only community support) or want to contribute to the development of OpenShift, there is OpenShift Origin.

CLI References

To help keep things simple, here's a quick reference for the most common commands and operations used to manage the application server via the CLI. For the sake of brevity, only the `jboss-cli.sh` script (in the Linux environment) is mentioned. Windows users should just replace this file with the equivalent `jboss-cli.bat` file.

Startup options

The following commands can be used to start the CLI in a noninteractive way:

- Pass script commands to the `jboss-cli` shell:

    `./jboss-cli.sh --connect command=:shutdown`

- Execute a CLI shell contained in a file:

    `./jboss-cli.sh --file=test.cli`

General commands

The following commands can be used to gather system information and set specific server properties:

- Show environment information:

    `version`

- Show the JNDI context:

    `/subsystem=naming:jndi-view`

- Show the XML server configuration:

    `:read-config-as-xml`

- Show the services registered in the container and their statuses:

  `/core-service=service-container:dump-services`

- Set a system property:

  `/system-property=property1:add(value="value")`

- Show a system property:

  `/system-property=property1:read-resource`

- Show all system properties:

  `/core-service=platform-mbean/`
  `   type=runtime:read-attribute(name=system-properties)`

- Remove a system property:

  `/system-property=property1:remove`

- Change a socket binding port (for example, the `http` port):

  `/socket-binding-group=standard-sockets/socket-binding=http:`
  `   write-attribute(name="port", value="8090")`

- Show the IP address of the public interface:

  `/interface=public:read-attribute(name=resolved-address)`

The domain-mode commands

Prefix the host name (and, if required, the server name) to indicate which host (or server name) you are issuing the command to. Examples:

- Show the XML configuration from the host master:

  `/host=master:read-config-as-xml`

- Show the IP address of the public interface for the `server-one` server running on the host `master`:

  `/host=master/server=server-one/interface=public:`
  `   read-attribute(name=resolved-address)`

Commands related to application deployment

The CLI can also be used to deploy applications. The CLI assumes that the `MyApp.war` file is in the working directory outside of the `jboss-cli`. Here's a quick reference to the deploy commands:

- List of deployed applications:
  ```
  deploy
  ```

- Deploy an application on a standalone server:
  ```
  deploy MyApp.war
  ```

- Redeploy an application on a standalone server:
  ```
  deploy -f MyApp.war
  ```

- Undeploy an application:
  ```
  undeploy MyApp.war
  ```

- Deploy an application on all server groups:
  ```
  deploy MyApp.war --all-server-groups
  ```

- Deploy an application on one or more server groups (separated by a comma):
  ```
  deploy application.ear --server-groups=main-server-group
  ```

- Undeploy an application from all server groups:
  ```
  undeploy application.ear --all-relevant-server-groups
  ```

- Undeploy an application from one or more server groups:
  ```
  undeploy as7project.war --server-groups=main-server-group
  ```

- Undeploy an application without deleting the content:
  ```
  undeploy application.ear --server-groups=main-server-group
    --keep-content
  ```

JMS

Here, you can find the JMS commands that can be used to create/remove JMS destinations:

- Add a JMS queue:
  ```
  jms-queue add --queue-address=queue1 --entries=queues/queue1
  ```
- Remove a JMS queue:
  ```
  jms-queue remove --queue-address=queue1
  ```
- Add a JMS topic:
  ```
  jms-topic add --topic-address=topic1 --entries=topics/topic1
  ```
- Remove a JMS topic:
  ```
  jms-topic remove --topic-address=topic1
  ```

Datasources

This is a list of handy datasource commands that can be issued using the datasource alias:

- Add a datasource:
  ```
  data-source add --jndi-name=java:/MySqlDS --name=MySQLPool
     --connection-url=jdbc:mysql://localhost:3306/MyDB
     --driver-name=mysql-connector-java-5.1.16-bin.jar
     --user-name=myuser --password=password -max-pool-size=30
  ```
- Remove a datasource:
  ```
  data-source remove --name=java:/MySqlDS
  ```

Datasources (using operations on resources)

You can also operate on a datasource using operations on the data sources subsystem:

- List the installed drivers:
  ```
  /subsystem=datasources:installed-drivers-list
  ```
- Add a datasource:
  ```
  data-source add --jndi-name=java:/MySqlDS --name=MySQLPool
     --connection-url=jdbc:mysql://localhost:3306/MyDB
     --driver-name=mysql-connector-java-5.1.30-bin.jar
     --user-name=myuser --password=password --max-pool-size=30
  ```

- Add an XA datasource (using an operation):

  ```
  xa-data-source add --name=MySQLPoolXA
    --jndi-name=java:/MySqlDSXA --driver-name=
    mysql-connector-java-5.1.30-bin.jar
    -xa-datasource-properties=[{ServerName=localhost}
    {PortNumber=3306}]
  ```

- Remove a datasource (using an operation):

  ```
  /subsystem=datasources/data-source=testDS:remove
  ```

Mod_cluster

Mod_cluster management can be carried out using the following CLI operations:

- List the connected proxies:

  ```
  /subsystem=modcluster:list-proxies
  ```

- Show proxies' information:

  ```
  /subsystem=modcluster:read-proxies-info
  ```

- Add a proxy to the cluster:

  ```
  /subsystem=modcluster:add-proxy(host= CP15-022, port=9999)
  ```

- Remove a proxy:

  ```
  /subsystem=modcluster:remove-proxy(host=CP15-022, port=9999)
  ```

- Add a web context:

  ```
  /subsystem=modcluster:enable-context(context=/myapp,
    virtualhost=default-host)
  ```

- Disable a web context:

  ```
  /subsystem=modcluster:disable-context(context=/myapp,
    virtualhost=default-host)
  ```

- Stop a web context:

  ```
  /subsystem=modcluster:stop-context(context=/myapp,
    virtualhost=default-host, waittime=50)
  ```

Batch

Here's how to handle batch processing with the CLI:

- Start batching:
  `batch`

- Pause batching:
  `holdback-batch`

- Continue batching after a pause:
  `batch`

- List of commands on the current batch stack:
  `list-batch`

- Clear the batch session of commands:
  `clear-batch`

- Execute batch commands on a stack:
  `run-batch`

Snapshots

Snapshots allow the storage and retrieval of the server configuration:

- Take a snapshot of the configuration:
  `:take-snapshot`

- List the available snapshots:
  `:list-snapshots`

- Delete a snapshot:
  `:delete-snapshot(name="20140814-234725965standalone-full-ha.xml")`

Index

Symbols

@EJB annotation 114
@Entity annotation 126
@javax.annotation.security.DenyAll
    annotation 316
@javax.annotation.security.PermitAll
    annotation 316
@javax.annotation.security.RolesAllowed
    annotation 316
@javax.annotation.security.RunAs
    annotation 316
@javax.ejb.Timeout method 77
@javax.persistence.Cacheable
    annotation 265
@Named annotation 114
@org.hibernate.annotations.Cache
    annotation 265
@org.jboss.ejb3.annotation.SecurityDomain
    annotation 316
@SecurityDomain annotation 318
@WebContext annotation 318

A

acceptor 81
access-log element 102
add-proxy command 286
address element 258
address-full-policy property 87
address-setting block 86
Admin console
    used, for deploying application 175-178
AdvancedADLdap login module 305
advanced batch commands 211
advanced deployment strategies
    about 185
    advantages 185
    Class-Path declaration, using 190
    server's automatic dependencies,
        excluding 186, 187
    single module dependency,
        setting up 185, 186
    sub-deployments, isolating 187-189
advanced Infinispan configuration
    about 254
    Infinispan threads, configuring 255, 256
    Infinispan transport, configuring 255
AdvancedLdap login module 305
Advertise class, mod_cluster
    URL 289
Apache
    installing 271
Apache Directory project
    URL 310
Apache web server
    Apache, installing 271
    benefits 270
    mod_jk library, installing 271-273
    mod_jk library, using 270
    mod_proxy, configuring 274, 275
    native management capabilities,
        adding 287, 288
Apache web server, advantages
    clustering 270
    load balancing 270
    security 270
    speed 270

application deployment, on WildFly domain
  Admin console used 175-178
  performing 172, 173
  to all server groups 173
  to domain, CLI used 173
  to single server group 174, 175
application deployment, on WildFly server
  automatic application deployment 162
  manual application
    deployment 162, 170-172
  performing 161, 162
application server
  filesystem 21, 22
  hardware requisites 9
  Java environment, installing 9, 10
  WildFly 8, installing 12
  WildFly, restarting 17, 18
  WildFly, starting 13, 14
  WildFly, stopping 16, 17
application server configuration
  core subsystems, configuring 38
  deployments 38
  diagrammatic representation 32
  extensions 33
  interfaces 35
  management interfaces 34
  paths 33, 34
  performing 31, 32
  profiles 35
  socket-binding groups 37
  subsystems 35
  system properties 38
  thread pool subsystem, configuring 39
application server logging configuration
  about 47
  async-handler 51
  console-handler 49, 50
  custom handlers 52
  logging implementation, selecting 48, 49
  logging subsystem, configuring 49
  periodic-rotating-file-handler 50
  size-rotating-file-handler 51
  syslog-handler 52
application server nodes, WildFly
    domain 134
AS process 320
asymmetric encryption 324

async-handler 51
asynchronous EJB
  about 71
  fire-and-forget asynchronous void
    methods 71
  retrieve-result-later asynchronous
    methods 71
asynchronous messaging 249
attributes 309
attributes/elements, bounded-queue
    thread pool
  allow-core-timeout 43
  core-threads 43
  keepalive-time 43
  max-threads 43
  name 43
  queue-length 43
  thread-factory 43
attributes/elements, unbounded-queue
    thread pool
  keepalive-time 44
  max-threads 44
  name 44
  thread-factory 44
authentication 300
authorization 300
autoflush attribute 50
automatic application deployment,
    on WildFly server
  about 162, 163
  CLI, used 164, 165
  deployment scanner behavior,
    changing 163, 164
  Eclipse deployments, configuring 169
  to custom folder 163
  web admin console, used 165, 167
  WildFly Eclipse plugin, used 168

B

basic access authentication 314
batch-delay parameter 83
batch processing
  handling 368
batch-related commands
  batch 212
  clear-batch 212

discard-batch 212
edit-batch-line 212
holdback-batch 212
list-batch 212
move-batch-line 212
remove-batch-line 212
run-batch 212
bin folder 22
blocking queueless thread pool
 about 45
 diagrammatic representation 45
bounded-queue thread pool
 about 40
 attributes/elements 43
 configuring 41
 core size 40
 diagrammatic representation 41
 maximum size 40
buffer cache
 about 106
 configuring 106

C

cache-container element 246
caching, entities
 about 264
 Hibernate annotations, using 265
 JPA annotations, using 265
caching, queries 266
caching strategies
 distribution 246
 invalidation 246
 local 246
 replication 246
caching strategy elements 248
Certificate login module 304
certificate management tools 326
CertificateRoles login module 304
certificate-signing request (CSR) 329
Certification Authority (CA) 324
classloading dependencies 179
Class Namespace Isolation 178
Class-Path approach 178
clear command 217
CLI
 about 15, 33, 140, 194, 195

application server 215
benefits 227
commands 196
commands, executing with 204, 205
commands, issued on resource 199
configuration snapshots, capturing 213, 214
datasources, creating 206-208
datasources, modifying 206-208
employing 195, 196
help command 209
history 216, 217
JMS destination, adding 205
mod_cluster, managing via 284, 286
non-interactive output, redirecting 213
operations 196
operations, executing 196-199
resources, navigating through 196-199
scripts, executing in batch 210
scripts, executing in file 212, 213
server configuration, reloading 195
snapshots, capturing 215
used, for deploying application 164, 165
used, for deploying application to
  domain 173
used, for managing web contexts 286
used, for server connection 15, 16
XA datasources, creating 209
XA datasources, modifying 209
CLI deployment options
 --all-relevant-server-groups 175
 --all-server-groups 175
 --server-groups 175
 --server-groups -keep-content 175
client authentication 325
Client login module 304
clients 80
cloud computing
 about 333
 advantages 335
 APIs 335
 cost reduction 335
 disadvantages 335
 elasticity 335
 hybrid cloud 336
 on-demand service provisioning 335
 options 336, 337
 private cloud 336

public cloud 336
services 337
versus grid computing 334
cloud services
Infrastructure as a Service (IaaS) 337
Platform as a Service (PaaS) 338
Software as a Service (SaaS) 338
types 337
cluster-connection name attribute 258
clustering
about 230
configuring 260
entities 263, 264
session beans 261, 262
web applications 267
cluster, setting up on same machine
multiple IP addresses used 234
port offset used 235, 236
command-line interface. *See* **CLI**
command line options, for managing OpenShift applications
configure 353
create 353
delete 353
deploy 353
force-stop 353
reload 353
restart 353
scale-down 353
scale-up 353
show 353
start 353
stop 353
tidy 353
commands, issued on resource
read-attribute 199
read-children-names 199
read-children-resources 199
read-children-types 199
read-operation-description 199
read-operation-names 199
read-resource 199
read-resource-description 199
write-attribute 199
concurrency
about 91
components 91

configuring 91
context service, configuring 92
managed executor service, configuring 93
managed schedule executor service, configuring 94
managed thread factory, configuring 92
configuration files, WildFly domain
domain.xml 137
host.xml 137
configuration levels, JVM
host level 144
server-group level 144
server level 144
configuration, OpenShift application
about 354
database cartridge, adding 355, 356
Eclipse, using 357-359
OpenShift Tools, using 357-359
ConfigureIdentity login module 304
connector 81
connector-ref element 258
context-service attribute 93
context service, concurrency
configuring 92
coordinator environment, transactions subsystem 90
core environment, transactions subsystem 90
core subsystems, application server configuration
configuring 38
core-threads attribute 93
custom handlers
about 52-55
bypassing container logging 57
loggers, configuring 55, 56
per-deployment logging 56
custom login module
reference link 308

D

database
connecting to 59, 60
DatabaseCertificate login module 304
Database login module
about 304-306

diagrammatic representation 315
passwords, encrypting 307-309
using 306
DatabaseUsers login module 304
data persistence, Maven web project
configuring 124, 125
data-source command 206
dead-letter-address property 87
declarative security 301
decryption 323
de facto standard 309
default configuration files
overriding 137
default domain configuration
about 134-136
elements 134
delete-snapshot command 216
Dependencies approach 178
deployment 159
deployments, application server
configuration 38
deployment scanner 162
digital certificate 324
DigitalOcean 338
direct-deliver parameter 83
disable command 217
distinguished name (DN) 309
distributed caching 250
docs folder
about 22
examples folder 22
schema folder 22
domain controller, WildFly domain
about 134
configuring 142
domain folder
about 22, 23
configuration folder 22
content folder 23
data folder 23
lib folder 23
log folder 23
servers folder 23
tmp folder 23
domain mode commands 364
domain.xml file
configuring 138, 139

durable element 86
dynamic modules 27

E

EAR file 160, 161
Eclipse environment
installing 18
EJB components
about 70
asynchronous EJB 71
configuring 71
MDBs 70
MDBs, configuring 76
no-interface EJB 71
SFSBs 70
SFSBs, configuring 74, 75
Singleton EJB 71
SLSBs 70
SLSBs, configuring 72, 73
timer service, configuring 77, 78
EJB container
about 70
configuring 70
messaging system, configuring 78-80
transactions service, configuring 89-91
EJB layer
adding, to Maven web project 114-116
EJBs
app-name parameter 120
bean-name parameter 120
distinct-name parameter 120
fully-qualified-classname-of-the-remote
-interface parameter 120
module-name parameter 120
securing 316, 317
enable command 217
enable-statistics property 91
encryption 323
Enterprise Archive file. *See* EAR file
Enterprise JavaBeans container. *See*
EJB container
entities
caching 264
clustering 263, 264
configuring 126-129
entry 309

[373]

entry element 85
eviction strategies, Infinispan
  LIRS 253
  LRU 253
  NONE 252
  UNORDERED 252
example, WildFly domain configuration
  creating 147-152
executable module 28
expiry-address property 87
expiry-delay property 87
explicit dependencies 182, 183
extensions, application server
        configuration 33

F

filesystem, application server
  about 21, 22
  application server modules 27, 28
  bin folder 22
  docs folder 22
  domain folder 22, 23
  modules folder 24
  standalone folder 23, 24
  welcome-content folder 24
  WildFly's kernel 26
filter-ref element 103
formatter element 50

G

Gartner Group
  URL 336
general commands 363, 364
Google Web Toolkit (GWT) 217
grid computing
  versus cloud computing 334

H

help command 209
Hibernate annotations
  used, for caching entities 265
hibernate cache
  about 252

configuring 252-254
replication, using 254
High Availability 245
history command 217
HornetQ
  about 257
  http 81
  inVM 81
  Netty 81
  URL 79
HornetQ persistence configuration 87, 88
host 140
host configuration, server element
  about 102
  access-log element 102
  filter-ref element 102
  location element 102
  single-sign-on element 102
host controller, WildFly domain 134
host parameter 82
host.xml file
  configuring 139, 140
http 81
http-client-idle-scan-period parameter 83
http-client-idle-time parameter 83
HTTP listener element
  allow-encoded-slash attribute 100
  always-set-keep-alive attribute 100
  buffer-pipelined-data attribute 101
  buffer-pool attribute 101
  certificate-forwarding attribute 101
  decode-url attribute 101
  enabled attribute 101
  max-cookies attribute 101
  max-headers attribute 101
  max-header-size attribute 101
  max-parameters attribute 101
  max-post-size attribute 101
  name attribute 101
  proxy-address-forwarding attribute 101
  redirect-socket attribute 102
  socket-binding attribute 102
  url-charset attribute 102
  worker attribute 102
http-requires-session-id parameter 83
http-response-time parameter 83

http-server-scan-period parameter 83
hung-task-threshold attribute 93
hybrid cloud 336

I

Identity login module 304
implicit dependencies 180-182
Infinispan subsystem
  about 229, 241
  configuring 245, 246
  hibernate cache, configuring 252-254
  replication and distribution, selecting between 250, 251
  session cache containers, configuring 247-249
Infinispan transport
  configuring 255
Infrastructure as a Service (IaaS) 337
installation
  Apache 271
  Java environment 9, 10
  Java, on Linux 10
  Java, on Windows 11, 12
  JBoss tools 19, 20
  mod_cluster 278-280
  mod_jk library 271-273
  WildFly 8 12, 13
interfaces, application server configuration
  about 35
  management network interface 36
  public network interface 36
Internet Service Provider (ISP) 239
Intrusion Detection System (IDS) 336
inVM, acceptors and connectors 81
InVmConnectionFactory 84
IP aliasing 234
isolation levels, Infinispan
  NONE 248
  READ_COMMITTED 248
  READ_UNCOMMITTED 248
  REPEATABLE_READ 248
  SERIALIZABLE 248
isolation level, WildFly classloading
  explicit dependencies 182, 183
  finding 180

implicit dependencies 180, 182
iText library
  download link 346

J

Java Archive file (JAR file) 159, 160
Java Authentication and Authorization Service (JAAS) 302
Java Development Kit (JDK) 9
Java EE 7 examples
  reference link 107
Java EE 7 tutorial
  reference link 77
Java EE security
  about 300-302
  declarative security 301
  programmatic security 301
Java Enterprise Edition (Java EE) 299
Java Enterprise services configuration
  about 59
  concurrency, configuring 91
  database, connecting to 59
  EJB container, configuring 70
Java environment
  installing 9, 10
  installing, on Linux 10
  installing, on Windows 11, 12
Java Naming and Directory Interface (JNDI)
  about 120
  Stateless EJB 120
  Stateful EJB 120
Java Non-blocking Input/Output (NIO) API 79
Java Persistence API (JPA) 97
Java Secure Socket Extension (JSSE) 325
Java security API
  approaching 300
  Database login module, using 306, 307
  EJBs, securing 316
  LDAP login module, using 309, 310
  UsersRoles login module, using 305, 306
  web applications, securing 313-315
  web services, securing 317, 318
  WildFly security subsystem 302-305

Java SE logging libraries (JUL)
  about 47
  diagrammatic representation 47
  formatters 47
  handlers 47
  loggers 47
JavaServer Faces Facets 110
JavaServer Faces (JSF) technology 107
Java Specification Requests. *See* JSRs
Java Transaction API (JTA) 89
Java Virtual Machine. *See* (JVM)
JBoss Enterprise Application Platform (JBoss EAP) 7
JBoss logging framework 47
JBoss tools
  installing 19, 20
JdbcLogger
  reference link 52
JGroups
  URL 244
JGroups protocols
  about 244
  discovery 244
  failure detection 244
  flow control 244
  fragmentation 244
  group membership 244
  reliable delivery 244
  state transfer 244
  transport 244
JGroups subsystem
  about 229
  Building Blocks 242
  Channel 242
  configuring 242, 243
  groups 242
  members 242
  protocol stack, customizing 244
JMeter
  URL, for downloading 291
  using 291
JMS commands 366
jms-queue add command 205
jndi-name attribute 93
journal-type property 88
JPA annotations
  used, for caching entities 265

JPA subsystem
  default datasource, using 126
JSF components
  adding, to Maven web project 111-114
JSRs
  about 8
  URL 8
JVM
  about 9
  configuring 142
  options, adding to server definition 143
  precedence order between elements 144
  server nodes, configuring 145

K

keepalive-time attribute 93
Kerberos login module 305
kernel, WildFly
  about 26
  architecture 26
  JBoss Modules 26
  MSC 26
keytool certificate 326

L

LDAP
  about 309
  attributes 309
  connecting, to WildFly 310-313
  DN 309
  entry 309
  RDN 309
LDAP Data Interchange Format (LDIF) file
  about 310
  using 311
LdapExtended login module
  about 304
  allowEmptyPasswords property 313
  baseCtxDN property 313
  baseFilter property 313
  bindDN property 313
  OBJECT_SCOPE, searchScope property 313
  ONELEVEL_SCOPE, searchScope property 313
  roleAttributeID property 313
  roleFilter property 313

rolesCtxDN property 313
searchScope property 313
SUBTREE_SCOPE, searchScope
    property 313
LDAP login module
  about 309
  using 309
LdapUsers login module 304
level element 50
Lightweight Directory Access Protocol.
    See **LDAP**
Linux
  Java, installing on 10
LIRS
  reference link 253
list-batch command 211
load-balancing
  with mod_cluster 276, 277
load-balancing, between nodes
  about 290-292
  example 295, 296
  load metrics, using 293, 294
load-balancing policy
  FirstAvailable 261
  FirstAvailableIdenticalAllProxies 261
  RandomRobin 261
  RoundRobin 261
load metric
  used, for load-balancing between
      nodes 293, 294
local-query cache 252
location element 102
log4j
  about 47
  URL, for documentation 50
logging implementations
  about 47
  Java SE logging libraries (JUL) 47
  log4j 47
  selecting 48
**logging subsystem, application server
    logging configuration**
  configuring 49
login modules, WildFly security subsystem
  activating 305
  AdvancedADLdap 305
  AdvancedLdap 305

Certificate 304
CertificateRoles 304
Client 304
ConfigureIdentity 304
Database 304
DatabaseCertificate 304
DatabaseUsers 304
Identity 304
Kerberos 305
Ldap 304
LdapExtended 304
LdapUsers 304
PropertiesUsers 304
RoleMapping 304
RunAs 304
Simple 304
SimpleUsers 304
SPNEGOUsers 305
UsersRoles 305
long-running-tasks attribute 93

M

managed executor service, concurrency
  configuring 93
**managed schedule executor service,
    concurrency**
  attributes 94
  configuring 94
managed thread factory, concurrency
  configuring 92
**management interfaces, application
    server configuration 34, 35**
management interfaces, securing
  about 318-320
  groups, configuring 322
  Role-based access control (RBAC) 321
management interfaces, WildFly domain
  configuring 140
management tools
  about 193
  command-line interface (CLI) 194
  web admin console 217
**manual application deployment, on WildFly
    server 170-172**
Maven web project
  creating 107-110

[377]

data persistence, configuring 124
default datasource, using for JPA
    subsystem 126
deploying 117, 118
deploying, to root context 118
EJB layer, adding 114-116
entities, configuring 126-129
JSF components, adding 111-114
persistence, configuring in other
    application archives 129
provider, switching 130
provider, switching with Jipijapa 130
remote EJB client, adding 119-122
remote EJB client, configuring
    programmatically 123
remote EJB client, configuring with
    properties file 122
web context, selecting 116, 117
max-delivery-attempts property 87
max-size-bytes property 87
max-threads attribute 93
MDBs
    about 70
    configuring 76, 77
    Does not Exist state 76
    Method ready Pool state 76
**message-counter-history-day-limit
    property 87**
message digest algorithm 307
message-driven beans. *See* **MDBs**
messaging subsystem
    clustering 257-259
    messaging credentials, configuring 259
Messaging subsystem 229
messaging system, EJB
    configuring 78, 79
    connection factories, configuring 84
    destinations, customizing with address 86
    HornetQ persistence configuration 87, 88
    JMS destinations, configuring 85
    point-to-point model 79
    publish/subscribe model 79
    transport, configuring 80-84
mod_cluster
    advantages 276
    configuration 281-284
    installing 278-280

managing, via CLI 284, 286
reference link 279
testing 284
troubleshooting 288, 290
URL, for downloading 280
used, for load-balancing 276, 277
mod_jk library
    installing 271-273
    using 270
mod_proxy
    configuring 274, 275
Modular Service Container. *See* **MSC**
modules, application server
    dynamic modules 27
    loading 27, 28
    static modules 27
modules folder 24
MSC 26
multihoming
    about 234
    configuring 235
    setting up, on Linux 234
    setting up, on Windows 7 234
mutual authentication 325

N

name attribute 93
Name property 167
Netty 81
network interface
    about 141
    configuring 141
    management 141
    public 141
    unsecure 141
Network Interface Card (nic) element 36
New Input/Output (NIO) 98
nio-remoting-threads parameter 83
node 242
no-interface EJB 71
Non-blocking Input/Output API 98

O

one-time password (OTP) 300
OpenShift
    about 339

applications, managing 352, 353
  Enterprise version 339
  Online version 339
  Origin version 339
OpenShift application
  building 346-350
  cartridge, installing 343-346
  configuring 354
  creating 342
  scaling 359, 360
  workflow 346
OpenShift client tools
  installing 340-342
OpenShift Online
  about 339
  account, accessing from different
      computer 342
  logging into 340
  URL 339
OpenShift server logfiles
  tailing 351
  viewing 351
  viewing, via SSH 352
OpenShift terms
  application 342
  cartridge 342
  gear 342
OpenShift Tools
  installing 357
  reference link 359
  using 357-359
Oracle
  URL, for downloading 9

P

page-size-bytes property 87
passivation 75
paths, application server configuration
  about 33, 34
  java.home 34
  jboss.domain.servers.dir 34
  jboss.server.base.dir 34
  jboss.server.data.dir 34
  jboss.server.log.dir 34
  jboss.server.tmp.dir 34
  jboss.home 34

  user.home 34
  user.dir 34
periodic-rotating-file-handler 50
persistence
  configuring, in other application
      archives 129
persistence-enabled property 88
persistence.xml file 125
Plain Old Java Objects (POJOs) 79
Platform as a Service (PaaS) 338
point-to-point messaging
  characteristics 79
pom.xml file 110
port parameter 82
private cloud 336
process controller, WildFly domain 134
profiles, application server configuration 35
programmatic security 301
PropertiesUsers login module 304
protocol servers 80
public cloud 336
public key cryptography 324
publish/subscribe messaging
  characteristics 79

Q

queries
  caching 266
queue-length attribute 93
queueless thread pool
  about 45
  diagrammatic representation 45
  sample configuration 45

R

Random
  reference link 259
RAR file 160
read-attribute command 199
read-children-names command 199, 203
read-children-resources command 199, 204
read-children-types command 199, 203
**read-operation-description
    command 199, 203**
read-operation-names command 199, 203

read-resource command
    about 199
    example 200, 201
read-resource-description
        command 199, 202
recovery environment, transactions
        subsystem 90
redelivery-delay property 87
Red Hat documentation
    reference link 340
reject-policy attribute 93
relative distinguished name (RDN) 309
RemoteConnectionFactory 85
remote.connections property 123
remote EJB client
    adding, to Maven web project 119-122
    configuring programmatically 123
    configuring, properties file used 122
Remoting framework 120
replicated caching 250
resources, application server modules 28
resources, deploying on application server
    about 159
    EAR file 161
    JAR file 160
    WAR file 160
rhc tail command
    using 352
Role-based access control (RBAC)
    about 321
    enabling 321
RoleMapping login module 304
root node path 18
Round-Robin
    reference link 259
RunAs login module 304
run-batch command 211
Runtime Name property 167

S

SAR file 160
scheduled thread pool
    about 46
    diagrammatic representation 46
Secure Socket Layer
    enabling 325, 326

security 299
security domain 303
security, WildFly
    about 299
    Java security API, approaching 300
    management interfaces, securing 318-320
    transport layer, securing 323, 324
selector element 86
server element
    configuring 99
    default-host attribute 99
    host, configuring 102, 103
    listener, configuring 100
    servlet-container attribute 99
    static content, serving 103
server group 140
server nodes
    configuring 145, 146
server profiles, web admin console
    configuring 220
    datasources, configuring 220-222
    JMS destinations, configuring 224, 225
    socket-binding groups,
            configuring 226, 227
    XA datasource, creating 222
service API 184
Service Provider Interface (SPI)
    about 184
    reference link 184
servlet container
    configuring 104
    JSP, configuring 105
    session cookie, configuring 105
    session state, saving 106
servlet-container element
    allow-non-standard-wrappers attribute 104
    default-buffer-cache attribute 104
    default-encoding attribute 104
    eager-filter-initialization attribute 104
    ignore-flush attribute 104
    stack-trace-on-error attribute 104
    use-listener-encoding attribute 104
session beans
    clustering 261, 262
session cache containers
    configuring 247, 248

session-cookie element
  about 106
  comment attribute 106
  domain attribute 106
  http-only attribute 106
  max-age attribute 106
  name attribute 106
  secure attribute 106
SFSBs
  about 70, 261
  configuring 74, 75
shared-cache-mode element, values
  ALL 263
  DISABLE_SELECTIVE 263
  ENABLE_SELECTIVE 263
  NONE 263
Simple Authentication and Security
    Layer (SASL) 120
Simple login module 304
SimpleUsers login module 304
single-sign-on element 102
SingletonBean 114
SingletonBeanRemoteImpl class 119
Singleton EJB 71
size-rotating-file-handler 51
SLSBs
  about 70, 261
  configuring 72, 73
  pool, configuring 72
pool size, configuring with CLI 74
snapshots 368
socket-binding attribute 100
socket-binding groups, application
    server configuration 37
Software as a Service (SaaS) 338, 339
SPNEGOUsers login module 305
standalone.boot.xml file 214
standalone folder
  about 23, 24
  configuration folder 24
  data folder 24
  deployments folder 24
  lib folder 24
  log folder 24
  tmp folder 24
standalone.initial.xml file 214
standalone.last.xml file 214

standalone.xml 31
startup options 363
Stateful Session Beans. See SFSBs
Stateless Session Beans. See SLSBs
static modules 27
statistics-enabled 91
subsystems, application server
    configuration 35
supported action hooks
  reference link 354
symmetric encryption 323
synchronous messaging 249
syslog-handler 52
system-properties, application server
    configuration 38

T

tab completion feature 165
TCP and UDP differences
  reference link 255
tcp-no-delay parameter 83
tcp-receive-buffer-size parameter 83
tcp-send-buffer-size parameter 83
thread factory
  about 40
  configuring 40
  group-name attribute 40
  name attribute 40
  priority attribute 40
  thread-name-pattern 40
thread-factory attribute 93
thread pools
  eviction-executor 256
  listener-executor 256
  replication-queue-executor 256
  transport 256
thread pool subsystem configuration
  blocking bounded-queue thread pool 42, 43
  blocking queueless thread pool 45, 46
  bounded-queue thread pool 40, 41
  elements 39
  performing 39
  queueless thread pool 45
  scheduled thread pool 46
  thread factory, configuring 40
  unbounded-queue thread pool 44

timer service
  configuring 77, 78
timestamp cache 253
transactions service
  configuring 89, 90
transactions subsystem
  coordinator environment 90
  core environment 90
  diagrammatic representation 89
  recovery environment 90
transport layer, securing
  about 323, 324
  certificate management tools 326
  HTTP communication, securing with
    certificate signed by CA 329, 330
  HTTP communication, securing with
    self-signed certificate 327-329
  Secure Socket Layer, enabling 325
troubleshooting
  cluster 239, 240

U

unbounded-queue thread pool
  about 44
  attributes/elements 44
  diagrammatic representation 44
Undertow
  architecture 98
  buffer cache, configuring 106
  configuring 99
  diagrammatic representation 98
  handlers 98
  listeners 98
  overview 97
  server, configuring 99
  servlet container, configuring 104, 105
  XNIO worker instances 98
use-nio parameter 82
User Account Control (UAC) 12
UsersRoles login module
  about 305
  roles.properties file 305
  users.properties file 305
  using 306

V

Verisign
  URL 330
version command 204
Virtual File System (VFS) 179

W

WAR file 160
web admin console
  about 217
  accessing 218, 219
  Administration tab 219
  benefits 227
  Configuration tab 218
  Home tab 218
  Runtime tab 219
  server profiles, configuring 220
  used, for deploying application 166, 167
Web Application Archive file. *See* **WAR file**
web applications
  creating 107
  clustering 267
  deploying 107
  securing 313-315
web context, Maven web project
  selecting 116
web contexts
  managing, configuration file used 288
  managing, with CLI 286
Web root context 24
web services
  securing 317, 318
web.xml file 109
welcome-content folder 24
Weld dependency 180
WildFly 8
  about 7
  installing 12, 13
  JBoss tools, installing 19, 20
  restarting 17, 18
  server connection, with CLI 15, 16
  starting 13, 14
  stopping 16, 17
  stopping, on remote machine 17

WildFly 8, features
  clustering 8
  command-line interface (CLI) 8
  Java EE7 certification 8
  logging 8
  port reduction 8
  security manager 8
  Undertow 8
WildFly 8, predefined roles
  Administrator 322
  Auditor 322
  Deployer 321
  Maintainer 321
  Monitor 321
  Operator 321
  SuperUser 322
WildFly classloading
  about 178, 179
  advanced deployment strategies 185
  global modules, setting up 184
  isolation level, finding 180
  module names 179
WildFly cluster
  configuring 241
  configuring, for domain servers 236-239
  configuring, for standalone servers 230
  Infinispan subsystem, configuring 245, 246
  JGroups subsystem, configuring 242, 243
  messaging subsystem, clustering 257-259
  setting up 230
  troubleshooting 239, 240
WildFly clusters, setting up for standalone servers
  cluster of nodes, running on different machines 231, 232
  cluster of nodes, running on same machine 233

WildFly domain
  about 133, 134
  configuring 137
  default configuration files, overriding 137
  domain controller, configuring 142
  domain.xml file, configuring 138, 139
  elements 134
  host.xml file, configuring 139, 140
  initiating 136
  JVM, configuring 142
  management interfaces, configuring 140
  network interfaces, configuring 141
  stopping 136, 137
WildFly domain configuration
  applying 146, 147
  modifying, at runtime 153-156
WildFly domain, elements
  application server nodes 134
  domain controller 134
  host controller 134
WildFly Eclipse plugin
  used, for deploying application 168
WildFly security subsystem
  about 302
  login modules 304
  security domain 303
Windows
  Java, installing on 11, 12
windows, icons, menus, and pointers (WIMP) interfaces 220
write-attribute command 199

X

xa-data-source command 209

Thank you for buying
WildFly Configuration, Deployment, and Administration *Second Edition*

About Packt Publishing

Packt, pronounced 'packed', published its first book "*Mastering phpMyAdmin for Effective MySQL Management*" in April 2004 and subsequently continued to specialize in publishing highly focused books on specific technologies and solutions.

Our books and publications share the experiences of your fellow IT professionals in adapting and customizing today's systems, applications, and frameworks. Our solution based books give you the knowledge and power to customize the software and technologies you're using to get the job done. Packt books are more specific and less general than the IT books you have seen in the past. Our unique business model allows us to bring you more focused information, giving you more of what you need to know, and less of what you don't.

Packt is a modern, yet unique publishing company, which focuses on producing quality, cutting-edge books for communities of developers, administrators, and newbies alike. For more information, please visit our website: www.packtpub.com.

About Packt Open Source

In 2010, Packt launched two new brands, Packt Open Source and Packt Enterprise, in order to continue its focus on specialization. This book is part of the Packt Open Source brand, home to books published on software built around Open Source licenses, and offering information to anybody from advanced developers to budding web designers. The Open Source brand also runs Packt's Open Source Royalty Scheme, by which Packt gives a royalty to each Open Source project about whose software a book is sold.

Writing for Packt

We welcome all inquiries from people who are interested in authoring. Book proposals should be sent to author@packtpub.com. If your book idea is still at an early stage and you would like to discuss it first before writing a formal book proposal, contact us; one of our commissioning editors will get in touch with you.

We're not just looking for published authors; if you have strong technical skills but no writing experience, our experienced editors can help you develop a writing career, or simply get some additional reward for your expertise.

WildFly Performance Tuning

ISBN: 978-1-78398-056-7   Paperback: 330 pages

Develop high-performing server applications using the widely successful WildFly platform

1. Enable performance tuning with the use of free and quality software.
2. Tune the leading open source application server WildFly and its related components.
3. Filled with clear step-by-step instructions to get to know the ins-and-outs of the platform, its components, and surrounding infrastructure to get the most and best out of it in any situation.

JBoss EAP Configuration, Deployment, and Administration [Video]

ISBN: 978-1-78216-248-3   Duration: 128 minutes

Detailed demonstrations to help you harness one of the world's top open source JEE projects

1. Learn about everything from installation, configuration, and debugging to securing Java EE applications—ideal for JBoss application developers.
2. In-depth explanations of JBoss EAP features and diagrams to help explain JBoss and Java internals.
3. Covers everything from JBoss EAP essentials to more advanced topics through easy-to-understand practical demonstrations.

Please check www.PacktPub.com for information on our titles

WildFly: New Features

ISBN: 978-1-78328-589-1　　　Paperback: 142 pages

Get acquainted with the exciting new features that WildFly has to offer

1. Learn about the latest WildFly components, including CLI management, classloading, and custom modules.

2. Customize your web server and applications by managing logs, virtual hosts, and the context root.

3. Explore the vast variety of features and configurations that can be implemented through CLI and the Management Console.

JBoss EAP6 High Availability

ISBN: 978-1-78328-243-2　　　Paperback: 166 pages

Leverage the power of JBoss EAP6 to successfully build high-availability clusters quickly and efficiently

1. A thorough introduction to the new domain mode provided by JBoss EAP6.

2. Use mod_jk and mod_cluster with JBoss EAP6.

3. Learn how to apply SSL in a clustering environment.

Please check **www.PacktPub.com** for information on our titles